D1449834

DAGGER JOHN

DAGGER JOHN

Archbishop JOHN HUGHES
and the Making of Irish America

JOHN LOUGHERY

Three Hills
an imprint of

CORNELL UNIVERSITY PRESS ITHACA AND LONDON

First published 2018 by Cornell University Press

Printed in the United States of America

Library of Congress Cataloging-in-Publication Data

Names: Loughery, John, author.
Title: Dagger John : Archbishop John Hughes and the making of Irish America / John Loughery.
Description: Ithaca : Cornell University Press, 2018. | Includes bibliographical references and index. |
Identifiers: LCCN 2017028804 (print) | LCCN 2017031290 (ebook) | ISBN 9781501711060 (pdf) | ISBN 9781501711077 (epub/mobi) | ISBN 9781501707742 (cloth : alk. paper)
Subjects: LCSH: Hughes, John, 1797–1864. | Catholic Church—Bishops—Biography. | Bishops—New York (State)—New York—Biography. | Irish Americans— New York (State)—New York—Biography.
Classification: LCC BX4705.H79 (ebook) | LCC BX4705.H79 L68 2017 (print) | DDC 282.092 [B]—dc23
LC record available at https://lccn.loc.gov/2017028804

Cornell University Press strives to use environmentally responsible suppliers and materials to the fullest extent possible in the publishing of its books. Such materials include vegetable-based, low-VOC inks and acid-free papers that are recycled, totally chlorine-free, or partly composed of nonwood fibers. For further information, visit our website at cornellpress.cornell.edu.

To Ty Florie (1923–2011)
aesthete, teacher, mentor, friend

Contents

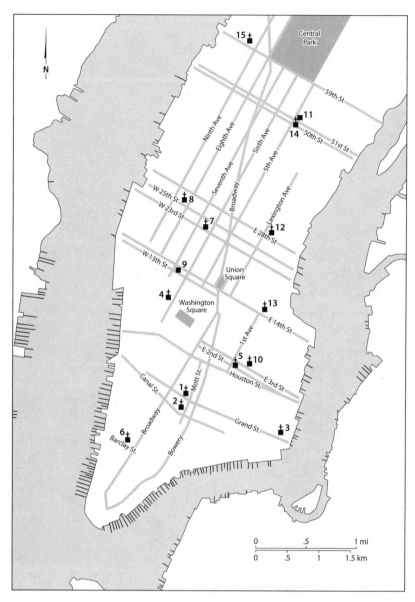

The Catholic Manhattan of John Hughes (see key on page x)

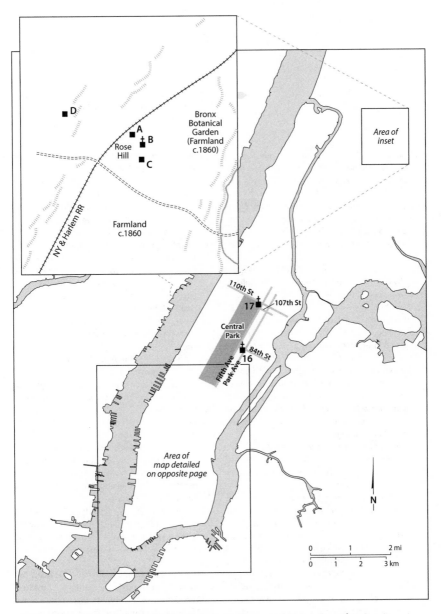

The Rose Hill campus of Saint John's College and Saint Joseph's Seminary,
now Fordham University, in the Bronx (see key on page x)

KEY

1. The original St. Patrick's Cathedral (now Basilica) on Mott Street (1815); the episcopal residence, stoned by anti-Catholic rioters in 1842, was located behind the cathedral on Mulberry Street.
2. The Church of the Transfiguration on Mott Street (1827), just north of the infamous Five Points neighborhood, was relocated more than once and served the city's most destitute Catholic residents.
3. St. Mary's Church on Grand Street (1833) was the only Catholic church on the densely populated Lower East Side when John Hughes arrived in New York.
4. St. Joseph's Church on Sixth Avenue (1834), still standing, was for many years the only Catholic church in Greenwich Village and was a popular posting for many priests under Hughes. It is the oldest unaltered church structure in the diocese.
5. St. Nicholas Church on 2nd Street and First Avenue (1835) was built to serve the German-speaking population of New York who had long complained about Irish priests who showed no regard for their culture and language.
6. St. Peter's Church on Barclay Street (1836), often, to Hughes's ire, on the brink of insolvency in the 1840s and 1850s, still stands today and serves the Wall Street area.
7. The Church of St. Vincent de Paul (1841, relocated to West 23rd Street in 1857) was founded to serve the city's French Catholic population, a group that also complained of neglect on the part of the Church's Irish hierarchy.
8. St. Columba's Church on West 25th Street (1845), built by the evening and weekend labor of Irish dockworkers whose families wanted a house of worship of Chelsea, was an inspiration to a hard-pressed bishop who constantly fundraised for more churches and parochial schools.
9. St. Vincent's Hospital (1849), staffed by the Sisters of Charity, was the first Catholic hospital in the city and was run by Hughes's sister, a nun of that order.
10. The Most Holy Redeemer Church (1852) on East 3rd Street and Avenue A was known as the "German Catholic Cathedral," but its construction failed to end John Hughes's many difficulties with his disgruntled German parishioners.
11. Orphanages were few in number in antebellum New York; the Roman Catholic Orphanage Asylum, one block north of the planned new St. Patrick's Cathedral, opened in 1851 with accommodation for five hundred homeless boys.
12. St. Stephen's Church on East 28th Street (1854), designed by architect James Renwick, served the city's most affluent parishioners and was ruled by some flamboyant, contentious pastors.
13. The Church of the Immaculate Conception on East 14th Street and Avenue A (1855) was the ninety-ninth house of worship John Hughes consecrated during his first two decades in New York.
14. St. Patrick's Cathedral, a Renwick-designed church known as "Hughes's folly," was not completed until long after its founder's death, but Hughes laid the cornerstone in a majestic ceremony in 1858.
15. The Church of St. Paul the Apostle (1858): the cornerstone of the grand, still-standing building dates from 1876, but on the same site Isaac Hecker, with Hughes's blessing, founded in a humbler structure the first Paulist church in New York. At the time, 59th Street and Ninth Avenue was far north of the city's center.
16. St. Lawrence O'Toole Church (1851), today the St. Ignatius Loyola Church, in Hughes's time the only Catholic house of worship on the East Side of Manhattan between Harlem and St. Patrick's Cathedral.
17. Mount Saint Vincent's Academy (1847), home to a school for girls and the motherhouse of the New York Sisters of Charity (led by Hughes's sister, Mother Angela) until the late 1850s when it relocated to the Bronx, later a hospital for wounded Union soldiers staffed by the sisters.

A. St. Joseph's Seminary
B. Our Lady of Mercy Church, a parish church (today the university chapel)
C. St. John's College
D. Edgar Allan Poe's house (still extant)

DAGGER JOHN

Prologue

To the Tuileries

NEVER HAD AN ELECTION in the United States—not the Jefferson-Adams contest of sixty years earlier, not the election that signaled the rise of the age of Andrew Jackson—been marked by so much rancor or fraught with more potential for national calamity. The talk of secession that had dominated the political landscape for decades had taken on a different, more immediate, and more threatening character. "The prospects are gloomy enough, but we must hope on," John Hughes, the archbishop of New York, wrote to a correspondent in Rome that spring.

The archbishop's hope was that William Seward, onetime governor of his own state, would be the Republican nominee in 1860. Hughes had been hoping for the better part of twenty years that Seward would one day occupy the White House. This fact in itself suggested something of the peculiar state American politics and religion had entered. Seward was a former Whig, member of a party long known to be antagonistic to the interests of Irish Catholics, and he was now a leader in the newest political party on the scene, a group whose ascendancy to the White House or control of Congress would only exacerbate growing tensions with the South. And Seward was the author of the famous 1858 "irrepressible conflict" speech, making use of an unfortunate phrase that seemed to imply the inevitability of a Northern clash with the slaveholding states. Like many New Yorkers, the archbishop believed that slavery would die a natural, unlamented death in the nineteenth century and that a bloody civil war was the last thing that would benefit either race or region; accordingly, he looked upon abolitionists as a dangerous breed.

Yet John Hughes knew Seward personally, trusted him deeply, saw him as a man of caution and sagacity. Seward's rhetoric and party affiliations mattered a good deal less than his actions: though a Protestant, he had stood with the Catholic Church in its fight twenty years earlier for public funding for New York's parochial schools, and that unexpected move—infuriating to many in Seward's own Whig Party—had been brave and wasn't to be forgotten. He knew Seward to be a man of both principle and compromise, with nothing of the fanatic about him. He couldn't say the same about the awkward, folksy former congressman from Illinois who had impressed so many New Yorkers with his Cooper Union address earlier in the year. Though he scrupulously avoided making overt political recommendations to his parishioners, most of whom were ardent Democrats anyway, and demanded the same restraint from his priests—believing, in fact, that it was best for the church to be circumspect in its political statements and for the Irish to avoid voting as a bloc—he was disappointed by Seward's loss at the convention in Chicago and made uneasy by Lincoln's election in November.

Fort Sumter changed all that. John Hughes believed in the morality of the cause—union, not emancipation—and saw no conflict with his role as a church leader in applauding New Yorkers, especially Irish Catholic men, who volunteered to fight in their country's defense. To the dismay of many priests and parishioners who questioned the righteousness of the cause or the appropriateness of the church taking sides, he ordered the United States flag flown over the cathedral on Mott Street. Though he hoped that the conflict would be short-lived and, like most Americans, never dreamed of the devastation that lay ahead, he strongly suspected that the war would represent a turning point in the fortunes of Irish America. If the sons of Tyrone and Roscommon and Kilkenny distinguished themselves in sufficient numbers, if they showed a willingness to sacrifice, if they proved their readiness to act for the greater good, they would finally, irrevocably, be accepted as what they never had been: authentic Americans, as worthy as anyone of the full rights and dignity of citizenship.

Hughes hoped that he would be able to maintain relations with his fellow bishops south of the Mason-Dixon Line after Lincoln's call for volunteers went out, but he was soon disabused of that idea. From his good friend of twenty years, the bishop of Wheeling, Hughes received a wrathful letter in May, demanding to know how in the world a leader of the church could in good conscience urge the Catholic men of New York to march south to kill Catholic men in Virginia. "In a few days the bloody tragedy will begin. . . . Are Catholics so numerous that you can spare them?" the letter railed. "The blood boils within me," Bishop Whalen wrote, to think that a fellow bishop could, directly or by implication, ask Catholics "to sacrifice themselves for the party that contains their most deadly enemies, abolitionists, infidels, and red republicans." Though Hughes tried at some length, nothing he wrote in response to Whalen could clarify his position or mitigate the bishop's fury. The previous year he had been invited to give a commencement speech at the University of North Carolina in Chapel Hill. Now few of his Southern friends wanted anything to do with him.

A month after Lincoln's inauguration, John Hughes—sharing the widespread view that the new principal member of the cabinet would actually be running the country while the president did his best to keep up—wrote to Seward, "*North and South*, all eyes are turned to the Secretary of State." The ensuing months brought many more missives from New York to Seward's desk, some with highly specific recommendations about troop movements, naval maneuvers, and budgetary matters. ("More attention should be paid to the forces at Cairo. . . . Fort Pickens ought to be strengthened," he wrote in June.) "Excuse me for offering these suggestions and consider them as coming from one who knows but little of statesmanship and still less of military science, but who does pretend to know a good deal of human nature," Hughes wrote when U.S. naval efforts in the Gulf were on his mind. Knowledge of human nature and suggestions about blockading and retaking Pensacola would hardly seem connected in any self-evident way, but the point—and Seward seems to have been at ease with it—was clear enough: the archbishop felt comfortable with Seward in a way he did with no other political figure. The secretary even shared some of Hughes's letters, or said he did, with Lincoln.

With the exception of several naval victories along the eastern coast, the first six months of the Civil War brought painfully little good news to the Union side. The charismatic Colonel Elmer Ellsworth, leader of the New York Zouaves, killed after hauling down a Confederate flag, had already been waked in the East Room of the White House, where the Lincolns shed copious tears for their friend, and in New York's City Hall; the debacle at Manassas in July had ended Union hopes of quickly retaking Virginia; and John C. Frémont's inept command in Missouri seemed more likely to push that state into the Confederacy than save it for the Union. Kentucky's neutrality had been violated by both sides, and newspaper coverage of the aging commander of the army, Winfield Scott, focused more on his bloat and his gout than his military cunning. The amateur quality of many officers and almost all the new politically appointed generals was obvious. The promised "Ninety Days' War" looked to drag on into the next year and beyond. Those who had urged compromise throughout the "secession winter" felt vindicated: a republic of thirty-four states could not be yoked together indefinitely by force of arms.

From a diplomatic perspective, the outlook was turning dark just as rapidly. Many Europeans were referring that fall to the division of the United States as a de facto reality, assuming it was only a matter of time before the North acknowledged its folly and sued for terms. Nervous that the result of this sentiment would ultimately lead to British or French recognition of the Confederate States of America (or even to intervention on their behalf), Lincoln and Seward began—belatedly, critics said—to give thought to how they might counteract this prospect.

In September, Henry Sanford, the U.S. minister to Belgium, wrote to Seward to say that he regretted that "no means have been adopted to act on public opinion in Europe." Another State Department official abroad, William Walker, reported that plenty of Southern gentlemen "highly gifted in their social qualities and mingling in various grades of society" had made their way across the Atlantic and were adroitly effecting the propaganda goals of their government. Why couldn't the North do the same? both men wanted to know. Charles Francis Adams and William Dayton, the ministers to London and Paris, respectively, seemed to Sanford to be too conscious of their official capacities, more patient and long-suffering than creative in their methods. "We need active useful men over here," Sanford urged.

On October 21, 1861, Archbishop Hughes received a telegram from Seward, asking to meet with him at his earliest convenience on a matter of some importance recently discussed by Lincoln and the cabinet.

Hughes lost no time in getting himself to the capital. Throughout the course of the year, Hughes had come to a better view of the commander in chief and was more sympathetic to the gravity of the problems he faced. "No President has ever been so severely tested as he," he remarked to Seward. The proposal put before him was that he, along with a few other carefully chosen men, would be sent to Europe at the government's expense for an indeterminate period "to promote healthful opinions" about the war, the righteous cause of national unity, and the need for foreign governments either to support the United States as a friend and ally or refrain from giving such support to the rebels. There was no question of any official status, any right to negotiate treaties or commitments, or even to speak publicly on behalf of the government. They would have to do all this "without seeming to do so." This would be very much an ad hoc endeavor, and, once on the ground, Lincoln's emissaries would have to determine on their own who their most receptive and influential audience might be and how their message could best be conveyed. Moreover, there was suddenly a heightened urgency to the mission: newspapers were reporting that week that two Confederate agents of some importance, James Mason and John Slidell, had run the blockade of Charleston and arrived in Havana preparatory to sailing to Europe to do their own propagandizing for the South.

The other men who had been approached were Edward Everett and John Pendleton Kennedy, prominent national politicians and former cabinet members, and Charles McIlvaine, the much-respected Episcopal bishop of Ohio and a confidant of Secretary of the Treasury Salmon Chase. Everett and Kennedy had already declined, to Seward's consternation, but McIlvaine was agreeable. Seward's idea, which Lincoln and the cabinet backed, was that McIlvaine would spend most, or all, of his time in England—Hughes's pro-Irish, anti-British fulminations were too well known to do the American cause any good there—while Hughes might see what opportunities presented themselves in France, Italy, and elsewhere to the south. Though McIlvaine was someone Hughes knew only by reputation (he probably suspected his anti-Catholic bent), he agreed with the reasoning behind having a Protestant divine who was intimate with many of the leading figures of the Church of England concentrate his efforts on Her Majesty's government and the press in London.

Discussing the topic with Seward and Chase at dinner at Seward's house on Lafayette Square that night, Hughes initially expressed more reservations than unqualified enthusiasm. It was an enticing but potentially awkward position for him to be in. To Seward's chagrin, he finally announced that he had to decline. Realizing that the cards were his to play, though, Hughes offered a "suggestion" later in the evening—one that was very likely on his mind all along—that he would reconsider if accompanied abroad, aided, guided, by another man whom the secretary of state knew well and had reason to trust: his closest political adviser from his time in the statehouse, a power broker in the Whig and later the Republican Party, and the publisher-editor of the *Albany Evening-Express*, Thurlow Weed. It was Seward's turn to be uncertain, even frustrated. Putting a friend like Weed on the government payroll for a nebulous purpose made him anxious. Seward was a favored target with Congress and in the press that fall. Weed had urged compromise before the shelling of Fort Sumter; and with Lincoln giving them so little, the abolitionists in the party were not in a forgiving mood. Salmon Chase, among other cabinet members, didn't like Weed. But Hughes was adamant about his terms (according to Weed in his memoirs, at least), and if all parties agreed, he would set out for London, Paris, Rome, Madrid, Saint Petersburg, with alacrity and eagerness—wherever patriotic duty called.

When Weed arrived at Seward's house by appointment after the dinner party and after Chase and McIlvaine's departure, Seward set him to try to talk Hughes out of this annoying entanglement: all so much wasted breath. Weed tried to steer Hughes to Seward's view but, in the end, was willing to go with his old friend even if he had to pay his own way. Seward was becoming more embarrassed and depressed by the moment. Hughes, as always, knew what was best for everyone. "I accompanied the Archbishop to his carriage," Weed wrote in a more-or-less appreciative tone, "where, after he was seated, he said with a significant gesture, 'This programme is not to be changed.'"

Just the thought of traveling with Weed, whom he had journeyed to Europe with twenty years earlier, was a source of undiluted joy for John Hughes. Thurlow Weed was someone Hughes marveled at, could relax with, whose company he found endlessly instructive and amusing. (Hughes had surely heard the story that made the rounds of New York politicos of a dinner party Weed had given at his home for some nativist politicians, vocally anti-Catholic, whose support he was wooing for Seward's reelection. On a tour of his house, they came upon a painting in the study of Hughes ecclesiastically attired; asked the identity of the sitter, their host didn't even pause, but explained that it was a portrait of Washington in his Continental robes that had been presented to Weed's father by the first president himself. No one lied on his feet better than Weed.) Weed would indeed have to travel at his own expense, Seward insisted. Weed had no problem with that condition.

Could Seward have held out and ultimately arranged matters more to his liking, excluding the controversial Weed? It is hard to tell. John Hughes was a political creature as much as a devoutly spiritual man, and he had never been averse to working with, or jousting with, men in power, friends or opponents. He loved a good bluff, and he was rarely called on it. The belief that religious leaders should remain above politics wasn't one he entirely shared, even when he pretended it was. It would be more accurate to say that he believed religious leaders should never *appear* to be engaged in political activity.

Rather, Hughes had been wooed by presidents, governors, and generals and enjoyed every minute of it, every encounter, every nod at his contributions to society and his potential as vote-getter and diplomat and peacemaker. James K. Polk had allegedly talked with him about serving as an emissary during the War with Mexico, with the intention of reassuring the conquered Catholics to the south that they had nothing to fear from their Protestant neighbor. It was a bizarre project, with no clarity as to whether it originated as Polk's or Hughes's suggestion, hatched amid a guarded nighttime conversation in the president's office and never realized, but it had appealed to Hughes's vanity, ambition, and belief in his destiny. He had been courted by Henry Clay and Winfield Scott. He had dined with Millard Fillmore in the White House and was on friendly terms with James Buchanan. He had addressed Congress at the invitation of John Quincy Adams. He had met two popes in Rome and, on his first trip to Europe in 1839, had been introduced to the emperor and empress of Austria. But a mission as an unofficial envoy to the court of Napoleon III was a different matter entirely.

There was some risk in asking a Catholic prelate to undertake such a mission, Seward and Lincoln realized. A greater risk for the prelate than for them, perhaps. Their request was not made lightly. A more timid bishop would have worried about what his parishioners who opposed the war would say, the never-to-be-mended rift with his Southern colleagues that such an action would precipitate, the very fact that he would be acting without prior permission from the Holy See.

FIGURE 1. *John Hughes, diplomat at large: the man Lincoln and Seward trusted to forestall the recognition of the Confederacy by Napoleon III and Pope Pius IX.* (Courtesy of the Archives of the Archdiocese of New York.)

It would seem that the president never doubted they had approached the right man and accepted that in the end he would have to be accommodated as he wished. If Hughes was known for his temper and iron will, he was also known for his social skills. He had a gracious and even ingratiating side. (A cousin of Mary Todd Lincoln, who met him at the White House, described him as "courtly.") He could be blustering and belligerent, but he could be persuasive and highly articulate. He still had the edge of his working-class immigrant roots, an early adulthood spent as a gardener and a stonecutter, but he was worldlier than he appeared and quick to grasp a point.

Nor was timidity a problem. It had never been a problem. John Hughes had weaned himself from timidity in his youth. As a priest new to Manhattan, he had walked the Five Points. He had stood up to crowds of jeering Protestants in public forums. He was anything but reticent. In an anti-Catholic riot that rocked New York City in 1842, his own home on Mulberry Street had been surrounded and stoned, its windows smashed. (Walt Whitman, in a less pacific phase of his career, had written in his two-penny paper, the *Aurora*, that if the rocks had landed on "the reverend hypocrite's head, instead of his windows, we would hardly find it in our soul to be sorrowful.") Two years later, when nativist fury again threatened the peace, he had been asked by the mayor if he feared for the safety of the city's Catholic churches; in Philadelphia, only weeks before, crowds had torched homes and churches, chasing Irishmen through the blazing streets at night. No, Hughes had purportedly told the mayor in what became a legendary exchange; he feared more for the Protestant churches in the event of such an attack. If the authorities could not keep order, he was said to have promised the mayor "a second Moscow."

Hughes was also no stranger to official vacillation and appreciated the fact that Lincoln, branded as hesitant in the press, was not showing a failure of will on this occasion. In 1859, the archbishop had been by happenstance visiting James Buchanan when word of John Brown's raid on Harpers Ferry reached the White House. Notoriously reluctant to take a stand about anything, Buchanan looked stricken. It was his job, Hughes reminded the chief magistrate, to be, at all costs, decisive. Weakness emboldened both the abolitionists and the fire-eaters. Invoking their shared North Ireland ancestry, he had written to the president on an earlier occasion, at the time of the Bleeding Kansas controversy, "I cannot imagine a descendant of the Buchanans that I knew in Ireland who, knowing or believing himself to be in the right, would ever give way." In Buchanan, gracious as he was to Catholic priests, Hughes saw his polar opposite: a man never intended by nature to be authoritative. He saw the price to be paid by leadership that would not be leader-like. He knew what tone he would take with the John Browns of the world.

Any review of the situation in France and the reasons it would take particular acumen and finesse to make an impression on the emperor and his advisers—a review that Seward, Chase, and Hughes surely engaged in at Seward's table that night—underlined the difficulty of this project. Buchanan's minister to Paris, Charles Faulkner of Virginia, had remained in place until May 1861, long past the time when the dilatory

Lincoln should have replaced him with a pro-Union man. Édouard-Henri Mercier, the French minister to the United States, was known to despise Seward and to believe that the Union could not be held together much longer at the point of a bayonet. He was rumored to have urged his government back in March to listen to Faulkner and offer formal recognition to the South. Édouard Thouvenal, Seward's counterpart in Paris, was notoriously hard to pin down, and the emperor himself had a habit of saying different things about America's troubles to different listeners.

What Seward couldn't have known that day was even worse: that Napoleon III had recently sounded out the British, inquiring if the time was not approaching when Anglo-French action to restore order in the Western Hemisphere might not be called for. The Union blockade of cotton shipments was affecting the French economy in perilous ways. (British prime minister Palmerston informed the emperor that he preferred for the moment to "lie on his oars.") As one twentieth-century historian of Franco-American relations summarized: "Not since the Revolutionary War had the Union stood in greater need of France's friendship," but that friendship was not forthcoming in the fall of 1861. A Catholic archbishop, if he could get the ear of a Catholic monarch—and the monarch's wife, the Empress Eugénie, a woman known to have a lively interest in foreign affairs herself—might, just might, do more than official communiqués and ministerial briefs.

Finally, knowing Hughes's penchant for dominating any situation he was a part of, Seward went out of his way to remind his friend, gently but repeatedly, that it would be important not to tread on the toes of the U.S. minister to France, who was, after all, his government's authorized representative to the Tuileries. In his official letter of instructions to Hughes dated November 2, he made three separate references to the need to work with, or through, William Dayton. A former New Jersey senator who had been John C. Frémont's running mate in 1856 and a favorite-son candidate at the Republican convention in 1860, Dayton was a smart and well-intentioned man but a diplomat who would be apt to stand on his dignity. Not surprisingly, Seward's prudent warnings turned out to be useless. When Dayton heard of the plan, he was incredulous and indignant and, in his impeccably gentlemanly way, was to prove anything but cooperative.

Hughes's presence in Washington occasioned comment, but the president had insisted that that the less publicity the mission attracted, the better. These were untested waters. Discretion would be crucial. As government secrets known to more than a dozen people tend to do, word got out rather quickly. The administration felt obliged to issue disclaimers and quasi-denials. On November 7, an unsigned item appeared in the Washington papers: "Thurlow Weed and Archbishop Hughes have *not* been sent to Europe as Commissioners Plenipotentiary, to counteract Mason and Slidell. The Archbishop sailed today, and I learn that Mr. Weed will soon follow, going to the continent upon an errand entirely voluntary, which will act upon the public sentiment there unofficially and without connection to either our or any European government." The author of this technically accurate but disingenuous bit of information was John Hay, Lincoln's personal secretary who did a fair amount of anonymous newspaper writing for his employer, and no one believed a word of it.

Back home in New York, Hughes packed for an extended stay abroad—he would be gone, as it turned out, for nine months—and refused to say anything about his intentions, even to his private secretary who was accompanying him, which in effect said everything. Worried about his health, he left instructions that William Starrs, his vicar-general, was to be the administrator of the diocese if he died abroad. He did decide to write to the Vatican before his ship sailed, asking the pontiff's blessing "even in this matter so apparently foreign to my sacred vocation as a prelate of the Catholic Church." His mission was essentially one of peace, he maintained, and as such "would redound to the benefit of Catholics and to the promotion of the interests of the Church." Of course, an unlikely reply in the negative from Pius IX would hardly have arrived in time to prevent his departure. He immediately followed this letter with a second, considerably more prevaricating, emphasizing that he was not going to Europe to advance the cause of the North or the Lincoln administration, which would indeed be a highly partisan, political act, but to advance the cause of the North *and* the South—that is, the need for a swift end to the killing.

It is a shame that the three members of the "entirely voluntary" civilian trio were not able to travel together. Hughes had been looking forward to time in close quarters with the genial Weed, and an Atlantic crossing with Charles Pettit McIlvaine wouldn't have been lacking in conversational possibilities. About the same age, McIlvaine and Hughes were alike in some ways, sharp-minded and opinionated and intimidating to underlings, though their backgrounds differed. McIlvaine, son of a U.S. senator, had graduated from Princeton and been appointed chaplain to the United States Senate while the impoverished Hughes was still hewing rocks in Maryland. McIlvaine had taught at West Point, where Robert E. Lee and Jefferson Davis had been his students, and knew New York City from his time serving at Saint Ann's Parish in Brooklyn and teaching at the University of the City of New York. At the age of thirty-three, he had been named the second president of Kenyon College before becoming bishop of Ohio. McIlvaine's standing among Protestant clergy on both sides of the Atlantic was rooted in his bold attacks on the Catholic-leaning Oxford movement within the Anglican Church—a movement dear to Hughes's heart.

Of this trio of envoys, about all one can say is: what a truly Lincolnesque arrangement of seafarers on a supposedly (but not in the least) secret mission—a party boss and newspaperman from Albany, an Episcopal bishop who remembered Jefferson Davis from his college ethics class, and a Catholic bishop responsible for the waifs and knaves of the Manhattan slums who was more than a little fearful of incurring the pope's displeasure. The whole enterprise, Charles Francis Adams felt, was absurd.

For his part, despite his sometimes crippling rheumatism and the Bright's disease that played havoc with his kidneys, John Hughes at sixty-four felt more invigorated than he had for many months. The crossing, after two stormy days at the start, was smooth. "Few passengers," he wrote Seward, "but very agreeable. English, Irish, Scotch, and Americans." When "misconceptions" about the war were voiced by any of the English passengers, he labored to set them straight but otherwise held fire. After two weeks at sea, he was in Liverpool and the following day in London. The *Times* took note of the American's arrival in the capital of the British Empire, dryly commenting that "Mr. Weed and Bishop Hughes, two of Mr. Seward's best friends, faintly disclaim the notion that their voyage to Europe is on diplomatic business." Hughes was described as "a prelate of attainments and political experience . . . skillful and anti-English."

Even though he understood that his bailiwick was to be on the other side of the Channel, the skillful prelate decided on his own to pay a courtesy call on Charles Francis Adams. He caught him in the middle of a dinner party, which he was not invited to join, and was granted an eight-minute interview. The son of John Quincy Adams wanted nothing to do with Lincoln's priest (he was to be far more hospitable to, and impressed with, McIlvaine and Weed), and the faintest display of politeness was all he felt obliged to manage. Hughes made light of the matter in his letter to Seward. Adams's son and private secretary, Henry, however, took note of the archbishop and thought more favorably of his intentions. If many at the legation believed backdoor efforts to influence public opinion were a waste of time, Henry's belief, recorded years later in *The Education of Henry Adams*, was that "the waste was only apparent; the work all told in the end."

Something momentous had happened the day after Hughes's ship set sail, though, something that no one had anticipated and that threatened to scuttle everyone's efforts to restore British-American amity. Mason and Slidell had left Havana aboard an unarmed British steamer, the *Trent*, which was overtaken in mid-Atlantic by a thirteen-gun U.S. sloop, the *San Jacinto*. Eager to make up for the navy's failure to prevent the Confederates' flight from South Carolina to Havana, Charles Wilkes, an overzealous commander indifferent to the niceties of maritime law, had his men board the British vessel and remove the two Southerners at gunpoint. British sovereignty and neutrality had been violated. Americans, including Lincoln, were thrilled by Wilkes's initiative, but that was before they awakened to the ramifications of what became known as "the *Trent* affair." Lord Palmerston's government, expressing his nation's outrage, demanded the release of the two men and an acknowledgment that the boarding and seizure were illegal. Short of that, war—an invasion of the United States—would be the result. Seward's most recent biographer has aptly called the *Trent* affair "the Cuban missile crisis of the nineteenth century," a moment of fierce anxiety when two major powers were, unintentionally and overnight, on the brink of a military encounter that would have catastrophic consequences.

Weed thought war was all but inevitable. Troops had been ordered to Canada to be positioned on the border of New England and New York. Shipyards went into overtime. Everywhere, not just in England, the British were clamoring to strike back at the United States. "The English here are very angry," the rector of the American College in Rome wrote to Hughes, though he offered the view that if Irish rebels had set out for Havana, the English would have "seized [the boat] without ceremony and would have refused satisfaction."

Uncertainty about how Lincoln and Seward were going to react to the British demands left the civilian envoys at a significant disadvantage. The best they could do was to issue vague, unfounded assurances that the dispute would be resolved without anything worse than more saber-rattling. The jingoist press in the North demanded that Mason and Slidell remain in prison in New York. Winfield Scott, recently retired from the army, had come to France on the same ship Weed had traveled on and wrote (with the help of Weed and possibly Hughes) a well-received pacifying letter for publication in the European press, though he thought the opposite and expected New York City to be attacked within weeks. It was a relief to the entire American community in Europe—a grudging relief to Hughes—when, after taking weeks to come to a decision, Lincoln and Seward defused the crisis by announcing in December that Wilkes had improperly acted on his own, not under orders from Washington, and that the rule of law would prevail and the two Confederate agents would be released.

A second issue, not at all resolvable, that left Hughes and his compatriots in an awkward position was the questioning they were subjected to in every city they visited about the cause the Union was fighting for. Everywhere they heard the same thing: if only the Lincoln administration would announce its commitment to ending slavery, European support for the North would be wholehearted. But that was exactly what no responsible American could mislead anyone about, and their statements concerning the nature of constitutional change in the United States, states' rights, and amelioration failed to lessen foreign skepticism or ire. To most Europeans, secession might well be a right; slavery wasn't. Hughes's own suspicion was that the end of the war would probably result in legislation phasing out a misbegotten institution, but he was certain that the overwhelming majority of men in arms from the North had signed on to fight secession, not to free the slaves. That reality had to be faced. European support couldn't be won on a false premise.

In Paris, William Dayton was more obliging to Seward's emissaries than Adams had been to Hughes—he hosted a welcoming dinner that included Winfield Scott, whose company Hughes had always liked—but the U.S. minister let the archbishop know that he did not feel comfortable seeking an introduction for him to Foreign Minister Thouvenal. He was on his own. Hughes had scarcely imagined that the situation would be otherwise. Socializing with the archbishop of Paris and meeting several well-informed cardinals, he discovered that Thouvenal had been perfectly aware of his movements and intentions from the minute he landed at Boulogne.

Playing a worldly part among Parisian sophisticates, Hughes accepted every invitation to mingle in high society to spread his message. One correspondent for a British paper who watched him at a diplomatic reception commented that the visiting American seemed to be "a gentleman with a very superior degree of intelligence," exhibiting a marked "strength and geniality" in his conversation. He talked to every priest he could find who seemed like a potential ally, including the bishops of Abyssinia and Peking, who were in France at that time. He was invited to preach several times at the Church of Saint-Roch. He compared notes and plotted strategy with Weed.

In particular, Hughes listened with sympathy to the many complaints about the toll the Union blockade was taking on French manufacturing, and he even made a trip to Lyon to meet with distressed textile workers and company managers. How much longer, they wanted to know, were they expected to wait for the cotton shipments that had stopped months before? To that, unlike the slavery question, there was an easy answer, Hughes felt: the sooner the French Empire informed the Confederacy that recognition and aid were never to be counted on, the sooner the war would be over and the sooner commerce all over the world would return to normal. Word that New Orleans, the key to all Southern import and export transactions by water, was likely to fall into Union hands in the coming weeks offered some hope that the needed shipments might resume.

Hughes's reports to Seward were always more optimistic than not, and like all ambassadors, he liked to convey the impression that he was winning hearts and minds every time he spoke; but he was undoubtedly alert to how truly divided and unstable French opinion was. Support for the South was substantially less in France than in Great Britain, but many Frenchmen saw some wisdom in hedging one's bets at this stage of the conflict. The press accounts he read were not especially favorable to the United States. Notable figures like Alexis de Tocqueville and Victor Hugo were ardent champions of the Union cause, but de Tocqueville's influence at court was nil, and the antimonarchical Hugo was in exile. Comte de Montalembert, head of the Liberal Catholic Party, with whom Hughes spent a morning, and the emperor's cousin, Prince Napoleon, who had recently visited the United States, were similarly pro-Union, but their influence was likewise nonexistent.

At last, on Christmas Eve, after Hughes had been kept waiting for more than a month, a private audience with Napoleon III and Eugénie at the Tuileries Palace was secured. Hughes had written to the emperor himself when the "cold shoulder," as he termed it to Seward, of William Dayton and the French officials exhausted his patience. "Being a bishop," he told Napoleon III, "it is not out of keeping with my character to pray and even plead for peace." Their conversation lasted for a surprising hour and ten minutes.

According to Hughes's memorandum to Seward, several topics were broached or covered. The resolution of the *Trent* affair was not yet known, and both talked as if hostilities were likely. Napoleon was of the opinion that America had violated British honor and would probably have to pay for it. Hughes offered the thought that His Imperial Majesty would be the best possible mediator between the two powers, should it come to war, a view Napoleon disputed (he had visions of mediating between the North and the South, not between Great Britain and the United States) and one that would have caused Seward to cringe. They chatted about a mutual acquaintance, General Winfield Scott, and their affection for him, after which the emperor expressed some pique at his own cousins from the House of Orléans who had offered their services to General George McClellan, the new head of the army. Napoleon wanted to discuss America's high tariff rates, and his guest was obliged to talk about economics for a while and make clear that decisions about those rates might more justly be laid at the feet of Southern than Northern businessmen, while Eugénie expressed her opinion that the blockade of the entire Southern coast could never be maintained, a point the archbishop declined to agree with. The bulk of their time together was given over, at the emperor's request, to the archbishop's version of the history of the American conflict: how had things come to this pass, what was the real story behind so many dead and so much heartbreak? Here the archbishop was at his most detailed and articulate.

Being able to speak to the empress as well as her husband was just what Hughes had hoped for. He was a practiced hand with the wives of the rich and powerful. The fund-raising he began four years earlier for the new, uncompleted Saint Patrick's Cathedral on Fifth Avenue had necessitated making inroads with a tightfisted bunch: the Irish gentry of

Manhattan. Wives spoken to meaningfully but deferentially sometimes yielded checks and pledges as readily as husbands spoken to bluntly.

Quite sensibly, Hughes did not feel it appropriate to break protocol and make an explicit appeal to the emperor not to recognize the Confederacy—he was not, after all, a bona fide representative of his government—but he did feel it fair and advantageous to allude to the empress's Spanish birth. He brought into the conversation, without belaboring the point, the South's long-standing designs on Cuba. If there was one observation that hit its mark, that was surely it. Before leaving the palace, the empress brought her little boy in to meet and receive a blessing from the archbishop, and on balance Hughes felt that day that he achieved, more or less, what Seward, with modest expectations, had hoped. "I think we might have fared worse in France than we have done," he wrote the secretary of state.

From New York, Hughes's sister wrote, "The Public on this side take it as a fixed fact that Archbishop Hughes is in Europe expressly to settle our National troubles and high hopes are entertained." Not everyone took so sanguine a view. An American priest in France at the time wrote to Bishop Francis McFarland in Hartford that "Archbishop John Hughes is still in Paris making the Emperor mind his own business and keep out of ours. But the French say that the Archbishop's presence is not felt and will not profit Uncle Sam." One French newspaper attacked Hughes as a pro-slavery man for his refusal to advocate abolition. Any judgment about Hughes's success in France, then, depended on whom one talked to, and no one doubted that in the end the emperor would act in his own best interests. If the new year brought one Confederate victory after another, no amount of earnest conversation would make any difference; if the Union's success seemed likelier, Napoleon would continue to bide his time. Hughes left Paris for Rome early in February. Thurlow Weed had since joined McIlvaine in England, who was having a much easier time of it among the Anglican elite.

More concrete, if temporary, good was accomplished in the Eternal City. Hughes went with great trepidation, as he knew that a fair number of American prelates had written to the pope and his secretary of state, Cardinal Antonelli, expressing something more than indignation—something closer to rage—that the Holy Father would allow a high-ranking clerical figure to act in an explicitly political capacity. Hughes was relieved to be warmly welcomed by the pontiff, who was willing to listen at length to all that the American archbishop had to say and seemed to find his remarks eminently plausible.

Seemed: that was always the important word with Pius IX, however. When the Catholic clergy of the Confederacy decided two years later to rethink their original disapproval about crossing any spiritual and political lines and sent Bishop Lynch of Charleston to do just what John Hughes had done, he made no inroads at the Vatican at all. That would suggest that Hughes's mission had been the successful one. Yet, in 1863, Pope Pius IX came as close as any European head of state to recognizing the Confederate States of America as an independent nation.

Hughes stayed at the North American College in Rome, the seminary for men studying for the priesthood who would be assigned to American parishes, an institution for which he had raised funds and wanted to inspect. During Holy Week, he attended or took part in all the major services at Saint Peter's and officiated at the stations of the cross inside the Colosseum. He dined with princes from the Borghese and the Doria Pamphili families. He also remained in Rome much longer than he had intended, as the pope announced that canonization ceremonies would be held in June for twenty-six Japanese Christians who had suffered martyrdom for their faith in the time of Francis Xavier, an august occasion to which all Catholic bishops worldwide were invited.

Despite the pain he was suffering from the lacerating rheumatism that had returned to plague his hips, knees, and ankles, the relief from which required constant hot sulfur baths, Hughes let Seward know that he would be willing to continue his sojourn, to Madrid, to Vienna, to Amsterdam, even to Warsaw, Moscow, and Saint Petersburg. President Lincoln decided that the submitted bills ($5,200 in total, by the end) were quite high enough and that the archbishop had probably done all that could be done. Hughes talked at length with the Spanish ambassador to Rome before departing and agreed that those conversations had served his purpose as thoroughly as a trip to see Her Most Catholic Majesty or the Spanish prime minister would have done.

One last stop Seward did want Hughes to make before setting sail was Ireland, and, as Hughes had already accepted an invitation to lay the cornerstone of Dublin's Catholic University that summer, his farewell to Europe was primed to be perfect in every regard. In Dublin and Belfast he was lionized, and the citizens of Cork, where he stayed with the mayor, entertained him with a great public dinner. Everyone wanted

to hear his views on everything. He recovered his vitality in the face of
this enormous, open-hearted adulation: no inscrutable Frenchmen, no
byzantine Vatican politics.

Unfortunately, at this stage of his wanderings and in this particular
tender setting, Hughes devoted his energies as much to public statements
about the historic barbarity of Great Britain in its treatment of the Irish
and of the United States as to the cause of the North against the South.
He went so far as to drop hints that one day his country would have its
proper revenge for the *Trent* affair. He implied that Ireland's freedom
from a forced union with Great Britain required only time and resolve.
In effect, in midsummer of 1862, it could be said that Bishop Hughes in
Ireland and Bishop McIlvaine and Thurlow Weed in England were all
but working at cross-purposes. "Your work in Ireland can never be forgotten in America [among the Irish immigrants]," a friend who read the
news accounts wrote to Hughes, "and England can never pardon you.
I know they are writing from every quarter against you."

A worse morass developed when, on the eve of his departure from
Dublin, a group of excitable young men from Tipperary came to call
late one night with a complimentary proclamation to read before their
famous guest and to have a chance to talk with him. His guard down,
he wasn't aware that they were members of a political society and that
a reporter was one of their number. Reading his own words thrown
back at him in newsprint in the light of day was a blistering experience.
He had meant what he told the young men—Ireland would have its
day, tyranny will inevitably fall—but he knew that William Seward and
Abraham Lincoln had not sent him abroad to stir the Fenian pot. It took
most of the voyage home for him to recover his equilibrium and subdue
the embarrassment that the "Nationalists of Ireland," as the Tipperary
boys called themselves, had provoked.

Archbishop Hughes returned to New York in August in a hopeful
frame of mind and was properly feted on this arrival. The Common
Council, some members of which—his antagonists for years—had no
doubt fantasized about a fatal storm at sea, sent a warm message of
thanks for his patriotic work, as did the governor, and his parishioners
were effusive in their praise. Seward gave a banquet in his honor at his
home in Washington, and Lincoln asked him to come by to provide
a month-by-month account of his impressions of European questions
and attitudes. Lincoln's gratitude extended to a willingness to drop a

diplomatic hint to *pio nono* about a cardinal's hat (it would be America's first) for the New York archbishop. Needless to say, Pius IX did not feel obliged to answer, let alone honor, the request.

These weeks after his return from Europe should have been the high point of a life whose trajectory could never have been imagined in the thatched house in County Tyrone where John Hughes spent his strapped childhood or amid the humiliating rebuffs he encountered in years of trying to gain admission to the Saint Mary's College and Seminary in Maryland. Yet the glow quickly and strangely faded. The criticism became as voluble as the praise and hit its mark more forcefully. He was accused of having gone to Ireland to raise troops for Lincoln. He was accused, even by some New Yorkers, of being a warmonger in clerical garb. Baltimore's *Catholic Mirror* referred to him as a "champion of desolation, blood, and fratricide." An elderly friend, a priest, only half-jokingly wondered where he had found a confessor in Europe to render him absolution. The *New York Sun* ran a satirical piece nominating Hughes for pope. The mood had evidently changed in Italy as well. Pius IX was quoted to him as wondering aloud if the United States had not grown to think of itself as too powerful and important, that world politics might not be better served by its breakup. For this he had spent almost six months in Rome? In an October letter the pope sent to both Hughes and Bishop Odin in New Orleans, the two men were admonished by their spiritual leader to join all their brother bishops in America, North and South, in praying for peace, as if no distinction were to be made between the rebels and aggressors and those who believed in union and never wanted to fight. Though couched in the language of piety, a more explicit rebuff from the Vatican to Hughes was unnecessary. There would be no cardinal's hat, ever.

It was almost as if, in a moment of depression such as he had never known, Hughes wanted to take back all the past year. Seward must have been astonished that fall to receive a letter from his friend that undercut all of his earlier, encouraging missives from Paris, Rome, and Dublin. But to whom should John Hughes unburden himself, to whom should he tell the naked truth when he wasn't playing a public role, if not William Seward, the smartest and kindest man he knew? "There is no love for the United States on the other side of the water," he wrote in bitterness and frustration. If the truth was finally going to be stated, he told his friend, we are "ignored, if not despised—treated in conversation in the same contemptuous language as we might employ toward the inhabitants of the Sandwich Islands, or Washington territory, or Vancouver's Island, or the settlement of the Red River or of the Hudson's Bay Territory." Self-doubt was not something Hughes had ever had to deal with in his rise to power, but he was forced to confront it now. He had thought a good man could devote himself, with equivalent passion and energy, to God and country. He had thought a good man could be vocal on behalf of the victims of imperialist brutality and nativist bigotry, tireless in attacking imperialists and nativists, and preach the loving gospel of Christ. He thought it was possible to see through the thickets of modern politics and still know the peace of the Holy Spirit. By the end of 1862, those convictions had been shaken and discarded.

About this, as about many other issues and problems in his final years, John Hughes was wrong. He did not live to see the end of the Civil War, just as he did not live to see the fruits of his labors—for his country and city, his ethnic group, and above all for his religious faith—inaugurate, in the not so very distant future, the more progressive modern age he longed for. In fact, more suffering—a break with Lincoln, the draft riots of New York—and far more despair lay ahead in the next eighteen months that called into question the aspirations and struggles of four decades. John Hughes's achievements would, indeed, for the moment be overshadowed by hatred and violence, but that moment would not last.

A SON OF ULSTER

LATE IN HIS LIFE, John Hughes received several letters from a Dublin antiquarian looking into the Hughes family history, investigating the possibility of some Welsh ancestry in the Hughes line. The archbishop's answer to his well-intentioned correspondent must have been surprising—unless, of course, the man was already familiar with the famous epistolary style of the prelate he was writing to. "I would beg leave to state, at once," Hughes responded, "that to me no derivation of life could be more highly appreciated than that which has descended to me from my Irish ancestry. Be assured that it would be rather a humiliation than a pride if it should appear that the genesis of the family came from Wales."

The letter was vintage Hughes, in all ways representative of a man who regarded his ethnic background—most of the time—as vitally important, second only to his religion in the evolution of his character and the unfolding drama of his life. John Hughes has been born a Roman Catholic in a country where it was scarcely possible to practice that religion and had come to a new country where the possibilities were greater but hardly free of conflict. By the time he was in his early forties, he was the most famous Roman Catholic in the United States. Yet he also, ultimately, saw himself as an Irishman in America, with all the pain and potential that concept entailed, and, more specifically, an Irishman who was a citizen of the nation's largest, most vibrant and contentious city. To be a Catholic, an Irishman, a New Yorker—these were core identities. No one, now that Hughes was in his sixty-second year, could have hoped to unsettle that sense of private or public self.

Yet Hughes had only himself to blame if John O'Donovan of Dublin was poking about for him in genealogical archives. Years before, for reasons known only to himself ("I fell into a great blunder"), he had floated the idea in a newspaper statement of a Welsh ancestry. It was the kind of lapse that, especially in his later, more exhausted years, few of his critics who followed his public utterances would let him forget. O'Donovan was attempting to be helpful. He may even have been initially encouraged in his research by his subject. He was certain he could confirm for the archbishop that he was indeed entirely Irish and in no part Welsh. But at that moment in the summer of 1860, all John Hughes wanted, really, was to be left alone on the topic.

Irish he was, for generations back. Hughes was born in Annaloghan, a mile from the market town of Augher, in the county of Tyrone in the province of Ulster—today, Northern Ireland, but at the time of his birth an island undivided but thoroughly subjugated. More hamlet than town, Annaloghan is gone today, but not all traces of the Hughes family have likewise vanished. Tourist-savvy Northern Ireland cultivates its ties to the New World. One can visit the Chester Arthur ancestral home and the Andrew Jackson Centre in County Antrim; in Tyrone, Woodrow Wilson's grandfather's dwelling stands; and, at Folk Park, with its costumed guides, so do the cottage that housed the founding father of the Andrew Mellon dynasty and—carted over stone by stone from its original location—the second of the two farmhouses John Hughes lived in as a boy.

The house is what one would expect: a plain white-painted exterior, a thatched roof, a four-foot-high fireplace, whitewashed walls stained by the burning peat a rusty orange above the hearth, sturdy wood furniture, a plate-filled hutch, oil lamps and milk pails, a jamb door meant to provide some privacy between the entry and the kitchen. The land where the cottage originally stood would have been used for growing vegetables, keeping livestock, and cultivating flax, so that during the long winters the family was also employed in spinning and weaving. The manufacture of linen was a reliable source of income for famers of the area. Once the Annaloghan establishment was doing reasonably well, Patrick leased a second property about three miles away, in Dernaved, and tried for a time to keep both going, dividing his time and his sons between the two.

The farms Patrick and Margaret McKenna Hughes managed placed them in that indeterminate middle—not the beaten Irish of the later Great Famine images, not gentry, not even necessarily middle-class by American standards of the time, but respectable country people. They were people who needed to be industrious or they could go under. Had they not left when they did, all safely on the other side by 1818, their children would have been confronted in middle age with a national nightmare as the potato rot set in and the soil turned against them. But Patrick Hughes was not one to bemoan a limitation when an opportunity to rise above it was in sight.

Born in June 1797 and baptized on the twenty-fourth—the feast day of Saint John the Baptist—John Joseph Hughes began life with two crucial advantages: a tight-knit, affectionate, eminently supportive family and the devoted regard of his mother. A letter from one brother in the 1840s even suggested that, as the family's last-born surviving son and a particularly bright boy, he had enjoyed a position as their mother's favorite. Of the original seven children, John was the middle child of the five who lived into adulthood. His two older brothers, Michael and Patrick, and two younger sisters, Ellen and Margaret, would make productive lives for themselves as Americans and be buried in the United States. John was especially close to Margaret and Ellen, whose paths—the one through her marriage, the other as a nun—would be most entwined with his. (The siblings born immediately after John, named Mary and Peter, both died when they were eleven and were buried in Ireland.) Their parents saw the benefits of a family in which lasting bonds were established not only between parent and child but between siblings as well. Patrick senior was acutely aware of how inhospitable the world could be beyond one's cottage and farm and circle of friends. The disadvantages of an outsider's status in his own country came, in time, to grate on him, enough so that he knew he would one day have to emigrate. He lived in an age and a place where the possibilities for the kind of advancement he wanted for his children were limited, where violence against Catholics was never far from his thoughts, and where, when his daughter Mary died, the priest was not even allowed in the cemetery but had to pour the freshly blessed earth onto the coffin at the gate.

History was not on their side. The various Catholic Relief Acts of the late eighteenth century had removed or mitigated some of the more draconian features of the old penal laws that kept Irish Catholics from enjoying the rights of citizenship or free worship under British rule, but the pace of real change was glacial. Disenfranchisement was no longer universal, the right of inheritance by any Protestant relative over one's own Catholic sons was no longer upheld, and restrictions on the purchase of land and time limits on leases were no longer in effect. The government had permitted the opening of the first Catholic seminary in 1795—with the proviso that all teachers and students swear an oath of allegiance to the king. Yet the obstacles to higher education, professional life, and access to the sacraments remained in place. The animus from London, despite the efforts of many liberal politicians, had been made clear from the time of the Gordon Riots (later memorably and frighteningly dramatized by Charles Dickens in *Barnaby Rudge*) to Prime Minister Pitt's statements in 1799 about the Irish "want of intelligence" and natural barbarism to George III's refusal to honor the parliamentary agreement to allow Catholics to sit in the House of Commons after the Act of Union came into effect.

In Ireland at the turn of the century, an Irish Catholic lived in the shadow of two abortive rebellions against the Crown—in 1798 and again in 1803—and the names of Wolfe Tone and Robert Emmet carried, for the politically minded, a mixed aura of patriotism, well-meaning enterprise, dangerous risk taking, and resounding failure. After a long quiescent period, Ulster in the decade of John Hughes's birth was a site of particular tension, even violent acrimony, and martial law had been declared in that province three months before he was born, as the British acted on fears of a French invasion of Ireland that would find ready allies among the Catholics and Presbyterians of the north. In 1797 "Ulster was effectively a military camp," one historian has written, with troops billeted on the people.

Not that this was an auspicious moment for Catholicism elsewhere in Europe. The French Revolution had displaced the faith in post-Bourbon France and seen churches padlocked, to be reopened as "temples of reason," as eight bishops and countless priests and nuns were murdered. John Hughes would one day be an outspoken defender of the papacy; in the year he was born, Napoleon Bonaparte was beginning his machinations against Pius VI that would lead several months later to the French occupation of Rome. The eighty-year-old pontiff was taken prisoner, the fisherman's ring forcibly ripped from his finger, and he died in France.

Within a few years, his successor, Pius VII, was famously humiliated
by the emperor at the coronation the pope was "invited" to attend and,
in 1809, during the second French occupation of the city, was abducted
from the Quirinal, where he had been under house arrest, and taken
from Rome. The tricolor replaced the papal flag over the Castel Sant'Angelo. Pius VII did not return to the Vatican until 1814, the year of Napoleon's exile to Elba and the Congress of Vienna. With the dissolution of
the Holy Roman Empire in the first decade of the century, hundreds of
German monasteries, abbeys, and schools were also closed. Anticlericalism was on the rise in Spain as well, leading in the ensuing decades to
savage outbreaks of violence against Spanish priests.

Patrick Hughes had opinions, but he was not an overtly political
man. He kept his head down, living in a largely Protestant area, and this
strategy worked to his family's benefit. John Hughes recalled as a teen-
ager coming upon a group of Orangemen bearing bayonets who stopped
him on a country road. He feared he was about to be assaulted until one
asked who his father was. Upon being told that he was Patrick Hughes's
son, his interrogator told his comrades to let the boy go. He knew the
father and that he was no enemy of theirs. What mattered to the Hughes
family, rather, was economic stability, the education of their sons, and a
proper religious upbringing for all their children.

The latter was not always easy to come by in Ulster Province circa
1800, unless nurtured within the home. The Irish novelist William Carleton didn't have much in common with John Hughes, not least because
Carleton renounced his Catholicism as an adult and perpetuated myriad
stereotypes in his stories about the Irish, but the two men were almost
exact contemporaries, and both grew up in County Tyrone in straitened
circumstances. In his autobiography, Carleton wrote about the difficulties confronting Catholic families of the countryside who wanted to practice their faith. This was a time, before a settled, expanding community
of churches, rectories, and convents, when priests were still an embattled
group, when it was estimated that there were no more than a hundred
nuns in all Ireland, and when "a chapel was a rare thing." "Within my
own memory," Carleton wrote in old age, "there was nothing in existence for the Catholic to worship of God except the mere altar," which
was covered by a shed roof open to the wind, leaving the officiating
clergyman who made the rounds with "nothing to cover him or protect
him from the elements. . . . During the winter months and wet weather in

general, those of both sexes who attended worship were obliged to bring with them trusses of hay or straw on which to kneel. . . . Indeed, I must say that during the winter months to worship of God was a very trying ceremony." And yet the people of Ireland who had access to instruction and the sacraments, and had sufficient education to read religious literature, which was true of the Hughes family, persevered in their faith and made sure that their children received the sacraments whenever possible. John Hughes's image of a priest from childhood would have been of a man who wasn't vocal about the civil rights of his countrymen but took risks for what he did believe in: the life of the soul and the hard-pressed dignity of the Roman Catholic Church on an enslaved island.

Education involved a similar kind of struggle. The day of the so-called "hedge schools" was slowly passing, as the places of education for Catholic children were no longer literally outdoors, on the other side of the hedge with a monitor's eye cocked for authorities on the prowl, but their "schools" as such were makeshift and elementary in their program and ambitions. Yet some accounts attest to schoolmasters who were more educated than one might expect and who were able to offer those of their charges who cared some instruction in Latin as well as literature, grammar, history, geography, and mathematics. The beginnings of John's erratic but fervent education and that of his less school-enthused brothers came at a small schoolhouse in the outskirts of the town of Augher; later John attended a slightly larger grammar school in Aughnacloy a few miles from the family farm. His parents were fully supportive of their youngest son's interest in scholarship. He grew up in a house with a small but cherished collection of books, and Patrick senior was said to be a serious reader by the standards of his time—even, according to a 1920 history of the diocese of Clogher, writing poems himself, one of which, "The Truagh Woods So Green," showed "an acquaintance with the classics."

One schoolmate in Aughnacloy had reason to remember John many years later. "I loved John Hughes," he wrote, "from the hour when, looking up from my book, I first saw his bright handsome face as he stood for a moment in the open doorway . . . on the day he came to enroll as a pupil." Terence Donaghoe and John Hughes became great mates, inseparable friends in early adolescence, before going their separate ways. They were to be reunited, on the other side of the Atlantic, when both were beginning their life as young priests in the heady world of Philadelphia in the late 1820s.

When Patrick and Margaret Hughes's third son reached the age of seventeen, however, his formal schooling came to an end in the way it did for so many book-loving eighteenth- and nineteenth-century young men, from Benjamin Franklin to Charles Dickens. Family finances demanded it. A bad year for crops and a bad year for the linen trade left Patrick in debt, forcing him to give up his second farm and unable to set aside any money toward tuition. John was put to work on the farm, an obedient but thoroughly miserable young man now, and given those tasks such as tending to the horses and running errands that might still leave him a little time for reading.

Several months later, seeing how unhappy he was at the farm all day, his father directed him down another avenue and secured a job for him as an assistant to Roger Toland, the head gardener at Favour Royal, an estate near Dernaved. Today a haunting wreck out of Brontë or Radcliffe, prey to vandals and arsonists (viewable as of 2014 on an eerie YouTube video walk-through), the manor of the Montray family was one of the grand homes of the region in its day. John Hughes would have learned horticulture at the hands of a master gardener on a lush property encompassing thousands of acres and was exposed to a standard of living which, at that time in his life, would have defied his imagination. The Montrays were not Protestant ogres, either. Thirty years later, their onetime gardener, now a New York bishop, would come for tea and find the remaining family members perfectly hospitable. Predictably, though, the job did not last long. Within a year, the family needed him back at the farm.

It isn't possible to know just when Patrick Hughes decided that the family had to leave Ireland. A decision that, absent some traumatic event, would probably need to ripen over time might have been in his mind for a good many years. The deaths of Mary and Peter, and Mary's insensitive burial, were a factor. International politics, however, inhibited any thought of emigration to Catholic-friendly Baltimore, the principal port of entry in America for most Irish at the time. The War of 1812 had made the seas a dangerous place and their objective an imperiled locale. In 1814 British troops were swarming over Maryland and had burned the White House and Capitol in the nearby District of Columbia. So it wasn't until a year after the Treaty of Ghent ended that strange, pointless conflict that Patrick Hughes presented his family with his plan. It was going to be difficult and disruptive, and if there was any reason to hope that things might be better for a Catholic Ulsterman in the years ahead, there would be no reason to attempt it, but that was not the case.

The family departed Ireland in three stages and endured a long separation. Patrick, along with his second son of the same name, sailed in 1816, landed in Baltimore, and eventually made his way to the Cumberland Valley area of southern Pennsylvania, where he had heard that land and opportunities were more plentiful. Michael and John were left to take charge of the farm. A year later, John joined his father and brother, once it had been determined that work was to be had and money could be made over time to pay for the rest of the travelers. Margaret, with Michael and her two daughters, had to stay behind to see to the sale of the farm and wait to hear that her husband had found a new place that would accommodate everyone; but the following year, they, too, made the crossing. First divided in 1816, the seven members of the Hughes family were not together again until 1818. About the uncanny strength of Mrs. Hughes—left behind, when her husband and two of her sons were gone, to handle weighty business dealings and then to make the crossing with Michael, Ellen, and Margaret—nothing needs to be said or doubted.

Two years before his death, speaking to an audience in Dublin, John Hughes referred to his family's departure in terms both nostalgic and bitter. Almost fifty years ago, he told his listeners, "like some disjointed or feeble spur, no longer useful to the wrecked and stranded barque of which it had once been a portion—I voluntarily floated off from the shores of this island. I was borne westward to another country beyond the Atlantic Ocean." The adverb *voluntarily* conflicts with the more passive verb and verb phrase, *floated* and *was borne*. How voluntary could such a move be? Who happily consents to be uprooted and carried away? Yet the promise of a better future lay elsewhere, as his father knew, and the hardships and anxiety would prove worthwhile. "In [my new homeland]," he recalled, "I had an opportunity of improving my education, for legislation there had not attempted to monopolise and appropriate to itself the key of knowledge, and there, although a Roman Catholic, I was made a freeman and an American citizen, long before the Act of Catholic Emancipation was passed by the British Parliament."

———

BALTIMORE IN 1817: John Hughes's first sight of America was designed to make a patriot. He sailed from Belfast and arrived alone, watched over on the voyage by a neighbor and friend of the family, an emigrating tradesman named Dixon, after what was a horrendous ordeal. Though he would later find sea travel bracing, life on board the kind of vessel Hughes journeyed on in 1817 was primitive. Passengers brought their own food, which was meant to last them up to four weeks in an era before refrigeration, had to get used to sleeping quarters and sanitary facilities that reeked on the best of days, and experienced pitching and rocking that induced not hours, but days, of nausea and headaches. But, at twenty, he was strong and healthy. And then he was there—in sight of Fort McHenry, in the harbor that had inspired Francis Scott Key, in a city, twice the size of Belfast, that was enormously proud of its role in repelling the British invaders and was often commented upon by European travelers as the most handsome on the Eastern Seaboard. Gas lighting had been installed in Baltimore only a few months before Hughes's arrival, making it the first metropolis in the county to do so.

It was also a city that was especially welcoming to Catholics. The late John Carroll, the first American bishop, was the brother of a signer of the Constitution and the cousin of a signer of the Declaration of Independence—no pedigree could be better in the time of Jefferson and Madison—and, as father of what is called "the Maryland tradition," had established a climate of respectability for his faith in "the premier see." A new archbishop, Ambrose Maréchal, had recently taken charge, and the construction of Benjamin Latrobe's imposing Cathedral of the Assumption, a project begun by Carroll, was well under way. Just to look at the country's first Catholic cathedral in the making, or to walk by Saint Mary's Seminary, the first Catholic seminary in the country, was to know that one had landed in a new place where, whatever obstacles lay ahead, the prospects for a good life were more likely than in Europe. For John Hughes, the brutalizing world of George III and the Orangemen belonged to the past. The inauguration of James Monroe that year had commenced what became known as the "Era of Good Feelings," and, as one historian noted, "The Catholic Church had never enjoyed a more secure and respected position on the American scene than it did at the beginning of the Era of Good Feelings." That harmony, of course, was not to last.

There were jobs to be had in Baltimore and its environs, even if this city of sixty-five thousand had not seen commerce restored fully to its prewar levels; and that was fortunate, as Patrick senior wasn't ready to have everyone join him in Pennsylvania just yet, where he was attempting to secure a property that would sustain the family. So John remained in

Baltimore, where his brother had found work, and, after a brief reunion with his father, looked about and considered his prospects. A plantation owner on the Eastern Shore of Maryland wanted an experienced gardener. The months at Favour Royal proved fortuitous, after all.

Presumably, John was put in charge of the slaves who labored in the gardens of this plantation as well, a situation that gave rise to the statement by some twentieth-century commentators that he had once worked as an overseer or, put less dramatically, as "superintendent of a slave plantation in his youth." Both designations sound inflated and imply an authority that the job did not likely possess. Indeed, six months later, as winter approached and his planting skills were of no further use, the immigrant Irishman was unemployed, told rather summarily that his services were no longer required. If he expected to be kept on in some other capacity, he was quickly disabused of that notion, though he claimed he had "worked with all [his] might" and apparently hoped for some consideration from his employer.

Whatever his exact relationship to the black men he directed—and bent and dug and mowed and planted with—in Maryland, it is worth stopping to consider the effect a first encounter with slavery had on John Hughes. It can't have been anything other than unsettling. No abolitionist, then or ever, and no special friend of the black man, he understood the unique degradation the lash and chattel status signified. He had had a taste of the attempt to enforce illiteracy and suppress political rights at home, but this was something different. Owner and owned: it was humanity at its most degraded, at both ends of the spectrum.

A few years later, in his mid-twenties, when he began to write and publish poetry in a local newspaper—a pastime quickly abandoned—he reflected on what he had observed in his first months in Maryland: "Hard is the lot of him who's doomed to toil, / Without one slender hope to soothe his pain, / Whose sweat and labor are a master's spoil, / Whose sad reward a master's proud disdain." In "The Slave," the young poet takes on—with very real poignancy—the voice of the black man who bids Columbia to "wipe the stain" from its codes, "to chase foul bondage from its Southern plains . . . to let Afric's sons feel what it is—to be." America has failed in her stated purpose, to bring freedom to all men, and the African captive, brought to this land not in steerage but in chains, can only cry: "Long have I pined through years of woe / Adown life's bleeding track, / And still my tears, my blood, must flow, / Because my hand is black. / Still boiling, still toiling, / Beneath the burning heats of noon, / I, poor slave, court the grave; / O Columbia, grant the boon!"

John Hughes was forced to relocate sooner than expected to Chambersburg, where his father had settled; for him, the next year was one of backbreaking and often ignominious labor. A high point of the summer was the arrival of his mother, Michael, and the two girls, and it was pleasing to see that his father was, by degrees, finding his footing in his new homeland. He had acquired a few horses and carts for hire and owned some small parcels of land suitable for planting crops to sell. It was also evident that his father was homesick and was never going to see himself as an American or forget what he had left behind. Emigration had been more traumatic than expected. For his sons, there was no choice. Heartsick that there seemed to be no opportunity to continue his education now that he was fifty miles from Baltimore, John took any job that came his way to help defray the family's expenses. He dug neighbors' gardens, he joined road crews mending roads, he wielded a pickax in the local quarry. He considered moving north to New York State to work on the Erie Canal.

Chambersburg, twenty-five miles west of Gettysburg, eighteen miles north of the Mason-Dixon Line, was a town of not quite two thousand people when John Hughes first saw it, and very little about the place provided an ambitious newcomer with reason to be optimistic about the future. Yet neither was it a frontier wasteland. Patrick had never had any intention of relocating his wife and children to an area where they might be the only Catholics or even part of a too-small minority as they had been in Ulster. Though Presbyterians formed the largest denomination, followed by Methodists and Lutherans, a Catholic community had been established as far back as the 1780s and a log church erected in the 1790s. In 1812 a stone structure replaced the original building, whose facade a county historian called a "marvel of stone masonry." The Hughes family worshipped twice a month at Corpus Christi, one of only several consecrated churches in the state outside Philadelphia. A priest said Mass and heard confessions on alternate Sundays as he divided his time among several smaller towns in Franklin County. Father Kearns was presumably a capable and pious man, to judge by his later postings.

The county seat, Chambersburg struck most people as having "a rough and unpleasant appearance" circa 1800, transformed into a muddy swamp during any heavy rainstorm, but more streets were being paved each year by the time Patrick Hughes arrived, and the town was proud of its hotel and tavern, courthouse and bank, grammar school and paper mill, the latter a going concern that printed a sizable percentage of the federal government's banknotes. Chambersburg also supported two weekly newspapers, one printed in English (replete with advertisements seeking the return of runaway slaves from the other side of the Mason-Dixon Line) and one in German. Still, life at home for John Hughes meant work of a kind for which he had little taste.

That grinding manual labor led to a meeting, which meant nothing at the time but must have seemed oddly coincidental later—though he never liked to speak of it, avoiding all his life any references to his time as a dollar-a-day laborer. One morning, while working on the new Pennsylvania Turnpike, he saw a carriage approach an unfinished stretch of the road. The rocky ground proved to be impassable, and the driver began to turn around. Hughes approached him and offered to help. He and the other members of the crew carried the gig over the rocks and set it down on the paved part of the turnpike. Conversation with the driver revealed that, though a native-born American, he was from a family in Ulster known to the Hughes family. Expressions of gratitude for the assistance were exchanged, and the lawyer from Lancaster was on his way. Thirty years later, Hughes would meet James Buchanan again as secretary of state. Hughes would also be an overnight guest at Wheatland, Buchanan's home in Lancaster. Forty years later, Hughes would be a welcome visitor of the same man in the White House.

Ultimately, the thought that he had journeyed three thousand miles to build roads or work the soil was unendurable to Hughes in a way that it never was to his brothers. He and Margaret were the restless ones of the family, a drive encouraged by their mother. Without money or family connections, though, for John Hughes the future was anything but certain—unless he could acquire an education. That was the key to everything in America. His thoughts turned definitively toward Emmitsburg, the education that might be had there—and something more than an education.

Twenty-five miles from Chambersburg, just across the border into Maryland, Emmitsburg was the one place where a community of scholars, such as they were, was to be located in the region in 1819. Mount Saint Mary's College had been founded only eleven years earlier and was a struggling as well as a hybrid institution. The Sulpician order had sponsored the establishment of a school there—a school, not a seminary—with the idea that its better students might then enter the Sulpicians' own under-attended seminary in Baltimore or their principal seminary in Paris. It was apparent soon enough, at least to the priests who worked in Emmitsburg, that enrollment numbers and dire finances were going to hinder, or ultimately preclude, the execution of this sensible plan. Mount Saint Mary's, severely debt-burdened from the start, needed to offer space to its own seminarians who would then act as unpaid teachers and tutors to the boys and young men who boarded there. Some of those seminarians would complete their religious studies in Baltimore, and a few would go to Paris; others, not.

Run by John Dubois, a French-born Sulpician priest who would several years later be named the third bishop of the New York diocese (hence, John Hughes's predecessor in that position), the seminary at the time Hughes first heard of it housed three priests and twenty young men who were studying for the priesthood who also served as teachers for the sixty to eighty students of the "college" (i.e., academy), mainly teenage boys who paid $135 per annum—when they actually paid—for their tuition and living expenses, to be instructed in Greek, Latin, English, French, geometry, mathematics, poetry, rhetoric, and moral philosophy. Some of those boys were considered likely prospects for the seminary—Dubois never lost sight of the original idea behind the founding of his school—but others were sent there by their families for the academic rigor the school promised and its reasonable fees.

Some were not even Catholic. It wasn't unusual in postcolonial America for Protestant families to send their children to Catholic schools, especially their daughters to convent schools, if those were the best educational institutions in the area and assurances were made that their sons and daughters would be safe from proselytizing for the Roman faith. From the point of view of the Sulpician fathers, though, the school had not developed as they intended, and they opposed any competition to their own seminary in Baltimore; but Mount Saint Mary's took on a sometimes desperate life of its own after a few years and proved harder than not to suppress. Ultimately, "the Mount," as it was colloquially known, would sever its ties to the disgruntled Sulpicians. There had never been any questions about where Dubois's loyalties lay.

Hughes's plans must have seemed quixotic to anyone outside his immediate family. A man who was too old and too poor to attend the school as a student was going to show up and ask to be admitted as a seminarian-tutor when he had only a few years' attendance at an Irish grammar school to recommend him. His initial query met with predictable silence. Mount Saint Mary's might be a makeshift, catch-as-catch-can institution at this early point in its history, but it was not quite that flexible. Nonetheless, Hughes moved from Chambersburg to Emmitsburg, looking for work and a way in. An Ulster man he met in a tavern helped him to find a job digging a millrace and later building a stone bridge. He found a family, the Mullens, to take him as a boarder. Mr. Mullen was an immigrant himself, an Irish schoolmaster. The old network counted for something. John became a communicant at Saint Joseph's Church. Repeated appeals to Father Dubois met with repeated rejections, though. By the end of the year the closest he was to his goal was when he was able to secure a job as gardener and groundskeeper for the school, living in a ramshackle log cabin on the property. A less determined person would have seen this trajectory as a sign that he should turn his thoughts in another direction or move back to Baltimore to look for work there.

Whether or not John Hughes knew or surmised as an adolescent in Ireland that he wanted one day to be a priest, or whether that thought took root after his arrival in Baltimore or during his stay in Chambersburg, is unclear. As an archbishop, Hughes himself liked the simpler story that he had known since boyhood, but his familiarity with any priests in childhood would have been very limited, nor does he seem ever to have mentioned to later acquaintances any priests he knew in Ireland, an odd omission if there were any who made an impression and inspired him to think about the priesthood. There is no doubt, though, that by the summer of 1819 he was certain that his future involved a commitment to the church.

Consider that the nature of a decision to become a Roman Catholic priest was no less momentous then than it is today. Yet its context is radically different. In the more secular climate of the Western world in the late twentieth and early twenty-first centuries, a young man entering the seminary is assailed by questions, potentially internal but certainly from those around him, so many of which imply sacrifice and loss: Are you prepared to do *without*?—without sex, without marriage, without children, without the comforts and entitlements of modern life? In Hughes's time, especially to a man coming from a religious family already attached to the faith—a situation very different from the dilemma faced by a convert—the perspective was different. With two sons following in the father's footsteps, a third son embarking on a religious path would have been a source of great pride to the family, especially to a pious mother. What one was giving up was obvious, but what one was gaining, if the calling were deeply felt, was much clearer.

The priesthood in the 1820s was not about loss for someone like John Hughes; to a good priest, it was about *being called*, and it was about a certain kind of empowerment. Not an empowered social status in the United States, to be sure, as priests enjoyed no such widespread respect in this country before the latter part of that century. But there was a sense that one was giving oneself to a formidable cause, both temporal and eternal, potentially living a life beyond what others lived as they circumscribed their concerns in plausible familial and material ways, and this drive was keenly felt by Hughes as he considered what his place in the world might be. The record for American priests in the first half of the nineteenth century is spotty—the loneliness and deprivation took their toll, and alcoholism and lack of education were undeniable problems—but the future archbishop had no doubts, had no reason ever to look back and wonder at roads not taken. His sister Ellen was to feel similarly called, entering the Order of the Sisters of Charity a few years later.

It would be instructive to know more about the American priests John Hughes knew personally who helped to shape his sense of a religious vocation, but any absolute clarity regarding that part of the story also seems lost to time. About Father Kearns of Chambersburg, only the faintest traces of biographical information remain. Hughes would have heard about the more famous American Catholic prelates of his day, however, and that list was not unimpressive. John Carroll was widely regarded as an exemplary representative of the church in Protestant America. Ambrose Maréchal (who visited Emmitsburg that year) was known as a man not afraid to speak his mind, had skillfully maintained the ties Carroll had established with the Federalist elite while still asserting episcopal rights, and oversaw the completion of the cathedral in Baltimore in 1821. The great orator John England was an even stronger, more conspicuous figure, and the Cork-born prelate's emigration to the United States and appointment as bishop of Charleston in 1820 would have been significant news among Irish Catholics. Voluble in his protests against British imperialism, he had refused to take the oath of allegiance to the Crown and, upon leaving Europe, announced his intention of becoming an American citizen as soon as possible. He brought to his new position a reputation as a force to be reckoned with. But these would have been names—legendary, perhaps, but rather distant to a young man in rural Pennsylvania contemplating a similar path.

One priest Hughes had personal contact with soon after relocating, according John Hassard, his last secretary, was merely passing through Emmitsburg in 1819, where he served at Saint Joseph's for nine months, but he offered an example of firm religious commitment and breathtaking if sometimes bizarre energy. Samuel Sutherland Cooper was a convert whose path to his calling was anything but typical. A good-looking rake and man-about-town in his younger days (the best billiards player in Philadelphia, it was said), he had been born into wealth, made plenty of money on his own as a sea captain, and for years indulged his tastes for travel, adventure, and great personal generosity to his friends. His conversion caused something of a stir in Philadelphia, where he had been known as a skeptic on all matters religious; but when he had decided that only the Catholic Church could provide him with the spiritual certainties he craved, he entered Saint Mary's Seminary in Baltimore and made a pilgrimage to Rome before being ordained in his forties—an age far beyond the norm for most priests beginning their pastoral work. Then, "a late-comer [to the faith], he strove to make up in ardor what he had lost in time," as one writer characterized his style. "Impulsive, impatient of results, over-zealous," Cooper held nothing back, giving a large part of his remaining fortune to Mother Elizabeth Seton and her Sisters of Charity to open a girls' school in Emmitsburg. (When he died in France in 1843, he was penniless, which surprised no one who knew him.) He was also by most accounts a passionate public speaker responsible for numerous conversions throughout the South and later in Europe, though his driving personality sometimes led to the opposite outcome. He made Bishop Carroll, who thought he detected signs of a "disordered imagination" in the man, rather nervous. He made many temperate people nervous.

John Hughes crossed paths with Father Cooper only briefly. Saint Joseph's Parish was Cooper's first assignment, and he proved a bit much for the town, especially in his attacks on the consumption of alcohol that led to parishioners leaving their empty bottles on his doorstep. It was typical of Cooper to insist on conducting a temperance crusade in a town with fewer than a thousand inhabitants that supported four taverns and several "tippling shops" and where even the dry-goods stores sold whiskey. He left before the end of 1819 to work as a missionary in several Southern cities. There he was much sought after by many pastors, though others found him too agitated, too doctrinaire. His charisma gave rise as well to some strange rumors over the years. At some point in his forties, he had all his teeth removed, rendering himself singularly unattractive, and did not replace them with dentures—not unheard of in a time of primitive dental care, gum disease, and ill-fitting replacements. Some of his admirers insisted that he had done this to mortify his flesh. A strikingly handsome man had, according to this unconventional mythology, become a penitent of the first order. Cooper himself always denied any such intentions.

The other priest Hughes met at this time was every bit as memorable and intense as Father Cooper, though in all ways deeper and far more stable. Theirs was an authentic and fruitful relationship. Simon Bruté would remain a close friend to John Hughes until Bruté's death at sixty in 1839. He had a quietly assured if sometimes scattered manner, and, more important, he was probably the first person who saw any latent talent in John Hughes and offered him the kind of encouragement he needed. Alienated from the start from John Dubois, Hughes needed to be believed in by someone outside his family. He needed a man of learning and culture to think that he might be the same one day. Bruté was that person. They met when Bruté succeeded Cooper as pastor at Saint Joseph's Church and was coming to Emmitsburg for a second time to teach philosophy and theology.

Like Hughes and so many priests of that era, Bruté was in the United States because of European politics. Eighteen years Hughes's senior, he had been born to an affluent Catholic family in Brittany and educated by the Jesuits. As an adolescent, he had witnessed firsthand the Revolution's brutality toward priests and nuns, the roundups and show trials and executions every bit as emotionally scarring in a town like Rennes as in Paris. He recorded in his last years his remembrances of the 1790s in France, when "death was a daily tale," mournful vignettes illustrated with his own pen-and-ink drawings. (Bruté's pronunciation of English was always imperfect, too heavily accented to be heard clearly from the pulpit; his written English, however, was better.) Graduating from medical school in 1803, he had decided not to practice medicine but to enter the newly reopened Seminary of Saint-Sulpice in Paris and was ordained

RT. REV. SIMON G. BRUTÉ, D. D.
First Bishop of Vincennes.

FIGURE 2. *Simon Bruté, John Hughes's earliest mentor, was a model of a dedicated, erudite, and tough-minded cleric.* (Courtesy of the Archives of the Archdiocese of New York.)

in 1808. He had no interest in remaining in France and, after teaching for two years at the seminary, left for the United States to teach at Saint Mary's Seminary in Baltimore. He craved a new world and a new life.

In 1812 he had been directed to go to Emmitsburg to assist John Dubois, serving as the overtaxed head of both the college and the seminary, pastor of the town, and superior of the Sisters of Charity. Dubois desperately needed another hand, and a fellow Frenchman was just what he wanted. Bruté remained there for three years, after which, following a sojourn back to France (to plead the school's case to the Sulpician hierarchy and to ship to America his sizable library), he was appointed president of Saint Mary's College in Baltimore, a job not to his liking or suited to his skills. By 1818 he was back in Emmitsburg, his true home, where he remained a beloved teacher for all the time that John Hughes was there. Eventually, in 1834, he reluctantly accepted the position of a newly created bishopric in Vincennes, Indiana. At the time of the appointment, John England wondered if the church was sending the right man. A literary Frenchman to be a frontier bishop, the spiritual leader of the far-flung Catholics of Indiana and the prairies of Illinois, a missionary to the Miami and the Potawatomi? He underestimated his man.

None of Bruté's students underestimated their teacher. Neither did Elizabeth Seton or the Sisters of Charity, to whose welfare he was devoted. Neither did John Dubois, really, although their relations were not always easy—Dubois eminently practical and often dictatorial, Bruté wildly impractical and ruminative, frequently exhibiting a nervousness of temper, ascetic, easily preoccupied, but courteous and generous to a fault. Bruté was also, unlike Dubois, free of the common French cleric's bias of the time, an antipathy toward the Irish. Rather, Bruté was everyone's ideal of a good priest, someone who would literally give a poor man the coat off his back and lived with the spiritual well-being of others foremost in his mind.

Bruté had a combative side, too. No matter how busy with his pastoral and teaching work, he found time to write for Bishop England's *Catholic Miscellany*, the nation's first Catholic newspaper, and other religious journals as far away as Hartford and Cincinnati, largely defenses of Rome and attacks on Protestant stereotypes. "That kind of work is continually called for by our position in this country," he once commented, "and the influence exerted by it too important to allow it to be neglected." That was a creed his devoted student from Ireland would share.

These two potential models—Bruté and, to a much lesser extent, Cooper—would have confirmed in John Hughes at least two impressions concerning his hopes for the future: to accept that God intended one to live a life in service to the church, to embrace a cause greater than oneself, did not mean that one's path would be smooth or predictable; and it did not mean forcing oneself into a mold, curbing one's temperamental or intellectual inclinations, or living apart from the world. On the contrary, in a land still unformed in so many ways, in a country in which one was part of a small religious minority, the call for action, persistence, and strength of personality was all the more pressing. Twenty-two-year-old John Hughes was certain that, if he could get the proper training, those were needs he could meet.

2

A VOCATION

IF DECIDING to become a priest and actually getting started down that path proved to be two very different things, the months spent at Favour Royal were not incidental in reconciling the two. Yet the difficulties of being accepted into Mount Saint Mary's on more than a horticultural basis were greater and more frustrating than John Hughes had anticipated.

A Catholic directory from the time refers to Mount Saint Mary's "terraces planted with trees [and] well-cultivated gardens"—a testament, in part, to Hughes's six-day-a-week labor, the fruits of his sweat and the dirt under his fingernails. The directory also noted the school's healthful climate and picturesque setting, architecture that sounded primitive by any standards, and (a proud boast) eight outhouses. The school's library was well stocked. More desperately with each passing month, Hughes wanted to be one of those seminarian-tutors with access to that library and the hope that he would one day be a celebrant at Mass and have a church of his own to lead. Nothing about his educational background impressed Dubois, though, as he made clear again and again to his earnest applicant. Nor should Hughes have been surprised by that response. At his age, he looked like what he was: a well-built Irish immigrant laborer with a square jaw, a prominent nose, and aspirations beyond his station. His manners were acceptable, his mastery of any one of the several academic subjects the school offered nonexistent, and his temerity vaguely annoying. Even after Dubois had hired him as the school's gardener and groundskeeper, he would have preferred his Irish-born employee to continue planting, mowing, and trimming, keeping his mouth shut. During those many months, John Hughes learned about patience and anger in equal measure.

The Cooper-Bruté connection might have been the crucial link in gaining him admission to the seminary and college grounds in the first place. Through either or both of these men he would have met their friend Elizabeth Seton, America's first native-born saint, whose fledgling branch of the Sisters of Charity was based in Emmitsburg. It is Seton (according to assorted commentators on Hughes's life) who spoke to John Dubois and managed to get him to reconsider his dismissive attitude toward the young man from Chambersburg. The story of her intervention with Dubois—"it took a saint to recognize John Hughes's talents" is the much-used line—has an apocryphal air to it, though that doesn't mean the facts are necessarily otherwise. Things too good to be true, too biographically pat, do happen. It is significant that Seton's most recent biographer makes no mention of this act (for the good reason that no documentation seems to exist), that Hughes's first and most comprehensive posthumous biographer did not verify the point in his 1866 book, and that Bruté's putting in the right word for the young man makes for an infinitely more plausible if less dramatic moment in the archbishop's life story. Saint Elizabeth Seton is a well-known figure; Simon Bruté is not.

Whatever the case, John Dubois relented under pressure, in a manner of speaking, and in the autumn of 1819 proposed an arrangement whereby Hughes could work for the seminary, living in a small log cabin on the grounds, and in lieu of salary be tutored in the coursework he would need should Dubois ever decide that he could become a candidate for the priesthood.

That arrangement, which was begrudging and humiliating and provided Hughes with living quarters no better than those of the slaves and the manumitted wage-earning black men who also worked the seminary land, lasted for several months. Only belatedly did Dubois recognize that he had judged the laborer thought so highly of by Seton or Bruté amiss. Hughes had a raw potential that belied his background, appearance, and résumé. Closer acquaintance suggested that he was energetic and conscientious beyond the call of duty, unwavering in his protestations of sincerity about his calling to a religious life, and actually voracious in his reading habits when finally provided with the books he wanted and needed. The only thing Dubois did not perceive at first—the result of a wise dissimulation on the younger man's part—was the depth of the resentment he had instilled in him. In the fall of 1820 Hughes was finally invited to begin his formal studies for the priesthood. Thus began a two-decade-long relationship between John Dubois and John Hughes

FIGURE 3. *The reluctant third bishop of the diocese of New York, John Dubois had grudgingly admitted John Hughes to his seminary in Maryland and, to his dismay, was replaced by him when the duties of his episcopal office became too much.* (Courtesy of the Archives of the Archdiocese of New York.)

that did much to affect the course of New York City history, immigrant history, and American church history.

The future third and fourth bishops of the diocese of New York—and how odd, how comically improbable, that designation would have struck both men in the early 1820s—were as unalike in background as in temperament. Dubois was a product of Bourbon France, a Latin scholar and son of a bourgeois family who at twenty had imagined ahead of him a long and satisfying life as a Parisian priest. The fall of the Bastille in 1789 and the Reign of Terror shattered that dream, thrusting him into the wilds of America in 1792. Thanks to forged papers from a powerful political figure who had been an affectionate friend and schoolmate at the Collège Louis-le-Grand—Maximilian Robespierre was a contradictory zealot—Dubois managed to escape France just as the roundups and murder of clerics who had refused to take the oath of loyalty to the state were beginning. He also took with him a letter of introduction to James Monroe from the Marquis de Lafayette, whose pious wife knew the young priest from the parish of Saint-Sulpice. Leaving his family behind and speaking not a word of English, he had no idea what to expect on the other side of the Atlantic; with his letter to Monroe, his way was both better paved than his gardener's had been, but more solitary and uncertain.

Emigration brought its share of culture shock. "I found myself in that vast country," Dubois later wrote, "where whatever I saw reminded me of nothing I had seen before." Yet he also encountered unexpected generosity in Richmond, Virginia. He experienced it from the Monroes, from Patrick Henry—who helped him to learn English—and from the state legislature that allowed him, in this area without any churches, to celebrate Mass in the courtroom of the Capitol in his first weeks in town. By the turn of the century, Dubois was settled in Maryland, at the urging of Bishop Carroll, where there were many more Catholics and hence a greater need for priests. He joined forces in the town of Frederick with a local Catholic attorney and rising politician, Roger Taney, to secure funds to build a church. He was known as a devoted and compassionate pastor.

In 1808, Dubois entered the Society of Saint-Sulpice and began the slow and arduous process of forming a school and seminary. Founding two such institutions in the woods of Pennsylvania would have struck Dubois as a far-fetched notion when he was a young priest back in cosmopolitan Paris. That he would manage to make a success of it against great odds, even seeing it in his old age as the most important accomplishment of his life, would have been past belief. Nothing in the 1810s suggested that such an endeavor would bear fruit. The French connection paid off on occasion: in 1821, King Louis XVIII of France, concerned about the growth of Catholicism in America, gave 3,000 francs (almost $600) to Mount Saint Mary's at a moment when every dollar counted. He would hardly have given a second thought to a seminary run by an Irishman.

More often than not, though, keeping Mount Saint Mary's going was a fierce uphill labor for all of the eighteen years Dubois was in charge. Ambrose Maréchal in Baltimore was anything but a faithful supporter. He made no secret of the fact that he considered Mount Saint Mary's a backwater institution that would never be anything better than that, and his particular complaint was that Dubois was running a haven for "a multitude of young Irishmen who would run the country." Too many students over the years to suit the French-born bishop would have names like McCaffrey, McCloskey, McGerry, Egan, Mayne, Whalen, and Hughes.

Those Irishmen were, in the main, a sturdy lot. The regimen at the seminary was especially appealing to John Hughes. He, like everyone else, rose at dawn, said his prayers, attended Mass, performed various chores, and took breakfast in silence. Reading was allowed at breakfast, which meant the day started, in effect, with a book in hand. Everyone, including Dubois, took a turn at serving dinner and performing various duties on the grounds. Classes throughout the day alternated with quiet study periods and time set aside for prayer. Relaxation was afforded by long walks with one's friends through the hillside. The directory hadn't misled: it was a healthful climate—for the robust—and a picturesque setting. For Hughes, those walking companions included seminarians Edward Francis Mayne and John McCaffrey; McCaffrey would later serve for decades as the director of Mount Saint Mary's. Hughes had a capacity for friendship in his younger years that wasn't seen, or quite believed in, by everyone who knew him later in his years as a bishop.

Hughes differed from all the other seminarians in that teaching was out of the question initially, and that was a problem. He simply didn't know enough, or know enough by John Dubois's standards, to be an instructor yet. He needed first to be a student himself. Yet sitting in classes with the rest of the student body (a twenty-three-year-old amid fifteen- and sixteen-year-olds) was not a situation designed to deal with a corrosive sense of inferiority in this setting or to instill respect in the other, younger pupils. Hughes was the butt of a fair number of jokes in a manner that the more respected seminarians never were. Put in charge of the daily study hall, he compensated in an ill-advised way and was a disciplinarian beyond what the situation called for. Corporal punishment was a standard practice at almost all schools of the time, but he was deemed by Dubois to have overstepped acceptable limits on one occasion, pummeling one surly boy, and was relieved of that duty.

Eventually Hughes was thought sufficiently informed to teach classes in arithmetic, grammar, and introductory Latin. The range of his charges was similar to that of teachers at any other academy, and he had to deal with the usual number of rude or lackluster scholars. Yet the caliber of the best students could be very high, as was the case with John McCloskey, who attended the Mount until the age of fifteen. Hughes's future private secretary and eventual successor as head of the New York archdiocese—and America's first cardinal—impressed everyone with his sober study habits and the quickness of his intellect. Richard Whalen, the future bishop of Richmond and Wheeling, was another, graduating in 1825 with "highest honors" before heading to Paris and his seminary studies there.

The caliber of his fellow seminarians would have been the real cause for concern in Hughes's first years at Mount Saint Mary's. Some of his new peers were no more distinguished than he was, but all of them were far better educated. To observe them in the classroom reminded him of the distance he had to travel, and quickly.

One person in that category, an Irish immigrant he took to immediately, was John Baptist Purcell, who had entered the seminary several weeks before him. Four years younger than Hughes, Purcell had left County Cork on his own at eighteen, disgusted with the limited educational prospects for a Catholic in his native land, and was sufficiently self-educated, especially in his reading of the classics, to secure a job within a few months of his arrival as a private tutor to a wealthy Maryland family. A pleasing blend of geniality and erudition, he made friends easily. Comparing himself to Purcell, Hughes felt keenly the difference in their backgrounds and the way in which others perceived them, but Purcell was a man to set someone he liked at ease. Hughes relaxed in his company, could joke with him, found him easy to talk to. Their arrival in the same year was a fortuitous development. Bruté also took Purcell under his wing, and the two traveled together to France in 1824 when Bruté needed to tend to matters connected to his late mother's estate, and Purcell then decided to complete his education under the Sulpicians and seek ordination in Paris.

Much more intimidating to anyone who had spent a larger part of his life with road gangs than fellow scholars was Charles Constantine Pise. Like Purcell, Pise was four years younger than Hughes, who studied under him, but when he arrived at Emmitsburg in 1821 for a one-year stay, he was already marked as an obvious future luminary of the church. Articulate, well-bred, intellectually inquiring, stunningly handsome, and (best of all from Dubois's perspective) not Irish, Pise was seen by Dubois as a highly desirable addition to his seminary. Educated at Georgetown College, Pise had entered a Jesuit novitiate before deciding that he did not want to commit to a lifetime with that order. The young man's historical sense and literary talents were regarded as exceptionally promising. One of his earliest efforts, a play about Montezuma and the conquest of Mexico, was performed at the Mount.

Indeed, Pise was an anomaly in an era when preparation for the priesthood in the United States was, to put it generously, inconsistent. A parish priest who was also a linguist, novelist, poet, and propagandist for Catholicism was a rare individual in antebellum America, and in his mid-twenties, not long after leaving Mount Saint Mary's, he was already at work on a five-volume history of the church from its beginnings to the Renaissance. That enterprise would bring him to the attention of Pope Gregory XVI, who in 1832 made him a knight of the Holy Roman Empire. In that same decade, Henry Clay would see that he was appointed for a year as the first Roman Catholic chaplain to the United States Senate. If anyone in Emmitsburg was going to be a figure of great renown in the American church in the coming decades, Pise would surely have been seen as that person. He and John Hughes would meet again, twenty years later, when Pise worked under the new bishop of the New York diocese, but their first encounter must have reminded Hughes of why it had been so difficult to secure admission to the Mount in the first place. He needed to work day and night if he were ever to be seen in the same league as a John Purcell or a Charles Constantine Pise.

That diligence and drive were not lacking. One instructor, comparing Hughes to John McCaffrey, who stood at the top of the Latin class, noted that "Mr. Hughes would at least be equal to McCaffrey if he had the same chance; excellent judgment in translation but does not know the meaning of words." Every evaluation stirred him to greater exertions. Hughes also devoted himself to the study of modern languages with particular diligence. He was nearly fluent in French by the time he left Emmitsburg, which pleased his mentor (Father Bruté sometimes wrote his lengthy letters to him in his native language), and made his first efforts at learning Spanish.

Public speaking, his forte only a few years later, did not come easily. The school's literary society, of which he was a member, required everyone to write an essay to be read aloud to the group. When his turn came, he was visibly nervous, his voice trembled, and he dropped his papers, leading to a wrathful outburst from Father Hickey, the society's cranky instructor who had scant tolerance for hesitation or incompetence. "That's pride, sir, nothing but pride!" he bellowed. "Put it under your feet. Pick up your essay and go on!" Refashioning himself into an effective orator became a major goal for John Hughes over the next year.

It was not easy for him to escape his past, though. Dubois liked the work he had done on the property and, treating him like the classic scholarship boy who ought at all times to be grateful, thought nothing of asking him between classes to assist in the planting when his help was needed or to superintend the men cleaning the grounds. On one occasion, Hughes was upbraiding a hired man who showed up for work drunk. "Who are you, I should like to know?" the man fired back. "You're nobody but John Hughes. Don't I remember when you used to work with your hands as I do?" His pupils could sometimes be as haughty on that subject, reminding him of what he wanted to put behind him but could hardly hope to at a place where everyone had watched him on his knees in the dirt, shirtless and wielding an ax at the edge of the woods, boots muddied, sweat-soaked in the sun with the other laborers, black and white.

His parents had no extra money to send him, and his poverty was ever visible as well. He had helped to put out a fire at the edge of the woods one day and, coming too close to the flames, had badly singed his only coat. Not having the money to replace it, he was forced for a considerable time after to wear a coat with a prominent patch and burn mark in the middle of his back. Hughes always held it against Dubois that he made no effort to help him acquire a new one or any other apparel to shield him from the winter winds, help he saw extended to other students. Dubois treated him like an unwanted stepchild rather than a member of the Emmitsburg family, Hughes complained—and eventually, before he left the seminary, he let Dubois know that those were his feelings.

A more serious fire the next year, in the summer of 1824, claimed the foundation of a large multistory building Dubois was erecting on a campus that badly needed more classroom and living space. Not having the money to rebuild, Dubois was obliged to have his seminarians spread out and take to the road on a summer walking tour, soliciting donations for their cause wherever they found groups of potential givers—in town squares, in private homes, in churches and taverns. Whether Hughes found this mendicant's task awkward or simply took it in stride he never said, but he did return to the Mount with a good story about being accosted by some vocal anti-papists in a tavern in a nearby town to whom he gave no verbal quarter. He seems to have found the idea of engaging in a battle of wits and insults with Protestant or agnostic opponents bracing, and in any event returned to Dubois with a tidy sum from his wanderings: four hundred dollars.

Hughes did have cause to be grateful for his position in one respect, though. In 1823, he had requested that his two sisters be admitted as boarding students at a reduced rate to Saint Joseph's Academy, the school run by the Sisters of Charity in Emmitsburg, with the stipulation that if either girl showed any inclination toward the religious life her tuition would be waived. If he had not already paved the way by establishing a good name for his family, that unusual arrangement would probably have been dismissed out of hand, and so sixteen-year-old Ellen and fourteen-year-old Margaret excitedly moved from Chambersburg to begin their first formal schooling. No doubt he knew Ellen's mind already ("There's a lot of John in that one," their mother had once remarked to their brother Michael). From the time of her first meeting with the nuns who would instruct her, she knew she wanted to be a part of their world as fervently as her brother longed to be a priest.

————————

THE CENTRAL SHAPING EXPERIENCE of Hughes's time at Emmitsburg was his work with Simon Bruté. Seminary education in the United

States at this time was not in any way systematic, with courses of study often decided by the individual bishops, who were, after all, the people who ordained the men deemed ready to be priests. Permission from Baltimore to teach theology at Emmitsburg had thus been a long time in coming, but Bruté was regarded as sound, and he would not be lured back to Baltimore. To read Augustine or Aquinas with him, to hear him discourse on Francis de Sales (one of the saints he most revered), or the finer points of dogmatic theology or canon law or ecclesiastical history, was all that Hughes hoped it would be. Bruté was a demanding but inspiring presence at the head of any study group, someone who expected his charges to keep up with him whether or not his exposition was quite clear. He could be digressive rather than comprehensive. His intellectual style was one of fits and starts; he had no capacity for the sustained focus and discipline needed to produce a book of his own, and his practice of reading aloud in French meant that his pupils who were not adept in both languages were at a disadvantage. Yet he was the teacher more students remembered fondly than any other.

From Bruté, Hughes first heard about Félicité Robert de Lamennais, a priest and political theorist who was making a name for himself during the years of the Bourbon restoration and had been a close friend of Bruté's in France. Though he later ran afoul of Pope Gregory XVI for his antimonarchical sympathies, at the time Bruté knew him and when his first books were being published, Lamennais was a leading spokesman for an ultramontane view of a church that was reasserting itself after the trauma of the Napoleonic years. His multivolume *Essai sur l'indifférence en matière de religion* was a much-discussed work in its day.

Bruté felt a great respect and affection for Lamennais, the anti-Enlightenment intellectual who eventually embraced republicanism, and the two corresponded, though Bruté was never a completely convinced adherent to the other's outlook. As one historian has summarized the matter: to judge from the evidence of his annotations in his copies of Lamennais's books, "we can conclude that Bruté leaned toward ultramontanism but was not entirely won over by its claims. He allowed that the Roman pontiff had the last say in matters of discipline (but not necessarily in doctrine). The opinion of the worldwide episcopacy counted for something." Some of Bruté's pupils at Emmitsburg, Hughes foremost among them, would have cause to appreciate that thinking about the vital importance of the bishops in the modern world—so many of them became bishops—but John Hughes would ultimately accept with more certainty than his teacher the absolute and rightful authority of the papacy.

Then there was the aura of Simon Bruté himself that captivated so many young men—a missionary and a mystic at heart who said Mass more zealously than any priest these seminarians had witnessed but who nonetheless had a broader experience and a wider culture than most of them had encountered. He could quote pages of Homer and Molière from memory. With the passion of an amateur cartographer, he filled his rooms with maps and added a geography class to the curriculum. The college's library, at its peak now, housed five thousand volumes, the vast majority on loan from him. It included a complete set of Diderot's Encyclopedias, polyglot seventeenth-century Bibles, a raft of religious histories and biographies, the Latin classics, and some antiquarian gems, including autograph letters from Saint Vincent de Paul and Pope John XXII. (That library and its acquirer must have had a reputation far beyond Pennsylvania. When Bruté left to become the bishop of Vincennes in 1834, John Quincy Adams remarked that "the most learned man in the United States is leaving the East to bury himself and his boatload of knowledge in the West.")

Bruté was a fount of personal lore as well, all peculiarly Bruté-esque, hard to believe but true—about the private audience he had had with Pius VII, arranged for by the superior-general of the Sulpicians, when His Holiness was in Paris as Napoleon's "guest" for the ill-fated coronation; about his thwarted effort to throw a petition at the feet of the emperor, seeking a pardon for an alleged conspirator, a friend from his medical school days; about his refusal of the emperor's offer to an appointment in the imperial chapel and his early plans to travel on foot to Syria to be a missionary. Bruté's could have been a life lived among the important, powerful men of his time, but he left none of his students in doubt that Emmitsburg is where he felt God had called him and where he was spending his happiest, most productive days.

About duty, Father Bruté could be a martinet, and he showed his sterner side when he felt his coreligionists were remiss in large or small matters. As a boy, he had known priests and those who sheltered them during the Terror who had gone to the scaffold. His standards of commitment were accordingly high. He impressed upon his students his belief that, if they chose a religious life, they had to accept that conventional guidelines would not apply to them. Devotion demanded more. When John Hughes was sent on an errand for the school to a town not far from Chambersburg and, of his own accord, stopped by for a visit with his parents before returning, he was the recipient of a blistering rebuke from his teacher for doing so without permission. He accepted a reprimand from Bruté in a way that he never could from Dubois.

The mid-1820s was the period in which Hughes first tested his own writing skills, producing a few verses for the Chambersburg and Gettysburg newspapers under the influence of the Romantic poets he had been reading. John Hassard, his first biographer, who saw copies in the 1860s of the seventeen poems of Hughes that had been published, observed that only one dealt with a religious theme. Others, like "The Slave," were more political. The plight of Ireland was a painful topic much on his mind—and always would be. "To the Home of My Fathers" begins: "Does Freedom yet breathe in the bard's rustic number? / Can his harp by the genius of Liberty strung, / Be mute, while the land where his forefathers slumber / Is bleeding in bondage, and bleeding unsung?" Like most Irishmen, he had hopes that in his lifetime British bondage would be countered, if not overthrown: "Is no Washington near thee, thou captive of ages, / To marshal thy brave ones and lead them to war? / Is no Franklin arrayed in the list of thy sages? / In that of thy heroes, no young Bolivar?" The lack in Ireland in the 1820s of a Washington, a Franklin, or a Bolivar was the crux of the problem, of course, as he saw it.

Even in a Fourth of July poetic declamation printed in the *Gettysburg Sentinel* on the occasion of the nation's jubilee in 1826, the poet made reference to "that ill-fated Isle" in contrast to his new country where the people were kingless and unconstrained. A hortatory line like "Columbia invites thee to rise and be free" would seem to be an invitation to armed rebellion in the spirit of 1776. Once he was a priest, Hughes would be far more reticent in suggesting that violence would be an acceptable means to the political ends he and all Catholic Irishmen desired. In 1826, though, the thought of active, physical resistance to the Crown was not something about which he had significant reservations.

By degrees, John Hughes was becoming a bookish man. One early biographer remarked on the fact that, as a bishop, Hughes owned a vast library—at several thousand volumes, it would have been among the larger private libraries in New York City—yet was rarely seen reading a book. (Newspapers he devoured for hours on end all his life.)

Given his command of language once he had a pulpit to speak from, that was hardly likely to be the case at the seminary, even separate from the extensive reading required for his religious studies. Indeed, one aspect of Hughes's talent rarely commented on in the literature about him is his linguistic facility. The cadences of impassioned oratory, the creation of a rhetorical arc, precision in wording: the elements of language he mastered early in his career fit him later in life to joust with men like Horace Greeley and Lewis Cass. These were not skills American priests were generally known for in the antebellum period. And if his sermons do not make especially gripping reading today, if for no other reason than their length (another hint of the attention-span differences between the mid-nineteenth century and early twenty-first), read aloud they have great force. So what was the origin of this blunt, cadenced, confident manner of expression? How much was in place, and how much was evolving, at the seminary? How much of this talent slowly developed throughout his twenties?

There are sufficient allusions to Shakespeare in his writings and letters to indicate that Hughes knew those canonical plays, but virtually every educated English speaker was well-versed in Shakespeare in the nineteenth century. References to Jonathan Swift, Samuel Johnson, Rousseau, Burke, Paine, Macaulay, and Carlyle suggest that he did at some point read the major prose writers of the Enlightenment and the early Victorian age. He also appears to have read Laurence Sterne, which in terms of sheer linguistic bravura is an interesting fact, though he regarded the irreverent Anglican as more an appalling infidel than not. A list of books he owned in New York, aside from the religious texts and biographies one would expect, includes the plays of Racine (a Bruté favorite) and the poetry of Milton. No one becomes a good writer who isn't, sometime before middle age, an omnivorous reader. His admiration for Simon Bruté, a collector of Jeffersonian proportions who could not live without books, who loved nothing better than to talk about what he was reading, played its part in that development.

Yet an instinct for language and its capacities might have been inbred as well. What kind of conversation did he hear at home growing up? Any reference to the verbal qualities of his parents, never to be found now, would be telling. Were they a taciturn couple, or were they great conversationalists like the raconteurs, voluble and alliterative and sarcastic, of Synge and O'Casey? The tart tongue John and his sister Margaret were known for hints at a common quality in their upbringing. The fact that Patrick Hughes worked with his hands in no way precludes a facile tongue. The stereotypes of the man of few words tilling the land or the pious and necessarily silent mother are just that, stereotypes. His sister Ellen was a very articulate woman, and even the letters of John Hughes's older brother, a farmer and his father's namesake, exhibit some impressive verbal skill. I imagine a word-savvy family.

Whatever the varied origins of his sense of the power of words, John Hughes was eager by the mid-1820s to speak from a pulpit of his own. That time was coming. In 1825, he was assigned to be a part-time deacon at a church in Philadelphia, which meant a monthly commute between Emmitsburg and Philadelphia, a trek that took the better part of twenty-four hours. At Saint Augustine's on Fourth and Vine Streets, he was taken under the wing of Augustinian pastor Michael Hurley. Father Hurley was a charismatic bundle of contradictions. A burly man, he was a heavy drinker who often had to be helped—more like carried—to bed after a night of "frolick and singing" and thought nothing of hearing confessions in his bedroom the next morning if he was unable to regain his legs. Affecting a thick brogue he didn't really have, he had adopted the peculiar practice of pretending he was from a rough, working-class background with no respect for Irish bourgeois pretensions, when in fact his father was a successful businessman, he himself had studied in Europe, and he had had his portrait painted (twice) by the noted artist Thomas Sully. Yet he deeply believed in his calling, preached the gospel with all his heart, and never turned away anyone who needed his help. His understanding parishioners loved him.

Hurley was full of advice for his young charge on every topic from his exercise regimen to his state of mind as a confessor to his sermon preparations. "Do not make your sermons long," he insisted, "—half an hour or thereabouts will be sufficient; you will then be able to deliver them with more energy and self-command, and to throw more soul into them, without which there is no true eloquence." Hurley had little use for a priest who did not "throw his soul" into his work. The advice was appreciated. When Philadelphia's Bishop Henry Conwell first heard Hughes in the pulpit, he was impressed.

Examined by Conwell when the time for his ordination approached, John Hughes passed muster: it was decided that he was indeed ready to be a priest. Bruté and his colleagues had done their job. The ordination took place on October 15, 1826, and after three months filling a vacancy in the town of Bedford, he was assigned to Saint Joseph's Church in Philadelphia, a ramshackle chapel on Willings Alley, where he took up residence with the bishop himself. (By coincidence, that same month John Dubois left his position at the Mount to be consecrated the new bishop of the New York diocese.) A short time later, Hughes was sent to the more upscale Saint Mary's Church on Fourth and Spruce Streets. The Philadelphia diocese at the time included all of Pennsylvania and Delaware and part of western New Jersey, a huge area in which approximately one hundred thousand Catholics (twenty-five thousand of them residing in Philadelphia) were served by only twenty-two churches and not even forty priests. Resources were obviously stretched thin, but that was far from the only problem the Catholic Church faced in Philadelphia.

Philadelphia when he arrived to stay was a more cosmopolitan center than any John Hughes had ever known. British travel writer (and mother of the famous novelist) Frances Trollope thought the city in 1830 a little pokey in comparison to Baltimore: "though much larger, it does not show itself so well," she wrote in *Domestic Manners of the Americans*, as "it wants domes and columns," and its better brick homes were "handsome" rather than "splendid." It was resistant to the gas street lighting Baltimore and New York had adopted. Nonetheless, she thought it beautiful, if a little dull and overregulated in the grid of its streets. "Distractingly regular," Dickens remarked on the same topic ten years later, suggesting the urgent need for a crooked street or two. Yet its bank buildings were stately and impressive. Most surprising to Trollope and her readers, given the state of most metropolitan areas then, was its neatness. Small wonder Americans pointed to Philadelphia as the young nation's finest city, the "American Athens," and many still regretted the removal of the nation's capital thirty years earlier to the swampland of the District of Columbia.

There were other sides to the city, of course, less attended to by Dickens and Trollope. In Hughes's time in Philadelphia, street crime and labor unrest were becoming more significant problems. At least two riots targeting black families led to the sacking of their homes, and an abolitionist hall was burned to the ground by an angry mob. Philadelphia wanted to hear nothing about that topic, any more than Boston or Baltimore did. Complaints about the growing influx of Irish Catholic immigrants were already being aired.

Philadelphia had also become a center, in a way no other American city had, for fallen monarchs and displaced aristocrats from postrevolutionary, post-Napoleonic France, Spain, the Caribbean, and Mexico. The exiled Joseph Bonaparte, Napoleon's older brother and the former king of Spain and the Two Sicilies, had a house in town and a huge country estate near Bordentown on the Delaware River, crammed with paintings he had managed to take with him. (Unlike his brother, he was a loyal son of the church and a patron in flush times.) Ana María Huarte de Iturbide, the widow of the last emperor of Mexico who had been displaced and executed by General Santa Anna in 1824, lived with her family in Philadelphia and was often seen riding about town in what residents thought a ridiculously ornate carriage for someone known to be living on a modest pension. Once-important counts, marquises, and barons made a home in Philadelphia—some religious, some indifferent or anticlerical; some philanthropic, and others tightfisted.

Yet if the city's best architecture and aristocratic fringe offered a superficial image of order and prestige, the same could not be said of the state of the Catholic Church there. Conwell's domain was an absurdly fractious place and had been so for some time. "Death would not be so frightful to me as Philadelphia," one priest had commented to John Carroll several years earlier when his name was mentioned for the episcopacy of that city. Conwell eventually had reason to think he should have resisted his own appointment as strenuously. Philadelphia in 1826 provided Hughes with his first glimpse of what a diocese looked like if its bishop were not sufficiently respected and lacked a commanding aura. "From my soul, I pity you," a friend from the Mount wrote when he heard of Hughes's appointment to that "miserable" city, "for I know something of Philadelphia."

Part of the problem was Conwell himself. In 1819, at the age of seventy-two and eager to lead his own diocese after years of waiting in the wings in Ireland, he had been offered a bizarre choice between two longtime vacancies: the bishopric of Madras, in India, or Philadelphia. Neither was a position anyone else wanted or could be talked into. His peers in Ireland could hardly believe the announcement of his "elevation," considering both his age and his obvious lack of leadership skills. "The thing was almost as impossible to believe as that he had been made Emperor of China," the archbishop of Armagh remarked. By the time Hughes met him, Conwell had probably come to think he could not have been more miserable had he opted for India.

The other problem was the cast of characters among the local clergy and the church trustees. Recent historians have argued that the trustee system, in which lay members of a congregation played an active decision-making role in the running of a church and assumed many or all administrative and fiduciary responsibilities, has been given a bad name by those who always write the first draft of history—the victors. The power of the final word exercised by Catholic pastors and bishops from the mid-nineteenth century to our own day was not the rule in the United States in the early 1800s; to many, it seemed, then and now, that the merits of a more Protestant system of governance, so to speak, made sense in a democratic nation far removed from the Rome-centered, hier-archically oriented world of Europe. In fact, some trustee boards worked very effectively with their resident priests, as several recent Catholic his-torians have acknowledged. That balance promoted a cooperative, inclu-sive spirit and suggested a hopeful future for Catholicism in the United States. Other boards were peremptory with their clergymen (and miserly about salaries), treating them like employees and wanting them to focus on their spiritual and pastoral duties and have no say whatsoever in any other aspect of parish or diocesan life.

Be that as it may, by the 1820s, Catholic bishops and pastors were at war with this entire philosophy and practice. They were doing so on good authority: in 1822, in an apostolic letter, Pope Pius VII had spoken out against the American idea of trustees appointing or removing priests as "something new and entirely unheard of" and not to be tolerated. The Vatican and the American bishops ultimately had their way. The battle, however, was not short, and it was not gentlemanly.

It was particularly ugly in Philadelphia. The Hogan schism was famous for years throughout the United States and Europe. A native of Limerick, Father William Hogan had come to Philadelphia just before Conwell and found an immediately adoring audience. He was handsome and energetic and, according to many accounts, roused Saint Mary's Parish from a lethargic period with his piety, charitable endeavors, and ardor in the pulpit. He also had opinions about everything and an unusual sense of self-worth for a man of the cloth. He eventually talked the church's trustees into voting him a stipend so that he could live alone and not have to cohabit with other priests in quarters not befitting his aesthetic needs. Gossip had it that he spent far more time in the draw-ing rooms of the well-to-do than was seemly for a man in his position.

Some parishioners suggested that his ardor extended beyond the pulpit. A housekeeper in the rectory preferred charges against him for sexual assault, though a jury acquitted him.

The independent-minded Hogan and his bishop were never going to be able to resolve differences this vast, and when Conwell suspended Hogan, the priest's admirers reacted with an avalanche of criticism that unnerved the new bishop, who had no talent for diffusing tense situations. Hogan refused to step down. "Jacobinical trustees" (Conwell's view of the matter) went to war with a prelate who didn't understand American ideas of due process and republicanism (the trustees' view), and the result went beyond name-calling at meetings and acrimonious exchanges picked up by the newspapers to an Easter Week riot in front of the church in 1822 when pro- and anti-Hogan forces went at each other with bricks, rocks, and pieces of iron railing torn from the church steps, and two hundred people were injured. The courts got involved, the Holy See was aghast, and Hogan, in open defiance of the pope, took to the press to defend himself. Excommunicated, he left the city and the church in 1824 and became an anti-Catholic writer in the 1830s. Conwell never quite recovered his equilibrium.

The Hogan scandal was over by the time Hughes came to the city, but the bitterness and territorial disagreements remained, and a new version of the old problem was brewing with another priest. Every bit as strong-willed as Hogan, William Harold had originally been one of Conwell's defenders but was now an antagonist. After their differences reached a breaking point, Harold was relieved of his duties as vicar-general of the diocese. Harold had plenty of supporters, and another schism loomed. This was the last thing the new priest from Emmitsburg wanted to be involved in—even Simon Bruté advised his former student to keep his head down and say as little as possible on the subject—but Conwell leaned on him to sign a petition condemning Harold, and Hughes eventually had to relent. Indignant and litigious, Father Harold saw a lawyer and threatened to sue those priests who had signed the document he claimed was libelous. Disgusted with the trustees who still backed Harold against the bishop and who threatened to withhold his salary, Hughes left Saint Mary's and returned to the humbler Saint Joseph's.

Though he wanted no part of the controversy, there wasn't any question in Hughes's mind as to the right and wrong of the situation. Like

Michael Hurley, he supported ecclesiastical authority. Those observers who saw beyond the clash of personalities in Philadelphia and recognized that what was happening was actually a clash of two entirely different value systems, the one calling for the restoration of a pre-1789 concept of the church and the other wanting an infusion of republicanism in a modernized, Americanized Catholic Church, were correct, but there was nothing about the manner or grandstanding of the latter group to win the support of someone like John Hughes. Harold went so far as to attempt to enlist the backing of President John Quincy Adams and his secretary of state, Henry Clay, in a petition to Rome on his behalf, but they wanted no part of crossing that line. It took two more years for the hierarchy to be able to send William Harold packing back to Ireland. Unlike Hogan, whose enmity to the church only grew over time, Harold was eventually reconciled with the hierarchy.

The one good aspect of having landed in Philadelphia was the proximity Hughes enjoyed to a few other priests who meant the world to him. There was Hurley, who made the priesthood seem like a kind of wonderful adventure, and, also at Saint Augustine's, the Irish-born Nicholas O'Donnell, five years younger than Hughes. He was newly ordained, exceptionally well read, and exceptionally generous. There was Thomas Heyden, for whom Hughes felt a warm regard, and—a remarkable, serendipitous occurrence—there, right at Saint Joseph's on Willings Alley at the bishop's side, was Terence Donaghoe. The two men hadn't seen each other since their schoolboy days in Aughnacloy. Donaghoe, coming from a family of more means, had been sent to study in Dublin after he and his good friend parted company, and later, when he had announced his vocation, to the Sulpician seminary in Paris. He had been a parish priest in Paris for a year before coming to the United States. A bond that was more than nostalgic, a deep closeness both men felt as intimate and brotherly, was quickly reestablished. Donaghoe was also an oasis of sanity in an increasingly volatile environment.

The pastoral nature of the work of a new, young priest in Hughes's place would have been overwhelming to anyone with an uncertain sense of vocation. Hours each week were spent visiting the sick, counseling the troubled, providing religious instruction to the young—the last a part of the job Hughes particularly enjoyed. (Some of the Hogan- or Harold-faction parents might have been spoiling for a fight, but their children were a welcome relief.) The round of baptisms, confirmations, weddings, and funerals never ended, given the shortage of priests, and it wasn't unusual for Hughes and Donaghoe to hear confessions on a Saturday for six or seven hours without cease. And at least two Sundays a month, of course, a new sermon. The more practiced Hughes became, the less he relied on notes or a prepared text. In the pulpit, Father Hughes was not exclusively about fire and brimstone, as some of his older fellow priests were; he could orate on "the mild and forgiving character of the Redeemer," a newspaper reporter later commented. Hughes could see that Conwell's leadership had not managed to forge a particularly devout community of Catholics. His own estimate of regular communicants among the city's Catholics was not heartening, he confided to John Purcell—a shocking one out of fifteen. He worked, then, to convey a sense of religion that was embracing as well as demanding, sustaining as much as it was challenging. Hughes was always proud to claim that he made thirteen converts to Catholicism in his first months in Philadelphia.

Two other sides of John Hughes's character came to the forefront as soon as he was settled in Philadelphia: an activist nature that took him away from a purely pastoral role to more organizational tasks, and a wish to be a publicist for the faith. As Protestant pamphleteering was on the rise, Hughes announced on his own authority that a counter-effort was called for, and he set about finding donors for a Catholic tract society that would publish inexpensive pamphlets and chapbooks for free distribution supporting the Catholic cause. In a similar spirit of rolling up his sleeves, when he heard about several Catholic children about to be sent to the city's almshouses after their parents' death because the two existing Catholic orphanages hadn't a single bed left, he formed a committee to look into donations and staffing for another facility. He found a house that could be rented for $400 a year, four Sisters of Charity willing to work there, and sixteen needy children to be the first occupants of what became the Saint John's Boys' Orphanage. He was, it was evident to those who worked with him, the sort of person who made things happen.

An inveterate letter-to-the-editor writer and a man who liked to see his words in print, whether signed or anonymous (as many newspaper articles were at the time), Hughes might have had ulterior motives in founding his short-lived tract society, as one of its first publications was his own—and, mercifully, his only—venture into religious fiction. His tale, *The Conversion and Edifying Death of Andrew Dunn*, was written

in response to a Protestant tale, recently republished in Philadelphia, that
told the story of an earnest young Irishman, born a Catholic, who begins
to have doubts about the faith of his fathers. He questions the priests
he knows about various aspects of Catholic doctrine and, finding their
answers unsatisfying (one even takes a whip to him), finds his way to
some more convincing Protestant divines. He assays to read and interpret
the Bible on his own and ends with the realization that the "Romish
communion" he had lived with all his life was a hoax and that true
happiness, self-respect, and salvation were to be found among the Protestants of Ireland. For some reason, despite the fact that this adversarial
story had no literary merit or particularly wide readership, it rankled,
and Hughes itched to write his own version.

That he did, even keeping the name of the protagonist, though of
course in his thirty-page novelette a Protestant-born Andrew Dunn, a
fellow of "a mild and amiable disposition," brings his religious doubts to
a kindly Catholic neighbor who instructs him in the history of his own
faith, refutes the charges of superstition and idol-worship that Andrew
has grown up with, and invites him to attend Mass with him. (This
neighbor, John Smith, seems to have an encyclopedic knowledge of the
minutiae of church history, one has to note.) The experience at Mass is
unnerving—strange and beautiful. His friends and family assail Andrew
with "every kind of abusive language" for having even set foot in the
Catholic church, but he sticks to his determination to investigate freely
the right path for him to take, ultimately concluding that the true church
of Jesus Christ was the Roman Catholic Church. When Andrew dies of
a sudden illness in middle age, he meets his end with the fortitude and
tranquillity of one of the early saints.

Hughes was thoroughly pleased with his wooden parable, though he
wrote to Simon Bruté—penning one of the more disingenuous lines of
his voluminous epistolary career—"I do not wish the thing to make any
noise because the Protestants will take alarm." He was, of course, hoping
for quite the opposite and looked to his friends to buy copies to peddle
or give away. Even Bruté, never known to have a dime in his pocket, was
talked into taking five dollars' worth—a small pile with few prospec-
tive customers in sight out in Emmitsburg. Writing *The Conversion and
Edifying Death of Andrew Dunn* was the kind of lark any pious young
man could have engaged in, but some people felt that a thirty-year-old
priest might have better things to do with his time. When the thrill of

publication wore off, Hughes agreed, more or less, and preferred not to be reminded about this literary endeavor again.

His next published "work" engendered a considerably more emphatic reaction, though, negative on both sides of the aisle, and it was one he would never fully repudiate or apologize for, even when he pretended to. In the first weeks of 1830, a new religious periodical had commenced publication in New York City. The editor of the *Protestant*, George Bourne, made no bones about his intentions; his weekly journal was about exposing "Romish corruptions" and warning Americans about a threat to which they needed awakening. It was so inflammatory, so vitriolic, that some Protestant ministers who had no sympathy with Catholicism nonetheless refused to have anything to do with it. Gleefully, Hughes took it as his personal mission to discredit Bourne's publication. Using the pseudonym "Cranmer," he sent in letters purporting to be from a Philadelphia Protestant who applauded the efforts of the *Protestant* to rouse his countrymen to the frightening fact that Catholics were invading the United States in greater numbers than anyone realized and that their plan, ultimately, was to subvert the Protestant, democratic character of a country that, to the servants of the pope, was merely fertile territory for conquest. Bourne was delighted and asked his Pennsylvania correspondent to keep sending him articles. Hughes obliged.

Over the course of several months, the *Protestant* printed one more ridiculous article after another, suggesting networks of priests and nuns ("she-wolves") spreading their tentacles throughout the Northeast. Bourne printed an editorial praising Cranmer for acting in the spirit of his real-life namesake, Thomas Cranmer, Henry VIII's Reformation ally and martyr to the fanaticism of Bloody Mary. Then, when he felt it had gone far enough, Hughes revealed that there was no Cranmer and that the letters had actually been penned by a Catholic priest testing the gullibility and exposing the ignorance of Bourne and his readers.

The delight Hughes felt in embarrassing Bourne and undermining the credibility of his journal was immediately mitigated by the fact that many Catholics, priests included, felt his ploy lacked dignity, was puerile and even un-Christian. Father Thomas Levins, who ran a New York City Catholic paper, the *Truth Teller*, was particularly hard on the exposed Cranmer. Lies were lies, he insisted, and the whole ruse had been vulgar, if not contemptible. He suggested its perpetrator should be reprimanded by his superiors. (At this point, all that was known was that a Philadelphia priest had authored the letters, not that Hughes was the culprit, though it didn't take long for most people to put the pieces together and make a good guess.) Part of Levins's anger stemmed from the fact that some readers thought he might be the real Cranmer. His back up, Hughes felt impelled to write to the *Truth Teller* a few indignant letters defending his actions, which was a tactical error—that much he could acknowledge later—as the whole fracas ended not with Hughes doing battle in public with a Protestant bigot but with a fellow Irish priest.

Politics, not religion, provided Hughes with his first significant appearance in print, a document about which he had no reason to be embarrassed, then or later. The occasion was not a religious one, but it was celebrated in a church, Saint Augustine's, on May 31, 1829, with Michael Hurley singing the Mass and John Hughes preaching, and it suggested, quite forcibly, that politics and religion—specifically, Irish ethnicity and Roman Catholicism—might have cause now to overlap in the modern world.

As a resident of a big city for the first time in his life, Hughes was also well placed to think more about what it meant to be Irish in America, what it might mean to see one's ethnic identity as not merely an emblem of victimhood or a source of frustration. As recent historians have been at pains to point out, definitions of "Irish America" have traditionally been rather narrow, associating or conflating Catholicism and Irishness in ways that more inquiry might not entirely bear out. Orangemen certainly saw themselves as Irishmen as much as their antagonists did. Vast numbers of Irish Americans felt no identification with the Catholic Church and never, or rarely, set foot in a church, let alone a confessional. But Hughes, like many men in his position, had—or developed by his late twenties—his own conception of what "Irish America" meant, and it was three things in equal measure: Irish, American, and Catholic.

The passage of the Catholic Emancipation Bill in Great Britain in 1829, then, was an event of epic importance, "a new era in the history of our hapless country," as Hughes wrote to John Purcell. Finally, after years of political agitation, Parliament had agreed to give the Catholics of Ireland a large measure of political and professional equality, even allowing Catholic Irishmen to sit in Parliament. Prematurely, as it turned out, Irishmen on both sides of the Atlantic felt they were seeing the beginning of the end of the oppression of their people.

In a sermon he labored over long and hard, Hughes wanted his listeners to consider what that phrase "their people" might mean. They now lived in a different country, and that meant they were citizens of the United States, a fact for which everyone should be grateful. That much went without saying. Yet Hughes wanted to remind his Irish audience that there was no reason a man need shed his past even as he welcomed a new and different present and anticipated an even better future. "There is in the heart of every man," he asserted, "that which interests him—the land of his nativity; and until his heart ceases to beat, no distance of either time or place will be able to extinguish the sensation." It was not a sensation one should resist, Hughes argued, and it was common to "the Jew, the Christian, and the idolator; to the barbarian as well as to the Greek." It was entirely possible—it made sense, it made for a fully grounded life—for those born elsewhere to feel a love and even a loyalty to two nations, especially if one were part of a group, as many of them were, who had left its homeland under duress.

Hughes reviewed in copious detail the history of an island never conquered by the Roman Empire, quicker to accept Christianity than any other nation, peopled by monks who kept alive through the Dark Ages the learning of the ancient world, battered by waves of Viking invaders. Their subjugation by the English had been a centuries-long nightmare, but now was not the time to continue to blame England or Protestantism (the first invader, after all, had been Henry II, a Catholic, not Cromwell); now was a time for reconciliation and even an acknowledgment that the brutality visited on the Irish was not so very different from the brutality white men of all religions and nationalities had visited "on the shores of Africa . . . putting manacles on hands that were free." It had become, sadly, part of the historical human condition to believe that *might made right*. The higher aspirations of our nature and the message of Christ said otherwise, and man's tragedy was everywhere evident in the cost of that pernicious outlook. The Catholic Emancipation Act, he trusted, would be a healthy, happy development for everyone in Ireland, Catholics as well as Protestants, and even in the long run for Great Britain itself. Mankind advanced when it rejected the doctrine that *might made right*.

All of Michael Hurley's earlier counsel about brevity in sermons was cast aside, and no one seemed to care. Hughes's almost two-hour oration on Irish identity, delivered to an overflow crowd, was received with great enthusiasm. It was also delivered at the right church—Saint Augustine's rather than the affluent Saint Mary's—where the parishioners were more middle class, more immigrant based, and less likely to want to turn their backs in embarrassment on their impoverished place of birth. Reaction to the sermon was sufficiently adulatory that it was printed as a pamphlet and circulated throughout the diocese and in New York; Hughes's brother even reported that people in Chambersburg were enthusing over the rhetoric of Patrick and Margaret Hughes's esteemed son.

Not everyone applauded the sermon or its sentiments, of course. The Episcopal *Church Register* of Philadelphia published a jeremiad expressing concerns that British leniency toward the Irish would awaken the sleeping, enfeebled lion that was the Catholic Church to feel emboldened in its efforts to undermine society. This time, Hughes was done with pseudonyms or unsigned articles and let loose in the pages of the *United States Gazette* with a fierce rebuttal under his own name. He was irate that an event such as had prompted his finest sermon to date, one in which he felt he had extended an olive branch to Britons and Protestants as well, should occasion more bigotry and mean-spiritedness.

One matter Hughes hadn't had to worry much about was what Henry Conwell thought of any of these forays into print. His bishop's power and influence were steadily on the wane throughout Hughes's first four years in Philadelphia. The Vatican had long noted with dismay Conwell's inability to win over the Catholics of Saint Mary's and restore order to the diocese, and then turned even more vehemently against him when he tried to make peace with the trustees by signing an accord that offered far too many concessions, including the right of the board to determine salaries and to veto his appointments (a step Hughes regarded as a dreadful mistake). Called to Rome to account for his ineptitude, Conwell delayed until Pope Leo XII ordered him to leave for Italy at once. Soon after his arrival the pope died, and Conwell took the opportunity to scurry back to America without anyone's permission. Finally, inevitably, it was decided that a coadjutor was needed to run the diocese; Conwell could stay, but he must understand that he was no longer in charge of anything. Explaining that to the bishop took some doing.

The only reason Conwell wasn't forced to leave Philadelphia was that everyone in Rome and in the diocese assumed, with the man now in his early eighties and tottering as he walked, it couldn't be long before he went to his final rest. How wrong they were: Conwell lived on, increasingly blind and always crankily at odds with his coadjutor, never for a day in the least reconciled to being sidelined, to the ripe age of ninety-four. He spent his final years dictating letters to other bishops telling them how to run their dioceses and finding ways to irk his successor. On one occasion, when the poor man was out of town, he had all his furniture removed from the rectory and put in storage.

That long-suffering successor, his ostensible coadjutor but in actuality the new bishop, was Francis Patrick Kenrick. Born in Dublin and ordained in Rome, he was two years older than Hughes, though in gravitas he might have been two decades older. Having spent most of his early adulthood studying in Europe, he was considered an unlikely candidate for missionary work in Kentucky, but the bookish, mild-mannered, soft-spoken, slightly effeminate priest was the sort to accept any assignment and rise to any occasion, and he handled himself well with the frontier Catholics and the local Presbyterians who took issue with his presence. In January 1830, the Propaganda Fide decided that he was the man to take on Philadelphia, a decision ratified by the new pope, Pius VII, and he set off from Kentucky to meet the reprimanded Conwell, now a figurehead, and the city's recalcitrant trustees and querulous parishioners.

Hughes got to know Kenrick as he joined him on visitations to parishes around the state; he had first met him at the first provincial council held in the United States in 1829, a gathering of American prelates and priests in Baltimore where the authority of the episcopate was reinforced, trusteeism put on notice, and other rules and reforms hammered out. (Maryland's Catholic attorney general, soon to be President Jackson's attorney general, Roger Taney, was on hand to advise the council about property and other rights.) Whatever his initial impressions of Kenrick, Hughes had reason to see the less mild-mannered side once he was installed in Philadelphia. He dismissed unsuitable priests from one end of the state to the other without a second thought, and he made clear to the trustees of Saint Mary's in a way that Conwell had never been able to that he meant business, even placing the church under an interdict. If parishioners could not see their way toward accepting Kenrick's views on governance, they could find another church to attend; no priest would stand at the altar at Saint Mary's until the interdict was lifted.

Kenrick and Hughes had periods of closeness, and there were many occasions on which each spoke well of the other. Hughes understood that it was his duty to be respectful and cooperative with his ecclesiastical superiors, and Conwell's supportiveness hadn't meant much as he approached his dotage. Kenrick eventually made Hughes his vicar-general. There was a wariness, though, born of great differences in temperament, that colored most of the Kenrick-Hughes relationship. Hughes always seemed to Kenrick so—so *busy*, so restless, so political, so opinionated. Kenrick was at heart a biblical scholar and theologian as much as, if not more than, a pastoral leader, and Hughes had a side, alien to Kenrick's nature, that was constantly in motion and almost seemed to long for a conflict. The Cranmer business, for example, struck Kenrick as unseemly and regrettable. That was the problem from the new bishop's perspective with this otherwise talented priest: you never knew what would come next. Though the two men would know and work together in many capacities for almost thirty-five years, they never fully trusted each other.

For some important assignments, though, Hughes was deemed by Kenrick to be eminently trustworthy. He served on a committee to explore the possibility of opening Philadelphia's first seminary, preached at Philadelphia's first diocesan synod, and was sent by Kenrick to Harrisburg to deal with an issue concerning state taxes allegedly due on the city's Catholic orphan asylum. For one project, Kenrick's feelings went beyond simple trust: he concluded that John Hughes was probably the only one in Philadelphia likely to pull off what he wanted done. He could see that the important Catholics of the city were gravitating toward Hughes now—he and the former empress of Mexico had taken a trip to the nation's capital together the year before to visit Georgetown College—and that the man liked nothing so much as a challenge others might shy away from.

What Kenrick wanted more than anything was a new church, one that would rival and eventually surpass in size and prestige the vexatious Saint Mary's, and one that would be built and owned by the church with no questions asked—that is, a trustee-less church. In December 1830, he authorized Hughes to take charge of this endeavor: to find the right architect, to oversee the designs, to form a fund-raising committee, to scout about town for the right location, to meet with the bankers—to make it all happen. It would be the city's new proto-cathedral. Hughes was delighted with the prospect and flattered to be asked to take it on.

After looking at several lots, some too expensive and some not advantageously located, Hughes decided on Thirteenth Street between

Market and Church Streets as an ideal location for what would be called the Church of Saint John the Evangelist. ("Ideal" for the future-minded; others thought that address much too far from the city's center.) His assignment also brought him into contact with two people who would become very important in his life—the architect he decided to hire, William Rodrigue, and a businessman, Marc Frenaye, who would become a close personal friend and an absolutely vital financial backer.

Rodrigue had much to recommend him. He was spoken of, by everyone who knew him, as a young man with a promising future who had obvious talents as an architect, surveyor, and civil engineer; he had studied art in Paris for three years and so knew all the major churches of that country. He was affiliated with the office of respected architect William Strickland, who had apprenticed with Benjamin Latrobe, but was eager to strike out on his own. Beyond that, both his parents were French-born Catholic refugees of some wealth who had left Santo Domingo in 1795 after the slave revolt made it impossible for them to remain; they were significant donors to a wide range of church projects in Philadelphia and stood with Kenrick against the trustees. They were overjoyed that their son was to be involved in the creation of a truly "Roman" house of worship. The plans called for an imposing edifice of stone—no Federalist brick—a neo-Gothic church with a soaring vaulted ceiling, interior arches framed by fluted columns, an ample balcony on each side, almost thirty stained-glass windows, seating capacity for a thousand, and frescoes painted by an Italian artist, Nicholas Monachesi, who was then living in Philadelphia.

To two of the people he trusted most, Hughes could not resist being boastful about the project that had been entrusted to him even when it was still in the earliest stages of construction. To John Purcell, he wrote, "It will make all the Bishops of all the churches jealous; cause those who give nothing toward its erection to 'murmur' at its costliness and those who did contribute to be proud of their own doing. As a religious edifice, it will be the pride of the city." He didn't want anything as squat and boxy as Saint Mary's, and, with room for so many worshippers, it would make Saint Joseph's or Holy Trinity, the German church, seem absurdly modest. To Ellen, now Sister Angela, he went even further: "The new church bids fair to be the handsomest in the United States. In point of grandeur, it is not, of course, to be compared with the Cathedral in Baltimore, but as far as beauty is concerned, it will exceed it."

Hughes was pleased that he and Rodrigue shared the same vision and worked so well together. The young architect introduced the priest to his family, and their fireside became a second home for him. He dined with the Rodrigues frequently and was "Uncle John" to William's younger sisters. The one problem, not a minor one, about this shared vision for a great new church that would not be in the "plain style" of the city's other churches was the cost. The land was acquired and mortgaged for a plausible but not inconsiderable sum—$13,000—but the estimates for what it would take to see a building of this size and elegance to completion should have given everyone pause. The total was projected to reach an additional $60,000. As might have been predicted, when Hughes moved to New York several years later, Saint John the Evangelist had still not cleared itself of its debt.

Without Marc Frenaye, a silk merchant and land speculator, the church might not have been built at all during Hughes's time in Philadelphia. Fifteen years Hughes's senior, Frenaye was another member of the émigré community devoted to the church. Born to a planter family in Santo Domingo, he and his siblings had been brought to France in 1788 by their parents to be educated, a colossal example of unfortunate timing. During the Reign of Terror, the Frenayes were lucky to escape with their lives. After returning to the Caribbean, Marc Frenaye moved to Philadelphia at the age of twenty-three, where he attached himself to an import-export firm that had him traveling extensively in Mexico and the Deep South. His marriage floundered—his attempts to get an annulment from his unfaithful wife were public and protracted—but his business prospered. When Hughes's fund-raising efforts for Saint John the Evangelist were at their lowest ebb and he was beginning to despair, Frenaye came through with a generous gift of $11,000 and an interest-free loan of $25,000 to enable construction to commence.

Hughes had hopes that his entire family would one day marvel at, and worship in, "his" new church, but that wasn't to be. On September 30, 1831, Margaret McKenna Hughes died in Chambersburg at the age of sixty-four. As she slipped away, she urged her family not to alarm her youngest son, as she knew how busy he was in Philadelphia and talked with pride of the importance of the work he was doing. She had also hoped to live to see Saint John the Evangelist rise but understood that that wasn't possible now. Apprised by his sisters of the situation, Hughes arrived home just in time to speak with his mother before the end in a painfully emotional scene in the middle of the night. Missing her death, he later wrote to a friend in Chambersburg, "would have been followed by regret for the remainder of my life as it would have deprived me of the consolation of receiving the last benediction of that tongue which first taught me to pronounce the name of God; and the last look of that eye which looked upon my childhood,—as well as of beholding the last throb of that fine heart which perhaps I had grieved, but which I know has forgiven me."

Margaret Hughes died comforted by the thought that her youngest son was set on a path to a life he never could have had back in Ireland, a life that promised great accomplishments for the faith—though, of course, she had few inklings of just how far that path would take him.

3

COURTING CONTROVERSY

THE *ANDREW DUNN* frolic and the Cranmer hoax had a giddy aspect to them, but in reality, John Hughes had entered the church and the fray at a time of momentous changes in the American perception of Catholicism. There would be nothing lighthearted about the contest that was just beginning.

More than a decade before the Great Famine and the massive influx of poverty-stricken Irish families to the New World, immigration numbers were rising, and as the nature of the Irish immigrant population changed in the 1830s, the vitriol in print, at the pulpit, and on the lecture circuit began in earnest. Middle-class arrivals from the north of Ireland had been an unthreatening, even welcome, addition to the republic as they were small in number, often readily employable, and frequently Protestant. Now that was no longer the case. Hughes could see this all around him on the Philadelphia docks. The new arrivals were more often poor and Catholic, or at least nominally Catholic. How many of the most economically pressed of the rural Irish immigrants had actually been baptized, received religious instruction at any time in their lives, or attended a Catholic church in Ireland is another matter. Nonetheless, class and religious anxieties quickly surfaced.

There was no single opening salvo in the anti-Irish, anti-Catholic campaign. There were dozens, depending on which part of the country one looked at and how unified the self-styled nativists in that region were. The British Catholic Emancipation Bill had stimulated concern about Catholic empowerment on both sides of the Atlantic, and the more than thirty religious newspapers in the country, reaching an estimated sixty thousand American homes, were sounding the alarm more vigorously each year. In the Northeast, the founding of the New York Protestant Association in 1831, an organization formed "to promote the principles of the Reformation," was instrumental in rallying adherents to the cause, disseminating pamphlets, sponsoring lectures, and arranging for debates with Catholic priests and laymen. Those debates sometimes led to mob assaults by angry Irish immigrants who took offense at Protestant insults, which in turn led to more publicity about the dangers posed by popish riffraff. Bishop Dubois in New York insisted that his priests and parishioners stop attending such gatherings; their defense of the faith, he told them, was only aggravating a worrisome situation. Then the books, a trickle in the years between Washington and Jackson, a torrent thereafter, began to pour forth. Indeed, in the field of religious literature, it could be said that a minor revolution in publishing was under way by 1830.

Books like *The Downfall of Babylon, or, The Triumph of Truth over Popery*, written by an ex-priest, or W. C. Brownlee's *Popery, an Enemy to Civil and Religious Liberty*, or James Horner's *Popery Stripped of Its Garb*—the monotony of the titles alone numbs the mind—found a sizable audience in the 1830s eager to read about an alien faith at odds with the theological and political mainstream of the United States. By one estimate, more than two hundred such books appeared in the United States in the first half of the nineteenth century, alongside thousands of pamphlets, chapbooks, and newspaper screeds. Some of the authors of these texts were obscure ministers looking to make a name for themselves, some were men genuinely disturbed by contemporary events who worried that Catholicism was antithetical to republicanism, and some, like Frances Trollope, were professional scribblers with an eye for a lucrative new trend. Others were highly respected national figures, such as Samuel F. B. Morse, painter and inventor, who returned from a stay in Rome ready to take up the cudgels in print. The result was a vituperative series of articles published in his brother's anti-Catholic newspaper in New York, the *Observer*, reprinted in book form in 1834 as *Foreign Conspiracy against the Liberties of the United States*.

Another was Lyman Beecher, the Presbyterian minister, acclaimed public speaker, supporter of the temperance and abolitionist movements, and first president of the Lane Theological Seminary in Cincinnati. (He passed his anti-Catholicism on, to varying degrees, to his preacher-writer sons and to his daughter, Harriet Beecher Stowe, who in an article for an evangelical newspaper described Catholics as "insidious, all-pervading, persevering.") In well-attended lectures and in *A Plea for the West* (1835), Beecher implored fellow Protestants to awaken to the threat that Catholic immigration posed to an expanding nation with so much unpopulated land. In Rome and Vienna, he warned, "tracts and maps are in circulation, explanatory of the capacious West, and pointing out the most fertile soils and more favored locations" where followers of the pope might settle. These settlers would arrive, like "an army of soldiers," sustained by their leader in the Vatican, who was himself "a creature of Austria . . . sustained by Austrian bayonets." Samuel B. Smith in *The Flight of Popery from Rome to the West* (1836) even implied that a blueprint and timetable existed for the Vatican colonization of the Great Plains.

Other sources of Protestant unease, diligently mined by publishers, appealed more directly to the modern vogue for the Gothic: the Jesuits with their vast networks and never-ending plots, the Catholic's love of florid pageantry, the crimes of the Inquisition, the hypnotizing qualities of incense and medieval music, the inappropriate possibilities of the darkened confessional. (The subtitle of Joseph McKee's compendium *Popery Unmasked* was "Showing the Depravity of the Priesthood and Immorality of the Confessional, Being the Questions Put to Females in Confession.") Intimate queries that ministers would never pose to their young parishioners were supposedly commonplace in the nation's Catholic churches.

Priestly celibacy was also coming to be regarded more skeptically by those who believed that healthy spiritual leaders should marry and father children. Indiscretions by the Catholic clergy only hinted at in the writings of the 1820s became explicit in the ensuing years, establishing the rapacity behind the Roman collar as a plausible trope even among the best writers. The protagonist of Herman Melville's *Omoo* meets three lecherous, wine-loving priests on Tahiti, tended to by "a set of trim little native handmaidens." Melville's publishers saw nothing untoward in that characterization, and in the decades before the Civil War the suggestion that few priests took seriously their vows of chastity was a safe charge to make in the literary marketplace, giving rise to more than twenty years of potboilers, from Scipio di Ricci's *Female Convents: Secrets of the Nunnery Disclosed* (published in Europe in 1829 and in the United States in 1834) to Benjamin Barker's *Cecilia, or the White Nun of the Wilderness* (1845) to Ned Buntline's *The Jesuit's Daughter* (1855).

Like the image of the prurient confessor or the debauched missionary, the convent was another subject of a persistent, explicitly sexual focus. The American fixation with the cloister and the convent school, lasting for the better part of two decades, made evident the voyeuristic impulse behind many discussions of Catholic practices. That a society of women should forsake marriage and motherhood to devote themselves to self-denial, prayer, and good works was a cultural tradition of long standing in southern Europe, but it was profoundly distressing to many Americans, especially American men, that it might be accepted here. "Taking the veil" implied an unnatural concept of womanliness. It was a rejection of democratic culture. It hinted at the potential for furtive misdeeds and sexual deviance. Even a highly ambiguous meditation on the subject, such as Nathaniel Hawthorne's 1836 story "The Minister's Black Veil," acknowledged the "strange awe" that emblem evoked, impressing some and repelling others, challenging everyone. Poles apart, though, from Hawthorne's artful tale of alienation and inner struggle were the works that the wider, cruder reading public was enthralled by.

Maria Monk's *Awful Disclosures of the Hotel Dieu Nunnery* is the classic of the genre, a phenomenal best seller in 1836. It wasn't the first "convent exposé" publishers offered to an eager readership, but it was the book that had the greatest impact, ultimately selling three hundred thousand copies, far outstripping George Bourne's erotic melodrama *Lorette: The History of Louise, Daughter of a Canadian Nun* (1833) and Mary Martha Sherwood's scabrous *The Nun* (1834). Monk's "memoirs" satisfied the most lubricious tastes. She wrote of taking her final vows in a Montreal convent only to learn, "to her utter astonishment and horror," that the younger, more attractive nuns were expected to provide "comfort" for the priests, while any children born of their comfort-giving were immediately baptized and strangled, sending them, unblemished, straight to heaven. Nuns who protested were similarly dispatched and buried in the convent's subterranean graves. Subsequent editions of her book related her life as a fugitive from the long, vengeful reach of the church, including a narrow escape in Philadelphia, where a "Father Hughes" was involved in discussions about what to do with the miscreant.

Maria's mother told a different story: that her daughter had never set foot in that convent, that she had been mentally unstable since jabbing a pencil into her head as a child, and that the father of her illegitimate baby was the lover who brought her to the United States and connected her to the organizers of her lucrative lecture tour. An inspection of the Hotel Dieu convent basements revealed no secret rooms or graves, but Monk's popularity, or notoriety, continued unabated for two years, until she became pregnant again, still unmarried. She purportedly died in 1849 in a New York City prison after being arrested in a brothel.

The drive to demonize convent life had consequences that were of more than theoretical or entertainment value, the most famous example of which is the burning of the Charlestown, Massachusetts, convent in 1834, an event that sent John Hughes, among others, into paroxysms of rage. The Ursuline convent was a large complex of buildings on Mount Benedict in the Boston suburb of Charlestown near Bishop Fenwick's residence, complete with gardens, terraced walks, and high stone walls. It symbolized to some area residents a newfound Catholic power and arrogance, with a mother superior who was withering in her scorn for anyone inside or outside the convent who questioned her authority.

The Ursuline convent was a target of local anger for reasons having to do with economic resentment as well. The girls who attended the boarding school all came from wealthy families. The majority, in fact, came from Protestant households who saw the nuns as suitable mentors for their daughters, so long as Catholic proselytizing was not an element of the program (which, apparently, it was not, at least in any overt sense). Moreover, according to one pupil, Protestant girls were preferred by the nuns, who were themselves largely Irish but educated in France. Some students came from as far away as Canada and New Orleans. It was a source of dismay to many Bostonians that Protestants would entrust their daughters to the Ursuline sisters, but the convent was one of the few, and one of the most respected, schools for girls in New England.

None of this mattered to nativist working-class men, who saw themselves as more ardent defenders of Protestantism than their wealthier, intolerably lax coreligionists. In 1829 gangs had attacked Irish Catholic homes in Boston and beaten the residents in a three-day rampage, and any excuse to vent their bile against the imposing and well-heeled convent would probably have sufficed. A young woman named Rebecca Reed helped to reignite old antipathies that spring as she went about Boston relating a tale of forced confinement on Mount Benedict and a narrow escape from a kidnapping plot that would have spirited her off to Canada. The truth was that she was a novice who had been dismissed from the convent for her unsuitability to the life, and who knew her audience. (The following winter, seven months after the attack in Charlestown, she published her story, *Six Months in a Convent*, timed to cash in on recent events.) But when an actual nun, suffering a breakdown that year, fled the grounds to seek refuge in a nearby house, rumors were widespread that Reed's story of underground cells and torture chambers had been verified. Lyman Beecher returned to Boston to preach against Romish plots. No matter that the nun in question, when recovered from her breakdown, and chagrined that she had caused so much trouble, asked to return to the convent and was accepted back by the sisters.

The crowd of drunken truckmen and brick makers who beat down the doors of the convent in the early hours of August 11 probably numbered between fifty and eighty, but more than a thousand bystanders, according to some accounts, stood across the street and watched, doing nothing to stop the carnage. Nor was the fire department anywhere to be found when the ransacked buildings were looted and set ablaze, the contents of the school's library was thrown into a bonfire, and the nuns and their pupils fled in panic-stricken groups in different directions into the night. A house-by-house search was conducted for the mother superior, who had good cause to fear for her life by this time, but she escaped unharmed. Afterward, many (including some of her pupils) did not choose to characterize her as an entirely innocent victim. Rather than attempting to plead with the rioters or allowing town selectmen to inspect her basements, as they had asked to do the day before, she had dug in her heels and audaciously told the crowd that ten thousand Irish Catholic men of Boston would stand by her and take up arms if anyone dared cross her threshold.

Lyman Beecher insisted that his presence in Boston that week had nothing to do with stirring any mob into action, and he was indignant that the city was turned into an armed camp for a few days after the incident, which he saw as kowtowing to the Catholics; but he did crow a short time later that some credit should be his for any increase in right-thinking in the area. Before he returned to Ohio, he wrote with pride to a correspondent that "the tide turned, and Catholicism forever in the Northeast must row upstream, carefully watched . . . and obstructed by public sentiment." Samuel F. B. Morse's response was similarly disdainful. Given what they believed was happening behind the convent walls, he attested, "had [the Charlestown men] viewed such an outrage with indifference, they would have shown themselves unworthy of American citizens."

Like every other priest in the country, Hughes was appalled at the news from Massachusetts (and his disgust with Beecher and Morse was unmatched), but unlike some Catholic clergymen, he kept his anger about the topic at a boil all his life. Few subjects elicited more agitated outbursts from Hughes over the next thirty years than the burning of the Charlestown convent. He fully supported the mother superior for not giving in to the mob or even to the town selectmen, who had insisted that they were doing all they could to prevent any violence. It was the state's responsibility to protect women and children, he maintained, and it was pure hypocrisy to find fault with the victims for their steadfastness—call it rigidity or call it standing by one's rights.

It was in this charged climate that Hughes honed his ideas about leadership and power. For the responses to Protestant ill will, stereotypes, and even violence were not uniform, even as Protestant responses to Catholicism were not uniform. Many Boston Protestants spoke out against the burning of the convent. The decades before the Civil War also saw some honest curiosity about the Roman faith on the part of American Protestants, some willingness to enter into a dialogue that could live within the terms of agreeing to disagree, and an appreciation of an anti-Calvinist, even gloriously and unapologetically Baroque aesthetic.

The Grand Tour, for instance, had become a feature of the well-rounded life for those who could afford it in the antebellum period, and a visit to Rome was regarded as even more essential than time spent in London or Paris. Recent scholarship suggests that the literature of tourism, written largely by Protestant travelers, reflects a conflicted but deep fascination with Roman churches, catacombs, confessionals, candlelit Masses, kneeling worshippers, penitential pilgrims, and papal processions set against a backdrop of the ruins of empire. The world of Bernini and Gibbon was like nothing else to be seen anywhere. The allure of Rome was reflected in a shelfful of antebellum fiction as well. The best-known example is probably *The Marble Faun* by the author of

The Scarlet Letter, America's most famous Puritan descendant, whose daughter converted after her father's death and became a nun.

Not surprisingly, then, some American priests thought that a too-combative response to the growing chorus of anti-Catholic feeling was the wrong approach, apt to alienate potential allies and likely to stir their enemies to yet more stridency. Bishop Fenwick's sermons in the days following the burning of the convent had been remarkably conciliatory, asking parishioners to turn the other cheek. He asked for clemency for the single rioter who was imprisoned—flagrantly a scapegoat, a seventeen-year-old involved in the burning of the library books who was not a ringleader or even a major participant in the assault.

Nothing about a counsel that urged moderation, silence, or a style of discourse conducted exclusively on an elevated intellectual plane appealed to John Hughes. In private life, he might—often did—accept the New Testament injunction to forgive fully and with alacrity. In the public realm, less so.

In this regard, Hughes took his models less from church life—though Bishop John England loomed as one example of the combative prelate—and much more from political life; and chief among the American statesmen Hughes respected was Henry Clay. It wasn't only that Clay's "American system" appealed to Hughes with its Whiggish emphasis on government-funded internal improvements, industry-protective tariffs, a strong central bank, and a balancing of sectional interests. It wasn't only that Clay got things done (the Missouri Compromise of 1820 was a signal accomplishment) and knew how to use the reins of power in Congress and the cabinet. It was the aura of the man, loved and hated by so many. Clay was ardent, charismatic, wry, self-possessed, and self-dramatizing. He had an openness to experience, a quick tongue, a sense of humor, a temper, and a constitutional inability to let a challenge go unaddressed. Whether or not Clay's reputation for card playing and deference to the belles of Washington was known to Hughes, and whether or not Hughes even cared about the man's private affairs and the criticisms showered on him, he cared about Clay. He was "a man much calumniated."

In another life, having chosen a different path, John Hughes could have been one of Clay's congressional lieutenants, an eager Whig politician himself. Only James Buchanan and William Seward elicited the same admiration at later points in his life. Hughes thought it best that

Catholic priests should not vote, should seem to be above such secular concerns, but he violated that principle in 1832 and voted for Clay in that year's presidential election. Moreover, he felt compelled to let his parishioners at Saint John's know that he had done so, to the vocal anger of some of his Democratic, pro-Jackson congregation.

But, then, it was an age of bravado and grandiloquence and dynamic personalities. Andrew Jackson's politics and personality were anathema to Hughes, but there was no denying that the man, with infinitely fewer accomplishments than Clay, was the occupant of the White House for two terms in part because of his public persona. Strong beliefs, strong words, righteous indignation, an appetite for conflict: these were potent forces to a populace that paid lip service to the moderation and gentility of a George Washington but thrilled to the spectacle of a leader who drew emphatic lines, never backed down, and never doubted himself. Jackson's anti-nullification proclamation in 1832 had been the paradigm of bold, clear leadership, and the country loved him for it. More than any other clergyman of his faith in his time, Hughes saw the potential for a Clay-like, Jacksonian approach to public discourse.

———

OPPORTUNITIES FOR ENGAGING in that discourse were not wanting. At the height of the Maria Monk boom, Hughes had written a lengthy article for a Philadelphia paper about the implications of this publishing coup. It was probably the most forthright, least defensive statement about the scandalous memoir published by a clerical figure in the country. "The immense circulation of Miss Monk's book," he wrote, "so full of obscenity and lewdness, is no equivocal sign of the growing corruption of morals." Yet he was willing to point the finger at those who promoted her more than at the pitiful, deluded young woman herself: "That a few lay and religious speculators should have been found to publicize it is not surprising for, among both, there are those who, it is to be feared, would publish a libel on the character of God if they thought it would be popular and that they should make money by it."

Hughes's ideal antagonist, though, wasn't someone from the gutter press or a third-rate journalist like George Bourne but a figure of more respectability and, therefore, of more danger to Catholicism among the burgeoning American middle class. He found that antagonist for a time in John Breckinridge, a Presbyterian minister with a formidable résumé and a reputation that extended far beyond Philadelphia. His father had been a U.S. senator from Kentucky and Thomas Jefferson's attorney general, and his nephew would become James Buchanan's vice president. He had studied law at Princeton before deciding on a career in the ministry and had served a one-year term as chaplain to the House of Representatives. He was also no friend to Catholicism.

In September 1831, Hughes had published an article in the *United States Gazette* addressing the widespread rumors that many Protestant clergy had fled Philadelphia during the recent outbreak of cholera while the city's priests and nuns had been praised for their refusal to abandon the sick and dying, even in the face of their own imminent peril. Hughes himself had stayed in town and done his part that blisteringly hot summer, visiting the sick and administering the sacraments. The Sisters of Charity had pressed themselves to the limit. Michael Hurley and Nicholas O'Donnell had turned Saint Augustine's rectory and school into a makeshift hospital with no denominational distinctions made among its four hundred patients. So Hughes indicated he was a little tired of being referred to by his Protestant counterparts as a member of the "popish" or "Romish" church—the proper term was the "Roman Catholic Church," as everyone well knew—when their own sense of vocation was so weak. He demanded the respect that Catholic clergymen and women religious had earned. Protestant ministers were "remarkable for their pastoral solicitude so long as the flock is healthy, the pastures pleasant, and the fleece luxuriant," he charged. Yet they were nowhere to be found "when disease begins to spread dissolution in the fold."

Reaction to the article was just what he had hoped it would be. Breckinridge, in particular, was offended and appalled and let it be known that he would be open to a debate, with Hughes or any other area priest, on the subject of which was the more authentic religion of Christ, the Catholic or the Protestant. Hughes declined the invitation for an oral debate at a local hall (possibly at Kenrick's insistence) but indicated that he would be agreeable to a literary exchange, a series of public letters in which each man made his case at sufficient length and answered the questions the other raised. That would do nicely, Breckinridge agreed; he would even allow Hughes the first word, then publish his response in the *Presbyterian*, with Hughes to follow in turn, using whatever journalistic forum he chose.

The terms of engagement the two men decided on in the fall of 1832 had the starchy precision of conditions usually settled on before a duel; all that was lacking were "seconds" appointed to confer on behalf of the principals. Both men agreed to allow themselves ample space for addressing the questions the other had raised about their respective religions, and they concurred that a six-month time limit felt about right, unless, of course, their eager public clamored for more. Healthy egos were at work here. They thought it desirable that one topic should be fully addressed before a new one was introduced. That intention went by the wayside pretty quickly. They also affirmed that politeness and decorum were essential. This was to be an "amicable discussion," best kept civil and straightforward at all times. That part of the agreement fell apart by degrees. Before they were done, their scathing dislike for each other was impossible for readers to overlook, with Breckinridge writing that he felt ashamed of Hughes for his "diarrhoea verborum" and pomposity, and Hughes blasting Breckinridge as a willful twister of words without an ounce of the gentleman about him.

Hughes's first problem was finding a forum for his letters. Philadelphia had been without a Catholic newspaper for more than a decade. Despite the misgivings Kenrick expressed about the whole undertaking—Kenrick, from Hughes's point of view, always seemed to be expressing misgivings about any project that excited Hughes—plans were quickly drawn up to begin a new weekly. Details about the origin of a revived *Catholic Herald* are sparse, but it appears that Hughes, the redoubtable Terence Donaghoe, and the ever-game Michael Hurley and Nicholas O'Donnell of Saint Augustine's, having found a few patrons, were the men who got it off the ground, with O'Donnell staying on as editor after the interests of the other men took them in separate directions. Contributing unsigned articles over the years always remained appealing to Hughes, when he had the time, but editing a paper on a regular basis was something he had no stomach for, and he and O'Donnell probably understood that from the start.

The first issue appeared on January 3, 1833, three weeks before the debate was scheduled to begin. Hughes was thrilled with their handiwork: the paper was cheap and the type plain, but its four pages, twelve by eighteen inches, gave space for him to answer Breckinridge's challenges with room left over for a handful of articles on religion and literature, book excerpts and reviews, some information want ads, and a scattering of news from abroad—meaning almost exclusively Irish political news, particularly anything that had to do with the Irish political leader Daniel O'Connell. Local or national politics was not ever to be touched on. Its subscriber base of four hundred (at three dollars for a yearly subscription) was scarcely adequate to pay the printer's bills, but the paper's founders didn't seem overly worried. Kenrick might initially have wondered if any of this justified the time and energy involved, but from his subordinate's perspective, he would just have to get used to the fact that he had a priest in his diocese who loved journalism, propagandizing for the faith, and polemical discourse.

(A word should be said in passing about the ads that appeared from time to time in the *Catholic Herald* in the 1830s. Many of them tell sad stories of family separation and social dislocation among the Irish Catholic population. Quite a number ask in quiet desperation for information about missing family members—young girls last seen on such-and-such a date, a husband who had evidently abandoned his family after promising to look for work in another county or state—or inquire about relatives who left Ireland aboard a certain ship but have never been heard from again. The pathos of these terse announcements is heartbreaking. They also serve as further proof that such a newspaper was needed in Philadelphia, however limited its reach.)

For the propagandizing intent of the paper, Father O'Donnell was especially useful. Only in his late twenties, he was a bookish man—he had made of the rectory library a collection that aroused Hughes's envy—with a talent for editing. His many obscure volumes came in handy when Hughes realized the daunting extent of Breckinridge's knowledge of the Bible and church history—there wasn't a pope, a church council, or a medieval doctrinal dispute the man didn't know something about—and decided he needed some serious help in preparing for these scholarly encounters. Hughes turned as well to Simon Bruté as a reference source, and letters made their way fast and furiously between Philadelphia and Emmitsburg. Hughes had plenty of questions. What did he know about Pope Liberius, whom Breckinridge kept bringing up, or the Calvinist synod of 1550, or Averroes's Muslim critique of Christianity? Nothing. How informed was he about the bulls of Boniface VIII or the martyrdom of Jerome of Prague or Melanchthon's writings on Luther? Not at all. Bruté always seemed to have a chapter-and-verse answer. Even Kenrick was pressed into bibliographic service.

The topics covered, in what ended up being thirty-five letters, totaling 326 pages when they were published as a book, ranged from the theologically serious to the historical and sociological, of varying degrees of importance, to the downright gossipy. The men debated doctrine, sometimes in truly meaningful ways, and they also aired personal prejudices.

Hughes's principal contention followed the standard argument: Protestantism represented a severing of a direct line from Christ through Peter and the Church of Rome, and it placed a misguided stress on the Old and New Testaments as the sole expressions of God's will, especially as interpreted by individual, sometimes conflicting, readings of the Bible (a process "flattering to human pride," he wrote, but not conducive to theological clarity). Its origins under the likes of Henry VIII, Calvin, and Luther suggested that its founders' motives were as much political as they were spiritual. It was a collection of sects, many of which warred with each other, and most of which openly attacked the Catholic Church in a very un-Christian spirit, while the term "Reformation" itself could only be considered "specious."

Breckinridge's strategy from the start was less about defending Protestantism per se and more about putting Hughes on the defensive and keeping him there. He naturally disputed any lineage that meant anything from Jesus to Peter and to Peter's successors—those popes and antipopes—just as he was ready to question the Catholic manner of baptism, belief in holy relics and exorcism, veneration of Mary, censorship of books, priestly celibacy ("occasions of sodomy"), indulgence selling, the impropriety of the confessional, the church's own equivocal attitude toward the Jesuits, the contorted reasoning of papal infallibility, the fiction of purgatory, and the damning record of the Inquisition.

In each letter, a correspondent was allowed to dwell on as many points and raise as many queries as he wished, giving his opponent a free hand in deciding what cried out for immediate rebuttal and what new questions should in turn be raised. It was an unwieldy method. Anything not fully answered in the immediately succeeding letter left the writer open to the accusation that he had been stopped in his tracks by a charge for which he had no ready defense. At times, it must have seemed as if each man was so overloading his letter as to leave the other with an unmanageable amount of material to respond to.

Sex got Breckinridge going at full speed, enough for Hughes to accuse him of producing a document no decent woman (not even a

Protestant woman) would read. If that was the case, Breckinridge countered, blame your own church's history, not my summary of it. Indeed,
his list of serious papal fornicators, spread out over several letters, was
long and juicy and gave him the opportunity to go beyond the obvious names like Alexander VI to bring in pontiffs like the boy-loving
Julius III or, more than once, Sergius III, whose Roman mistress had
the unique distinction of having been the lover of one pope (Sergius), the
mother of another, their son (John XI)—she looked after her boys—and
the grandmother of a third, the great libertine John XII. On the topic
of the celibacy of the Catholic clergy, including women religious, Breckinridge was sure that "the worst, the half, has not been told!" (Excla-
mation points proliferated on both sides as the debate went into the hot
summer months.)

About the lascivious and irreligious popes from the early medieval
period to the Renaissance, there wasn't much Hughes could say other
than that no institution should be judged by its worst failures, that pre-
tenders to the throne of Peter were never accepted as true vicars of Christ;
he knew that Breckinridge was simply trying to bury him in a mountain
of indefensible smut. Nor was there much to comment about the treatment of Galileo or the Saint Bartholomew's Day massacre of the Hugue-
nots ("I condemn it as much as you"), though, he pointed out, it was
not as if Protestants "were immaculate on the subject of persecution."
Hughes was more at ease, and more adept, for instance, at explaining
and defending transubstantiation, which Breckinridge had repeatedly
attacked as one of the most "false, shocking, novel" notions put forth
by the Catholic Church and which he insisted had been unknown to the
faithful before the thirteenth century. Interestingly, a large percentage
of the letters are concerned with explanations of this doctrine, which in
fact serious readers would have found instructive if they were willing to
overlook the increasingly bileful tone of the letters and the spectacle of
two clergymen slugging it out like pugilists. Hughes could be an eloquent
explicator of the church's belief in the living presence of Christ's body
and blood in the bread and wine offered at Mass.

A long-winded "slugging" is just what the whole thing became by the
end, though, with both writers falling into belligerent repetition of earlier statements, finger wagging, and name calling. Yet some readers managed to separate the wheat from the chaff, and others found it plainly
entertaining. No surprise: Protestants were sure that Breckinridge had

put Hughes in his place; Catholics, that Father Hughes had held his own against an erudite and annoying adversary.

One unexpected benefit of the debate for John Hughes was that it raised his profile in Philadelphia even outside Catholic circles. He was invited to become a member of one of the city's elite groups, an offer he happily accepted. Kenrick's reaction can only be surmised. Yet the Wistar Club was less a snobbish, restrictive social enclave, the kind of organization no priest has any business being a part of, than it was an invitation-only intellectual and fraternal body of men who gathered a few times a year at different members' homes for oysters and sherry and no-holds-barred discussions of current events, civic doings, and scientific, literary, and philosophical questions. It was also a decidedly Whig-centered group. Here Hughes met congressman John Sergeant, Henry Clay's running mate in the last presidential election. He socialized with publisher Matthew Carey, whom he knew from his Saint John's fund-raising committee, and his famous economist son Henry (the former an Irish Catholic nationalist, the latter a convert to Protestantism with no interest in Ireland). He met Horace Binney, one of the great lawyers of his time, a friend of John Marshall's, and an outspoken foe of anti-Catholic bigotry. Unlike most other Catholic clergymen at the time, Hughes saw an advantage to having social contacts with Protestant men of business, lawyers, and scientists, quite aside from the mental stimulation the gatherings provided. The very fact that his presence was desired at these purely intellectual suppers indicated that not all his Protestant countrymen thought as Breckinridge did—that to be a Roman Catholic was, by definition, to be unlettered and opposed to progress.

Hughes's energy and initiative—his breadth of vision—did not go unnoticed by the hierarchy in Rome. As early as 1833 there had been talk of promoting him to a bishopric. That first opportunity passed him by in a quirky fashion. When John England, who happened to be in Rome that year, was approached for his opinion about which American priest might be the most suitable to be appointed the new bishop of Cincinnati, he offered two names, that of Hughes and John Purcell, who was at that time the director of the Mount. He further suggested that a self-made man like Hughes might be the better choice and more agreeable to the residents of a rough-and-tumble frontier community like that of southern Ohio. The cardinal who headed the Propaganda Fide, the office in charge of the American hierarchy, either misheard him or misremembered their conversation, because the next time he saw Bishop England, he was pleased to tell him that the pope fully agreed with his reasoning and had named John Purcell to the position. Hughes's disappointment can well be imagined. He was then talked about as Purcell's replacement as the director of the seminary in Emmitsburg, but on second thought that did not seem to anyone the right place for the man, even in Hughes's own view of the matter, and the job went to someone else and eventually to his friend and fellow Mount Saint Mary's alumnus, John McCaffrey. He was also discussed as a potential bishop when there was talk of a new see being created in Pittsburgh in 1837, but that restructuring of the diocese did not take place until several years later. Still, Hughes's strengths were known, and, everyone who knew him agreed, his future as part of the church's hierarchy looked promising. "He pants to do good, widespread good," John McCaffrey wrote to Simon Bruté.

One strength Hughes did not exhibit, assuredly, was a capacity for dynamic fund-raising, though to get the money he needed for his new church out of Philadelphians in the early 1830s, especially given his interest in an imposing facade and a lavish interior, was probably a task beyond any one man's abilities. The consecration of Saint John the Evangelist had taken place on Passion Sunday in 1832, even though its exterior was still not completed. It was a major occasion: dignitaries and journalists were invited, the former Empress of Mexico was in attendance, and Annibale Carracci's painting *The Flagellation of Christ* was on display, donated by Joseph Bonaparte, who handed out artworks about town like visiting cards. Hughes had asked John Power, the vicar-general of the New York diocese, to deliver the opening sermon. That turned out to be a serious miscalculation, as Power took no notice of the fact that his host had asked many of the city's more prominent Protestants to attend the service and launched into a pointless attack on Protestantism when his assignment had been purely celebratory and forward-looking. Hughes was horror-struck and let Power know that. He was afraid that any interfaith bridges he had been building had been definitively demolished. More important, though, the consecration ceremony raised only $850, an ominous sign that the church was going to be in financial trouble before it had even assumed its intended central role in the religious life of the city.

In 1834, not long after the church escaped a major fire in the neighborhood with minimal damage, and a grammar school had already been set up in the basement, the situation took on a critical dimension. Payments to angry creditors could not be met. Appeals to individuals and pleas from the pulpit by Hughes and his assistant, Father Francis X. Gartland (the future bishop of Savannah), were not bringing in the money that was needed. A concert open to the public presenting the American premiere of Mozart's *Requiem Mass* netted only a few hundred dollars. Marc Frenaye suggested that Hughes consider taking his appeal much farther afield: to Mexico, where he could put him in touch with many wealthy, devout Catholic families. Frenaye, who was living in the rectory now and serving as the diocese's key financial adviser, even offered to accompany his friend. Hughes agreed this might be the only solution and set about to learn Spanish, subjecting himself to an intensive course of study that several weeks later had him well on his way toward a working knowledge of the language. Hearing of his plans, his guilty parishioners, at the urgent behest of Father Gartland, decided to dig deeper into their pockets to meet the next schedule of payments. After Gartland's imploring sermon, checks were written for $4,000, and another $15,000 in long-term pledges came in. The trip was canceled.

The thought of such an arduous journey and begging for funds in a foreign country while speaking a foreign language was not something Hughes could really have been looking forward to, no matter how good a face he put on it, but the priesthood, he was learning, sometimes called on men to change their initial self-image, to adapt to unexpected contingencies and pressures.

———

OTHER CHANGES, both joyous and sorrowful, were more personal and familial. In 1836, William Rodrigue, the thirty-six-year-old architect he had now known for four years, joined the family circle when he and Margaret Hughes were married. This wasn't a surprise: the Rodrigues had practically adopted Hughes from the day they met him, and Margaret's visits to Philadelphia from Chambersburg had been frequent enough to allow a courtship to blossom. The two older Hughes brothers, Patrick and Michael, had long since married and started their own families, and Ellen had taken her final vows with the Sisters of Charity eight years earlier. Their father had entered into his decline. It was time for Margaret, in her late twenties, moderately attractive and self-assured, never particularly shy or modest, to find a life partner, and it was past time for William.

Her brother couldn't have been happier that the two were attracted to each other. Courteous, cosmopolitan, well-spoken, talented—and ten years Margaret's senior—William had been brought up in a family with social aspirations, a respect for learning, and an unshakable devotion to the church.

The Rodrigue family also had decided views on slavery, and theirs was not a perspective John or Margaret Hughes would have been personally exposed to previously. The Rodrigues had fled Santo Domingo after the slave revolt and told stories of atrocities against white slave owners that would have fueled any white American's fears of what another Nat Turner uprising could mean. They had settled in Philadelphia, with its sizable Caribbean and Mexican Catholic émigré population, determined to recoup their fortune and see all their children well educated, properly wed, and comfortably settled. They didn't want to hear anything about abolitionism. William's brother, a physician, was not merely opposed to abolition, though; he seems to have been a strong proponent of the peculiar institution. Aristide Rodrigue eventually relocated west and, with the grandson of Daniel Boone, became one of the founders of the town of Lecompton, Kansas, a famous center of the pro-slavery, anti-abolitionist movement of the Midwest.

William's marriage to a woman whose brother was an up-and-coming figure in the church can't have seemed anything but advantageous to the Rodrigues. (They might also have been pleased considering that his most recent romantic dalliance had been with a Presbyterian young woman who was doubtful about converting.) If Saint John the Evangelist became the renowned church it was intended to be, their son's reputation would be made. William's new brother-in-law was becoming more well-connected to the business elite of the city each year, and although the newly married couple lived at first in Chambersburg, they moved to New York soon after John Hughes relocated. Margaret had a taste for urban living and social advancement that her two farmer brothers did not.

As expected, Patrick Hughes, father of this now very Americanized brood, died several months later, a stranger in a land he never came to love. Margaret looked out for him until the end. At the time, John Hughes was in Baltimore with Bishop Kenrick, attending the second provincial council, and he did not have the chance for a final parting with a man he deeply respected, but he was present for the funeral and burial. From there he was talked by his friend John Purcell—now Bishop Purcell—into visiting Ohio, where he was supposed to allow himself some time for rest and renewal, but his name preceded him, and he was asked to deliver sermons throughout the state and as far away as Saint Louis, offers he found impossible to decline.

By now, Hughes was a speaker in demand. Back in 1835, he had been goaded by John Breckinridge into an oral debate before a Philadelphia audience, the debate that Breckinridge had always wanted—the result of which was an exhaustive recapitulation of their previous letters, even more grandstanding on both sides, much heat and little light, some truly ugly language from Breckinridge, and another, even longer book publication. For Kenrick, enough was enough, and he had ordered the *Catholic Herald* not even to cover the event. Simon Bruté, now in Indiana as the first bishop of the newly formed diocese in Vincennes, shook his head. His old pupil liked the stage too much, he felt. Nonetheless, as a result, Hughes's fame became more than local—Aristide Rodrigue asked for copies of the book to distribute to Catholics in Kansas—and even Bishop John England was willing to attest that Hughes had "won unfading laurels for himself" in taking on the odious Presbyterian. In 1837, Hughes's moment was at hand.

John Dubois had never had an easy time of it as bishop of New York, and everyone knew it. While he was not as inept as Conwell—far from it—very little had gone his way, and he no doubt wished he had never been "elevated" from the work he loved in Emmitsburg to his thankless post in Manhattan. The Irish of the city refused to accept that their first choice for the position several years earlier, John Power, had been passed over by the hierarchy. They were relentlessly hard on the Frenchman sent to lead them, a man whose English was less than perfect and whose preaching style left them cold. Power claimed that when Dubois spoke from the pulpit, numerous members of the congregation took that as an opportunity to visit the rum shop across the street from the cathedral.

Aging rapidly, crushed by the economic and demographic problems he faced, Dubois carried on as best he could, and the wonder is that he hadn't been asked to be relieved of his duties by the time it was decided that a coadjutor was essential. But the man had a healthy sense of pride, even if he was sometimes paralyzed by an indecisive nature. Power, not an objective source but probably correct nonetheless, had summarized the situation in 1834 to Paul Cullen, an Irish cleric in Europe: "Our good old prelate means well, but unfortunately never does anything right. His time is spent in planning and scheming, never in executing." The badly needed seminary for which he had fund-raised to the point of exhaustion burned to the ground before completion, foreclosure hung over the heads of more than a few churches in the city, and trustees and parishioners were loud, and often appallingly rude to the bishop's face, in voicing their many complaints.

John Hughes's name, not surprisingly, was on the short list of men to send to New York to deal with this critical situation. He wasn't anyone's first or even second choice, though. Bishop Dubois had let it be known that he wanted John Timon, a Vincentian missionary who was making a name for himself out west, though the fact that Dubois was supporting him probably scuttled Timon's chances pretty quickly. Dubois had argued over the years for Francis Kenrick, but the hierarchy in Rome had no intention of letting him leave Philadelphia, and Kenrick had no intention of attaching himself to another Conwell. The Irish of the New York diocese let their views be known: Power, one of their own, it had to be. Dubois's response: never in a million years. It was not even to be thought of. They would have to kill him first. John England thought it would be wise to give the people of New York a leader they would rally behind, and in fact the generally capable if gossipy and self-serving Father Power had much to recommend him.

Kenrick was probably Hughes's most damaging critic, or nonsupporter. He never felt at ease with his protégé's volatile nature, too-visible ambition, and penchant for stirring the waters, and he did not want him posted elsewhere while the debt situation at Saint John's was unresolved, especially now that the Panic of 1837 had wrecked the national economy and charitable giving in Philadelphia had precipitously fallen off. Honorable men both, Kenrick and England felt obliged to let Hughes know that they had not written to the Propaganda Fide in support of his candidacy. Hughes was stung by the lack of two such important endorsements, but in the end it didn't matter. The Vatican disregarded their opinions.

In November 1837, Hughes received word that he should conclude his affairs in Philadelphia as soon as possible, as he was to be John Dubois's coadjutor with right of succession and would be formally installed in that position at Saint Patrick's Cathedral on Mott Street early in the new year. Given Dubois's health, the hierarchy's decision obviously meant that John Hughes, just forty years old, would soon become the bishop of the diocese of New York. John Power was bitterly disappointed. His local supporters were angry. Hughes's friends and family were thrilled. One person the coadjutor-to-be could not share the happy news with, though, was his early local mentor, that most dynamic and eccentric of priests, Michael Hurley, who had died of bronchitis a few months previously at the age of fifty-seven. Hurley, above all men, would have thought Father Hughes and the troubled diocese to the north to be a good—an even—match. He had served as a priest there while Hughes was still at Emmitsburg, and he knew all too well the problems any serious leader would have to confront in that minefield on the Hudson.

In his biography of Orestes Brownson—the aggressive New England Catholic journalist whose path was to cross, in both productive and unpleasant ways, with that of Hughes in years to come—Arthur Schlesinger Jr. wrote, "Brownson may indeed have brought rudeness to Boston, but he also brought strength, and strength was badly needed." Exactly the same could be said of John Hughes and New York. Rudeness and strength were the future; drift and patience were the past.

4

CONFRONTING GOTHAM

PHILADELPHIA HAD ITS slums, its social problems and growing pains. It had its rapacious businessmen, its fallen women, its needy and contentious immigrants. If one believed any part of George Lippard's *The Quaker City; or, The Monks of Monk Hall* (1845), the most popular American novel of its day, the City of Brotherly Love was actually a lively cesspool of vice and crime, a site of rampant debauchery and unbridled greed. New York City was something else, though—less a product of a Gothic writer's imagination and more a shocking, ever-expanding, seemingly intractable reality.

The mythologizing of Gotham, island of inexhaustible variety and energy, enviable center of ambition and innovation, dominated thinking about New York City throughout the twentieth century. That perspective belonged to a far distant future when John Hughes arrived. Most visitors to the city in the 1830s were more astonished by its chaos, dirt, poverty, and crime. Wealthy New Yorkers lived comfortably in Greek Revival town houses on tree-lined streets—picture the Slopers in *Washington Square*—and the truly rich had country villas on or near the Hudson River or East River in upper Manhattan. Bolstered by the completion of the Erie Canal a decade earlier, an energetic, entrepreneurial middle class had made New York City a commercial mecca. Prior to the Panic of 1837, the shops were always full. The waterfront, a forest of masts, was never quiet. Yet most of the three hundred thousand residents lived in tight quarters south of Fourteenth Street, cleanliness was hard to come by (Charles Dickens thought New York had nothing of the Bostonian and Philadelphian sense of tidiness), and the city was better known for its pickpockets and aggressive gangs than its culture or amenities, despite its five theaters, art academy, athenaeum, and the efforts of the competing Knickerbocker and Young America writers to foster a literary fraternity. The cockpits and rat-baiting arenas did a brisk business around the clock. Anti-abolition riots, anti-brothel riots, theater riots, Election Day riots, and "flour riots" had kept the hard-pressed constabulary, such as it was, busy in the mid-1830s in what was a particularly unsettled period. Walt Whitman later celebrated Manhattan in his poetry, but his pre–Civil War newspaper journalism was more honest about what he called "one of the most crime-haunted and dangerous cities in Christendom."

Much more so than Boston, Philadelphia, or Baltimore, it was also a highly sexualized city. Street prostitution was more public and becoming more brazen all the time. The head of the Magdalen Society estimated the number of "girls on the town," the preferred euphemism of the decade, at a staggering ten thousand. Many thought that number absurdly high; but even halved, that figure is remarkable. "The oyster shops swarm with them," one visitor wrote, and "the theaters are disgraced by them." Pornography was more readily available, hawked on the streets, and abortionists and brothels were more widely advertised. (The ax murder of the beautiful prostitute Helen Jewett and the sensational trial and acquittal of her boyish client-slayer had dominated the news two years before Hughes's arrival.) The penny papers, "receptacles of scandal," in the words of former mayor Philip Hone, like the "flash press"—the weekly male sporting papers of the early 1840s, *New York Flash*, the *Whip*, the *Libertine*, the *Subterranean*, *New York as It Is*—were flourishing enterprises that contributed to the view of New Yorkers as a racy people short on decorum.

One particularly disgruntled British traveler remarked that New Yorkers in the 1830s were no more reserved on the Sabbath than they were on weekdays and expressed his amazement at seeing women selling oranges and oysters in the porticoes of churches while crowds of young men beneath the church windows, "many in a disgusting state of intoxication," made a nuisance of themselves, volubly urging on the pigs fighting at the curb. And the pigs, the famous pigs—they were everywhere before the mid-1840s, it seemed, rooting, rutting, defecating, devouring the occasional dead dog, the bigger ones jostling pedestrians off the street. "Ugly brutes," Dickens commented about these peak-snouted scavengers of the metropolis.

Government was of little help at this stage in the city's history. The mayoralty, only four years old as a purely elective office, was a toothless, one-year position, shifting back and forth between Whig and Democratic candidates, with most of the real power residing with a corrupt or inept Common Council. "The city is virtually without any municipal government," James Gordon Bennett's *New York Herald* complained. Reform societies were in their boisterous infancy. The police and fire departments were largely volunteer affairs, and those volunteers were not themselves always the most reputable or law-abiding of men. The real power of this city lay with what Whitman called "the divinity of trade," a driving spirit manipulated by investors and real-estate speculators who forced a disruptive rate of growth and change upon residents as even downtown's consecrated graveyards and potters' fields were regularly emptied (none too respectfully) to make room for new housing, stores, and office buildings. With good reason, Alexis de Tocqueville had written five years earlier, "I look upon the size of certain American cities, and especially on the nature of their population, as a real danger."

The collapse of sanitation wasn't something even the most ardent city booster could talk away. A Barbados planter, shocked at the changes since the time of his last visit ten years earlier, wrote in his journal that Broadway by 1837 had become a "pig sty" in a city where "dead rats, cats, and every kind of refuse are thrown onto the streets." Tobacco spittle was everywhere, he observed. No one took responsibility for cleaning anything. The rich could afford private street sweepers, but most residents were at the mercy of a small and underfunded sanitation system. "The city has some fine large buildings," Nathaniel Carrington admitted, "but in consequence of the extreme filth of the streets they lose their effect on the stranger." Worse than the dismal aesthetic impression was the fact that sidewalks, gutters, alleys, wells, and ponds became breeding grounds for disease.

What mattered to John Hughes, of course, was not the state of urban life in general in the country's now-largest city, but the extent to which these problems affected its Catholic population. And that gave cause for grave concern. By some estimates, almost 20 percent of the city's population—over fifty thousand men, women, and children—were Catholic, or were presumed to be Catholic, based on their countries and counties of origin, statements made upon arrival, the neighborhood they resided in, blood relations who identified as Catholic, and other factors. By no means was church attendance a reliable factor in any kind of serious census taking, as the majority of those fifty thousand people, native or foreign-born, did not attend church. Most were among the city's poorest inhabitants and lived in those downtown wards that were the least healthful and most crime-ridden. How connected to their supposed faith should they be when exhaustion, despair, and a struggle for survival were their more common lot, all made worse by the recent economic troubles? Psychologically battered, they knew, too, just how they were viewed by their Protestant countrymen: "the filth and offscouring of all Europe." *Offscouring* was a popular, potent word in this context. The fact that some British, Swiss, and German towns were said to deport or facilitate the emigration of their undesirables added fuel to the indignation of New York City taxpayers who had to support the poorhouses, asylums, and orphanages that the immigrants were filling. There was no doubt in Hughes's mind that the church was the most likely avenue, possibly even the only avenue, by which poor Irish immigrants might advance toward a life of dignity and self-respect, but how one unknown priest leading a handful of other committed priests was to effect a social transformation on a scale that would make any difference was far from clear. He had come to New York with no reputation among the masses of the destitute and the working class, just as he had left Philadelphia with a reputation for unseemly vociferousness among the genteel.

Of equal consequence, there was the matter of Hughes's reception among the clergy in the diocese. Father Power's admirers had not reconciled themselves to the fact that he had been passed over again, few people seemed inclined to say a good word about the newcomer, and several of the city's priests boycotted Hughes's consecration at the cathedral. This in itself said something about Dubois's lack of control over his clergy. It was a slight that stung and was not soon forgotten. The situation called for some fortitude on the part of the coadjutor, and he took pleasure from a well-attended ceremony that included the presence of Bishop Benedict Joseph Fenwick from Boston and Bishop Kenrick, his sister and brother-in-law, Marc Frenaye and other dear friends from Philadelphia, and a sermon preached by Father Mulledy, a noted Jesuit and future president of Georgetown College. One of the local priests who was present, John McCloskey, had known Hughes at Mount Saint Mary's. He remembered the consecration as a "grand and imposing scene" with the object of everyone's attention displaying great "composure and self-possession." Hughes appeared to him to be standing at the altar "in all the fullness of health and vigor." The truth was that the coadjutor was just recovering from a debilitating cold, but he was determined to appear strong, alert, and articulate. The Protestant lawyer George Templeton Strong, who heard him speak a few weeks later, concurred: the new prelate was an impressive speaker, the best he had ever heard. "His manner is very good—plain, candid, and serious," quite unlike the more bombastic Power. "He is no hypocrite, I think," Strong wrote in his diary.

FIGURE 4. *The old Saint Patrick's Cathedral (now basilica) on Mott Street was the site of John Hughes's consecration as coadjutor of the New York diocese. It was only several blocks from the infamous slum district, the Five Points.* (Collection of the Archives of the Archdiocese of New York.)

Then, settled into his rooms at the diocesan residence on Mulberry Street directly behind the cathedral, a building shared with Bishop Dubois and three other priests—it was down to work. To Marc Frenaye, he wrote in March, "I shall like New York in proportion as I forget Philadelphia," adding "and to this latter the Philadelphians seem disposed to allow every chance."

Down to work meant, first, confronting some frightening fiscal facts. To whatever extent he knew the broad picture before leaving Philadelphia, Hughes must have been dismayed when he studied the ledgers in detail and contemplated the economic crisis the New York church was facing. The churches of the diocese labored under a collective debt of $300,000—more than all its properties were worth on the open market—at a hefty interest of 7 percent, and most priests lived in rented rooms, as very few parishes could yet afford their own rectories. Five of the city's seven Catholic churches were eyeing potential bankruptcy in the near future. A few blocks south of the cathedral, the Church of the Transfiguration reported an annual deficit of over $1,000 on a $4,700 yearly operating budget and was contemplating auctioning off its organ to meet its creditors' demands. When a $1,800 loan at Saint Joseph's Church on Sixth Avenue in Greenwich Village came due the following March, the trustees were able to pay the bank only $200 on the debt and had to resort to a new loan to meet their obligations. The total debt on the parish at the time exceeded $35,000. Saint Peter's Church on Barclay Street, a smaller parish, listed in a similar period of several months its expenses for the water bill, interest on the mortgage, taxes, oil and lamp cleaning, salaries for the organist and sexton, wine, candles, insurance, new locks and brooms, lumber, plastering, and work on the rectory, all of which came to $1,270.44. Donations, pew rentals, and Sunday plate collections for the same period came to $1,271.38, leaving the church at that juncture ninety-four cents in the black—and that was supposed to represent a financial victory. But it wasn't a victory of any kind: that accounting came from a rare flush period for a church that normally confronted an annual deficit of over $6,000, and the church's total debt to the banks and individual creditors was over $135,000.

Elsewhere around the state, the picture was no brighter. A church in Utica recorded $1,455 in receipts and roughly the same in expenditures, but that tidy zero balance was possible because no money was set aside for the priest's salary or the rent that was owed on the house he lived in. A church in Albany noted that it took in $3,182 a year to cover its annual expenses of $3,177, including priests' salaries, leaving the pastor with a balance of five dollars. Unfortunately, a local bank was holding a $5,000 mortgage on the building, and the church owed $1,781 in other loans. The Church of Eden in Erie, New York, reported an income of $173 for a seven-month period, suggesting a spartan edifice, candle-less Masses, and, once again, unpaid priests who had to rely on relatives or generous parishioners for food and pocket money. Some priests were concerned about the erratic payment of their salaries. Others were models of near-saintly patience. A priest from Schenectady closed his report to the bishop by noting with relief that his church owned outright the vestments and chalice he used, that the cruets and ciborium were his, and that "the congregation promises and *sometimes* [his underlining] pays for my support." No provisions were in place for those clergy who became ill or needed to be looked after in retirement. And in more rural areas, there was scant hope of finding more resources. A priest near Syracuse reported (as of January 1839) a total of 365 parishioners—"170 who can read"—of whom 131 were able to give the church anything.

More robust fund-raising was essential; that much was readily apparent. Most of the regular parishioners of Saint Patrick's Cathedral were the city's working-class Irish, but a fair number of middle-class and affluent Catholics attended other churches in better neighborhoods around the city. Hughes had it in mind to make the acquaintance in his first year of any and all communicants of significant means and influence. Just as clearly, though, it was evident that the best local efforts would never breach so prodigious a gap, growing each year, between income and expenses. That wasn't going to be possible in New York City or anywhere else in New York State and the large part of New Jersey the diocese claimed as part of its own. That grim situation would stabilize over the next two decades, especially in New York City, as the economy improved, but in the late 1830s there were too few Irish Catholics who could or would write the kind of checks that were needed. The diocese would have to look farther afield for assistance.

Education and child welfare were the other pressing concerns on Hughes's mind that winter. It was estimated that not even half of the city's Catholic school-age children attended school at all, either the public schools or the six parochial schools in the city. At that rate, a vicious cycle of poverty would remain unbroken for generations. There were only two Catholic orphanages in Manhattan and one in Brooklyn, serving not quite three hundred children. Many children whose parents had died and who had no other family willing to take them in were left to roam the streets on their own. There was a grave danger of losing tens of thousands of Catholic children to destitution and cholera and, by their adolescent years, to alcoholism, atheism, vicious criminality, and prostitution. Girls who became pregnant and couldn't afford an abortionist resorted to infanticide at home with dismaying frequency. Hughes left no record of his first walk through the Five Points, a neighborhood made luridly famous by Herbert Asbury's book and Martin Scorsese's film *Gangs of New York*, but it was only ten minutes on foot from his new home (south through present-day Little Italy and Chinatown to the intersections of what are now Worth and Baxter Streets) to witness a level of blight that rivaled London's East End and left most tourists who ventured there speechless. One visitor from South Carolina referred to the area as "the bowels of the city."

On the other hand, a look back could, on a good day, provide some perspective. The law barring Catholic priests from even entering New York State, passed in 1700 at the height of anti-Catholic fervor in England under William and Mary, had only been repealed in 1784. When the first bishop of New York, John Connolly, arrived in 1815—just twenty-two years before Hughes—he found a diocese with three churches (two in Manhattan and one in Albany) and four priests. During his decade-long tenure, he oversaw the construction and staffing of thirteen more churches across the state. Under Dubois, five more churches were built in Manhattan alone, bringing the diocesan total of consecrated churches to over twenty, with the number of priests statewide reaching sixty-three. (Many religious services were held across New York and New Jersey at the time in chapels, rented spaces, and unfinished or unconsecrated churches serviced by circuit-riding priests.) The increase in population meant that the crisis of a leaderless flock was growing exponentially, but the neediness of the diocese could also signal a kind of unnerving vigor. At least, from one perspective, it offered something—raw material, albeit of a ferocious sort—that might be worked with. To a person not easily daunted, the New York diocese was just what John Hughes took it to be in 1838: a challenge of the first order. Indeed, in a moment of downright bizarre optimism, he told John Purcell in February, "Conditions in New York might be worse."

Nor was Hughes entirely alone. John Dubois was in decline, but John Power was an intelligent man of energy and fortitude. The fact that he couldn't stomach his new superior might not have to mean all that much in the future, or so both men hoped. Several other priests Hughes would be in regular contact with were in his camp and impressed him with their abilities and an outlook similar to his own. William Starrs, rector of the cathedral, was a sensible, capable man, ready to work with him, while Felix Varela, pastor of the Church of the Transfiguration in the heart of Five Points and, with John Power, vicar-general of the diocese, was always ready to work with anyone. A thin, shaggy-haired, bespectacled Cuban exile in his fifties, Varela was the closest to a saintly figure—or a saint/intellectual—the diocese offered and was revered by the poor of his parish for his piety and compassion. Born to a wealthy family, he had pretty much used up all of his inheritance keeping his impoverished church going. Charles Constantine Pise, whom Hughes knew at Emmitsburg and had invited to Philadelphia to preach at Saint John the Evangelist, was away when Hughes came to New York but returned to work at Saint Peter's later that year. He was no adversary (yet), while John McCloskey at Saint Joseph's Church—last seen by Hughes as a fifteen-year-old graduate of Mount Saint Mary's—struck the coadjutor as "one of the best educated and most exemplary priests of the diocese . . . prudent and studious." Not wanting to see McCloskey promoted away from New York, Hughes would eventually employ him as his personal secretary, ask him to serve as president of Saint John's College (Fordham University today), and, two decades later, arrange his appointment as bishop of Albany. Two priests Hughes desperately wanted to lure to New York were Terence Donaghoe and Nicholas O'Donnell, though he had success only with the latter, who was assigned to head a Brooklyn church.

And then there was John Urquhart, an Irish Dominican with a "fine, commanding figure" who served as pastor at the cathedral. A bookish man, he seems to have been tailor-made to work with the new coadjutor. He had a way with words, a waspish tongue, a great sense of humor, and sufficient judgment (or so it seemed at the time, later events proving otherwise) to win his superior's warm regard. During Hughes's first three years in the diocese, he sent Urquhart to Albany, Rochester, and elsewhere to conduct inspections of churches and to look into parishioners' complaints that Hughes himself didn't have time to attend to. Urquhart was a tireless investigator. He also appeared to be the only priest who could tell his superior home truths and get away with it. Reporting back on a priest accused of spending too much time in local grog shops, a man Hughes did not want to think ill of, he pulled no punches: "I am sorry to say you know not your man." He not only kept the taverns open until one or two in the morning, Urquhart wrote, but he was "a knave and a consummate intriguer."

Winning the respect of the other priests of the diocese took a good deal longer and, in some cases, was never achieved. In time, the subject mattered less and less to Hughes, who simply expected—demanded—loyalty, professionalism, and obedience. In any event, when Bishop Dubois suffered a paralytic stroke two weeks after Hughes's consecration, an attack that left him in a greatly diminished state for the next four years, personal feelings suddenly counted for rather little. At that point, there was no question of who was going to be in charge. John Dubois's haphazard leadership was a thing of the past.

———

WHERE TO BEGIN? A listening and inspection tour was a start, through Manhattan, Brooklyn, Westchester, and eventually into New Jersey and as far north in New York State as the Buffalo area. The coadjutor wanted to hear about what was going well and what wasn't in each parish, wanted to know the issues and personalities involved, wanted to be seen and known himself. Trustees at odds with their pastors were willing to give him an earful. Pastors treated imperiously by their trustees were equally voluble. The laity wanted to talk about priests who drank too much, had a roving eye, were suspected of financial malfeasance, or begrudged them home visits. The books in many parishes were in appalling shape, with pew rents uncollected for months or years and numbers not quite adding up. Pew rents themselves were a touchy subject: seating arrangements assigned by ability to pay—by class and social standing—might do for purse-proud Episcopalians, but that antidemocratic approach was abhorrent to most working-class Catholics who were expected to stand at the back or in the aisles during Mass. Yet the hard fact remained: without pew rents, many churches would go under. Some churches were forced to charge admission at the door. Others held concerts of classical music, open to interdenominational audiences. Weekly plate collections, individual donations, and bequests from wills did not provide Catholic churches at the time sufficient income to meet their bills. Pew rents and bankers kept the doors open in the 1830s and 1840s.

The bad feeling throughout the diocese had to do with ethnicity as well. Bishop Dubois, a Frenchman, had all but given up hope of being treated fairly by New Yorkers. Charles Constantine Pise, an Italian American, was also not warmly regarded by his Greenwich Village parish of largely Irish congregants, in part for the same reason. (Viewed as an intellectual snob who exhibited a thinly veiled disdain for his working-class congregants, he had been the subject of many complaints. His trustees had tried to fire him the previous year, leading to an ugly battle with Dubois. Hughes suspected the charge was unjust.) German Catholics naturally wanted to be served by German-speaking priests, and regarded the Irish priests they were sent as completely insensitive to their culture. The French Catholics of the city felt ignored altogether. The still-fewer Italian Catholics might as well have been invisible.

To sort out the justice of each complaint, let alone devise a remedy, would have been beyond the capacity of any one administrator. The problems were systemic and long-standing and not unconnected to numbers: too few priests, too few churches, too many laymen whose needs were not being addressed. Hughes also understood that he needed to evaluate the priests in the diocese more exactingly than Bishop Dubois had done and be more concerned with the image of the church. (It is hard to imagine Hughes putting up with, as Dubois did, the student from the Mount who lodged at the episcopal residence for a time and declined to leave when told to do so, as he had "taken to city life with a passion," openly patronizing nearby brothels and strolling down Broadway arm in arm with some of the women he met there.) Hughes agreed with Simon Bruté: nothing undermined a person's faith faster than a representative of the church who was neither caring, or at least dutiful, nor theologically sound. Yet the shortage of priests meant that a juggling act was called for. If a priest was dismissed, a successor was rarely waiting in the wings. Only the most extreme cases of misconduct could be swiftly dealt with, and Hughes had to hope in some instances that a reprimand would suffice.

Over the next few years, though, he was able to move with greater speed in weeding out the unsuitable, and he became notorious for his letters that dispensed with any gentleness on the point. A priest who had taken a sacred vow to serve God and man and was unable or unwilling to live up to that vow was, for John Hughes, a figure of contempt. "If you ever possessed the true spirit of a priest," he wrote to one man he was relieving of his duties, "I fear you have lost it. How your account stands with God, as such, your own conscience may decide." To another he wrote: "Retire and do penance. That is the only reparation you can make now to the Church of God for your past but unforgotten scandals." Alas for posterity, not a single letter specifies the scandals in question.

There was inspiration to be had, though, as Hughes traveled about the state. Near Syracuse, he encountered a community of eighteen Catholics, all converts from an extended family, and two more who were about to be baptized. They met in the private chapel the paterfamilias had set up in his house, taking communion from visiting priests, adorning their altar "in the richest manner that the resources of the country would allow." In December, they had traveled over nearly impassable winter roads to reach Utica, fifty miles away, for Christmas services. Spending a day with them, Hughes wrote, "I hardly spoke; I listened in silence, and with secret emotion, wishing my own heart to share in all the *feelings* of faith and joy which I saw abounding in theirs." He was reminded of the simplicity and quiet fervor of the early Christians.

Unfortunately, truculence was more the order of the day than early Christian piety, and one battle he was not willing to put off was that having to do with the power of the church trustees. Kenrick had taught him well. There would be no progress without peace, and there would be no peace without clarity and order. Dubois had done his best to bring the European model of hierarchy to the diocese, but his success was limited, and even the occasional victory took too much out of a man now in his mid-seventies. Hughes, on the other hand, might be said to have been eager for a roustabout. This business of trustees wanting to hire and fire priests, withholding salaries or rents, and making decisions about expenses and expansions without consultation with their pastor or bishop had to end. It might be an American tradition, but it was an American *Protestant* tradition. The hydra of trusteeism wasn't going to be vanquished overnight, he acknowledged, but he was going to make sure the battle lines were clear. He intended to draw a picture of an inevitable future in which trusteeism as it was then known was phased out, and he was going to make absolutely certain that anyone connected with his new church—Saint Patrick's Cathedral—knew that that future had already arrived on Mott Street.

At the end of his first year in New York, the trustees handed Hughes a perfect occasion in which to assert his views. Dubois sometime before had fired an insubordinate priest, Thomas Levins (the same Levins who had attacked Hughes over the Cranmer episode in the pages of the *Truth Teller*), from his post at the cathedral. The trustees liked Levins and instructed him to remain where he was, which he did. They increased his salary and refused to pay the priest Dubois had appointed in his place. When Levins in turn fired a man who taught at the cathedral Sunday school, that man refused to leave without Dubois's consent, and, at the direction of the trustees, Levins called in a constable and had him forcibly removed in front of the children. That was all Hughes had to hear. He gave the trustees a week in which to apologize for this ridiculous incident, but he heard nothing from them. He did hear that Levins had been emboldened by the board members who supported him to suggest that Hughes was not going to get away with telling him, or the trustees, what to do any more than Dubois had.

Hughes then released a pastoral letter, written by him but signed by Dubois and read at Sunday Mass the following week, which put the matter in the starkest terms. Either the trustees agreed to relinquish their rights, legal as they might be, and allowed their bishop and his coadjutor to rule their church, or he would close the cathedral. They would be free to worship elsewhere. Saint Patrick's would be placed under an interdict, its priests sent to other postings, and not reopened until the bishop was satisfied that a new, more appropriate arrangement was in place. He cordially invited everyone interested in the new policy, pew holders or otherwise, to attend a meeting that evening. Several hundred people, many fairly agitated, showed up. They might have been expecting an exchange of views or an attempt at a diplomatic resolution. They might have been expecting an admission that the letter had been a bit of grandstanding, an opportunity to search for some common ground. What they got, instead, was a searing diatribe.

Hughes's tactic was to appeal to his unnerved parishioners over the heads of the trustees—acting as if the trustees weren't present—and to suggest that the parishioners were innocents being gulled by men who comported themselves more like Anglicans than sons of Rome. The law maintained that the trustees were the legal custodians of the building they occupied and the revenues of the parish. He did not dispute that fact, inconvenient as it might be. He did, however, dispute the belief that the trustees should have any say over the clergy whatsoever or anyone appointed by the clergy to teach or perform any other duty required of them. The lines between the temporal and the ecclesiastical were being blurred. To hand that power to the trustees was to become, in effect, like any Protestant church here or in Europe, a decision with which he and their bishop would have no part. What is it you really want? he asked his audience. Your parents left Ireland because they could not worship freely and their priests were dictated to by civil authorities. If that was their wish, to continue that form of constrained Catholicism, now was the time to say so. "If so, then it is almost time for the ministers of God to forsake your temple and erect an altar to their God around which religion shall be free, the Council of Trent fully recognized, and the laws of the Church applied to the government and regulation of the Church." He invited a response then and there. A few trustees resigned, others were cowed into silence. The parishioners, in the main, seemed willing to stand by their bishop rather than the trustees. No one wanted the church closed. They realized—or feared—that Hughes meant what he said. Father Levins departed.

"We have brought them so low that they are not able to give a decent kick!" Hughes crowed in a letter to Marc Frenaye. He used the same exultant line in a letter to Archbishop Eccleston of Baltimore. The following month, in April 1839, he predicted to Frenaye that it would not be at all difficult to reform the principles of trusteeship "through the whole diocese." He followed up on his attack over the next few weeks with a series of didactic lectures, coached by Simon Bruté, on the history of the government of the church and the damaging effects of trusteeism.

In relating his victory over trustees in succeeding years, Hughes never ceased to present his speech that day, and one the following week, as a deciding battle. It might have been, more or less, for one church—Saint Patrick's—but it wasn't for many parishes throughout the diocese or even for the rest of Manhattan. No man, no matter how assertive his personality, could effect that near-miracle. The truth was less clear-cut, less grandiose.

Saint Nicholas's Church on the Lower East Side, for example, was only one of many where the trustees chose rather pointedly to ignore their new episcopal leader. A German church, Saint Nicholas had been founded in 1833, but the parishioners had never taken to their first Austrian-born pastor, John Raffeiner, and made life miserable for him until he finally asked to be moved elsewhere in 1840. Over the next two years, pastors came and went on Second Street, and Hughes was in despair that this fractious congregation would ever become a peaceable house of worship. Nothing he could say did any good, confirming him in his belief—more like an ingrained prejudice—that German immigrants were a people naturally prone to obstinacy and strife. He eventually asked the Redemptorists to step in to see what they could do, and they appointed a particularly strong, charismatic young priest, Gabriel Rumpler, to take the helm. He lasted for a heroic two years. It was said that Redemptorist priests were afraid to walk the streets near Saint Nicholas after dark, so intense was the enmity they met from their parishioners.

The reality was that the defeat of trusteeism and the rise of a hierarchical view of Catholicism in New York was a gradual, fits-and-starts process that, in some areas of New York State and New Jersey, took the better part of two decades to effect. But there was no doubt in Hughes's mind that the process called for combative confidence, and that quality was precisely what John Dubois was no longer able to provide.

Relations between John Hughes and John Dubois went from bad to worse throughout 1839. The elder man simply could not accept that the younger man was there to supersede him, that he might be what the church in New York actually needed at this moment in its history, and—most glaringly—that he wasn't just another upstart Irishman come to make his life miserable. That Hughes had been his gardener at the Mount, an Ulster nobody begging entrance to his seminary, made Dubois's situation that much more humiliating.

Even his dwindling number of supporters recognized that Dubois was not physically or mentally able to cope with the demands of his position anymore. Vatican authorities were well aware of the situation, and in August 1839, Archbishop Eccleston was delegated to go to New York to break the news to Dubois that, for all intents and purposes, he was to hand over authority for the governance of the diocese to Hughes. The atmosphere at the rectory became unpleasant. It was the Conwell/Kenrick situation all over again. In need of friendly faces, Hughes invited Marc Frenaye and his old assistant at Saint John's, Francis Gartland, to visit New York as often as possible. For the moment at least, Hughes felt very much on his own in his struggles. To make matters worse, back in June, his long-distance friend and mentor, Simon Bruté, had died. It was a hard loss to bear, and for several years Hughes contemplated writing a biography of Bruté.

It was especially important to Hughes that Dubois be relegated to a secondary position at this time because he wanted to proceed—vigorously—with what he regarded as a crucial mission. That mission was the founding of a seminary, an institution modeled on the Mount that would be supported by a school on the same or nearby grounds. Dubois himself agreed that a college and seminary were vital to the future of the New York diocese, to educate the sons of the Catholic middle and upper class who were currently attending Protestant or secular schools and might thereafter be lost to the faith, and to provide the diocese with more priests. He had done his best to bring such an institution into being, but nothing had gone right. In 1833, he had purchased 160 acres in the town of Nyack on the Hudson River, thirty miles north of the city, but all that Dubois had to show after four years was a school that was no more than a glorified farmhouse occupied by several students, a formidable debt, a display of massive indifference from Manhattan's monied Catholics, and a hostile community in Nyack.

When the three-story building under construction that would have been the proper schoolhouse caught fire in 1837, crowds of local Protestants gathered to cheer; and as there was no insurance to pay for rebuilding or compensation, the bishop's efforts in that realm came to an ignominious close. He had lost the diocese $25,000. Not long after arriving in New York, Hughes toured the site of Dubois's "splendid folly," as he termed it, and decided that the fire had been a blessing. Nothing he heard about the place suggested that it would ever have been a going concern.

Hughes and Dubois agreed on a plan to have a school closer to home and a bucolic seminary even farther away. They secured a promise from a wealthy Brooklyn Catholic, Cornelius Heeney, for a gift of land in Brooklyn on which to build the school, while Hughes was apprised of a bargain in the upstate town of Lafargeville, a plantation and 650 acres that could be had for $20,000. He leapt at the opportunity. Unfortunately, after an argument with Dubois over the title to the land, Heeney withdrew his offer, and Lafargeville, three hundred miles north of the city, turned out to be almost as calamitous a choice of location as Nyack. There might not have been crowds of Protestants to make Catholic seminarians feel unwelcome, and the fresh air might have been as healthful as the diocese's brochure insisted, but there were other problems. Only Hughes could have imagined that a seminary in the snowbelt of the state only a few miles from the Canadian border would have broad appeal. Worse, Dubois insisted on being allowed to appoint the instructors. They were a pious lot, the coadjutor agreed when he visited the school, but woefully inadequate as teachers of anything. The Saint Vincent de Paul Seminary was closed in 1840. Though he didn't care to admit it, Hughes's Lafargeville enterprise had been as poorly thought out as Dubois's Nyack venture.

Finally, and more sensibly, Manhattan's Catholic real estate men directed Hughes's attention to the north Bronx, then still a part of Westchester County. Land of the right acreage in the right location was available, and an intermediary, Andrew Carrigan, believed he could negotiate a purchase price of just under $30,000. Rose Hill, an estate of just over one hundred acres in what was then "the town of Westchester," was bounded on the east by the Bronx River and to the west by a sharp ravine and a stream, Mill Brook. (The stream, long since gone underground, was near the current railroad tracks parallel to what is now Webster Avenue.) Its acreage extended well into what is today the New York Botanical Garden. As the site was only ten miles from Manhattan, students and seminarians would presumably not be so hard to attract. Word in the business community that the Harlem rail line was to be laid that far north within a year or two made the site seem all the more plausible.

Hughes launched a fund-raising campaign that September. The initial results were encouraging, with several thousand dollars coming in over the first three months. Thereafter, donations tapered off to a trickle, and a third of his pledges did not come through. Hughes was getting a hard, quick lesson in New York economic realities. People meant well, but when business slumped or a family's expenditures unexpectedly rose, a school and a seminary were not the same crucial priorities to his flock that they were to their spiritual leader. Moreover, recovery from the Panic of 1837 was by no means an accomplished fact two years later. Hughes understood that he would have to look to Europe for help, and sooner rather than later.

Looking to Europe in 1839 meant not merely hoping that lay donors and wealthy cardinals might help one's cause. It meant applying for assistance, and even making in-person appeals, to a few key philanthropic organizations that had come into existence after the Napoleonic wars, specifically to aid in securing a more durable foothold for Catholicism in the Western Hemisphere and in Asia. The Society for the Propagation of the Faith, based in Lyon, France, had been the first. It was followed a few years later by the Leopoldine Society of Vienna, named in honor of Emperor Francis I's late daughter, Maria Leopoldina, who had been the wife of Brazil's Pedro I. More recently, in 1838, a German body for the same purpose had been established in Bavaria, the Ludwig Missions Society, under the imprimatur of Ludwig I. American clergy fell over one another to become mendicants in the 1830s.

These groups doled out funds in a fairly unsystematic way, it would seem. Everyone had probably heard of the good fortune of Bishop Edward Fenwick, Purcell's predecessor at the Cincinnati diocese. He had allegedly received a healthy $35,000 from Europe over his decade-long tenure. Simon Bruté, on the other hand, could not get anything to speak of for his new diocese in Vincennes when he beseeched the same organizations for help in 1838. But then Edward Fenwick, an indefatigable Dominican, had done his asking in the flesh and was a personable salesman. Other prelates reported various outcomes for their own efforts. Francis Kenrick had received money ($5,000 in one later account, $2,500 in another version) as seed money for a seminary he wished to establish near Philadelphia. One's odds presumably improved on-site, and if the donors could associate a face with a cause. John Hughes was ready to be that face for the New York diocese.

In going on what was indecorously known as a "begging trip," Hughes was actually following in his bishop's footsteps. Dubois had traveled to Europe in 1829 and remained for two whole years, leaving his diocese in Power's hands. He had done his best, but he brought back no new priests or nuns and, given his expenditure of time and money, a rather meager financial return of $3,000. The Dubois expedition was actually something of a scandalous bust. If he went, Hughes asserted, he intended to show results.

John Purcell had recently made one of these begging trips himself and had related to Hughes the details of the experience when he stopped in New York on his way back to Ohio. He had first sent a capable priest from his diocese, John Henni (later bishop of Milwaukee), but that decision, he told his friend, had been a major mistake. A priest had neither the prestige nor the entrée of a prelate, and Henni returned to Cincinnati, Purcell complained, "without bringing a priest or an ornament or a single franc." An ambitious, articulate, socially inclined bishop, on the other hand, necessarily did better. Purcell had returned in 1839 with $7,000 and the promise of some priests. He worried, in fact, that Hughes would do even better, to the detriment of his own need for priests. He complained to Samuel Eccleston that he didn't think his good friends in New York were above waylaying European priests originally intended for his diocese. He probably had a point.

5

WHO SHALL TEACH OUR CHILDREN?

ON OCTOBER 16, 1839, John Hughes boarded a packet ship, aptly named the *Louis-Philippe*—after the monarch he would meet on the other side of the Atlantic—in New York harbor. He got no farther than Staten Island, though, as the winds turned against the vessel, which remained docked with everyone on board for another four days before being able to set sail again. The *Louis-Philippe* encountered a fantastic storm eleven days out of port, which the bishop, a heavy sleeper, managed to ignore until dawn, when he climbed unsteadily onto deck to see several sails in ribbons, the crew racing about to secure twisted lines, and nervous fellow passengers clinging to anything secure and preparing to enter the deck-top "hurricane house," for all the good that would do. "The winds were howling through the cordage," he wrote to his sister, "the rain dashing along furiously and in torrents." Waves formed valleys, their peaks a "transparent emerald . . . crowned with a toppling of white foam, which, as the wave approached, would . . . come tumbling down with the dash of a cataract." He was reminded of his recent visit to Niagara Falls. It was an experience that was "beautiful, terrible, and sublime," he decided, but offered "as much of the *terribly* sublime as I ever wish to witness concentrated in one scene." The gale lasted for twenty-four hours.

Arriving safely in France, Hughes stopped in Caen and Rouen, where he was entertained by the archbishop, before moving on to Paris, where he settled in with the curé at Notre-Dame, was asked to say Mass, took in the sights—Sainte-Chapelle, the Louvre, the Rue de Rivoli—and heard all about daguerreotypomania, the subject everyone was talking about as Louis Daguerre that very month had made public his process for the making of photographic images. Of Paris itself, he wrote home, "Great luxury and great misery—great impiety and great sanctity, all are here." He made use of his letters of introduction to other priests, prelates, and potential donors and honed to a fine point his story of the worthiness and need of his diocese. He spoke before the laymen of the Paris branch of the Society for the Propagation of the Faith. He was then brought to the Tuileries by a leading American politician and future presidential candidate, a man with whom he would clash in the future. Lewis Cass had been appointed U.S. minister to France in Andrew Jackson's last term in office, kept the post throughout the four years of Martin Van Buren's administration, and even continued to serve in Paris during the first years of the Whig reign of Harrison and Tyler. Not yet wary of Hughes, he provided excellent entrée to any level of French society.

Dressed in "full episcopal costume à la française," as he told his sister, Hughes enjoyed a private audience with the king, the queen, and one of the princesses. The conversation at the palace, if not buoyant, went smoothly, as Louis-Philippe—his face famously placid and pear-shaped in the renderings by Daumier—was even more fluent in English than Hughes was in French and had positive memories of his four years in American exile during the French Revolution, which he spent in Philadelphia, New York City, and Boston. The mendicant from New York also dropped subtle hints about how lacking in ornamentation American churches were, but, he told Margaret, he feared those comments fell on deaf ears. The bishop's pessimism was premature. On a later trip Hughes made to France, the king gave him a lavish present: six superb stained-glass windows for his cathedral depicting the apostles and evangelists Jean, Luc, Mathieu, Marc, Pierre, and Paul. (They proved an unsatisfactory fit on Mott Street and were removed in 1846 to the chapel at Fordham University, where they remain today.)

Meeting the citizen-king and his family was a satisfying start to his trip—the contexts this farmer's son from Ulster found himself in were quite dizzying—though Hughes was anything but impressed by the heir to the throne. Attending Mass one Sunday a few pews away from the duc d'Orléans, he observed the dauphin talking during the service and not even removing his coronet or bowing his head at the elevation of the host. It was an infuriating sight, he told his Philadelphia friends. He was probably even more shocked when he learned that the dauphin was not even married to a Catholic. When Louis-Philippe's son died in a carriage accident two years later, Hughes even debated the propriety of a memorial service in New York for so indifferent a Catholic. He ended up absenting himself on business and left John Dubois to officiate and Charles Constantine Pise to deliver a eulogy.

Hughes's notes and letters about this first trip to Europe are frustratingly meager, especially compared to those of many of his traveling peers, but given the distance he covered and how full his days were, it is not surprising that he had limited time for correspondence or journal keeping. Did he meet with Hyacinthe-Louis de Quélen, the renowned archbishop of Paris, ill with dropsy as he was then, two months before his death? It would seem likely, and their conversation would have been worth recording. The archbishop had been a friend of Talleyrand and was a member of the Académie Française; he had ordained John Purcell when he was a student at Saint-Sulpice. A devout and erudite man, he had stayed by his parishioners during the cholera epidemic of 1832, just as Hughes had in Philadelphia, though he had suffered an indignity several months before at the hands of Parisians that Hughes could hardly fathom being inflicted on an archbishop—though it might have reminded him of the Charlestown convent episode. Known to be sympathetic to the deposed Charles X, a reactionary Catholic, and skeptical about the legitimacy of Louis-Philippe's right to the throne, he had seen his residence on the river vandalized, his library and furniture thrown into the Seine, and his money stolen. Churches had been sacked that year. The sacristy of Notre-Dame had been looted. Catholicism in the 1830s was not a stable entity. In America, it was threatened by Protestant nativists; in France, by anti-church republicans.

From Paris it was on to Lyon, where he spoke before the principal branch of the Society for the Propagation of the Faith, and then to Genoa, Florence, and finally Rome by Christmas Eve. Rome struck Hughes as infinitely more beautiful than pre-Haussmann Paris and the winter climate more congenial ("the sky too is all that the poets have said of it"). He wasn't overly impressed with the residents. "The Romans seem to care very little about foreigners except for the improving of their taste and lightening their purse," he noted, scandalized at the six dollars a day he was expected to pay for the rooms he rented, which came with a mandatory private valet. Yet the ecclesiastics who welcomed him were more than gracious, and, of course, his audience with the pope of far greater moment than his visit with the French monarch.

Gregory XVI, who had allowed the visiting American to assist him at Mass in Saint Peter's on Christmas Day, "received him with great goodness," the introducing cardinal felt. Hughes found the Holy Father to be, as expected, a pious and imposing man. Unlike his successor, though, Gregory was not a progressive leader and found modernity threatening—he even opposed both railways and gas lighting (Hughes disagreed about the former and shared the papal antipathy toward the latter)—but he had done something extraordinary the month before Hughes arrived to meet him. *In supremo apostolatus*, issued in December 1839, was a papal bull condemning the international slave trade. Hughes had read about this important apostolic statement in Paris and knew full well what it meant for American Catholic priests and the bind the church in the United States would find itself in, especially in the wake of the current *Amistad* crisis. The Jesuits of Maryland had only divested themselves of—meaning, *sold south*—the last of their slaves earlier that year. Many Catholic priests in the South owned slaves and continued to do so until the time of the Civil War.

To this day, historians disagree about *In supremo apostolatus*, some arguing that the language (in Latin) implies an attack on the institution of slavery itself as well as the slave trade, others insisting that the prohibition pertained to the slave trade alone or (at most) to the "unjust" treatment of those already in bondage, and still others maintaining that its condemnation of even the slave trade is equivocal. Reactions in America caused much consternation among bishops outside New England, who foresaw more persecution if they were suddenly perceived as threats to an institution that was still legal in the United States and whose overnight collapse would endanger the nation's economy. Bishop England of Charleston, for one, had his work cut out for him explaining to South Carolinians that one might not be pro-slavery and yet could still be vehemently opposed to the abolitionists. Even before Hughes was back in the United States, Martin Van Buren's secretary of state, John Forsyth, was making pre-election political capital out of the pope's statements, suggesting that Catholics were taking instruction from the Vatican and were out to undermine the American economy and way of life.

This moment forms the second unfortunate gap in Hughes's papers from this trip to Europe: Did the bishop from New York discuss with Gregory XVI the ambiguities and potential repercussions of the papal bull? It seems plausible to assume that, if asked, Hughes could have explained that opposition to bringing new slaves from Africa was something everyone agreed on now and that an expression of regret that slavery existed might likewise be acceptable, but that any hint of abolitionist sympathies on the part of American Catholics, especially Irish Catholics, would drastically impede their assimilation into society and might even lead to more violence against them. The very fact that no evidence of a conversation found its way into the Hughes archive or the posthumous recollections of those who knew him suggests the delicacy, the awkwardness, of the whole matter. It was, potentially, the kind of conversation Hughes as a famous archbishop could have had with Gregory's successor, Pius IX, whom he greatly admired, but not with Gregory.

Hughes stayed several weeks in Rome. When not working, he didn't want to leave a ruin, a church, or a painting unexamined. He spent time ingratiating himself with Cardinal Giacomo Fransoni of the Sacred Congregation for the Propagation of the Faith—the Propaganda Fide—the body that oversaw church affairs in America and controlled some important purse strings; learning from Paul Cullen, the future archbishop of Dublin, about the organizational issues involved in running the Irish College in Rome; discussing with Jan Roothaan, superior-general of the Jesuits, the need for teachers at the new seminary and college Hughes would soon be opening; and reveling in the architecture and aura of the Eternal City. "Other cities are beautiful, if you please," he wrote to Felix Varela, "but to me insipid if compared to Rome." When he felt he had accomplished all that he could, he then headed north after a quick visit to Naples, stopping again in Florence, as well as Lucca, Pisa, Bologna, Modena, and Ferrara, finally reaching Venice and Trieste in the early spring, and, a few weeks later, the all-important Vienna. All along the way, he accumulated donations and letters of introduction. An invitation in Florence to dine with the Grand Duke of Tuscany, Leopold II, meant an acquaintance with his wife, a great-niece of Marie Antoinette, who was more than happy to provide him with effusive letters to her relatives among the royal family of Austria. To be in a country where the principal rulers, without exception, were deeply attached to the Catholic faith was in itself a strange and exciting sensation.

In the capital of the Austrian empire, the American consul, John Schwarz, a Catholic himself, arranged for an interview with Emperor Frederick I and Empress Maria-Anna of Savoy and dinner with the great diplomat of the age, Prince Metternich. John Purcell had supplied a letter of introduction to Vincent Milde, the archbishop of Vienna, who in turn introduced him to a Monsignor Gaetano Bedini, secretary to the papal nuncio, whom he would meet again in New York under fairly extraordinary circumstances. This leg of the trip would have required some discretion. The Austrians were not particularly interested in hearing more about the needs of destitute Irish Catholics. In fact, they had been hearing for too long from German and Austrian Catholics that in the United States everything was skewed toward the Hibernians and that, under the authority of the Irish bishops, they were the unjustly ignored members of the faith.

Sensibly, Hughes spoke to the Leopoldine Society of a more universal condition: how the wealth of the native-born Americans, their manners, their language—everything—reminded the humble Catholic immigrant, wherever he was from, "that he is not in the land of his fathers nor among the companions of his youth." It was a picture of emotional disruption and spiritual alienation that he painted, which might well have described his own feelings on landing in Baltimore in 1817. "It is only when he has the consolation of his religion within his reach that he feels comparatively happy in his new position," he urged. And how difficult it was for that reach to extend to so many over so vast and still-growing an area in the New World. Tremendous strides were being made—he did not want his audience to perceive the Catholics of America as unresourceful and unmotivated, passive dependents on Old World charity—but progress, he reminded his listeners, was inhibited at every turn by Protestant aggression, a population explosion, and a serious lack of priests and money.

Hughes must have done credit to his cause. The society gave him 4,000 florins (specifically, he was reminded, for the benefit of German Catholics), and the emperor's mother provided him with 500 florins for his seminary. Hughes had gone out of his way to mention that German would be taught at Rose Hill.

From Austria Hughes made a short trip to Pressburg (modern-day Bratislava) in Hungary, where he met a Hungarian Franciscan, Zachary

Kunz, who agreed to come to New York to take charge of a new German church then under construction. (Kunz's experience with the trustees of the Church of Saint John the Baptist on West Thirtieth Street was anything but smooth, but he proved to be the indomitable man Hughes was looking for.) Visits to Munich to speak to the officials of the Ludwig Society, to Stuttgart, and to Strasbourg followed, before he returned to Paris for a few days, where he made an unsuccessful appeal to the Sisters of the Sacred Heart, and then one more time to pass the hat in Lyon, before finally crossing the Channel. There was no real reason to stop in London ("city of gloom and gorgeousness"), a center of Protestantism and colonialism, but he had decided to head home by way of Ireland and was curious to see Westminster Abbey and Saint Paul's Cathedral (profoundly unimpressive after Saint Peter's, he felt) and to get a taste of the art and politics of the British capital. Most importantly, though, he wanted to meet the public figure about whom he felt the greatest interest and hopefulness.

Daniel O'Connell, known to Irishmen as "the Liberator," was the Irish member of Parliament for County Clare celebrated for his ceaseless labors on behalf of the repeal of the Act of Union that had yoked Ireland to Britain, and for the widening of Catholics' rights in their own land. An inspiration in another century to men like Gandhi and Martin Luther King Jr., he stood firmly by the principles of nonviolence, scorning the bloodshed Robert Emmet had provoked. He believed in working for change within the parliamentary system. O'Connell was a problematic figure for American Irish Catholics, though. As notable as his work for Ireland's independence was, he was equally outspoken on the subject of slavery. An Irishman enslaved to a Briton, a black man enslaved to a white man: how were the situations so different, he wanted to know, except in degree and duration? He had no reservations about addressing Irishmen in the United States on the subject and letting them know which side of the debate they should be on. Irish Catholic racism, Irish Catholic fear of an emancipated black labor force, Irish Catholic fear of alienating the majority of their new countrymen by aligning themselves with a radical and despised social movement—the reasons to regret O'Connell's bluntness, honesty, and ethics were numerous across the water.

Simon Bruté had probably spoken for many when he wrote to Hughes on an earlier occasion: "I read with exceeding disappointment that virulent and truly intemperate letter of O'Connell about American affairs, Texas . . . slavery . . . from the pen of a foreigner . . . prostrate at the feet of a girl of eighteen [a reference to the newly crowned Queen Victoria]." If there was anything he understood about his adopted countrymen, Bruté insisted, it was that Americans had nothing but contempt for anyone with ties to the British monarchical system and a "horror and irritability" when corrected by foreigners. And these were the observations of a man who was himself opposed to slavery. Journalist Orestes Brownson (not yet a famous Catholic convert) thought the cause of repeal a desirable one but that O'Connell's abolitionist sympathies might be a ploy to conciliate the British for his own political purposes.

Hughes wanted to think well of O'Connell. He loved his earnestness, his culture, his style, his ambition. He probably didn't know about his lax church attendance. He obtained a letter of introduction and, after some polite conversation, decided to broach the potentially unbroachable. "It would be strange, indeed, if I should not be the friend of the slave throughout the world—I, who was born a slave myself," O'Connell told him. Hughes wrote to Varela: "He silenced me, although he did not convince me."

The two men evidently got on well, as they saw each other both in London and on a subsequent trip in Ireland. Hughes went to hear O'Connell speak in the House of Commons, where he felt he witnessed a model of judicious oratory. He watched him at a large dinner party captivate a table of MPs and elegant ladies with his detailed knowledge of James Fenimore Cooper's novels. With O'Connell at his side, Hughes attended the annual meeting of the Catholic Institute of Great Britain in May, in the Freemasons' Hall, at the conclusion of which he was flattered to be invited to speak on the state of the American Catholic Church. His descriptions of the rawness and energy of New York and the struggles of priests in the wilderness could be mesmerizing. If Europe was an object of wonder to the untraveled American, he was at times an object of wonder to the locals.

Hughes found Ireland not much changed from the time of his adolescent years. It was still an impoverished country "crushed by an apostate nation." He wanted to go back to County Tyrone to meet with the cousins he hadn't seen in twenty-three years but decided that would have to wait for a future trip. Instead, he talked to audiences throughout the southern part of the island of the needs of their Catholic countrymen who had emigrated, and encountered one pleasant surprise in the form of a social crusade in progress. He was told on this visit, he wrote to Felix Varela, "wonderful things of the moral revolution which has taken place on the subject of temperance." He attended a temperance rally led by the charismatic Theobald Mathew, a Capuchin friar, in which thousands of Irishmen pledged themselves before God to complete abstinence from "spirituous liquors": if this was possible in grog-soaked Ireland, what could be said to be impossible in New York? Temperance was to be added to the long list of projects to be undertaken.

Preparing to return to the United States, Hughes had secured fewer commitments than he had hoped for regarding the emigration of new priests, but the individuals he met who had agreed to emigrate to New York, or who had been assigned to him, seemed promising, and at least the process was under way and the word was out. Felix de Villanis, who was coming to head the seminary at Rose Hill, knew very little English, but Hughes was sure he could master that obstacle in short order. Hughes had collected needed funds, or promises that sounded reliable, from the Leopoldine Society and assorted bishops and private donors ($12,000 in all, he told Margaret in confidence), including some money earmarked by one bishop for the outraged Ursuline sisters of Massachusetts.

That sum did not represent a stunning success, but neither was it a sign of complete failure. He was also loaded down with fine-art engravings, crucifixes, vestments, and expensive altar cloths to distribute and books for the diocesan library, more than seventy of which had been given to him by a Florentine patron. To Frenaye, he wrote, "I have had every success that I could have anticipated; some anxiety of mind; much fatigue of body; and now and then little fits of spleen that *you* were not with me, as you should have been."

On July 1, Hughes set sail for New York—on a ship, one of the first of the new steamers making the Atlantic crossing, less pleasingly named than the one that took him eastward: the *British Queen*. His time abroad had been exhilarating, but he was eager to see Mulberry Street again. Letters from Varela had kept him abreast of the news of the diocese. Hughes had sent reports of his progress to be published in the *Catholic Register*, a small paper Father Varela had founded a few years earlier. Two items of business would require his attention, he knew, as soon as he docked. One was fully expected—the acquisition of the property Father Villanis was supposed to head, about which he complained not enough had been done—and the other, something of a surprise.

————

THE MAN WHO RETURNED to America in the summer of 1840 had worshiped in the great cathedrals of Paris, Rome, Florence, Venice, and Vienna, more historic and resplendent than any to be seen on this side of the Atlantic. He had been introduced to two major reigning monarchs. He had been welcomed to the center of Christendom by a pope and dined with cardinals and princes. He had had his first encounters with the genius of Michelangelo's labors for Julius II, the martyrs of Caravaggio and Rubens, Borghese's treasures. He had bandied words with Metternich, who seemed to believe that Catholicism and an intolerant Protestantism were not made for coexistence; in the end, one must prove stronger than the other—intriguing food for thought. He had shared a platform with the Liberator. His imagination fired by the thought of an imposing cathedral in his own city someday, his sense of mission deepened by his audience with the pope, his belief in the majesty and hierarchy of the Catholic Church renewed by the weeks spent in Rome, his self-confidence steadied, if not inflated, John Hughes was not the same person who had departed New York on the *Louis-Philippe*.

He was a man at a pitch of enthusiasm and more determined than ever. He instructed Andrew Carrigan, the businessman and real-estate speculator who had overseen the purchase of the Rose Hill property, to get moving and to bypass the procrastinating Dubois on any decisions that needed to be made. He wanted those schools opened soon. He set about tackling the mountain of correspondence that had accumulated in his absence and resumed his tours of outlying parishes. He made preparations for the priests he had met in Europe to take their new posts as soon as possible. (Not all of them worked out as planned: one young man, Daniel McManus, appears to have found the transition from Ireland to the more unbuttoned New York rather full of temptations. Within a few months, he was involved with a woman who introduced herself around town as his wife. When Hughes wrote to his bishop in Ireland about sending him back, William Higgins at Ballymahon expressed his shock and disappointment that one of his star seminarians turned out to be a reprobate but thought, all things considered, that the problem was Hughes's now. Father McManus's chagrined brother came to America to attempt to retrieve his erring sibling in 1842. The trail goes cold at that point.)

John Power and Felix Varela had been especially busy in Hughes's absence. Their flurry of activity had to do with a great cause, or what was fast becoming a cause célèbre—the education of Catholic children in New York City—a cause that was to shape a defining moment of John Hughes's episcopacy. A great deal had happened in the several months Hughes had been away, and Power and Varela found themselves, along with several prominent laymen (church trustees and otherwise), in the midst of an unexpected political battle over public funding for parochial schools. They had recently submitted a proposal to the Common Council of New York, requesting that monies be made available to Manhattan's several hard-pressed parochial schools, which, operating in church basements and rented halls, taught approximately three thousand children. The financial help was needed to enable these schools to stay open and to expand to include the many Catholic students who refused to attend the public schools on the grounds that the discrimination they faced there was intolerable. This request was not necessarily as radical as it may sound. There was a precedent behind what the clergy and trustees were asking for. The city had on occasion provided modest funding to Catholic schools up until the mid-1820s, if not for the reasons that were now put forth.

His administrators' petition to the Common Council was nothing Hughes had anticipated before his departure for Europe, but the basis for concern was not unknown to him. Catholic complaints had been growing more urgent over the last decade. It was more than an irritant—it was a source of genuine theological consternation—that the daily Bible reading that took place in the public schools was taken from the Protestant version of that text, the King James Bible. Catholic children had no choice but to sit and listen to, or be forced to read aloud from, what their parents and priest told them was a corrupt rendering of scripture produced under the sponsorship of an apostate English monarch. Bishop Dubois had complained of this situation to city officials before, but his words fell on deaf ears. Perhaps of greater moment to the children themselves was the attitude of many of their teachers toward their ethnicity and their faith. Public-school teachers in New York City were overwhelmingly native Protestants. Their view of their immigrant charges was often anything but enlightened. Their view of Irish Catholic immigrant children in particular could be especially dismissive or disdainful and was widely recognized as a factor in declining attendance among school-age immigrant Catholic children.

Parental and clerical anger went beyond the use of the King James Bible, though, or any purely anecdotal information about the frequency of teachers' bias-infused comments. The textbooks and school library books themselves were an even more pressing issue. One popular history text, by the best-selling S. G. Goodrich, told schoolchildren about Martin Luther, "an Austrian friar" and "daring innovator," who had aroused Europe from a "long lethargy" of enduring papal corruption. Goodrich felt particularly free to let go when describing clergymen of a darker hue: Mexican priests were known to "spend much of their time in gambling." Oliver Goldsmith's *History of England*, used in many American schools, referred to Queen Mary as "strongly bigoted to the popish superstitions" whose "zeal had rendered her furious." Noah Webster's *History of the United States* was a hymn to New England Puritanism for having rescued the world from a superstitious and grasping Catholic clergy. Nathaniel Huntington's *A System of Modern Geography*, published in 1836, pointed out that in Latin America "priests are very numerous. Many of them possess great wealth and influence, live in palaces, and minister in magnificent and sumptuously ornamented churches." Italy under the popes fared no better in Huntington's hands. Italians were characterized as "reserved but effeminate, licentious, and superstitious. They are singularly pompous in religious exhibitions and pay great homage to images." The 1819 edition of *The New York Reader: Selections in Prose and Poetry from the Best Writers Designed for Use in Schools* contained an imaginary dialogue between Hernando Cortez and William Penn in which the Protestant Penn ("A Papist talk of reason!") decisively bests the Catholic explorer.

Not every textbook was as crude as *The Village School Geography*, written by "a teacher in Hartford," which had gone into its fourth printing by 1840 and informed its grammar school readers that "a part of Italy is governed by the *Pope*, who makes such laws for the people as he pleases. . . . Though often very wicked, the Catholics say he cannot do wrong." Antebellum texts that aimed to be more moderate in tone existed, but they were hardly widespread and certainly never presented

Catholicism as equivalent in wisdom and nobility to the Protestant ethos that had given the world George Washington, the Bill of Rights, and universal education. Rather, Catholicism was always about autocratic government, image worship, benighted foreigners, and slavish obedience.

Had textbooks purchased with taxpayers' money taken a similar jaundiced view of any Protestant sect or northern European ethnic group, the outcry would have been formidable. It had long been infuriating to Catholic clergymen and laymen alike that no one seemed to take their complaints seriously or to recognize blind prejudice for what it was. But, of course, that was because the prejudice was so widespread, common to all levels of society. Even Charles Dickens, writing *Barnaby Rudge* that year, a depiction of anti-Catholic violence at the height of brutishness, felt compelled to note in the novel's preface that, despite his detestation of the rioters, he was "one who has no sympathy with the Roman Church" itself. "A bad foundation for liberty, civil or religious," respected journalist Lydia Maria Child wrote in 1842, deprecating the church's "tendency to enslave the human mind."

Sympathy had come from an unexpected quarter, though, in 1840 while Hughes was in Europe. When Whig governor William Seward, elected to office in 1838, delivered his annual message to the state legislature, he had addressed the issue head-on. On two trips to New York the year before, he had fulfilled his campaign pledge to be an education-conscious state leader by examining the city's schools, which were not a part of the state's district system but were administered separately by a body called the Public School Society. The Public School Society—in actuality, despite its name, a private body of philanthropically minded citizens—had been founded (under a different name) in 1805. Controlled by a fifty-member board of trustees, it was responsible for expenditures, hiring, and curriculum. While Seward saw much that was impressive and effective in the way the society discharged its duties, one fact shocked and distressed him. A large number of Catholic families boycotted the system and kept their children home. As more Catholic immigrants poured into New York each year, many with sons and daughters who desperately needed to learn to read and write, the future was plain to Seward—an America of mass illiteracy and social disorder—and he was not inclined to remain silent when a solution could be found. Accordingly, he urged the establishment of new schools that would be more welcoming to the foreign-born and specifically to the

Roman Catholics of New York. He asked that public funds be set aside for what would be, in fact, denominational schools staffed by Catholic teachers. He also suggested that newly arrived immigrant children would be better taught by those who could speak their language and knew their culture, an idea he would later abandon as problematic and unworkable.

The vehemence of the opposition to the core of his proposal caught Seward off guard. He was immediately put on the defensive. "Knowledge taught by a sect is better than ignorance," the governor declared to an outraged correspondent. "I desire to see children of Catholics educated as well as those of Protestants, not because I want them to be Catholics but because I want them to become good citizens." He regarded any constitutional objections to his plan as "trifling," as it was manifest to him that no good could come from perpetuating a system in which so many children were truant, quite possibly for good reason, and which the Public School Society, left to its own devices, was not able or willing to rectify. Few Whigs shared his concern.

What Seward was confronting at this moment early in his career was the depths of class hatred and ethnic bigotry within his own party. When answering a fellow Whig who had written a letter chastising him for being too solicitous toward the Irish immigrants, who were obviously an inferior people, he was both eloquent and concise: "Why should an American hate foreigners? It is to hate such as his forefathers were. Why should a foreigner be taught to hate Americans? It is to hate what he is most anxious his children should become. For myself, so far from hating any of my fellow citizens, I should shrink from myself if I did not recognize them all as worthy of my constant solicitude to promote their welfare." About the Irish themselves, he maintained that he found the common stereotypes offensive. "I think them eminently and proverbially grateful, confiding, and devoted. I believe the institutions of their adopted country are as dear to them as to us who are native citizens." It was for sentiments like these, voiced to the very men who controlled his fate as a party leader, that John Hughes came to love William Seward. In August, once he had entered the fray himself, Hughes wrote applauding the governor for his "high, liberal, and *true* American views" on education.

There were some who suspected Seward of toadying to a political bloc that might help him in the future. Even well into the twentieth century, historians' doubts about the governor's motives lingered. Historian

FIGURE 5. *A Protestant ally of Irish Catholic causes when he was the Whig governor of New York, William Seward was the politician John Hughes most admired and hoped to see in the White House.* (Courtesy of the Library of Congress Print and Photography Collection.)

Sean Wilentz called Seward's proposals "a masterstroke of Whig opportunism." But there is no reason those motives couldn't have been both altruistic and self-interested. Seward's interest in education was of long standing, and if he expected the Irish Catholics of New York to be sufficiently grateful to abandon the workingman's Democratic Party, he had to have known the odds of that happening were slim. In the end, supporting the idealist's cause of Catholic education only hurt his standing within the Whig Party, possibly costing him the presidential nomination in 1860, and he made few inroads with immigrant voters. Yet Father Power and several Whig ward politicians, without Seward's permission, took care that copies of a pro-Irish speech he had given on Saint Patrick's Day made the rounds of Catholic congregations and Hibernian clubs;

that action contributed to the idea that the governor's motives were not entirely altruistic. Democrats cried foul.

Seward had opened a Pandora's box, to be sure. Jewish and Scottish Presbyterian interests demanded to be heard. Members of those faiths claimed to be discriminated against as well in a largely Anglican school context and felt that if Catholic schools were going to be paid for by the state, so might schools that could be devoted to the needs of their own people. Nor were all Catholics on board in this fight, either. Some Catholic New Yorkers, whose views were expressed in the pages of the anti-Whig *Truth Teller*, one of the two Catholic papers in the city, wanted to see movement in the opposite direction—wanted the public schools made truly and entirely secular, with religion (even reading from any version of the Bible) kept out of the classroom and left in the students' homes and houses of worship. That idea was too far in advance of its time for most Protestants and Catholics, and Varela's *Catholic Register* argued that its rival publication was recklessly jeopardizing the moral education of the city's children.

So, emboldened by Seward's words but not at all confident that the state legislature would ever look favorably on the governor's proposal, Power and Varela formed a Catholic action committee and petitioned the appropriate committee of the Common Council and pressed their case. The response was an emphatic rejection of the idea. This occurred only a few weeks before Hughes's return. No one assumed Hughes was going to accept *no* as a final word on the matter or that the process was in any way winding down. Indeed, though his two priests and their lay associates had been doing a creditable job in leading this fight and in articulating the Catholic position, as soon as he settled in on Mulberry Street, Hughes let everyone know that, as the de facto bishop of the diocese and with Dubois unable to rise from his bed some days, he would take charge of the entire campaign for Catholic education that was already in motion.

From Hughes's perspective, several things were needed. One was a more detailed account of the toll the current system took on Catholic children and a lengthier exposition of what would be accomplished for all of society by subsidizing parochial schools. Another was a more aggressive tone, a less respectful acceptance of setbacks. A third was a greater display of passion and unity among the city's Catholic population—that, Hughes believed, was vital. Finally, a more capable spokesman and prosecutor, a single face to put forward and rally the faithful, was called for, and no one need look too far to locate that individual. That autumn Hughes met with Seward's confidant and closest political ally, Thurlow Weed, and began a correspondence with Seward, cementing a friendship that both men hoped would be of long duration. They met later in the year for the first time when the bishop was upstate visiting a parish in the Utica area. Knowing that his own effectiveness would be limited by his party ties and obligations, Seward was more than willing to see what Hughes could accomplish on his home ground downstate.

With consummate naïveté, the Public School Society had hopes that some accommodation could be reached with Bishop Hughes. The society was now ready to make amends about any offending texts and obligingly sent boxloads of books to Hughes's office, promising to expurgate troublesome passages (loads of paste and cardboard at the ready) or eliminate entire books from the curriculum. Hughes was pleased to accept the boxes, but he never intended to serve as the society's grateful editor. He wanted the books for evidence, as quotable material to use in writing his brief. He was particularly incensed by *An Irish Heart*, found in many school libraries, a novel for young readers that equated alcoholism in Ireland with those who "followed the dark lantern of the Romish religion." Through August, September, and October, he worked in several fiery addresses to stir the diocese to a heightened level of interest in education. When the municipal government agreed to accept a new formal petition and reopen the debate by the end of the year, he also announced, to the surprise of everyone, that he would not hand the presentation of the church's case over to its lawyers or any other prominent laymen of the action committee, but would speak before the Common Council himself, something no prelate had ever done.

His performance was mixed. With Power, Varela, and Pise at his side, Hughes spoke at extraordinary and not always effective length over a two-day period before a packed chamber. It was a discussion, with prepared speeches and badinage (sometimes courteous, sometimes sarcastic) between the two sides, that encompassed the history and reality of a church-state separation since the time of the Founders, the purposes of taxation, the hyperbolic charges that had been made in the press by both the society and the church, the need for some form of moral instruction in schools (the one point almost everyone could agree on), the disgrace of *An Irish Heart*, and the differences between the Douai and the King

James Bible. As expected, the now-wearied Common Council proved unsympathetic once again. The vote was 15–1, and the Public School Society's authority was reconfirmed. Yet Hughes had garnered enormous press coverage and made a citywide impression, for himself and his cause. The *New York Observer*, the most outspoken anti-Catholic daily in the city, conceded that "no one could hear him without painful regret that such powers of mind . . . and such apparent sincerity of purpose were trammelled with a false system of religion." Hughes announced that the battle would now be taken to Albany. That had probably been his hope and intention all along.

"We come here denied of our rights, but not conquered," he told a massive crowd that filled Washington Hall on Broadway and Reade Street, one of the largest meeting spaces in the city, on February 11, 1841. "We have an appeal to a higher power than the Common Council—the Legislature of the State. And I trust it will be found that the petty array of bigotry, which influenced the Common Council, cannot overawe the Legislature." The issue went beyond Catholic rights, he told his wildly enthusiastic audience. It could apply to people of any faith—the Jews, the Unitarians—who did not believe in the King James Bible as a suitable text for their children and the pretenses of the Public School Society to impartiality. "This is a question of right," he asserted, "and though a whole Board should be found to bend to the knee of the Baal of bigotry, men will be found who can stand unawed in its presence, and do right." Gulian Verplanck, the sole Whig assemblyman from the city who was sympathetic to the Catholic side, was approached by way of Father Pise, a friend, and agreed to present the church's proposal to John Spencer, New York's secretary of state, who was in charge of the state's education policies. Spencer, who several months later would serve in President Tyler's cabinet and be nominated by him (unsuccessfully) for the Supreme Court, was known to be an open-minded man free of religious prejudice.

Spencer's own investigation of the situation in New York confirmed the growing doubts that the governor was having about the Public School Society's claims of success. Of approximately sixty-three thousand school-age children in the city, records indicated that no more than thirty thousand attended the public schools, only thirteen thousand on what could be called a regular basis. A 20 percent attendance rate did not inspire confidence. Spencer's view was that a major realignment of

the system was needed in the city, and he asked the legislature to consider a plan in which decentralization was the key: localized schools and
localized elected school boards would best know how to work with the
children of their neighborhoods and thereby increase regular attendance.
He saw the issue as larger than one of religious instruction. More diverse
elements of the public needed to be more involved in deciding what was
taught to their children and how it was taught. He was also uncomfortable with the state's involvement in the sectarian/nonsectarian dimension of the problem, believing that district control made more sense.
A school in a Catholic neighborhood with a largely Catholic student
population could lay aside the King James Bible and any offending texts
without a second thought.

While no one thought this an ideal solution—Spencer's bill was
obviously going to solve some problems and create new ones—Hughes
was willing to call it Solomonic. In the wake of Spencer's report,
which one recent historian has termed "a landmark challenge to the
Anglo-Protestant cultural power in New York City," Hughes directed his
forces toward a period of tactical silence. Gloating would be premature
and impolitic. The state assembly began hearings in the spring on a bill
crafted from Spencer's recommendations. Lawyers for the Public School
Society fought back tenaciously and not without a degree of reason on
their side. Ward partisan politics would determine the composition of
these new school boards, they argued; there would be no uniformity or
stability for such a school system in a city with a constantly growing,
changing population, and children of minority families would be forced
to receive religious instruction based on the wishes of the majority in
their district. None of that made any sense or even really resolved the
Catholic complaints. When the state senate decided to postpone a vote
on the bill until the new year, Hughes was caught off guard, and Seward
was dismayed. Postponement smacked of derailment. Hiram Ketchum,
one of the Public School Society trustees and a lawyer who represented
the society in both the Manhattan and the Albany hearings, had recently
been nominated by the governor for a judgeship. To make a point of his
displeasure, Seward withdrew Ketchum's nomination.

Hughes had no intention of letting the momentum he and his followers had achieved subside over the course of several long months. He
held still more large-scale public meetings during the summer, attacking
the disdainful Ketchum (who had referred to Hughes throughout the

Manhattan hearings and in the press as "the mitred gentleman"), the Protestant editorialists who claimed that the city's Catholics wanted to highjack the school system, and the Whig Party across New York State, which with the strange exception of its leader, the governor, was lining up almost to a man against Spencer's bill. To those, like Ketchum, who had insisted during the course of this debate that the United States should be recognized for what it was, a fundamentally Protestant nation, Hughes responded with oratory that transcended the school issue itself: "That a great majority of the inhabitants of this country are not Catholic, I admit. But that it is a Protestant country, or a Catholic country, or a Jewish country, or a Christian country in a sense that would give any sect or combination of sects the right to oppress any other sect, I utterly deny." He challenged the nativist chorus that used the controversy to tar immigrant Catholics as citizens unsuited to a republic, suggesting that the members of the Protestant elite were the people with a faulty sense of democracy, fair play, and equality of opportunity.

Hughes also labored to situate the debate in the larger context of power and vulnerability. It behooves every citizen, he insisted in a speech at Washington Hall in June, "to see that all are protected alike—the weakest as well as the strongest, but the weakest especially. No matter what sect is assailed, extend to it, in common with all of your fellow citizens, a protecting hand. If the Jew is oppressed, then stand by the Jew." What was not acceptable, what was never acceptable, was to allow those in power to perpetuate an injustice uncontested.

Just before leaving Europe for New York, Hughes had written to Felix Varela to say that their cause was right—Catholics taxed to pay for education should have the benefit of a bias-free education—but he fervently hoped that the churchmen could steer clear of politics or "even the appearance of politics." It was necessary to proceed "without the necessity of admitting party politics into the discussion." In September, he had written a letter to William Cullen Bryant to be published in the poet-editor's *New York Evening Post*, to assuage those who had similar concerns. "We exclude politics from our deliberations," he insisted, as Catholics could be found in all parties (a slight stretching of the truth). "Our object is to seek justice from just and upright men, who will comprehend our grievances, without distinction of party." That cautionary sentiment was long gone from the bishop's mind in the summer and fall of 1841.

Four days before the November election that would determine the makeup of the 1842 state assembly, Hughes was ready to take a calculated risk and wade into the political waters in a way no man in his position in America had previously done. He dined with Thurlow Weed, who was fast becoming one of his closest friends, at the episcopal residence on the night of October 29 and outlined the plan he and his inner circle were prepared to unveil. Weed loved the string-pulling spectacle of politics (he was one of the architects of William Henry Harrison's log-cabin-and-hard-cider campaign) but knew better than to accompany the bishop to the meeting that was being held that night at Carroll Hall on Duane Street. Rather, he followed his new friend downtown at a safe distance and slipped into a balcony seat unobserved.

What Weed witnessed was a tour-de-force of strategy and rhetoric. It had never been his wish to meddle in politics, Hughes announced to his expectant audience of two thousand, but it was time, he told them, to be more direct in their tactics, a shift that everyone present knew would be highly political. America was the land of the ballot box, and through the ballot box they would be heard. It was time for Catholics throughout the city to cast their votes for men who would take their concerns seriously and work to end a school system that was indifferent to their children's spiritual welfare. He had a list of approved names to be read aloud by the committee's secretary. Hughes exhorted the crowd that those candidates who were "disposed to make infidels or Protestants of your children, let them receive no vote of yours." It was an audience that required little convincing. The response to his torrent of rhetorical questions—Will you stand by the rights of your offspring? Will you adhere to the nominations made? Will you be united?—was thunderous.

The Carroll Hall slate, as it became known, was at heart an anomalous, even absurd concoction. It included thirteen candidates for the state assembly and two for the state senate, ten of whom were running on the regular Democratic ticket. Only five candidates ran exclusively on the Carroll Hall independent slate. Men who had been with Power and Varela at the start of the fight, like the estimable journalist and publisher Thomas O'Connor, and others who were on record as supporters, like John L. O'Sullivan, editor of the *Democratic Review*, were included, as were some who hadn't even been approached about associating themselves with this enterprise and didn't approve. Men with impeccable credentials, like future congressman William Maclay, and an Andrew

Jackson intimate and ex-diplomat, Auguste Davezac, received the bishop's endorsement along with party hacks. Some of the politicians hailed that night at Carroll Hall had contradictory things to say about Spencer's report and the Public School Society, depending on which reporter they were talking to, a circumstance that confused a fair number of voters. The next day a few disavowed any connection to a "Catholic party." The bishop insisted, though, that he had been privately assured that, when the time came, these were men who could be relied on. Most incredibly, the list also included the notorious Mike Walsh, a hard-drinking Bowery b'hoy, labor-agitating journalist, and brawler extraordinaire, an Irish Protestant immigrant on the make who was using the school issue and the Catholic vote to forge a name for himself and force Tammany Hall to recognize his potential as a vote-getter. Each name on this pro-Catholic, or ostensibly pro-Catholic, slate "was received with the most deafening and uproarious applause," one eyewitness reported.

Reaction the next day to a Catholic bishop's attempt to influence the electoral process "filled the city with utter astonishment," one paper noted, and elicited a storm of criticism. The *New York Sunday Times* saw no reason a prelate shouldn't attempt to sway voters on an issue that affected his people, and Weed's paper supported Hughes, of course, but few other newspapers, in or out of the city, took anything less than an alarmist view. The *New York Sun* ominously warned Catholics of the nativist reprisals they would bring down on their own heads, suggesting that the naturalizations laws might be revised in a penalizing fashion, and the *New York Evening Post* (a more genteel paper than the *Sun*) branded Hughes's decision a grievous misstep, smacking of a plot hatched behind closed doors in Albany. William Cullen Bryant wrote, "Nothing can be imagined more fatal to the demands of the Catholics than this bringing the Catholic hierarchy to contend for it in the battlefield of politics." The *Journal of Commerce* urged New Yorkers to fight "priestly dictation." Even the *Baltimore Sun* weighed in on the dangerous thinking behind the Carroll Hall plan.

By far the most belligerent remarks in a major paper came from the pages of the *New York Herald*, the freewheeling daily owned by James Gordon Bennett, a Scottish immigrant and a practicing Catholic but hardly a respectful or doctrinaire one. He ran his paper on the assumption that the New York reading public had no use for journalism that pulled its punches, a view vindicated by his sales figures. Writing in the spring of 1840, while Hughes was still in Europe, he had called upon "the Catholic Bishop and clergy of New York to come forth from the darkness, folly, and superstition of the tenth century." He had doctrinal as well as social views to air: "We have no objection to the doctrine of Transubstantiation being tolerated for a few more years to come. We may for a while indulge ourselves in the delicious luxury of creating and eating our divinity. A peculiar taste of this kind, like smoking tobacco or drinking whiskey, cannot be given up all at once." He called on the College of Cardinals to think about electing an American pope and to stop placing one "decrepit, licentious" Italian after another on the throne of Peter. From this source, which he regarded as beneath contempt, Hughes expected no mercy.

About the doings at Carroll Hall, Bennett was adamant. Clergymen should keep their noses out of politics and stick to what they did best: "saying masses for the dead—forgiving the sins of the living—giving the sacrament—marrying young couples at $5 a head—eating a good dinner and drinking good wine at any generous table—or toasting their shins on a cold night at their own fire-sides." From that point on, the *Herald* considered Hughes fair game on any topic, never missing an opportunity to go after him in print. He became a favored target for the next twenty years, both for the papers his name sold and the sheer delight Bennett took in knowing how angry he could make the bishop.

For now, Catholic voters were urged by the *Herald* to ignore "the impudent priest . . . the abbot of unreason" who was leading them astray on the electoral field and who was nothing better than "a mere tool of Governor Seward." Bennett especially loved to remind his readers of the bishop's humble résumé, which included work as "a highly respectable and industrious gardener." The only editor in town who even approached Bennett's level of scorn for Hughes in ensuing months was Walt Whitman in the bile-filled pages of the *Aurora*, where amazement was expressed that "this cunning, flexible, serpent-tongued priest has had the insolence to appear in the political forum."

Hughes's scheme did not quite pay off, but neither did it backfire. A Democratic landslide across the state brought both houses of the legislature into the Democratic camp. Closer to home, Hughes analyzed the results and concluded that his mission had been accomplished—if his mission had been to suggest to both Whigs and Democrats, especially to Democratic Tammany Hall, that Catholics could no longer be discounted as a negligible political force and could even hold the balance of power in some elections. All the official Democratic candidates who had been endorsed as part of the Carroll Hall slate had been elected, and the three Tammany Democrats who had not been so endorsed had lost to their Whig opponents. No one could mistake that message, Hughes felt. (Not one of the candidates on the ballot solely as part of the Carroll Hall ticket was elected, but that was expected.) A partial victory, a purely symbolic victory, a Pyrrhic victory, not even a victory at all: political historians throughout the next century characterized it in different ways. Hughes had no regrets, not even when James Gordon Bennett went on a postelection tirade about the gardener-bishop from Emmitsburg, a man "with a deficient education and an intellect half made up of shreds and patches, like a piece of second-hand clothes" who was manifestly incompetent to hold his office. And a fact that speaks volumes about antebellum New York politics: the rough-and-ready Mike Walsh received the fewest votes of any candidate running for the legislature—twenty-three hundred, compared to Thomas O'Connor's eighteen thousand or John L. O'Sullivan's seventeen thousand—but nonetheless went on to have exactly the career he wanted in the 1850s, in the U.S. Congress, before he drank himself to death at the age of forty-nine.

The real and pressing problem—Hughes, Seward, Weed, and the Carroll Hall men all knew it—was that the legislature about to convene was as unlikely to approve the use of state funds for Catholic schools as its Whig predecessor had been. No one was going to approve that now. The solution of Hughes's allies upstate was to have William Maclay, the most noncommittal member of the Carroll Hall slate, head the committee in charge of continuing the inquiry John Spencer had started and fashioning a bill that had some chance of passing the legislature. Maclay had been a Latin teacher before going into law and politics; though he was a Baptist—the son of a Baptist minister, in fact—Hughes liked him and was ultimately pleased with the choice. A petition on behalf of school reform signed by over twelve thousand New Yorkers was presented to the legislature by Maclay, at Hughes's request. It can be assumed that the two met for private conferences when Maclay was in the city visiting schools and gathering information. Word everywhere was that Hughes had even been given a copy of Maclay's bill to revise and approve before its official release. His prevarication and denials on that subject would have meant the need for a confessor, for surely the bishop never told a more flagrant lie. Not that Maclay's bill thrilled him, but he understood it was the best that he was going to get. It kept the crux of Spencer's recommendation, affirming that each ward in New York City should be considered a separate school district and that the Public School Society, which had never been truly "public," be disbanded. Funding for parochial schools was neither approved nor forbidden. No mention was made of the subject at all. Hughes accepted that that part of Spencer's bill would prevent the new bill's passage and negate any progress his side had made, in which case the Public School Society would live on for years to come. What mattered now was to render that body null and void and then trust to local school district elections in the city to advance the Catholic immigrant cause.

The moderately phrased Maclay bill passed the assembly on March 21 by a vote of 65–16 and was sent on to the senate for consideration. (For this, Maclay, more wily Jesuit than honest Baptist, shall be made a cardinal, one New York City newspaper sarcastically predicted. Actually, he was elected to Congress in 1842.) Hughes communicated his satisfaction to Seward with the assembly vote and, mindful of how much closer the senate vote would be, expressed his hope that the governor would remind his fellow Whigs that a defeat of the bill would push Catholics forever back "into the faithless arms that have embraced and wheedled them so long"—namely, the Democratic Party. Seward knew perfectly well that Catholics, especially Irish Catholics, had never left those arms and were never likely to in numbers that meant anything, but Hughes loved to dangle that possibility before his friend. The hatred Hughes felt toward Tammany Hall was never to be shared by his flock.

To make sure that everyone understood the stakes, Hughes called yet another meeting at Carroll Hall a few days before New York City's April 12 mayoral and Common Council election and drew up another slate of independent candidates, headed by Thomas O'Connor for mayor, who were on record as firm opponents of the Public School Society. Alert for once to the consequences of his too-high public profile, he did not attend the meeting. As was the case with the previous slate of names, no one thought these men could be elected. What Democrats feared, what Hughes wanted them to fear, was that they would be spoilers, taking enough votes away from their party to bring about a Whig victory. The very next day, four days before the municipal election, the Maclay bill was passed in a contentious late-night session by the

Democratic-controlled upper house of the legislature. The independent Catholic slate of municipal candidates was withdrawn, and a promise was made to support all the official Democratic candidates.

The last act of this religious-political-legislative drama was ugly. On election night, April 12, gangs roamed the streets. Nativist and Irish Protestant men in the Democratic Party who felt their concerns had been shunted aside by their own party, which had truckled to, or been blackmailed, by the papists and their scheming bishop, were in a disruptive mood. This group included the Spartan Band, whose leader was none other than Mike Walsh. The Spartans met up with an Irish Catholic gang, the Faugh-o-Ballagh, on Centre Street, and skulls were cracked. Club-wielding police appeared on the scene and added to the bloodshed. The anti-Catholic participants of the fight fanned out in several directions, vandalizing Catholic residences and gutting the Sixth Ward Hotel, where some Irish immigrants had hoped to find sanctuary. They then moved on to Mulberry Street, where cobblestones and bricks were used to smash every window on all three floors of the episcopal residence. Hughes was in Philadelphia that day, but the elderly Dubois was home, alone in his bedroom, frightened and unprotected. Several area priests rushed to help Dubois, and a cordon of Irish women from the neighborhood gathered to surround the cathedral across the street, fearing that their church would be ransacked or torched. The mayor and the police finally arrived to drive the rioters away and restore order.

Most press coverage of the riot expressed the shame that all right-minded citizens felt, but Hughes was not left unscathed by criticism. Had he known his proper place, his home and church would not have been threatened. "Had it been the reverend hypocrite's head, instead of his windows, we would hardly find it in our soul to be sorrowful," Walt Whitman wrote. More temperately, George Templeton Strong simply called the riot "the first fruits of that abominable tree—the School Bill."

The disapproval of Hughes's decision to involve the diocese in an electoral cause was never really to abate. Clerical involvement in matters explicitly political and traditionally secular made too many people nervous. That a double standard existed is past question; there was no equivalent outcry when numerous Protestant ministers *from the pulpit* urged their parishioners to vote against the first Catholic candidate for mayor in 1880. Yet Hughes has sometimes been written about as if he were blithely unaware of what he was doing, a bullish and unthinking man, and that was far from the case.

The unworldly cleric, his mind more intently focused on spirituality and the next world, could be a figure of admiration, a force for good in the world, Hughes fully acknowledged. He also knew he had nothing in common with that paradigm. His temperament, interests, and beliefs pointed in another direction. Whatever critics might say, there was something more bracing—more immediately useful—in considering how religious values and worldliness overlapped, conflicted, asserted and defended their spaces. There were also moments when society, not the church, caused the lines to blur, and this, Hughes felt, was one of them.

Hughes had long been fascinated by the fractious relationship between Napoleon Bonaparte and Pius VII, for instance. He had read a good deal about the two men and was pleased to deliver a lecture on the topic when invited to do so by the Mercantile Library of Philadelphia in November 1841. It was "rich and instructive" to contemplate the era of Napoleon's rise and fall, the stresses placed on the papacy in those years by those who saw the church as too weak to defend itself and wished to marginalize it still further, and the details of Pius's strategizing. The story had everything: "What ardent hopes, what trembling fears, what daring resolves, what vacillations, what treacheries, what courage, what inconstancies, what defections and untruth of character preceded or followed the march of events during this dazzling and astounding period!" Hughes's version acquits Pius for able leadership in the face of a nearly crushing political force, for knowing when to advance and when to retreat and when to allow moral example to carry the day. His audience understood that Hughes was, in effect, speaking that night about the church in America as well. The Maryland tradition had served its time in another era. This was a moment for action, strategy—a rowdy commitment to public life. His enemies wanted to pretend that Catholics like Hughes were at fault for meddling with a secular, public school system and the electoral process in a country that insisted on a separation of church and state. How truly secular this school system was, why one wouldn't want to use the ballot box to end a blatantly discriminatory state of affairs, how real this separation was—Hughes's perspective on the issue was entirely different.

When the story passed from the front pages of the news, though, many asked what Hughes had achieved. There was no money to set up an effective Catholic parochial school system. Many Catholic parents felt their children stood a better chance of a stable education and advancement casting their lot with the public system. Plenty of his fellow Catholic contemporaries and later chroniclers of this episode, approaching it from a secular or a church history position, have suggested that it was a grave error on Hughes's part to push matters as far as he did, exacerbating existing tensions with no tangible gains to show for the effort and the stress. The chief justice of the U.S. Supreme Court, Roger Taney, a Catholic who followed the situation in New York, thought Hughes's engagement with politics a mistake. More than a century later, Daniel Patrick Moynihan termed the whole morass an unmitigated disaster. Yet Hughes did not see it this way. Unquestionably, he had no regrets. If nothing else, he saw his community as more united than ever. To Bishop Antoine Blanc in Louisiana, contemplating a similar fight several years later, he urged full engagement with the forces of Protestant school control. "The contest in New Orleans should be a bold one," he advised. Even a loss sometimes represented a certain kind of victory. Pius VII was imprisoned by Napoleon. Yet he outlived the French emperor and saw himself restored to power.

The school controversy also brought Hughes into a relationship with a man in public life for whom his respect and affection were never to diminish. Had his hopes been realized and William Seward occupied the White House one day, Hughes would have had a great deal to show for his labors and allegiance. It was always a source of irritation to him that his fellow Irishmen and coreligionists did not see Seward for the friend he was ("they are exceedingly stupid on these matters," he told the governor). He did, however, expect that his clergy would appreciate Seward and his values, Protestant or not. When the New York senator delivered his famous "higher law" speech in Congress in 1850, suggesting that conscience might trump the Constitution over a heinous immorality like slavery—a perspective that made Hughes very nervous—Seward's secretary sent copies of the speech to all New York City's priests. One returned the packet to Washington with a crude retort scribbled on the envelope. Seward's secretary informed the bishop, who was so shocked by the wording that he never revealed the language the priest had used. Anger scarcely describes his reaction. The offending cleric was dismissed from the diocese, never to be mentioned again.

6

"The Baal of Bigotry"

THE TESTING TIME was upon him. As Bishop Dubois's condition declined by increments, it fell to John Hughes to confront what was, from any point of view, a rapidly worsening situation in the diocese. The two most pressing problems throughout the 1840s were what they would always be—money and priests. Too little money, too few priests. Too many urgent needs unmet.

The debts that so many of the churches of the diocese labored under were the source of Hughes's greatest anxiety at the time. His first attempt to meet this problem head-on and prevent foreclosures focused on the situation close to home and was a project of an idealistic bent. If the Catholics of New York City could come to see themselves as part of the same congregation or group—in effect, as *Catholic New Yorkers*—rather than as members of a specific parish with no link to the other parishes of the city, then those who had money might be disposed to help those who did not. The Church Debt Association, founded in May 1841, called on every Manhattan parish to appoint a collector who would be in charge of a monthly subscription, the funds of which would be distributed equally to the ten churches on the island. Those churches with a smaller mortgage could pay it off sooner than they had intended; others, like Saint Peter's or the Church of the Transfiguration, which lived on the brink of disaster, could buy time, keep their creditors at bay, and handle their debts in a slower but still less despairing manner. It was a call for altruism, for reaching into one's pocket for the benefit of people in another part of town whom one would never even meet—but who, Hughes insisted, should be regarded as brothers in a common cause.

The skeptics, including Marc Frenaye, were proved right. The Church Debt Association raised $8,000 in its first three months and $17,000 for the year—not a negligible sum but far short of Hughes's expectations in the face of a collective debt of $300,000—and immediately thereafter died a natural death. The wealthier parishes did not want to contribute to the maintenance of the poorer parishes, and the Germans especially did not want to be tapped for money to go to Irish parishes. For that matter, Hughes had hardly unpacked from his European trip when he began receiving letters from Austria. The Leopoldine Society wanted an accounting of the money he had received from them and wanted some response to the letters they were receiving from disgruntled German and Austrian Catholics who claimed he was more interested in helping "his people" than the emperor's former citizens. John Schwarz, the American consul in Vienna, warned him to be careful. Particularly unnerved by the thought of Saint Peter's Church going under, Hughes authorized Charles Constantine Pise, the one priest in the city with a reputation that extended to European Catholic circles, to travel to Ireland and see what he could do on the fund-raising and recruitment front. The result did not amount to much.

The need for more clergy felt like an equally intractable problem. Each year the Catholic population of the city grew, and there were simply not enough priests to say Mass and to baptize, confirm, marry, absolve, and bury these people. Not only were there too few of them, but the better men were always being snatched from him, often for the best of reasons. Andrew Bryne, for one, was an effective pastor at Saint Andrew's, a new church opened on the site of Carroll Hall in 1842, and a person he had entrusted to go to Ireland as well to see if he could enlist Christian Brothers to come to New York to be teachers. Bryne was in his new position only several months when he was called by the hierarchy to become the first bishop of Little Rock. In the same year, the able William Quarter of Saint Mary's Church left New York after being consecrated at Saint Patrick's Cathedral as the first bishop of Chicago. It was always going to be that way, Hughes knew: the men of real talent would be needed to exercise leadership elsewhere, just as he had been taken from

Saint John's in Philadelphia. But he himself was forced to engage in the same juggling of his best priests.

In August 1840, Hughes had opened Saint Joseph's Seminary in Rose Hill, and on June 24, 1841 (his forty-fourth birthday, or thereabouts), he had opened Saint John's College a few hundred feet away. Twin goals were being realized—a place to ensure the education and ordination of more priests and a place to educate more young men, some of whom might later study for the priesthood. Yet Hughes had to move his favorite, John McCloskey, from full-time work at Saint Joseph's Parish in Manhattan to head the college—what Hughes himself called "an unfinished house in a field"—while he had to employ Felix Villanis, whom he had recruited in Europe to run the seminary, to double as a Greek and mathematics instructor at the college. (Villanis lasted a year.) Mindful that he had promised the Austrians that German would be offered at Saint John's, he had to hire someone who wasn't even a priest. A German immigrant and Lutheran minister, Maximilian Oertel, had recently been received into the church, a conversion that received a fair amount of attention in New York when Oertel published a propagandizing pamphlet about it. His English was spotty and his teaching skills negligible, but at least he knew German and was an obliging sort. He lasted a year as well.

Finding a Hebrew instructor was all but impossible, and late in the semester Hughes settled on a man he didn't even know but whom McCloskey had met in Italy. Ambrose Manahan was an American priest in his early thirties but had been studying in Rome for several years when he arrived in New York at the end of the year with letters of recommendation from church officials sufficiently glowing to have him appointed as faculty member and vice president. His Italian mentors neglected to mention that he was almost impossible to get along with.

As Hughes might have suspected at the time, opening a seminary and a college and ensuring the success of both at the same time, with accommodations that were at best rudimentary, were going to prove beyond his—beyond any one man's—capacity. The college, which by the end of the century was known by the more familiar name of Fordham (as it will be in these pages from this point on) would ultimately prosper in its location; the seminary would not. But, as it was always to be when it came to educational endeavors, Hughes was indefatigable. There had been no Catholic college in the Northeast before he set his mind to it. Now there was one. It was a little embarrassing that the school was opening with only six students, the faculty outnumbering their charges by a wide margin, but a start was a start. By 1845, enrollment stood at 145. By 1850, it was 212.

Fordham boasted a curriculum that was top-heavy on languages (Greek, Latin, Hebrew, Spanish, French, Italian, and German) and included mathematics and chemistry as well as rhetoric and belles lettres—McCloskey's province—literature, mythology, bookkeeping, and moral philosophy. Hughes employed his brother-in-law, William Rodrigue, to undertake the construction of a three-story seminary (the present-day Saint John's Hall) and a small church and to teach drawing and civil engineering. The Rodrigues moved from Manhattan into the small stone house (still extant) next to the present-day Saint Robert's Hall. A newspaper advertisement touted the school's location "in one of the most picturesque and healthy parts of Westchester County." McCloskey declared that "its system of government will be mild and paternal." Students found only one of those adjectives accurate. Parents were assured that no books were allowed on campus that were not approved by the administration. The six students for the opening summer session were joined by forty others in the fall, paying $200 per year (washing, bedding, and mending included).

The seminary opened with twenty-one young men studying for the priesthood, who were also expected to help out at the college. Rodrigue's designs for proper, more commodious facilities were immediately approved. But how this mammoth undertaking was to be paid for in the long run was anybody's guess. In attempting to lure qualified priests to staff one or the other institution, Hughes was a powerful salesman, often putting on a more optimistic face concerning the immediate prospects for the seminary and the college than he actually felt. Within two years, Fordham and its neighboring seminary would be $19,000 in debt, and John McCloskey had returned to Manhattan to become Hughes's coadjutor, leaving the contentious Manahan in charge.

From the green spaces of Rose Hill to the docksides of Manhattan was another matter. It was impossible to put a hopeful face on the conditions that the waves of Irish immigrants were being subjected to upon their arrival at any one of the sixty wharves that lined the East River. The numbers were staggering, even if they had tapered off for a time after the depression of 1837, and the appalling treatment started very literally upon their arrival, as "runners" sometimes took advantage of

FIGURE 6. *Saint John's Hall (still extant on the campus) originally housed Hughes's ill-fated seminary and later became a part of Saint John's College, now Fordham University.* (Courtesy of the Archives of the Archdiocese of New York.)

steerage families even before they disembarked, bribing their way onto the ships as soon as they were moored, offering to help disoriented passengers find lodgings, taking charge of their luggage for them, telling them how they could put them in touch with potential employers. The stories Hughes heard were heartrending. The immigrants' money often disappeared as fast as their luggage, or, when brought to boardinghouses near the wharf with purportedly modest rates, the new arrivals were presented with exorbitant bills the following morning, the landlords threatening jail or the confiscation of all their guests' worldly goods if their demands were not met. Defenseless men were plied with liquor or roughed up by hooligans, and their daughters were not always safe from the more unscrupulous predators they encountered.

The Irish Emigrant Aid Society was born—or, more accurately, was reborn (an earlier organization had closed its doors ten years previous)—out of frustration with this situation. It was an undertaking commenced by several philanthropic Catholic businessmen, including physicians William Macnevan and Robert Hogan, elder statesmen of the Irish community in New York, and it was a cause to which Hughes happily lent his imprimatur and his support as a fund-raiser. Operating out of an office at 62 Gold Street, the aid society opened its doors in the spring of 1841 and advertised its mission as working "to afford advice, protection, and information to Irish Emigrants." It established an employment bureau that kept lists of jobs that had been vetted and compiled a registry of reputable boardinghouses, with warnings about those that were known to be part of the con artists' web. Soon-to-be citizens had a place to go where, if their language skills or experience of urban life seemed a frightening impediment to them, they could talk to someone who might provide counsel and encouragement. Help was provided with getting prepaid tickets to Ireland when it was time to bring the rest of the family over and with locating relatives who had preceded them to these shores.

The aid society's goals were modest, and for once Hughes had his hand in an enterprise that wasn't entirely daunting, and—a source of pride to him—it was a cause that suggested to their enemies that the Irish could look out for their own, that Catholics could look out for their own. Even Walt Whitman wrote plaintively of the lines of nervous Irish women who would appear at the society's office in thick woolen capes, worn leghorn hats, and heavy boots, desperate to land a job as a domestic.

Yet Hughes's hope that the country's newest Catholics would turn to their church in large numbers was thwarted by other realities he couldn't ignore, especially as he visited more churches and met more priests. There was an air of disorder about everything connected to the church, a lack of clarity and consistency that did not inspire respect. Hughes felt the need to reverse that course. He called the first synod of the diocese in the summer of 1842 and let every priest from northern New York State to central New Jersey know that he expected them to attend and to bring with them copies of the decrees of the Council of Trent and past provincial council decrees. After a prayerful retreat at Fordham, they settled in at Saint Patrick's Cathedral to "discuss"—meaning, to hear—their bishop's plans for the future and their part in it. "The previously leaky vessel of the Church in New York," as one writer put it, "would now be a taut ship." Priests were to be properly attired at any ceremony they performed, the precise Roman rituals of the Mass were to be observed at all times, and the laxness of those who were not to be found in their diocese on Sundays, usually for questionable reasons, was to come to an end. Marrying people who appeared on one's doorstep was to come to an end. That bigamy among immigrants was widespread and that ill-advised unions were being formed on the docks beside arriving vessels troubled the bishop; he insisted that proof of bachelorhood and the announcement of banns that allowed for four days' notice before any wedding were to be required. He also insisted that priests not officiate at mixed marriages or at funerals in city cemeteries if Catholic cemeteries were nearby. Baptisms were no longer to be performed at home if there was a Catholic church within three miles of the home, unless the child was seriously ill.

Hughes had pointed comments to make about the social lives and clannish commitments of the new immigrants as well. Many were joining "secret societies" soon after their arrival, groups with oaths and closed meetings that carried fierce regional and familial ties from the other side to the New World. Warring factions would refuse to attend Mass together. Animosities carried over into the workplace as "Corkonians" fought "Connaughts," and jails and courthouses filled with street-fighting toughs who saw their own countrymen, fellow Catholics, as enemies to be subdued based on their place of origin back in Ireland. The Irish were never going to become reputable American citizens if they couldn't leave this primitive form of tribalism behind them, Hughes insisted, and he told his priests to let their parishioners know that membership in any such group would be grounds for excommunication. It was time for the clergy to pay more attention to how their flock was perceived and to how adequately their charges understood the demands of citizenship.

It was also high time for Catholic clergymen to pay more attention to how *they* were perceived. He understood that, no matter how forceful a proclamation he issued, the trustee situation was not in everyone's power to control absolutely. If he were to be honest—and in this case he was by no means inclined to be so—Hughes would have admitted that every parish within the city limits of New York had not fallen into place as he had hoped. Arguments, some vociferous, erupted from time to time in different parts of town. The personality of the pastor and the makeup of the trustees in any given parish determined a great deal. Nonetheless, he told those present at the synod, he expected more from them than the previous leadership had asked. Inventory your property, keep accurate financial records, refuse to allow church property to be used for meetings without the approval of the pastor, refuse to accept the hiring or dismissal of any church employee without the authorization of the pastor, and be models of propriety: those conditions formed a starting point. When the trustees became overbearing, keep your bishop informed and fight them as best you can—that was the heart of his message—but in all cases give your critics fewer grounds for complaint. We must be the figures who command respect in our community. A pastoral letter in September articulated the new policies (minus the implicit but barbed criticism of the errant clergy), heavily emphasizing the baptismal policies, secret societies, and new trustee parameters, and it was read in every church in the diocese.

How he would handle a board of trustees that remained recalcitrant was made clear some months later when the laymen who had run Saint Louis's Church in Buffalo with a free hand for years refused to surrender all financial and other administrative decisions to their pastor. They "respectfully declined" to submit to the bishop's request, they wrote in a letter, to which he responded that he had not *requested* anything. They were much mistaken. His pastoral letter, he informed them, was a statement of "an ecclesiastical law which is to be general throughout this diocese." The trustees could manage the church as they wished, if that was their fixed purpose, he told them, but no Catholic priest would say Mass there, no baby would be baptized, no wedding or funeral performed. In 1843, Saint Louis's Church in Buffalo was placed under an interdict, and its priests moved to other churches. When nervous parishioners in Buffalo wrote to Hughes, he explained he would be pleased to lift the ban once it was clear that he was dealing with "true Catholics, in their souls," who understood the proper governance of a parish church. When a Buffalo newspaper picked up the story and the cause of the now-enraged trustees, he wrote to offer a clarification of his position, firmly but calmly phrased. The interdict lasted for seventeen months.

If Hughes alienated a significant number of priests during his time as bishop of the New York diocese, he probably did the largest share of that yeoman's work over the course of those three days in the summer of 1842. While he said he welcomed open discussion of the topics he brought before the assembled clergy, while he hoped for a reasonable exchange of ideas about how best to implement them, he had an agenda, and he did not intend to see it diluted or sidetracked. His priests knew that he was expressing disappointment with many of them—that he knew their parishioners' complaints had some justice on their side, that not all of them were as reliable or caring or even as educated as they could be—and he wanted them awakened to the arrival of a new order.

The secular press in New York, primed by the schools controversy, was properly awakened, and several papers went after Hughes for his many promulgations. Singling out four writers in particular—David Hale, a Congregationalist; William L. Stone, "some kind of Presbyterian"; Mordecai Noah, a Jew; and "the fourth, the editor (whose name I do not know) of a little paper called the *Aurora*"—as his sharpest assailants, he marveled that he had managed to unite a Congregationalist, a Presbyterian, a Jew, and possibly a barbarian in their view of their own competence to judge Catholic doctrines. His letters to the press defended his positions on these myriad issues, and with David Hale, editor of the *Journal of Commerce*, he continued a caustic exchange through two more public letters. It was at this time that the first mention of the stiletto purportedly appended to his signature was raised in print. Hughes could only express astonishment that an adult of any faith could fail to distinguish a cross from a dagger, but the damage was done. "Dagger John" entered the mythology of New York and Catholic life. The name would stick and outlive him to this day.

In a city with so many newspapers, the lack of a well-regarded Catholic newspaper with a strong subscription base was yet another problem. In this instance, Hughes pretended to no false optimism whatsoever. Felix Varela's *Catholic Register* had a tiny circulation, and as it was run by a very busy parish priest, no one could have expected it to be a more substantial publication, while the *Truth Teller*, whose editor disagreed with the bishop about trusteeism and the Spencer bill, was to Hughes's mind worse than useless. When two Catholic brothers, James and John White, expressed interest in starting a weekly with their own funds soon after they first met Hughes, he delayed answering them for quite some time. But on July 4, 1840, the *Freeman's Journal* made its first appearance with his skeptical blessing, and several months later it absorbed what was left of the dying *Catholic Register* and incorporated the name into its own title.

Hughes could not have asked for a publication more in line with his values. It became, in essence, the house organ of the diocese. Though its coverage of international news was extensive—articles about the Irish Repeal movement dominated the front page for months at a time, and the American eagle on the masthead shared space with an Irish harp—the *Freeman's Journal* was a useful vehicle, especially during the battle over school funding. The only problem was the one Hughes had anticipated from the start. The paper lost money hand over fist. The Whites, and the editors who succeeded them after they bailed out, needed to ask for handouts, hundreds of dollars at a time. In 1842, Hughes confronted a hard choice: let the paper go under or buy it himself. He did the latter, thus beginning six years of more financial headaches.

Finally, educational conditions at schools for Catholic immigrant children did not provide any cause for optimism in the aftermath of the fight with the now-defunct Public School Society. District elections upon which Hughes had placed his hopes did not yield school board members willing to see state funds used even obliquely for sectarian purposes, not even for instruction or readings from the Douai Bible after regular school hours. So children were forced to attend their local public schools much as they did before, listening to the King James Bible in districts where that was still approved—with, presumably, the more offensive texts now withdrawn from classroom or library use—or attend the struggling parochial schools. And those schools were struggling. One board of education inspector described the church-basement schools he visited in the summer of 1842 as "crowded to overflowing," appallingly lighted and ventilated, disastrously understaffed. It was estimated that as many as seven thousand Catholic children in the city were turned away because of lack of space. Hughes preached regularly about rising to the challenge to provide funds for schools that could be staffed by nuns or Christian Brothers, but the money just wasn't forthcoming. (Nor were the Christian Brothers right away: the first did not arrive from Europe until 1848.) The economy in New York was still, several years after the panic of 1837, in a weakened state. Even his own clergy tired of hearing Hughes on this subject.

A report from a church near Buffalo in 1850 could be seen as representative of the entire diocese in that period. A pastor there reported 400 Catholic children who were of school age. Ninety of those children attended the church school, their parents paying fifty to seventy-five cents a child for the term, while 200 attended the state's free district school—the "infidel" schools, as the pastor mournfully put it—and 110, as far as he could tell, attended no school at all. In the same month, the pastor at Saint Francis's Church in Manhattan at Thirty-First Street and Seventh Avenue estimated that 100–120 children attended the church school, kept open by the church itself and private contributions. "The rest of the children [of the parish, presumably more than double that number] frequent the public schools or no schools at all, as the case may be," he noted sadly. A flourishing parochial school system remained a dream for the future, but it was not a dream Hughes was willing to abandon. The consequences of having children attend schools in which their faith was disparaged were too dire.

FIVE DAYS BEFORE CHRISTMAS in 1842, eight months after he endured that terrible night when rioters smashed the windows of his home and called out threats to drag him from his bed, John Dubois died. He was seventy-eight. He and his coadjutor, now the de jure as well as the de facto bishop of the diocese, had had as little to do with each other as possible in Dubois's last year, but it was a moment for John Hughes to reflect on how much, in an indirect way, he owed to a man with whom he had so little in common. It was a moment, too, to contemplate the Catholic American past receding before one's eyes: bishops John England and Henry Conwell had died that year as well, within days of each other.

A Protestant observer at Dubois's funeral was impressed by the city's outpouring of grief and respect, given how rare it had been to hear a kind word said about the man by many of his parishioners. "The crowds that flocked to his funeral testified to the strong veneration of the Catholics for his memory," Lydia Maria Child wrote. "Masses for deceased relations and friends are now redoubled; with the hope that the good old bishop will help them in purgatory, as he was ever ready to help them in life. This gives rise to some jests among the unbelieving; but I despise no thought that is born of the affections. . . . We Protestants are too prone to pull up our flowers, to see whether they have any roots."

Child also related an anecdote she heard that, if true, suggested what a purgatory Dubois had been living in in New York. A few years earlier, Dubois had been seen on the roof of the cathedral, nervously watching a fire in a neighboring building. "As the danger increased, he knelt across the roof, his venerable white hairs streaming in the wind, and prayed fervently for the preservation of his church." He was spotted by the firemen who thought it a great joke to direct their hose toward him, forcing him off the roof. Child was certain that the offenders could not have been Irishmen, but she had that wrong. They had always been Dubois's real antagonists.

The Irish of New York had an Irish bishop now, and they wanted him to make the most of the opportunity. This came at a moment, though, when Hughes's own inner resources were waning, though he would rally soon enough. At the Fifth Provincial Council in Baltimore in May 1843, where he was asked to deliver the eulogy for the three recently departed bishops, he raised the question of his need for a coadjutor. The work was too much for one man and was undermining his health. His fellow bishops agreed, and the request was forwarded to Rome. Various names were bandied about, but in the end Hughes had his way. It would be another Irishman, in effect, but this time a native-born American. The following spring, John McCloskey was consecrated a bishop and became Hughes's much-needed second-in-command. As far as Hughes was concerned, the appointment came none too soon.

That council also made recommendations to Rome to establish new dioceses at Hartford, Chicago, Little Rock, Milwaukee, and in the Oregon Territory. Catholicism was expanding in all directions in the early 1840s, with 579 priests serving throughout the twenty-five states, 71 now in the New York diocese. New rulings covered a range of topics, including a stipulation that laymen were no longer to be allowed to deliver orations in Catholic churches, that any Catholic attempting to remarry after a civil divorce should be excommunicated, and that priests were not to borrow money for their parishes without prior approval from their bishops. John Purcell wanted to raise the matter of how to extend religious instruction to African American Catholics, but that issue seems to have gone nowhere. The council did acknowledge that Catholics in the United States were enduring a period of calumny and hardship, which would require from them a renewal of faith and great forbearance.

Forbearance was not Hughes's strong suit. Yet despite his growing reputation as a man with a healthy ego, Hughes at no time assumed that he could fight the good fight on his own. He needed to be one among many. Establishing a presence in the city, in a way that Dubois's personality and physical infirmities—and ethnicity—had prevented him from doing, thus became another priority during his first years as bishop. He had done that, of course, with the school funding battle and his many

letters to the editor, but that was not the kind of high profile he had originally intended. Rather, he wanted to seek out and forge relationships
with those men who could be useful in creating a community of power
and influence. If this seemed like a secularization of his priestly role,
such a shift, Hughes believed, was inevitable given the drift of the times.
A man in his position had no choice in modern America, as the power of
the trustees declined, other than to become something of a "lawyer and
merchant, a contractor, a money-payer, and a borrower." In the 1840s,
a bishop would simply have to pay more attention to public opinion and
the power of the press, to political contacts, real-estate values, interest
rates, and refinanced mortgages. Whoever could help him in these varied
roles was a desirable person to know.

Most of those gentlemen were Catholic, like Andrew Carrigan,
who oversaw the sale of the Fordham property, or publisher Thomas
O'Connor of the Carroll Hall slate, banker Gregory Dillon and hardware
merchant Felix Ingoldsby (both early leaders of the Irish Emigrant Aid
Society), and assemblyman and future judge Charles Patrick Daly, who
had opposed his bishop's decision to endorse a Carroll Hall ticket. Peter
Hargous was a shipping magnate whom Hughes was to ask to head the
Fordham board of trustees, a man he came to regard as a close friend.
Congressman John McKeon, as knowledgeable about city and national
politics as any man, was a Democrat in and out of office in the 1830s
and 1840s before becoming a U.S. Attorney under Franklin Pierce. The
elderly and generously philanthropic Cornelius Heeney, a onetime business partner of John Jacob Astor, had been—along with Francis Cooper,
another Hughes ally—one of the first Catholics to serve in the New York
state legislature in the 1820s. Some of these American success stories were
shockingly reactionary men, such as Charles O'Conor (son of Thomas
O'Connor, despite the different spelling of their last names), one of the
great lawyers of his day and a vehement supporter of slavery and states'
rights. Some were not Catholic, Democratic, or reactionary: Gulian Verplanck, for example, an ardent Episcopalian, Manhattan literary intellectual, and Whig state senator had been Hughes's liaison, via Charles
Constantine Pise, to John Spencer in the fight on behalf of the school bill
in the legislature and cared deeply about the plight of the immigrants.

This process also meant socializing with those families of means
who supported the church or, if Protestant, exhibited tolerance and a
cosmopolitan view of the world. One well-placed member of Manhattan

society, a girl at the time, remembered first encountering the bishop at the home of an affluent Catholic friend on LeRoy Street and being impressed by his affability and "attractive conversation." A friend of the Winfield Scott family, Marian Gouverneur also met Hughes later on numerous occasions through the convert daughters of the famous general. She recalled as well a Protestant schoolmate, Sarah Jones—daughter of one of New York State's most prominent barristers, Chancellor Samuel Jones—who was equally taken by the bishop at these social gatherings and began to attend Mass at Saint Patrick's Cathedral. Sarah eventually converted and became a nun. Her family's reaction can only be surmised.

Not surprisingly, John Hughes found himself enjoying the company of men of the world, men who knew how to wield power for the causes they believed in. This was especially true of what became a long-lasting relationship with Seward's right-hand man, Thurlow Weed. That friendship that began during the public school controversy is telling. The résumés of the two men have a good deal in common—born in the same year to families of modest means, they were self-taught, knew from an early age what they wanted to do in life, and were well established in their fields in their thirties—though their temperamental affinities are the real key to their comfort in each other's company. Each appreciated in the other a clarity of mind, a strategizing outlook, a sense of humor, a passion for journalism, and a delight in brisk, informed, unsentimental political conversation. As his biographer describes him and as his memoirs attest, everything about Weed's appearance and manner reflected "joy in living, his love of power, and his zest for action." Now that Hughes was an important New York personage himself, those were exactly the qualities in the men with which he felt most at home—imperiousness and conviviality.

Yet, at the same time, there was a complementarity between Weed and Hughes. The latter could be—intended to be—at all times, front and center in executing the business of the church. Weed was a behind-the-scenes figure, never running for office himself, and committed to calculation and persuasion: "the wizard of the lobby," as he was called. For Hughes, there was a fascination in seeing how a man pulled the strings, though his own efforts were never to be as supple and subtle as Weed's.

When Hughes decided that a second trip to Europe was called for in the summer of 1843, he was delighted that Thurlow Weed asked to accompany him. At that moment, Weed desperately needed a break from the brutal pace and internecine warfare of New York politics. They were joined by Bishop John Purcell and Pierre-Jean de Smet, a Jesuit missionary of Purcell's acquaintance, a man Hughes took to immediately and thereafter considered a lifelong friend, and a better quartet for intelligent, amiable transatlantic companionship Hughes would never know again. The travelers' plans did not go unnoticed. Reading a newspaper mention of their ship's departure for Liverpool, Whig lawyer Philip Hone (New York's Samuel Pepys and the model of the acidic diarist) remarked in his journal, "I do not believe Mr. Weed is an adjunct of the right reverend apostles of the papacy or that he is to assist them in preparing a report to the sovereign Pontiff of their successful efforts to introduce the true faith into this susceptible nation by means of a judicious exercise of political influence of their band of foreign dictators." But he did believe that Weed and his boss in Albany had done more than their share to advance the Catholic cause. "As for Bishop Hughes," the ex-mayor wrote in his diary, "he deserves a cardinal's hat at least for what he has done in placing Irish Catholics upon the necks of New Yorkers." A cardinal's hat had, in fact, been on Hughes's mind even from the time of his first trip to Europe, but he had wisely warned his family then not to raise their hopes.

Of the six Atlantic crossings John Hughes made after his emigration, this was one of the best. He was with three people whose company he relished. With Purcell, he had a personal history to look back on and a church future to look forward to. The garrulous Weed was always ready to share political lore, and de Smet had stories of his own—and trunks full of Native American clothing and tribal artifacts from his time in the Iowa Territory and Wyoming. Hughes might also have learned something on this crossing from de Smet about solicitation tactics. Perhaps the Native American garb did the trick, but the missionary was a master in that area. On this trip, de Smet collected a staggering $26,500 in donations and found eight Jesuits and six nuns of the Sisters of Notre Dame de Namur who agreed to accompany him back to the West Coast of the United States.

Hughes did not intend this crossing to be as extensive and prolonged a trip across the continent as his previous venture. He planned to visit Ireland and England and Paris briefly, but his real destination—the point of the whole voyage—was Brussels and Antwerp, home to the major bankers of Catholic Belgium. The interest rates in New York were defeating his hope to prepare for a time, however distant, when the church's debt could be retired or rendered manageable. Twenty thousand dollars in annual interest (a sum that would have built a new church each year) was, to his mind, an intolerable burden, and he imagined that consolidating the debt and approaching the right lenders abroad for an interest rate of 3 or 4 percent might not be an entirely quixotic venture. Presumably, the men of finance he consulted in New York thought it at least worth the attempt.

The travelers departed for Liverpool on June 7 aboard the *George Washington*, the same packet boat that had brought Charles Dickens home the year before. William Seward, out of office now, came to see them off. "For the first ten days our ship bounded gayly over the billows with fair and fresh winds," Weed wrote, before the sea calmed and their progress slowed, though they were offered the compensation then of numerous whale sightings and schools of porpoises surrounding them for hours. A hundred and fifty steerage passengers were aboard as well (another underside of the immigrant story), disappointed Irish and Scottish emigrants returning to Europe after finding that America had not lived up to their expectations. The passengers with whom their party dined and socialized included a range of American, British, and German businessmen, two British army officers, and a Bavarian Catholic priest returning home for his health. On the first Sabbath out, Hughes preached a sermon standing on a step of the mizzenmast for any who were interested, which occasioned, according to Weed, a huge, enthusiastic crowd. "He made the ocean a witness in favor of the truth of Revelation," the Protestant Weed wrote, as he compared the majesty of the Creator to the pretensions of man's creations in a "truly impressive" sermon. Sea voyages brought out the best in Hughes—the salt air, the breeze, the time to read, the absence of harrying visitors and correspondence, the hours of chess and relaxed conversation—and he had no complaints about the way he passed his forty-sixth birthday that summer.

Things went somewhat awry off the coast of Ireland. "The wind has baffled us," Weed observed, bringing them not toward the Irish Sea and on into Liverpool but ten miles off the coast of Ireland, where a "mountain of rocks with their Druidical towers" came into full view. Days passed with no progress toward heading in the right direction. Small boats came alongside each morning, offering to take those passengers ashore who were willing to land near the Cove of Cork and make the rest of their journey overland to Dublin and thence across the water to

England. Hearing from the boatmen that Daniel O'Connell was back in Ireland and going to give a series of addresses that week, Hughes's party decided to avail themselves of this opportunity to meet him.

In the little village where they landed, news that two American bishops were in the area spread quickly, and they were made much of before departing for Cork, where Purcell left them to visit relatives in the north. Spending time with O'Connell in Dublin—a second meeting for Hughes—and watching him address a large gathering at nearby Donnybrook made everyone in the party glad that their plans had been forcibly altered. Weed was astonished at the charisma and oratorical skill of the man. De Smet was no less impressed: "After being buried five years in the heart of the American desert," he wrote, it was thrilling to meet "one of the greatest men of the day—the only agitator who has ever instituted a revolution without spilling one drop of blood." Back in Cork on his own, later, Weed also had the chance to meet Theobald Mathew, with whom he was almost equally taken. He was glad to hear that Mathew had plans someday to bring his temperance crusade to the American side of the water. Between O'Connell and Mathew, Weed felt, there was hope yet for Ireland.

Thurlow Weed the traveler, on his first trip to Europe, had something of the wide-eyed child about him. In Ireland, he looked with awe upon the landscape, the ruined abbeys, and the dire poverty to be encountered on their wanderings along the eastern coast—crowds of child-beggars, hovels of one room shared by families with their poultry and livestock. In London, he wanted to see everything, and he wanted Hughes, when he was free from his own rounds of business, to accompany him to likely and unlikely spots. That zealousness entailed a visit to both houses of Parliament, Westminster Abbey, the British Museum, the National Gallery of Art, the Royal Academy, and the Royal Observatory in Greenwich, but it also meant joining the gawkers at Madame Tussaud's and inside the "frowning, gloomy walls" of Newgate Prison. They made a mad dash to Saint James Park when word went round the hotel that Victoria and Albert were out riding in an open carriage, though the royal couple were the last two people in the world the bishop of New York needed to see in the flesh. He was game for anything to please his friend, though, especially as Weed had consented to attend Sunday Mass with Hughes when in Ireland. There were limits. When Weed, his travel bag loaded with letters of introduction, set out to arrange an interview with

Charles Dickens, Hughes suggested that he might want to dip into the American chapters of *Martin Chuzzlewit* first. He did, and the idea of paying homage to the famous novelist was quickly put to rest.

In the letters Weed mailed home, intended for publication in his Albany paper, he summarized his ecclesiastical friend as the ideal traveling companion, curious and flexible and energetic, a man "in the prime of life, with tastes and habits and aspirations which will not rest while there are treasures of knowledge unexplored." The same could have been said of Thurlow Weed. After London and a parting with his friend, who was heading to Scotland before going back to Ireland and on to France, it was time for Hughes to cross the Channel in search of precious funds. De Smet, a Belgian native, went with him to Belgium, before going to Rome himself to meet the pope. But not even de Smet's presence helped Hughes's case. He couldn't find a single banker interested in loaning money to a debt-wracked Catholic diocese three thousand miles away with dubious collateral, situated in the midst of a generally hostile culture. All he had to show for his weeks in the British Isles was a meeting with several priests who were willing to consider emigrating to work for him and an afternoon spent with a Fordham seminarian on the Grand Tour, a promising convert named James Roosevelt Bayley, who was a nephew of Mother Elizabeth Seton and a man who would one day be a second McCloskey to him. All he had to show for his time in Belgium was an immersion in Flemish art and a fantastically expensive pectoral cross given to him by Queen Louise-Marie, to whom he was presented at court by the well-connected de Smet. A brief stopover in Paris yielded even less: sympathetic ears, but no practical solutions and no aid.

Disappointed and a bit depressed, Hughes returned home only three months after departing New York harbor. He also returned to an America fractured by even more unstable relations between Catholics and Protestants than when he had left.

———

EVEN IN THE CONTEXT OF A PARTICULARLY VIOLENT DECADE in the United States, the Philadelphia riots of May and July 1844 are an unnerving moment in American history to contemplate. The "Baal of bigotry" that his adversaries had bowed to in the schools controversy, as Hughes termed the opposition, was nothing compared to the physical violence that religious and ethnic hatred could provoke, an enmity that left bodies in the street and churches smoldering.

On the afternoon of May 6, 1844, as many as three thousand nativists held a rally near a Catholic school in the heavily Irish Philadelphia suburb of Kensington—a location chosen to make a point. The rhetoric was the usual tirade against the foreigners who were strangers in the land, people of questionable loyalty and un-American traits. A fight ensued with the area's Irish Catholic residents in which an Irish ex-constable, attempting to make peace, was shot in the face. The mob attempted to storm a Sisters of Charity convent school, but the defenders fought them off, killing one would-be arsonist in the process. The next day, a larger, enraged mob rallied outside Independence Hall demanding revenge. A procession was formed with a ripped American flag held aloft on which were painted the words "This is the flag trampled under foot by the Irish papists!" The crowd proceeded to march on Saint Michael's, a church that had been founded by Terence Donaghoe, and burn it to the ground. Donaghoe, serving in the archdiocese of Dubuque now but on a visit to his old parish, managed to escape unharmed. The convent (its occupants gone), an Irish-run open-air market, and the Hibernia Hose Company were torched as well. The following day, Saint Augustine's Church went up in flames. The library Hughes had so valued during the Breckinridge debates was taken from the rectory, piled up in the street, and set ablaze. Gravestones were overturned in Catholic cemeteries. Priests and nuns fled their rectories and convents and were sheltered by their parishioners. The more affluent Catholic families decamped from the city, and Bishop Kenrick himself was ushered out of town by his nervous staff. The authorities could do little to stop the three-day rampage, and an estimated thirty homes of Irish residents were vandalized or burned to the ground before order was restored.

In June, the city's Catholics endured the frustration of reading the report of a grand jury investigating the violence, a report that settled all blame on the Irish Catholics who had provoked the nativists and prevented their exercise of free speech in Kensington. Nothing about the verdict was designed to ease tensions, and another outbreak of violence and an assault on Saint Philip Neri Church in the Southwark neighborhood took place in early July. That episode was as much a battle between the state militia and the nativists as it was between the nativists and the Irish. The toll for these two outbreaks of mob rule in Philadelphia was estimated to be thirty men killed and more than a hundred seriously injured, both immigrants and nativists.

FigURE 7. *The burning of churches and assaults on Irish homes during the
Philadelphia riots of 1844 confirmed John Hughes in his belief that Catholic
strength and solidarity were essential.* (Courtesy of the Library of Congress
Print and Photography Collection.)

The cause of the uproar was Philadelphia's own version of the school
controversy. Not many months after the Maclay bill was passed into
law in New York, Francis Kenrick had approached Philadelphia's school
commissioners with the same complaints. His tone, however, was considerably milder than Hughes's, and he never so much as hinted at a
threat of political retaliation. The commissioners were amenable to his
appeal and had agreed in January 1843 that students should be allowed
to read from whatever Bible their parents approved of during school
hours. Protestant groups took this gesture as a sign of weakness, more
bowing to the political influence of Rome. A public letter from Kenrick
insisting that he had no objections to the King James Bible being read
in public schools—*for and by Protestants*—failed to quell the growing
agitation. Anti-Catholic pamphlets were circulated throughout the rest
of the year, speakers at rallies lashed out at "power-mad clerics," and the
Protestant Banner in March 1844 finally declared, "The decisive blow
has been struck, the Pope reigns in Philadelphia!" It was a city primed
for violence.

The fast-hardening association of Catholicism with Irish birth or
ancestry was made especially apparent by the fact that no German

Catholic churches were torched in Philadelphia. One such church was actually in the path of the rioters as they left Kensington, but it survived without so much as a window broken or a threat made. Philadelphia nativists were underscoring a perceived link that would promise even more trouble in the years ahead as Irish immigration radically increased. The problem, to those who shared this view, was not with Catholics per se; it was with those Catholics who emigrated from a particular place, arrived here in sufficient numbers to make demands, were led by priests of their own ethnic background, had diligently worked their way into the political system, and were ready, if pressed, to use their fists or their firearms.

Many residents and editorialists expressed sympathy for the Catholic losses, and years later one of the two churches was rebuilt with public funds, but some Protestants were even inclined to include John Hughes—eighty miles away—in their assignment of responsibility for the disorders. "Blame attaches to both parties," a prominent Philadelphia businessman noted in his diary, "but I hold the Irish Catholics the most culpable as the original aggressors. Bishop Hughes of N.Y. stirred up the flame in that city by preventing the use of the Bible in public schools & his indiscreet interference with the popular elections." The Catholic clergy in Philadelphia were allegedly following his lead, Thomas P. Cope felt, and the indignation of the nativists was understandable. A death threat came in the mail from a Philadelphia man claiming (falsely) to be the brother of a nativist killed in the riots, and Hughes asked the police in both cities to investigate.

Allies like William Seward rallied to the defense of the victims. Speaking in upstate New York, the former governor expressed sorrow that "men, women, and children were compelled by American citizens to flee from burning dwellings in the night time," their only offense "that they and their ancestors were born in Ireland and that they worshipped God according to the creed and ritual of the Roman Catholic Church." Former Philadelphia mayor and U.S. senator George M. Dallas, who would be nominated that summer to be James K. Polk's running mate, served as defense attorney to some of the Irish participants arrested during the riots.

Fears that the same kind of attacks might occur in New York City were widespread that spring and summer. This is when Hughes's most oft-quoted remark was purportedly made to New York's mayor, who asked Hughes if he were worried about his own diocese's churches. The rejoinder: no, because if a single church under my care is touched, the Protestants would need to look to their own houses of worship, as the city would be turned into a "second Moscow." This image has a wonderful, visually allusive ring to it, and one might well wish Hughes had expressed himself thus—indeed, he might have. It evokes his backbone and his manner of expression. That no source of the time quotes such a strong, newsworthy statement, however, raises suspicions that it might be an example of retrospective phrasing, a line Hughes passed on to his secretary and future biographer, John Hassard, twenty years later. The sentiment is accurate, nonetheless. Hughes was outraged by what had happened in Philadelphia, disgusted that Kenrick had fled the scene and his priests and male parishioners had done nothing to protect their churches, and ready to threaten defensive physical force if necessary to safeguard Catholic property in his own city, the mayor and the police be damned. Immigrant New Yorkers loved him for the strength of his response. Men with guns patrolled the streets outside the cathedral with his permission.

National politics that summer also provided evidence that one had to be leery of counting too much on anyone to look out for Catholic or Irish interests other than Irish Catholics themselves. The Whigs nominated Henry Clay for a third and final time to head their presidential ticket, a development that pleased Hughes. He and his coreligionists would finally have a friend in the White House, an anti-Jacksonian who would oppose a land-grab to the Rio Grande and the creation of more slave states. He was anything but delighted, though, when he learned that Clay's running mate would be Theodore Frelinghuysen, a former mayor of Newark and senator from New Jersey who was thought to harbor Protestant evangelical or even nativist attitudes toward Catholicism. He was known to be an advocate of tight Protestant control of public schools. With cause, Whig politicians worried about Hughes's reaction to that nomination. Clay men in the city paid calls on the bishop. He chose not to commit himself publicly. Some Clay men in Kentucky wrote to him specifically on the subject of Frelinghuysen, to which he replied, "I look upon him as a sincere, honest . . . honorable bigot." He instructed the *Freeman's Journal* to express the paper's disapproval of the vice-presidential choice. The selection of Frelinghuysen certainly stood out in sharp contrast to the Democrats' choice of immigrant-friendly George M. Dallas for the second spot on their ticket.

Henry Clay's surprise defeat that November only increased the enmity felt by many Whigs toward immigrant voters, most of whom were Irish and Catholic. Given Polk's slim five thousand-vote margin in New York State and the fact that, had Clay carried New York, he would have won the election, Whigs like Millard Fillmore and Daniel Webster cast suspicious eyes in the direction of Hughes. A coalition of "abolitionists and foreign Catholics have defeated us in this state," Fillmore stormed. "We are to be prostrated in the dust by an army of Irish paupers, set on and marshaled by their infernal priest!!!," another Whig complained to Senator Thomas Crittenden. "God Almighty save us!!!"

The "infernal priest" tried to stand above the fracas. He knew, even if no one else did, that he had no legitimate power by which to direct the voters of his diocese, and that any explicit announcement for one candidate or another would be entirely inappropriate. That didn't mean he held back in private conversation or failed to let his views be known among influential people. Quite the contrary.

In this case, he might personally have wanted to see Henry Clay in the White House rather than Polk—so he told William Seward—but he might also have wanted to see the Whigs pay for the insult of adding Frelinghuysen to the ticket and taking his support for granted. Cutting off his nose to spite his face was not a practice unknown to the bishop. Yet what he wanted had only a limited bearing on what ballots were dropped into the Whig or Democratic ballot boxes. His alleged influence was bottomless fodder for the daily press, though always too good to pass up. Votes could be marshaled by John Hughes for Whigs or Democrats "at the wave of his crozier," James Gordon Bennett told his readers, who were eager to believe in the myth of a papist autocrat pulling the strings from his cathedral office.

Hughes was not devoid of ideas, though, or a wish to proclaim those ideas, about how the urban immigrants of his religion and nationality should position themselves in relation to the native mainstream. As the national debate about slavery—its morality, its future, its containment or, post–Mexican war, its expansion—heated up in the 1840s, he was perfectly clear in private conversation and public utterance about what he expected. If Catholics were perceived as a threat to America because of their religious beliefs, they must never be perceived as a threat because of their political beliefs. Most Irish Catholics did not hold radical views on race in any case, so there was hardly much convincing to do, but he worried incessantly about the southern failure to see that the differences between their people and the urban Irish were differences of manners and class, to be mitigated over time, not differences in fundamental values. He worried that the Irish would be seen as a socially destabilizing force. Hence, the anxiety caused him by Daniel O'Connell or the rare abolitionist priest like Father Thomas Farrell, whom he ordained in 1848 and who served five different parishes in Manhattan in the decade before the Civil War, bringing his unsettling politics with him everywhere.

And what of Hughes himself and slavery, Hughes himself and the ultimate emancipation of those souls in bondage? There isn't the remotest possibility of turning John Hughes into that favored subject of modern biographical writing, the individual of another era so far ahead of his or her time that the subject's beliefs remarkably, pleasingly, coincidentally dovetail with ours. Thomas Paine, the Grimké sisters, Herman Melville, Margaret Fuller, Susan B. Anthony, Eugene Debs—the list of people who often appear to be, at heart, one of our intellectual contemporaries, just clothed differently and set amid an odd cast of characters, is long. Hughes isn't of that number. He was a man of his times, most especially on the subjects of race and social disorder, and he can only be known and encompassed in that context. An Irish Catholic abolitionist like Henry Kemp, a member of the Massachusetts Anti-Slavery Society who thought Hughes and other prelates should be excommunicated for their refusal to take an active stance against slavery, represented a minuscule minority among Catholics. Hughes always thought Daniel O'Connell would have done better had he focused on Ireland's struggle to free itself from Great Britain and left slavery to the Americans to figure out, and he repudiated O'Connell's later, stronger statements on the subject. Likewise, he probably regretted ordaining the rabble-rousing Thomas Farrell.

That said, it does not follow that Hughes shared all of the more aggressive opinions of other Irish Catholic men he knew or associated with, such as New York lawyer Charles O'Conor, who wanted to see every escaped black family returned to their rightful master in chains, or California politician Peter Burnett, who promoted immigration bans on black freemen moving to the West Coast. Like John Purcell, who used the word "ill-advised" when discussing slavery, Hughes was sorry that the institution had ever come into being. "I am no friend to slavery," he told the editor of the *New York Courier & Inquirer*. He never defended it as a positive good in the manner of John C. Calhoun or many of his fellow bishops in the South.

In one sermon at Saint Patrick's Cathedral, he referred to slavery as "an evil" that had been revived in modern times only because of the unconscionable avarice of white men. As far back as 1829, he had referred to the slave trade, "putting manacles . . . on hands that were free," as oppression pure and simple. He saw the point of *In supremo apostolatus*. In an address on Christianity and social servitude delivered at the Broadway Tabernacle in the winter of 1843, he questioned the repeated use of the statement that the Bible unequivocally justified slavery by reminding his listeners of the different culture the Jewish patriarchs had been part of and listed numerous early church fathers who set a noble example by freeing their slaves. But his countrymen were stuck with Jefferson's metaphorical fox caught by the tail, and the resolution to the problem was going to have to be effected gradually. He stood with Seward, Clay, and Webster on this point. The cry of the abolitionists was a call for social disorder. It was a cry, for that matter, made by a group that included plenty of outspoken anti-Catholics like Harriet Beecher Stowe, Theodore Parker, and the late Elijah Lovejoy with whom he never wanted common cause.

His personal relations with black Americans were practically nil. He had nothing to do with Pierre Toussaint, the ex-slave who had prospered in New York City and become a significant Catholic philanthropist. By the standards of our day, John Hughes was a racist man. By the standards of progressive thinkers of his own day, John Hughes was a racist man, though the charge carried less weight then, of course. Like most Westerners, he regarded Africa as a continent lost to religion and civilization, and so he could even term slavery "not an unmitigated evil" in that it led a lost people to Christianity, with the hope that these once-heathen people would be Christians for all time, once slavery was ended. Like Henry Clay and Abraham Lincoln, though, he never doubted that the two races had not been created equal. Like Nathaniel Hawthorne and Orestes Brownson, he felt a distaste about any physical proximity to black men and women. He could not even imagine black and white Americans worshipping in the same church together. His interest in the hard lot of people treated unjustly by society lay elsewhere—with the

Irish of the Five Points, the mother unable to feed her children, the job-less immigrant and the orphan who, unless educated and better cared for, would produce children similarly bereft, and above all with those individuals who, spiritually bereft, might be saved if they found their way to a viable, sustaining religious tradition.

At the end of 1844, a few weeks before Christmas, Hughes delivered his most explicit address, at venues in Baltimore and Philadelphia, on the earthly causes of that destitution and despair. In what was probably the longest speech of his career, a man not known for brevity wished to offer a portrait of the times and a statement of belief that political economy and the traditional Catholic values of duty and charity could not, or should not, be separated. The portrait of the age was unsparing: "There perhaps never was a period when men entered on the pursuit of wealth with so much of what might be called almost desperate deter-mination to succeed as the period in which we live." Cupidity, bribery, extortion, exploitation of the weak, the sacrifice of the public good for private gain—these values and practices, Hughes told his audiences, were becoming part of the very fabric of Western culture to an unprec-edented extent.

Hughes took Great Britain as a prime example, a nation often lauded for its standing as the richest country of the world and a shining example of the Protestant mercantile spirit. All that may be true, he admitted, but the "destitution of her millions" was part and parcel of that standing. Honorable as it was that Britons "should sympathize in the sufferings of those who are in the condition of slaves throughout the world," it was pure cant to talk about black emancipation while ignoring the plight of colliers, ditchdiggers, factory workers, and seamstresses who were paid subsistence wages and lived in the most degraded conditions, cast off by their employers like so much refuse when they were no longer of use to them. The wealth of Britain was unsurpassed, but the extent and the intensity of the misery Briton's industrial poor endured were also unsur-passed. He had seen it himself on his trips to London and Liverpool. "The spectacle of the starving laborer maintaining a contest of compe-tition with the bloated capitalist" was never going to result in a humane resolution for the laborer.

Hughes was no socialist. He respected the free-enterprise system—but not when its adherents acted as if workingmen had no rights and their economic system had nothing to do with divinely inspired moral expectations first articulated by Jesus and the early church fathers. If patience and respect for the social order were expected of the poor, as indeed the church taught, then "moderation in enjoyment and liberality toward the poor" were expected of the rich. Social Darwinism, fast becoming an article of faith in the new industrial age, was for Hughes a moral travesty. Though he spoke primarily of Great Britain, always a pleasing target, and felt that the dissolution of the convents and monasteries in Henry VIII's time had removed one crucial source of aid to the most abjectly destitute on that island, Hughes did not intend his American audiences to assume that his remarks did not also pertain to the United States. On the contrary. His fear was that the worship of God in the United States was being replaced by a worship of money, personal success, technological advancement, and national pride.

These topics—a concern for the plight of the working class, a demand that men of business be held ethically accountable for their wealth, a refusal to accept the law of supply and demand as the sole basis for a well-functioning society—constitute an ongoing theme in Hughes's lectures at this period of his life. It was after hearing a similar speech in New York that year that Isaac Hecker, a Brook Farm utopian and recent Catholic convert who was planning to enter the priesthood, wrote to Orestes Brownson in Boston that he thought Hughes and Brownson might have a good deal in common, at least on the topics of labor and economic justice. It was a speech that displayed a fierce social conscience. It was a speech, Hecker said, that Brownson himself could have given.

Among the politically minded, Brownson's was a name heard more and more frequently in this period, and Hughes would have appreciated the compliment at the time. An intellectual of a particularly mercurial nature, Brownson had been born a Congregationalist but converted at nineteen to Presbyterianism. Finding that faith too narrow and doctrinaire, he became in his twenties a Unitarian minister before losing his faith altogether and drifting into the orbit of radicals Fanny Wright and Robert Dale Owen and the Working Men's Party. From there he became a tangential figure in the Boston Transcendentalist circle and a well-regarded essayist. He was the sort of man, so obviously intelligent and passionate about social issues, from whom everyone always expected a good deal. "The hero wields a sturdy pen, which I am glad to see," Ralph Waldo Emerson wrote in 1840. "I had judged him from some [earlier essays] & did not know he was such a Cobbett of a scribe."

The allusion to William Cobbett, the British political radical and pamphleteer, was apt—at the time.

What Emerson was not prepared for, what few who knew Brownson were quite prepared for, was his conversion to Catholicism in 1844, a decision that occurred only after a prolonged inner struggle. Bishop Fenwick of Boston, who met with Brownson for many months prior to his baptism, had kept Hughes apprised of the situation. Hughes was naturally pleased with Brownson's final decision—it was the talk of intellectual circles that fall—and despite Brownson's ties to the Democratic Party and never-wavering support of John C. Calhoun's presidential aspirations (and his detestation of Henry Clay), Hughes hoped for a close association with the publisher of *Brownson's Quarterly Review* someday. He felt he was wasted in Boston.

Hughes takes "a great interest in you," Hecker wrote to Brownson. "There is no question Bishop H. is the most able bishop we have, and a Review started here with his patronage would have much greater advantages than at any other place in the union." A prolific writer of the first rank, a political thinker of consequence, was too rare a commodity in Catholic circles not to be kept in one's sights, Hughes agreed. Hecker never stopped pressing upon that his friend that he would find a more appreciative berth in Manhattan, but for the time being Brownson remained where he was.

War and Famine

MORE AND MORE, Hughes felt the need to have around him some staunch allies. McCloskey had been the correct choice for a right-hand man. He was quick, he was hardworking, he shared the same values, and he had an entirely different personality. "His modesty was of a kind that might often be mistaken for timidity," Cardinal John Farley later wrote of him, but in actuality he wasn't timid. He was merely diplomatic, less prone to public displays of indignation. He would never outshine his bishop, but he was extremely useful in myriad situations—dealing with obdurate trustees, sizing up politicians, investigating complaints, and calming the waters. Cardinal James Gibbons made a biblical comparison: John McCloskey was Moses at prayer, Hughes was Joshua fighting in the field. That is just how the Joshua of New York wanted it.

William Starrs, who remained with Hughes at Saint Patrick's for his first five years in New York, was another rock. He left to become pastor of Saint Mary's on Grand Street in 1844 but returned to the cathedral a few years later as rector and Hughes's vicar-general. While he was condescended to by some of the more intellectually inclined priests of the diocese, Hughes saw in him a man who was both caring and competent. He wanted more like him. Terence Donaghoe—a priest more than caring and competent, almost inspirational—was someone Hughes never stopped hoping he could entice back from the Midwest to New York.

He was the only person whom he addressed in his letters as "*Cher Ami*" and at least once paid for him to come east for a long visit. Chiding him for not being as faithful a correspondent as he would have liked, Hughes joked in an 1845 letter that "living in the wilderness and having nothing to do but watch the Indians and wolves" should leave a man time to write back more frequently. Hughes valued his company so much that he even made the arduous trip to Dubuque, Iowa, himself a few years later.

Another priest Hughes had high hopes, and even a special affection, for—a young man who probably reminded him of Donaghoe—was John Harley. Educated at Emmitsburg, Harley had been employed as a mathematics and bookkeeping teacher at Fordham and was ordained by Hughes in June 1842. But Harley soon found himself at odds with the new head of the college. Ambrose Manahan quickly proved uniquely unsuited to that position, and his tenure was brief and acrimonious. No one liked him. That winter, Harley had written to the bishop that "Mr. Manahan has come among us full to overflowing of wild and useless schemes, schemes not at all suited to the wants and needs of the institution." Harley offered to tender his resignation. It was impossible to continue to work with the autocratic Father Manahan. Harley was concerned "for the ultimate prosperity" of the college, as the students were "almost in a state of rebellion, and nothing but the paucity of their number [was] restraining them from eruption." Even for the faculty, "what was before the home of harmony and happiness," he reported, "is now the abode of discord and unhappiness." Hughes went to Rose Hill and investigated for himself and dismissed Manahan at the end of the school year, sending him downtown to work at Saint Joseph's Church. He appointed the twenty-seven-year-old Harley to be the new—the third—president of Fordham. What Harley lacked in age and experience, Hughes felt, he would make up in sense and collegiality, two qualities Manahan had never displayed.

One reason Hughes gravitated toward those priests like Harley, who seemed capable and socially at ease and with whom he might feel some kind of rapport, was that so many other relationships with his clergy were not working out. Most of the diocese's priests had never worked under anyone who was as management-conscious as their new bishop. By 1845, Charles Constantine Pise let John McCloskey know that he could not remain in New York indefinitely. He found Hughes too prickly, too demanding. It is also possible, though he never said so, that the bishop felt the same lack of regard. With his book publications and national reputation, Pise was an easy man to inspire envy in a superior never eager to share the limelight.

Then there were priests whom Hughes liked—who had even lived at the episcopal residence—like John Urquhart, who proved in the long run to be very disappointing. After vanishing from New York for a few years, Urquhart wrote a lengthy epistle to Hughes from California in the hopes of clearing the cloud of scandal that had attached to his name when it was discovered that he has been secretly supporting a teenage boy in Manhattan. He maintained that the young man wasn't his child, as the gossipmongers had assumed, but was the abandoned offspring of his sister, and his tale of familial woe had an honest and poignant ring of truth to it; but there was no possibility of his return to the diocese. Priests were either above question on moral grounds, Hughes made clear on numerous occasions, or their usefulness was at an end.

All did not go well with Harley, though, when his health broke down. This was a source of grave concern to Hughes, who had invested high hopes for Fordham in Harley's leadership. Deciding that a third, shorter trip to Europe was needed, more to find priests and nuns to bring to the diocese than to fund-raise, Hughes took Harley with him to see if doctors in Dublin or London could offer any hope. (Harley's illness was never specified in any Hughes letters but was identified as diabetes in the diary of James Roosevelt Bayley.) Even before they departed in December 1845, the Fordham president's condition was worsening, and Hughes was under no illusions about the gravity of the situation. Consultations with the best doctors he could find in Europe were, he told Bishop Blanc of New Orleans, "his last hope for that dear and valuable young ecclesiastic."

The itinerary for this four-month trip included Dublin, London, and Paris, but not Rome or Vienna. There was neither the time nor the money to visit the Holy City again, and it is likely word had reached New York that Hughes would not find Austria as open-pursed as he had previously. German complaints that all the money went to the Irish were unabating, and the financial demands from across the water were becoming too much for European Catholics. "Here in Germany," one Bavarian chaplain wrote to an American priest in 1844, "our people are astounded that American bishops and missionaries travel so much; indeed, our people resent it. Vienna sent word to us that they do not wish to see another

American bishop." The day of the hat-in-hand bishop spending so much time away from his diocese was on the wane.

Yet, if asked or confronted, John Hughes would have been happy to answer any critics: wealthy European Catholics had no idea what American Catholic priests were up against, no conception of how vast their needs were if they hoped to forge a viable nation for Catholic immigrants. If the price was, in effect, humbling one's pride and begging from those with money—then beg he would. There were, he calculated now, approximately two hundred thousand Catholics in New York State and the part of New Jersey for which he was responsible, an area roughly the size of England and Wales, and he estimated that yearly conversions were close to five hundred. Those people were attended to by 106 clergymen (59 of whom, he noted, were Irish-born). Be that as it may, as a realist, he focused his efforts in 1845 on personnel rather than money.

Harley was ill on the voyage over and required his companion's tender ministrations. Once on land, he seemed better. The Irish leg of the trip was reasonably productive. Several nuns from the Order of the Sisters of Mercy and some Christian Brothers in Ireland tentatively agreed to come to New York City, and to anyone in authority who would listen he outlined his hopes and plans for the future. The pair visited Hughes's birthplace in the north in company with the bishop of Clogher, and Hughes had a chance to see some aunts, uncles, and cousins, all now suitably impressed with the rise of Margaret and Patrick's boy. He was invited to preach in the cathedral at Clogher on the Feast of the Epiphany and promised some pecuniary help for those of his relatives who were in particularly straitened circumstances. It was also interesting to see his homeland in company with someone who had never been there. "Riches and poverty are to be met side by side," Harley wrote home to a friend. At the dinner parties they attended in Dublin, Harley was struck by the indifference to the poor that he encountered among affluent Irishmen, many of whom were now impugning Daniel O'Connell's sincerity and talking about the more radical Young Ireland movement in the making.

Everyone was also talking about this strange new fungus affecting the potato crops, a blight that left entire fields that were healthy during the day ruined almost overnight. As harvest time approached, the crops might look fine, one Munster immigrant remembered, but suddenly "there was a cry around that some blight had struck the potato stalks." The leaves blackened, crumbing into ash when touched, and the air itself became "laden with a sickly odor of decay." Inexplicably, sometimes one field was infected and another nearby not, and, still worse, sometimes wagonloads of healthy potatoes were harvested only to turn stinking and putrid within days.

No more than 40 percent of the 1845 crop was affected, so no one knew whether this would be the extent of the damage in succeeding years or whether the fungus had run its course, or whether some means to counteract the damage might be found. Harley's opinion was that "the distress likely to accrue from the potato rot will be fully as great as represented in the papers [which were not yet envisioning anything like massive famine and exodus from the countryside]. Still, with care and economy, there will be no starvation." At about the same time, Thomas D'Arcy McGee, an Irish journalist who had recently returned to Europe after a year in the United States, was expressing the same caution in a report to the *Boston Pilot*: "On the whole, though we expect some serious degree of scarcity, I think I may safely add that there are as yet no sufficient grounds for apprehending anything like famine." That was the line of the day.

Hughes and Harley arrived in London in time to witness the opening of Parliament, where the repeal of the Corn Laws, which maintained a high tariff for imported grains that was a hardship in times of shortage, was a subject of acrimonious debate. Nothing of what he heard there convinced Hughes that Great Britain would rise to the occasion if a critical food problem lay ahead. He was particularly interested in meeting some of the recent converts that the Oxford movement had given rise to, though John Henry Newman does not seem to have been one of the men he met, and he found time to send several travel letters home to Thurlow Weed to publish under a pseudonym in his Albany paper. About his brief time in Paris, Hughes had little to say, but he did return with six beautiful stained-glass windows, a gift to his cathedral from Louis-Philippe. By April, Hughes was back in New York while Harley stayed behind to escort the Sisters of Mercy to their new home.

As Hughes feared, however, the trip did John Harley no good, and the doctors they saw had nothing to offer. Hughes asked James Roosevelt Bayley, the convert he had met in Europe on his last trip and whom he had ordained in New York two years before, to take the helm at Fordham. Hughes then employed Harley as his secretary to keep him close by on Mulberry Street. He was dead by the end of the year.

Writing to John McCloskey just after his boss had departed on this European expedition, John Purcell acknowledged what everyone felt, that Hughes's bailiwick was now the preeminent diocese in the country. "The Diocese of New York is like a racer," he wrote, "leaving all that started since or before she left the post far, far behind."

———

RENOWN DID NOT REALLY bring peace, though, in the mid-1840s. Troubles continued to confront the diocese that six years of intense labor had not abated. Hughes especially hated being blindsided by bad financial news that had been kept from him. A circular he sent to all diocesan churches in 1845 demanding a full financial accounting of expenses, income, and debts—*for once*, he told his priests, he must have specific, detailed, and verifiable information—had caused a panic in some rectories while he was away. As a result, some churches reported breaking even to the penny, which seems highly improbable, if not miraculous, but those priests knew that they would prefer any fate to that of being called to Mulberry Street in New York City to explain questionable expenses or a suspiciously high overhead or a balance sheet that involved guesswork or even a hint of creditors starting to bang at the door. Other priests simply told him, flat out, that their parishioners could give no more, and he should stop harassing them for what they did not have.

Trustees, near and far, continued to be an issue. Saint George slaying the hydra of trusteeism with one awe-inspiring address made for a good story, and Hughes liked good stories, but the fact of the matter was that even in Manhattan not everyone had quaked at the new bishop's last word on the subject. On his first trip abroad, Hughes had lured Zachary Kunz from Hungary to lead the city's second German parish, Saint John the Baptist on West Thirtieth Street, only to see the poor man placed in an untenable position when his trustees became progressively ruder and more intractable with him. Eventually, Hughes shut the church down (it would be reopened and then placed under interdict again and reopened again in the next decade: they were a tough group at Saint John the Baptist), and he suggested that Kunz scout about for affordable land for a new German church, if he had enough loyal followers in his congregation. He did, and Saint Francis of Assisi on West Thirty-First Street became the city's next new parish in 1845.

Similar troubles rocked other parishes. The Redemptorists, whom Hughes had asked to take charge of Saint Nicholas Church, the city's first German parish, on Second Street and First Avenue, had never been welcomed there by the church's lay trustees and in 1847 obtained permission to build a new church on Thompson Street. Germans were always impossible to deal with, Hughes complained. More to his liking was the fervor of the Irish who so desperately wanted churches in their neighborhood that they would take matters, literally, into their own hands. Westside Irish dockworkers labored, unpaid, unsupervised, at the end of their shifts and on weekends constructing, brick by brick, Saint Columba on Twenty-Fifth Street between Eighth and Ninth Avenues, so that the Irish Catholics of Chelsea would have a house of worship close by.

Geographical distance meant that misunderstandings might abound. Five trustees of a church in Troy, near Albany, had resigned after disagreements with their pastor, but they decided they wanted a hearing with the bishop. They saw Hughes, either on a trip they made to Manhattan or when he was passing through Troy, but if they expected any satisfaction from that quarter, they had a limited familiarity with the man they were approaching. The bishop took a pretend so-be-it stance, acting as if the whole business were a minor matter, and he told them (they subsequently wrote to their pastor) that "he leaves it to the people to choose whether they will have trustees or not, as he commands nothing." Putting ink to paper could not have been easy when it came to writing those last four words.

When it wasn't trustees, it was priests. Ambrose Manahan did not work out downtown any better than he had at Fordham and was fired a second time. "You can no longer be pastor at St. Joseph's," Hughes wrote him, "when you have but too well succeeded in destroying all confidence." He was told to find employment elsewhere. Hughes hoped, he told him, that in the future he might "disappoint the melancholy anticipations which the past is too well-calculated to inspire."

Yet if the concerns involving wayward priests, recalcitrant trustees, and empty coffers seemed at times endless, significant victories sometimes came unexpectedly. Nothing was going right at Rose Hill, but in 1845 Hughes made the momentous decision to pass on responsibility for the success of his college and the seminary next door, which had originally been managed by the Vincentians, to another source altogether. Not that he hadn't tried already, several times. He had raised the topic

with Jan Roothaan, superior-general of the Jesuits, frequently—even at
their first meeting in Rome in 1839—to no avail. But now conditions
were right: the Jesuits' school in Kentucky, Saint Mary's, was flounder-
ing, Roothaan was finally amenable, and all parties were able to come
to financial terms. That summer, twenty-nine members of the Society
of Jesus made the eleven-day trip from Kentucky. Some months later,
another twenty arrived from Europe. These new New Yorkers included
Augustus Thebaud, a prolific writer, and the highly educated John Larkin, who became the first Jesuit dean of the college and later served as
its second Jesuit president (after Thebaud).

The relationship between Hughes and the Jesuits was not destined to
be smooth. When disagreements arose, the new faculty had no intention
of being dictated to by anyone other than a superior of their order. About
the only member of the order with whom Hughes established warm
relations was Father Thebaud, who found Hughes "an affectionate and
pleasant companion" and would come round to the Rodrigues' house
on Rose Hill whenever he knew the bishop was visiting his sister and
brother-in-law. The other advantage to letting the college pass out of
diocesan hands was that the eminently capable James Roosevelt Bayley,
Harley's successor, could be brought downtown to serve as his secretary,
which Bayley did for the next several years.

That same year, Hughes had appealed to the Common Council for
undeveloped land north of Forty-Second Street for a large Catholic
orphanage. The Roman Catholic Orphan Asylum on Prince Street was
dangerously overcrowded, with 250 children in its care, and the Saint
Joseph's Half-Orphan Asylum on West Eleventh Street was in a similarly
dire condition, looking out for one hundred young residents whose single
parents could not care for them. He had good reason to know how inadequate the West Eleventh Street building was: Sister Angela—his own
sister Ellen—was assigned by her motherhouse to work there in 1846.

The same civic body that had thwarted him at every turn on the
schools question was more open to this proposal, and, to his delight, the
bishop was offered, for a rent of one dollar a year, property on which
to build—an entire city block in a largely wooded area, between Fifth
and Madison Avenues and Fifty-First and Fifty-Second Street. It took six
years to erect the ample four-story boys' orphanage and to pay off the
loan (Hughes insisted it would not open until the debt was retired), but
when the bishop signed the deed for the property in 1846, he knew this

was an accomplishment of which he could be proud. Thousands of boys in Manhattan, barefoot "street Arabs," lived an existence straight out of *Oliver Twist*, but now five hundred of them had a chance of a better life. Visitors never described the orphanage as a cheery place (far from it), but the alternative was worse. Within a decade, the orphanage housed over eight hundred boys and thereafter raised a second substantial building for girls.

Smack in the midst of these successes, though, came a debacle of Hughes's own making. When Hughes arrived in the city, the Sisters of Charity were the only women religious on the scene in any significant numbers. A small contingent of nuns of the Religious of the Sacred Heart ran an elite girls' academy (with a startling tuition of $250 a year). In time, these women religious would be joined by the Sisters of Mercy, the Sisters of the Good Shepherd, the Ursulines, and the School Sisters of Notre Dame, who came from Germany to open a German orphan asylum in the Yorkville section of Manhattan. The Sisters of Charity worked in the city's parochial schools and its Catholic orphanages but remained under the jurisdiction of their order, answerable to their local mother superior, to their mother-general, Mother Etienne Hall, in Emmitsburg, and to their superior-general, Father Louis Deluol, in Baltimore. Their order had never been subject to the authority of a local bishop. This was more than a tradition; it was a long-standing policy wherever sisters of the order were stationed—in the United States, in Mexico, in Europe, or in Africa.

Hughes chafed under this system from the beginning. He was trying to open new schools and needed teachers, yet he had no official power to reassign one of the nuns in his diocese from an orphanage to a school or some other task. He did just that, of course, when he felt it was called for, and ignored the complaints. Over time, the complaints to the motherhouse grew and became more embittered. At least as important, he expected the sisters to provide care at the boys' orphanage as well as the girls'. This was explicitly counter to the order's founding charter, which specified that sisters would work only with children or adolescents of their own sex. Hughes's rationale for demanding that the sisters, in effect, sidestep their vows of obedience to their order was one of necessity: there was no one else in the city yet to look after the boys. The numbers of the needy grew each year. Someone had to do it, and he was the church official who would decide how best to serve the Catholics of New York. Mother Etienne got involved when rumors reached her that Hughes was suggesting that her sisters be formally placed under his jurisdiction. She let the bishop know that that was not going to happen. He talked of appealing to Rome but was told by numerous sources he would find no support in that direction.

Finally, in the summer of 1846, Hughes corresponded with Father Deluol in Maryland and put forth his proposal that changes in leadership should be made in his favor. Warned by Mother Etienne, Deluol had been expecting this letter for a while. His reply was testy and unequivocal: the Sisters of Charity cared for female foundlings and orphans. Boys, housed separately and only those under the age of seven, were looked after by lay matrons under the sisters' supervision. That is the way it was to remain. As Hughes was, in Deluol's words, assuming a presumptuous "higher ground" in insisting that the needs of his diocese required a revision of these time-honored rules, Deluol informed his correspondent that the time had come for *all* the Sisters of Charity in New York to return to Emmitsburg. Any who chose of her own free will to stay could do so but would have to consider herself forever separated from her order. He also let Hughes know that, in overstepping the bounds of his authority so egregiously, his request was "calculated to inflict a deep and dangerous wound" on a valued religious community and one that, if adopted by other bishops, would be a mortal blow to the Sisters of Charity. Hughes was put in his place.

At first, Hughes tried to be conciliatory with Deluol, but when that didn't work, he became truculent. Hughes informed him that if he withdrew the sisters entirely, he, and he alone, would be responsible for the "wreck and ruin" of all of the diocese's efforts to stabilize a calamitous social situation. Hughes was emphatic that he would never encourage anyone, least of all a nun, to violate a vow of obedience, but that the consequences of a mass withdrawal from New York would be dire, and Deluol should know that Hughes wouldn't hesitate to say who should be blamed. Deluol's view was clear: you have brought this on yourself; no bishop has ever asked such a thing; Mother Etienne and I have no confidence that you will respect the sisters' independence from your rule. The problem is yours.

To Sister Angela, Hughes wrote in frustration that he was not "a promoter of anarchy," and of course she and her fellow sisters would have to go where they were told by their superiors. He would not countenance a division within any religious order. "Let schools and asylums fall to the ground," if that was the way it had to be. Let the orphans go hungry. Let the boys be sent to a Protestant orphanage. Let the children of the Irish immigrants remain illiterate. Yet, he told his sister, he planned to protest Deluol's actions "solemnly, publicly, and privately," which he did. The superior-general, on the assumption that he had sufficiently intimidated the New York bishop by that time, then offered to restore the status quo ante, so long as Hughes understood his place in the scheme of things. But by no means was that the case. "This kind of business has gone far enough," Hughes wrote to one of the nuns in New York who had been a persistent critic and, it seems, might have been crowing over her victory. She was told to leave the diocese as soon as she could pack her bags. If all the others wanted to follow her, they should feel free to do so: "I shall look for others to take their place."

Push had come to shove. The nuns were placed in an excruciating position. Some did not want to leave the children and the work they had grown attached to in New York and return to the motherhouse. Others couldn't wait to get away from Hughes, and others were racked with indecision. The man who had said he would never countenance division was now the direct cause of it and, what's more, felt he had to accept that prospect as the lesser of two evils. Now he had to hope that many of the sisters would abandon their order. Even with the Sisters of Mercy he had met on his last trip to Europe arriving soon from Dublin, he could not manage if all sixty-two nuns departed. His was an empty bluff.

When the time came to make the wrenching decision, thirty-three sisters decided to stay in New York. That number included Sister Angela. They then formed a new community, the Sisters of Charity of Saint Vincent de Paul, under the jurisdiction of the bishop of the diocese, with some members kept at the orphanages and some given teaching duties. Hughes's one stipulation about their choice of leadership was that his own sister not be voted in as their new mother superior. (Popular with the other sisters, she was nonetheless elected to that position nine years later.) Mother Elizabeth Boyle, their first superior, was a pleasing selection to Hughes, a devout convert he felt he could work with. Within forty years, this new community had almost a thousand members in the city, providing a huge teaching workforce for the city's parochial schools.

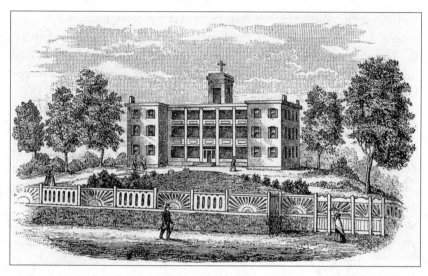

FIGURE 8. *Occupying land at what is today Fifth Avenue and 110th Street, the motherhouse of the Sisters of Saint Vincent of New York, under the leadership of John Hughes's sister, served as a school and, during the Civil War, a hospital for Union soldiers that earned the respect of even the anti-Catholic Walt Whitman.* (Courtesy of the Archives of the Archdiocese of New York.)

All this came at a cost. The bad feeling about this episode permeated the diocese for the rest of Hughes's days. Attacking Protestant bigots and taking on insulting journalists was one thing. Browbeating nuns was another. Some of his own priests and parishioners were shocked. Even a man he liked, a good friend from his Philadelphia days, Father Nicholas O'Donnell of Brooklyn, was incredulous. If the bishop had his way, he would be "the center of power and authority" over everyone, male and female, lay or religious, O'Donnell wrote to Mother Etienne, and he very much doubted the wisdom of that course. John Hughes was "arrogating a jurisdiction no other bishop claims." Hughes's response, had he known of O'Donnell's disapproval, would have been emphatic. No one knew what he was up against or had the vision necessary to see what it would take to alleviate the social problems the city's Catholics confronted. He regretted discord, he regretted his own temper, but he would see those schools staffed and those boys looked after if he had to make an enemy of everyone in the church hierarchy on this side of the Atlantic.

In a letter written at the end of the year, when the dust had more or less settled, Hughes tried to be gracious to Deluol and expressed regret that in their correspondence he had lapsed into "a certain pungency of style." What had transpired had been "the most painful controversy of my life," he wrote, and he hoped that never again would he be so aggressively at odds with a fellow leader of the church. That kind of war left no one feeling victorious.

———

NOT SO THE war with Mexico.

James K. Polk had, in effect, promised war when he stood for annexation in the election of 1844, and in 1846 he delivered on that promise. As a nominal Whig and a Catholic, John Hughes had grave reservations about his country's action in so defiantly, so transparently, concocting a pretext for the invasion of its Catholic neighbor to the south and for the instability that a hotly disputed armed conflict—its first in more than thirty years—would inflict on the nation. Given the war fever and expansionist rhetoric gripping the country, he instructed the *Freeman's Journal* to take a noncommittal tone. The Catholic press would not give Protestant Americans any reason to question Catholic or Irish immigrant patriotism. Indeed, only one Catholic writer spoke out against the conflict and published pointed attacks on the administration that summer—Orestes Brownson, who labeled Polk's land grab "uncalled for, impolitic, and unjust" and questioned the honesty of the government's official statements about Mexican aggression.

When the long-awaited call to arms was finally heard in May, Hughes had just arrived in Baltimore in company with his coadjutor and Fathers Varela and Pise. The occasion was the American church's Sixth Provincial Council, the fifth Hughes had attended. As always, Hughes was glad to meet other leaders of the church and to take part in the discourses, debates, and spiritual communion of these infrequent gatherings. The opening ceremonies, the *United States Catholic Magazine and Monthly Review* noted, were "grand and imposing, beyond anything ever before witnessed in the United States." Sixty priests were in attendance, as well as twenty-three bishops, for a gathering that offered fewer consequential pronouncements than past councils had but made one very important announcement: its intention to petition the Holy See to name the Blessed Virgin Mary the patron saint of the nation, a decision that left Hughes overjoyed. His peers also approved Hughes's request to the pope to deal with the now overextended, overpopulated

New York diocese through the creation of two suffragan sees, centered in Buffalo and Albany. John Timon and John McCloskey would be asked to lead them the following year.

Along with John McCloskey, John Purcell, Francis Kenrick, Michael O'Connor of Pittsburgh, and Martin Spalding of Louisville, Hughes was invited to deliver an address to the assembly. Rare was the occasion now when he was not asked to be one of the principal speakers at any event he attended. It was accepted by this time that he was one of the best orators the Catholic Church had on this side of the Atlantic. It was further agreed by all members of the hierarchy that any mention of the war with Mexico should be avoided, but the council's closing pastoral letter did remind Catholic men that allegiance to the church did not exempt them from a "civil allegiance." Enlisting to fight would be a matter of politics and conscience with which the church would not interfere. The difficult position the American church found itself in during other, later conflicts—the Spanish-American War, Vietnam, Iraq—was presaged by events in the 1840s.

Before the final session, an unexpected missive arrived in Baltimore that was the talk of all the council participants, especially as it was not directed to the bishop of Baltimore. The secretary of state asked if Hughes, along with Bishop Mathias Loras of Dubuque, could come to the capital before they headed home. "I desire to confer with you on public affairs of importance," James Buchanan wrote, "and this will afford me an opportunity of making your personal acquaintance, which I very much desire." (Buchanan did not then recall their earlier meeting near Chambersburg, and there is no reason he should have. Hughes evidently reminded him.) The two prelates left early the next morning. Buchanan met them at the State Department and explained the reason for his cryptic communication.

Worried that the war was going to take on an anti-Catholic character that the administration was eager to avoid, President Polk wanted to talk with one or both of them about the advisability of sending some Catholic chaplains to join Zachary Taylor's troops in the hope that, as U.S. forces penetrated into Mexico with what Americans hoped would be a short and glorious excursion, they could assuage Mexican fears about American intentions. Mexicans were perfectly clear about the most pressing of the invader's intentions—the claiming as spoils of war of California, Baja California, present-day Arizona and New Mexico, and as much of central Mexico as Taylor's troops could take—but Polk did not want anyone to think that the destruction of the Catholic Church in the conquered territory had ever been a part of his thinking when the hostilities commenced. If the people of Mexico thought that, they would fight all the harder and prolong the conflict; if other nations came to that sorry conclusion, what the president saw as a great, divinely inspired cause would be sullied.

Polk was exceedingly nervous about Mexico's priests. Like many American Protestants, he assumed that the Catholic clergy had an unbreakable hold on the faithful and were de facto political leaders of their people. He told Thomas Hart Benton, "If the Catholic priests in Mexico can be satisfied that their churches and religion would be secure, the conquests of the Northern Provinces of Mexico will be easy, and the probability is that the war will be of short duration; but if a contrary opinion prevails, the resistance to our forces will be desperate." He had a proclamation drawn up in Spanish to be distributed throughout Mexico promising its people freedom of religion once U.S. troops had liberated them from the "tyrants" who ruled them.

What happened with Bishop Loras that week is not clear. He may have met with Polk separately as the president also met with Bishop Peter Kenrick (Francis Kenrick's brother) of Saint Louis the following day, but on the evening of May 19, the president met alone with Hughes in his office. It was the New York bishop's first time in the White House. As neither Buchanan nor any other third party was present, the details of the conversation remain conjectural. Hughes informed the president that there would be no problem finding Catholic chaplains to go to the front; he had already spoken to the priests at Georgetown College. The desirability of sending a high-level emissary to Mexico was also discussed. In his diary, Polk said—or implied—that Hughes ("a highly intelligent and agreeable man") had offered his own services for that role. Hughes later dropped hints to confidants that the president had been the one to suggest the possibility of his assuming the part. It could be supposed that the president's view is the accurate one, as he would have no reason to alter the facts in his own diary, though it also had to be said that few occupants of the White House have been more calculating and flexible about veracity than James K. Polk. If the president had made such a suggestion, he had taken leave of his senses. From the other side, it could be argued that the extraordinary compliment the bishop wanted others to know had been extended to him by the chief executive might well have been a self-serving fabrication on Hughes's part. Eighteen years later, ex-president Buchanan would confirm to Hughes's first biographer that the suggestion had been Polk's, not Hughes's. Buchanan's doubtful access to the facts and later close friendship with Hughes do nothing to settle the matter.

It might also be said that if Hughes made the offer, or for a moment actually considered going to Mexico on behalf of his government, he too had taken leave of his senses. A large recruitment rally in New York City that month had led the Irish in the crowd to drown out a speaker with hisses when he imprudently shifted his remarks from the justice of America's expansionist aims to the possibility of leveling "Mexican temples"—by which he did not mean remnants of the Aztecs or the Mayans. And anyone who kept abreast of the publishing world, as Hughes did, was familiar with the trove of books that had appeared over the last three years—from William Prescott's scholarly *History of the Conquest of Mexico* to assorted travelogues and memoirs, some by American diplomats stationed in Mexico—that made, to varying degrees, the same point: America's southern neighbor was a backward, despotic, theocratic society in need of liberation and better government. *Theocratic*, of course, meant *Roman Catholic*. Only the most naïve jingoist could believe that anti-Catholicism didn't play at least a part in the enthusiasm Protestant Americans felt for an assault on Mexico. "One nation is full of Christians, the other is full of Catholics," the *New York Journal of Commerce* summarized the matter. Evangelicals were ecstatic at the thought of the fertile fields that awaited them when the halls of Montezuma fell open to American might.

In any case, the idea of a mission to Mexico City went nowhere. Its only significant result was to make John Hughes feel enormously flattered and important. Hughes stayed in the capital to attend a reception at the White House that night, his presence was duly noted by the press and important Washingtonians, and he returned to New York the following day. Two highly respected Jesuits, John McElroy and Antony Rey of Georgetown College, were eventually dispatched to the front in an unofficial capacity. (McElroy was a particularly pleasing choice to Hughes, as he had been his sister's mentor during her time in the novitiate.) How effective they were meant to be among any Mexican Catholics they encountered is an open question, as McElroy knew no Spanish, and Rey's command of the language was limited. They were just as likely being sent to provide support for American Catholic soldiers, some of whom complained bitterly about being forced to attend Protestant services on the Sabbath; but that was a concern Polk was reluctant to advertise. McElroy came back in one piece and went on to become one of the founders of Boston College; Rey was killed by brigands at the end of the war, his lanced body found in the desert. (McElroy in particular made a favorable impression even among some Protestant soldiers. "If all Catholic priests were like him," one wrote, "there would not be half so much prejudice against Catholicism.")

Leaked word of the meeting between the president and the bishop did neither man any good in the short run. Members of both parties questioned Polk's judgment in seeking the advice of Catholic bishops on any topic whatsoever. The editor of the *Philadelphia Daily Sun*, a nativist congressman who had been a rabble-rouser at the time of the 1844 riots, accused the administration of shamelessly bowing before a foreign power (i.e., the Vatican) and referred to McElroy and Rey as "Mr. Polk's Romish priests." The editor went further and asked if Americans were to cater to Catholic needs at government expense "because a certain Bishop of that Church can influence a certain number of Catholic voters for any party who may choose to purchase them." James Gordon Bennett in the *Herald* accused Hughes of ingratiating himself with the White House as a means to win a cardinal's hat.

In reality, Hughes hadn't thought much of Polk—a pygmy was seated in the presidential chair, he told Thurlow Weed, hinting that it was time to begin grooming their mutual friend—most definitely not a pygmy—for higher office. The only immediate benefit for Hughes was an unanticipated reunion at the State Department with the man whose carriage he had helped to carry across a rock-strewn stretch of a Pennsylvania turnpike in 1818. Buchanan marked Hughes as worth knowing better.

It was a whirligig moment in politics on both continents, to be sure. The death of the reactionary Gregory XVI a month after the Baltimore Council and the surprise elevation of a liberal cardinal, Giovanni Maria Mastai-Ferretti, to the papacy, as Pius IX, stunned the West, alarming conservatives like Metternich but allowing progressive people of all faiths to think hopefully about the church for the first time. Mastai-Ferretti was known to oppose the Austrian military presence on the peninsula and to see no need for the aggressive police state his predecessor had relied on. When he amnestied more than a thousand political prisoners and exiles in his first month in office, relaxed censorship of the press, and abolished Leo XII's anti-Semitic edicts, Pius IX became the most popular man in Italy and the subject of lavish praise in the United States.

Several months later an interdenominational celebration was held in New York City in honor of the pope—about as unimaginable a concept as Catholics in the city could ever have entertained—at which the mayor and numerous dignitaries, including Horace Greeley, Whig editor of the *New York Tribune*, spoke warmly about the new occupant of Peter's throne. Letters of encouragement were read to the crowd from Vice President George Dallas, Secretary of State James Buchanan, former president Martin Van Buren, and Senator Thomas Hart Benton. Polk remained silent. Hughes attended the New York fete, optimistic about a relationship with Greeley, who was becoming a name in Manhattan circles. Hughes's hopeful frame of mind about the powerful editor of the *Tribune* lasted about as long as Pius IX's liberalism.

There was a desperate need of any occasion for good fellowship between native-born Americans, especially Protestant New Yorkers, and Catholic immigrants, as a crisis, unexpected and unprecedented, was unfolding that year. The predictions of Harley and McGee about the potato blight had proved them less than prescient. The 1846 harvest of potatoes had been only 20 percent of the accustomed level, a devastating loss for the masses of subsistence farmers for whom potatoes were their main, or often only, source of food. The blight abated for a time in 1847 but returned thereafter with renewed virulence. A Cork landlord, only one of many, reported with astonishment and horror the cabins on his estate now populated by "famished and ghastly skeletons," the children with bloated bellies, the parents fever-wracked and waiting for death. The first news reports of the reality of the famine had seemed too horrendous to be credible, but then the evidence began to turn up on the city's docks. The "Irish hemorrhage" started in earnest in the first months of 1847. The resulting stigmatization would quickly make "Irish Catholic," more so than ever before, bywords for *dirty, dangerous,* and *socially destructive.*

In 1847, the number of Irish immigrants arriving at the port of New York doubled from its yearly average in the earlier part of the decade, climbing to almost 53,000. The next year, just over 90,000 desperate travelers poured off the ships. (The number nationwide was 151,000.) Almost 113,000 people landed in New York in 1849. These were unfathomable, unnerving immigration statistics to longtime residents of the city, proper cause for panic, as many of the new arrivals looked like nothing New Yorkers had ever seen before—wasted, ill-clothed, numb with grief, dazed by their horrendous experience on the water. They had been "stowed away like bales of cotton," as Herman Melville described their plight in *Redburn* (1849), living for weeks in what smelled like an "open cesspool [and] abused by the seamen and cuffed by the officers" when they came up for air and dared approach too near to the space reserved for the first-class passengers. Complicating a dire situation, many of these people were unskilled and so not immediately employable, a large number spoke only Irish, and almost all were completely unused to urban life.

Between 1847 and 1851, 850,000 Irish men, women, and children left Europe rather than die on what remained of their tenant farmland. Even if the estimate is accurate that 55 percent of these people eventually left New York to make a new life elsewhere in smaller cities, villages, and in the countryside, by 1860 there were more Irish-born people living in New York City than lived in Dublin, Cork, or Belfast. No aspect of New York would be, or could be, the same ever again, given the transformation these numbers would effect.

"My feelings, my habits, my thoughts," Hughes noted to an aide, "have been so much identified with all that is American that I have almost forgotten that I am a foreigner." The Great Famine brought him back to a consideration of his origins, and the sight of disembarking survivors of the so-called "coffin ships" and their stories of evictions at home by "crowbar brigades," workhouses filled to capacity, coffin shortages, skeletal remains of relatives left unburied, and British inaction struck him "as a great personal grief." In February 1847 he had ordered a collection taken up in all the churches of the diocese for his new seminary. Now he announced that the $14,000 would have to be diverted. "It is better that seminaries should be suspended," he declared, "than that so large a portion of our fellow-beings should be exposed to death by starvation." He sent the money to relief agencies run by the church in Ireland.

Correspondents in Ireland confirmed that a tragedy of awesome magnitude was upon them. Edward McGinn, the bishop of Derry, a strong nationalist priest and a compassionate man whom Hughes had met on his trip with John Harley, wanted him to know that no exaggeration was involved in any reports he might be hearing: "We never had, not even in the days of persecution, anything to equal the distress of the present season. In every hamlet, in every village, our poor people are starving. . . . The most clear-sighted cannot see their way through this calamity. . . . The government and aristocracy are perfectly confounded and running in their bewilderment from one remedy to another as if they were demented. . . . What they have been doing hitherto must tend to aggravate rather than diminish the calamity. Disease and death have, in a hundred shapes, set in, and our poor clergy can scarcely attend the living or bury the dead." Whenever he was able, Hughes sent money of his own to Bishop McGinn to distribute as he thought best.

The month after sending his seminary collection abroad, Hughes gave an angry lecture at the Broadway Tabernacle on the subject of the famine. His purpose was to raise money for relief aid and to hammer away at Britain's history of exploitation of its colonized neighbor and indifference to Irish suffering. His theme: We should not be asking "Why has God allowed this to happen?" (a question he considered blasphemous), but "Why has man allowed this to happen?" and, in particular, why is Her Majesty's government doing so little in the face of what would become 1,000,000 deaths and 2,000,000 people in forced exile out of a population of 8,200,000? He acknowledged that some would want to single out the rapacity of landowners as the primary cause and others would focus on Irish indolence and a foolish reliance on one crop for subsistence, but he wanted his listeners to think about what government was becoming in their time. Society had organized itself into sovereign states "to accomplish the welfare of all its members," a goal endorsed by Christianity. "The system which now prevails," he believed, "has lost sight of [that premise], to a great extent. It is called the free system—the system of competition," and it accepts that some will be forever safe from want and others will live like beasts of burden. This was not an acceptable philosophy. Great Britain's failure to do more in a time of crisis was a religious as well as a political indictment of the empire.

From their very different angle, American relief efforts were not able to handle the crisis in their own streets much more effectively, and slums that had looked scarcely livable in the 1830s spread out and took on the quality of habitations of hell. Concerned about the likelihood of immigrant girls turning en masse to prostitution, the Sisters of Mercy opened a refuge for indigent Irish immigrant women in 1848 on the corner of Houston and Mulberry Streets, a venture Hughes applauded and raised funds for, but he and the good sisters were well aware that efforts like these were going to make only the smallest difference. Police precinct houses had to open their doors as nighttime homeless shelters. Clothing drives were organized at churches to keep the new arrivals, some of whom had arrived in rags, decently attired on the streets. Emigrant aid societies were overwhelmed, and street crime rose precipitously. Some of the new arrivals moved north of the city limits, to what is today Central Park and the Upper West Side, to build shanties, scavenge for food, and look for day labor as best they could. Predictably enough, compassion vied with anger among longtime New Yorkers. Native artisans held mass meetings to demand restrictions on this influx of "pauper labor" that was undercutting them at every turn.

Most of the very poorest of the Irish did not, of course, make it out of Ireland. Passage in steerage could cost as much as 5 pounds, and to them that might as well have been 500 pounds. Many of these people could only hope to make it across the Irish Sea, going the other way on cattle and coal barges, to find a place for themselves in the slums of Liverpool, Glasgow, or London. The mix of those who were now, theoretically at least, John Hughes's concern ran a gamut at one end from battered souls who would be dead within a few months of arrival, to those who would survive by crime or the lowest forms of labor, never become literate, never see their way out of their anguish and alcoholism. These were not, it goes without saying, churchgoing people. But the boats also disgorged huge numbers who represented every minute gradation on the social spectrum: out-of-work laborers, servants, craftsmen, clerks, schoolmasters, shopkeepers. Some were devout Catholics, some were antagonistic or indifferent to religion, and some had experience and ideas about the church that were as hazy and undeveloped as their ideas about citizenship and ethnic identity.

A catastrophe on this scale was nothing that any individual or group, however well meaning, could have coped with in a transformative way. The American government, firmly committed to a laissez-faire approach to economics, rejected the idea of federal aid and urged private and religious charities to do their best. When a bill was debated in Congress concerning aid sent directly to Ireland, President Polk let it be known that he would veto it if it came before him. The modestly hopeful—or at least less despairing—reactions to the crisis, then, had to come from the people themselves. A group in need that attempts to look out for itself becomes a group with a more cohesive identity, and Hughes hoped that development would be one outcome of the horror they were living through. Every bit of succor we can offer our suffering compatriots, he reminded his flock, had the potential to make better Catholics and better Americans out of the new arrivals. True, many middle-class and wealthy Irish Americans wanted to pretend they had nothing in common with what the coffin ships were bringing to their shores—a perfectly plausible response—but Hughes kept his eye on the decades ahead, certain that poverty and alienation from the church were not the unchangeable fate of the Irish in America. A crisis can call forth a sense of a solidarity that was not as deeply felt before that crisis began. A crisis can call forth a differently imagined future.

A vibrant Irish press could also help to counsel against despair. Some of the new papers that tried to participate in such an effort barely got off the ground. The *Irish Advocate* "made two questionable appearances and vamoosed," a competitor noted. The *Irish-American*, however, started by an immigrant of energy, determination, and a wisely diplomatic nature, Patrick Lynch, found an audience rather quickly and became the most influential Irish paper in the city. Lynch's acumen was evident, in part, in his pricing of his paper at two cents a copy and his ability to stay on the good side of the bishop. He produced a better publication than the *Freeman's Journal*, and within a few years could boast a healthy circulation, for an ethnic paper, of twenty thousand readers.

The paper explicitly stated its intention to defend and vindicate "the interests of the Irish American and American Irish race," dwelling not only on its problems but "statistical proof of [its] numerical strength, property, station, influence, genius, military prowess, eloquence, literary ability and statesmanship." Lynch also helped to fashion an Irish version of what would later be called a Horatio Alger mythology, something Hughes agreed was much needed by a people so disdained. In the late 1840s and early 1850s, Catholic friends and associates of the bishop's like Charles O'Conor, Felix Ingoldsby, and John McKeon were frequently written about as useful reminders that plenty of Irish immigrants before the current arrivals had started at the bottom and worked their way to positions they might not have attained back in Europe. O'Conor's name was constantly in the news—he had one of the most successful legal practices and commanding public personalities in the state and served on countless political and charitable committees—while Ingoldsby was touted as the kind of successful merchant all right-thinking men would want to be: wealthy, reliable, approachable, civic-minded. When John McKeon was named New York County's district attorney, the *Irish-American* singled him out as the perfect role model: "Young countrymen from Ireland! And you! Sons and daughters of the Irish stock! Study the character of John McKeon. *What he was, you are;—what he is, any of you may be.* Be honest, faithful, industrious, and energetic, and the highest honors in the land are open to you."

The best story of all, though, was that of the ditchdigger from County Tyrone who walked with presidents and popes, who protected the city's churches from harm and never backed down from a fight. It was an image John Hughes knew, now, he had been right to cultivate.

8

A WIDENING STAGE

FAME BROUGHT ITS own gratification, of a kind that even a humbler man might have found hard to resist. In 1847, a rather breathless British travel writer, a Protestant named Susan Minton Maury, published her *Statesmen of America in 1846* and was sufficiently impressed (not to say awed) by John Hughes to devote twenty-five pages of her book—more space, in fact, than she gave to Daniel Webster, Chief Justice Taney, William Seward, or Martin Van Buren—to someone she described as "the historical man of the day" and the most impressive cleric in America. With his name appearing regularly in national newspapers, Hughes was certainly the most talked-about clergyman in the country.

Politicians took notice. Twenty senators and thirty-three congressmen invited the bishop that December to speak before Congress, an invitation that had been offered only once before to a Catholic prelate, to John England in 1826. Among those who signed the invitation were John Quincy Adams, John C. Calhoun, Lewis Cass, David Wilmot, Stephen Douglas, and Thomas Hart Benton, as well as the Speaker of the House, Robert Winthrop. "I do not feel at liberty to decline a compliment," Hughes answered, "with a wish so kindly expressed on your part and so flattering to me." His now-closest friend among the episcopate, William Walsh of Halifax, was visiting New York at that time and accompanied him to the capital.

The invitation—like the jubilation that greeted Pius IX's ascension— suggested that times might be changing; more than a few of those men, including the ailing former president and Massachusetts representative, were known to have made anti-Catholic remarks in the past, some of which had been reprinted in the *Freeman's Journal*. But James Gordon Bennett saw a subject of more mirth than gravity in Irish New York's spiritual leader luxuriating in that "menagerie of politicians and roguery" such as Washington, D.C., offered. "If he preaches there," the *Herald* publisher declared, "it cannot be with the hope of saving many of the sinners in that department of human life. Bishop Hughes must know the value of a politician's soul too well to think it worth saving at all."

Others suspected an ulterior motive that had little to do with saving sinners. Hughes's meeting with President Polk several months earlier still rankled in more extreme nativist circles. Rumors made the rounds of the capital that the administration was considering replacing Nicholas Trist, the peace negotiator in Mexico the president was openly unhappy about, with John Hughes—as bizarre a notion as it was baseless. Other rumormongers took a different tack, suggesting that Hughes was in town to plead his case to be named American minister to Rome. As usual, Hughes paid no attention to personal innuendoes in the pages of the Whig *National Intelligencer* or, back in New York, the *Herald*. Better-informed sources would have known that the Polk-Hughes relationship had run aground that summer when the administration's paper, the *Washington Daily Union*, had published a crude attack on the Mexican Catholic Church, later retracted, and the infuriated bishop had warned the president that it would be a serious mistake for the Democratic Party to take the Catholic vote for granted.

Despite inclement weather, the floor and gallery of the House were filled with a standing-room-only crowd when the bishop took to the podium on December 12 and observed in his audience not only the noted men who had invited him but such equally prominent figures as the great orator Daniel Webster. The new Whig congressman from Illinois, Abraham Lincoln, might have been in attendance as well; he had arrived to take his back-row seat in the House ten days before and would make his own first remarks in the same chamber ten days later. It was a shining moment for John Hughes. Exactly thirty years earlier, a poor immigrant had disembarked to begin a new life not so many miles from the capital. Now, for two hours, he had the ear of many of the country's leading figures.

For this occasion, Hughes knew enough to avoid remarks that could give offense to any group and to avoid any mention whatsoever of Mexico or the famine exodus. Not surprisingly, then, "Christianity: The Only Source of Moral, Social and Political Regeneration" pleased everybody—except, of course, Jewish and Protestant evangelical readers and those nativist legislators appalled at the lack of judgment the leadership had shown in letting a Catholic priest address Congress in the first place.

The most intelligently calculated element of the address was the honor it accorded to the United States as the first true republic in the world. As concerns grew that these unwashed immigrants pouring into the harbors along the East Coast were, by virtue of their intolerant religion and blind obedience to their priests, going to make poor citizens, inappreciative of the kind of culture they were now a part of, Hughes unreservedly embraced the characterization of America as the exceptional land that its founders and the current members of its national legislature believed it to be. All the more reason, he noted, for its lawmakers to be godly men with caring hearts and its voters to believe that they, too, must answer to God for the purity of their motives and their concern for the common good, even in the casting of their ballots. He concluded with a comparison of George Washington and Napoleon as the exemplars of two differing views on the exercise of power: the one self-sacrificing and thoroughly Christian; the other, imperial and self-aggrandizing. Stephen Douglas, for one, was particularly impressed, and he wrote to a friend a few years later that he entertained "a very high admiration for the character of the bishop" and would be glad to let anyone know that. Correspondents as far away as Ireland read of the speech and sent their plaudits.

Numerous invitations to speak came in in the wake of his address to Congress, some even from Protestant organizations. The New England Society asked the bishop to lecture at its annual dinner commemorating the Pilgrims' landing—an odd occasion, perhaps, for a man who regarded the Puritans as anything but praiseworthy or theologically sound. One member of the society who had opposed the invitation noted that the Winthrops and the Bradfords would be turning in their graves at the thought of their descendants toasting a representative of "the Whore of Babylon" and then raising their glasses to the pope himself. Even Hughes felt the pleasing strangeness of the evening. "Were I to give way to my feelings," he told William Cullen Bryant, seated next to him at dinner, "I should almost doubt the reality of things around me, or question my own personal identity."

Nonetheless, there were moments when the old barbs were still being thrown his way, when editors delighted in getting his goat. The *New York Observer*'s anonymous religious columnist, who signed himself "Kirwin," began a series of articles several weeks after Hughes spoke to Congress that took aim at the superstitious nature of Catholicism and questioned whether a man as smart as John Hughes, an "intellectual pugilist," could actually believe many of his church's more far-fetched teachings. The paper gave the articles the appearance of a debate being conducted in public by attaching excerpts from Hughes's past speeches as responses to Kirwin's assertions, giving the impression that the bishop was actually engaging in a contemporaneous rebuttal of the charges. Sensing a market for his ruse, the columnist saw to it that *Kirwin's Letters to Bishop Hughes* eventually made it into book form. Hughes held fire until Kirwin finally stepped forward and identified himself as Nicholas Murray, a Presbyterian minister from New Jersey, at which point Hughes published his own series of long-winded and defensive letters in the *Freeman's Journal* under the heading "Kirwin Unmasked."

Hughes would probably have been well-advised to ignore "Kirwin" altogether, but the problem was that his antagonist was not a lone voice of bigotry finding its way into print in the wake of the war. After Santa Anna's defeat, American Catholics had to absorb the disturbing news brought by returning troops of looted churches and convents, priests assaulted, and religious mementos ("Mexican curiosities") taken north by the sackful. They had to listen to journalists, historians, orators, and fiction writers expounding at length on the theme of historical inevitability and the Protestant missionary work that might now commence. Progressive educator Emma Hart Willard published her own history of the war within several months of the signing of the treaty, observing that God had ordained America's armies as the means to end the benighted Mexican enslavement to Rome, paving the way for the good work that tract societies might now accomplish there. (How far the evangelical reach could realistically extend was an unresolved topic of discussion. That the United States had seized only Mexico's northern provinces and not the entire country was a relief to many: there were limits to how many more brown-skinned people and how many more Catholics most

Americans wanted to have to deal with within their borders. Daniel
Webster was particularly concerned with this issue.)

If Hughes ever believed that President Polk's assurances of respect
on the eve of the war would mean something in the field and among the
wider populace, he knew better now. Whig senator John Bell of Tennessee, who wanted to see the wealth of the Mexican church confiscated for
war reparations, taunted Hughes from the floor of Congress in 1848. He
realized that a Democratic president would never agree to his proposal
to seize Catholic property and sarcastically suggested that Hughes and
his pope had managed Polk deftly for their own ends. The opposite, of
course, was true.

Some returning soldiers and officers spoke well of the Irish Catholic
gallantry they had witnessed in battle and did their part in dispelling
stereotypes. An Ohio major, Luther Giddings, was particularly clear
about that in an engrossing 1853 memoir of the war, and Fathers Rey
and McElroy had impressed many with their devotion to the men. Yet
it is doubtful that the events of 1846–1848 did much to improve the lot
of those Hughes thought it would help. The tragedy of the Saint Patrick,
or San Patricio, battalion, made for a particularly depressing coda to
the conflict. The fate of hose soldiers encapsulated everything that was
wrong with Protestant-Catholic and native-immigrant relations in the
United States.

No one has ever determined the exact number with any degree of
accuracy, but well over one hundred and possibly as many as two hundred U.S. soldiers had gone over to the other side, some before war
was formally declared and others after Polk's declaration of war. They
fought especially valiantly in the defense of Mexico City. These men
were almost all recent immigrants, a large number of them Irish Catholic, and their motives were varied. Some refused to stomach any longer
the brazenly anti-Catholic attitudes and actions of their commanders,
and others questioned why they were being sent to kill fellow Catholics
in support of the "madness of [Polk's] plans," as one angry deserter
put it. A few were disgusted by the barbarity of their countrymen once
they crossed the Rio Grande, and others—some hard drinkers among
them—just couldn't take the brutal regimen of army life. The San Patricios fashioned their own green flag as an emblem to fight under, featur-
ing on one side the Harp of Erin and a row of shamrocks and on the
other Saint Patrick and the words "Republica Mexicana." They paid the

predictable price when Mexico City fell and they were captured. Fifty of them were hanged before assembled U.S. troops in the largest mass execution in American history. Others were tortured and branded with a *D* for deserter.

Protestant America had its prejudices confirmed by the San Patricios, and Bishop Hughes could see how little his efforts amounted to in this instance as he sought to align himself, and by extension his fellow Irish Catholics, with the powers-that-be and to prevailing political creeds. Rather, many Americans agreed with Protestant minister Charles Sperry, who, in *The Mysteries of Romanism*, depicted American bishops— Hughes in particular and by name—as foreigners disdainful of American law and American ways.

———

CHANGE, SO MUCH OF IT uncontrollable and most of it unpredictable, was fast becoming the order of the day. The violence that overtook Europe in the "year of revolutions"—1848—demanded any American bishop's attention no less than the war or the famine exodus. When Louis-Philippe was forced to abdicate in February and fled to England, republicans in Europe and the United States hailed the end of the French monarchy; the Catholic hierarchy on both continents was less sanguine, fearing the coup would inaugurate another brutally anticlerical period in France. Simon Bruté had painted a vivid picture for his students of what that could be like. When Metternich fled Vienna and Emperor Ferdinand was forced to abdicate, the cheers in the American press were even louder. The fight of Hungary to break free of Hapsburg rule was a cause dear to the heart of progressive Americans. A new Europe seemed to be in the making almost overnight as Danes forced an end to their absolute monarchy, Germans demanded constitutional rights, Italians rose up against their Austrian overlords, and even in John Hughes's homeland a new group—the Young Ireland movement—announced that the day of Daniel O'Connell's tepid parliamentary efforts to secure freedom from Great Britain belonged to the past, like the great man himself who had died two years earlier, and that the time for more forceful resistance had come.

Hughes had multiple concerns about these developments, even when some of them seemed positive enough at first glance. First, there was the question of their origin in physical violence. Cobblestones torn up, soldiers attacked, and crowds fired upon, houses of authority besieged, civilian martyrs to liberty: these might be images that some could romanticize, but he looked upon them as deeply troubling. New York City was still a tinderbox itself, populated with people too volatile—including many of his coreligionists and fellow Irishmen—for their own good. Men who should know better, like Horace Greeley, acted as if the violence that saw the success of their liberal causes was always justified, even inevitable. (The headlines of Greeley's paper of April 10, which brought the first news to New Yorkers of these developments from Europe, cried out, THE PROGRESS OF FRANCE / GREAT NEWS FROM ITALY / BLOODSHED IN BERLIN.) New Yorkers had fashioned a city grown too accustomed to violence, Hughes insisted. They lived in a time where men could burn down a theater and turn Astor Place into a site of carnage to make a point—a point that cost twenty-five people their lives—about which actor, a native American or a suspect Briton, had the right to play Macbeth before New York audiences. This was not the moment or the place, he felt, to glorify blood in the streets over legislative reform or a Burkean gradualism. The fact that so many of the radical movements in Europe, particularly in Hungary, Austria, Germany, and Italy, were overturned the following year simply confirmed Hughes in his judgment about the mistaken glamour of revolutionary violence.

Then there was the problem of the expectations that were raised by a rapid rearrangement of the social and political terms men had long lived under. In Italy, this issue was especially evident with the tenuous position Pius IX had been placed in. When the movement to unite the peninsula under republican rule began, many Italians assumed the new liberal pope would give his sanction to raising arms against Austria, which occupied large sections of the peninsula in the north and the south. Though privately pleased when it seemed as if the Austrians might be dislodged from Italy in a timely way and with minimal bloodshed and willing initially to commit a small number of his troops to the cause, Pius quickly concluded that events were spiraling out of control. He was horror-struck at what the ravages of a full-scale war in Italy would unleash and let it be known he could not countenance a nationalist attack against a fellow Catholic nation. He scorned the politicians' talk of a "holy war." The nature and extent of his progressivism had been misread. Thus, to republicans, the papal hero became a papal traitor in the space of a few days—in both Italy and in the United States. When one of his chief ministers was stabbed to death in the fall, and the Swiss Guards were finding it harder each day to restrain the discontented crowds outside the Quirinal Palace, Pius decided Rome was no longer safe for him and fled in disguise to Gaeta in Neapolitan territory controlled by Austria. Giuseppe Mazzini arrived in Rome, a republican government was proclaimed, and once again, echoing events of the Napoleonic years, a pope was in exile.

To someone intent on binding men and women to a view of the church as the bedrock of a sane life, as a source of allegiance deeper than all others, this was a calamitous development. Hughes's goal of fostering civic, ethnic, national, and religious pride was going to lose one—for him, the most crucial—of its four pillars if, for the second time in fifty years, a pope could no longer occupy the center of Christendom without fearing for his life. Hughes took to the pulpit and the lecture platform to raise money for Pius, now cut off from most of his revenues. Greeley complained that this fund-raising was playing into the hands of the Austrians, as the collected funds would go to bolster the antirepublican cause. There was even some discussion among American bishops of inviting Pius to seek asylum in the United States.

An Italy without the pope was almost impossible to contemplate. Unnaturally raised political expectations had the potential, then, to cause the greatest harm of all in the eyes of a Catholic bishop—an alienation from one's faith. It was bad enough when this occurred among Italians, Hughes felt, but even worse when it transpired among "his people," the Irish. The men of the Young Ireland movement were idealists who led the least formidable of that year's uprisings. Some accounts of this momentous year in European history don't even mention their efforts, for a plausible reason. The Irish "1848" moment was a debacle and a humiliation. And when it was all over, some of the participants wanted to lay the blame for their defeat on Ireland's Catholic clergy. They seemed to be suggesting that the Irish would be better off without their priests, that the church stood for passivity and opposition to change. This sentiment Hughes found intolerable.

The Young Ireland leadership was a disparate, fractious group of journalists, poets, politicians, firebrands. Most—Thomas D'Arcy McGee, Thomas Francis Meagher, Richard O'Gorman, Michael Doheny, Joseph Brenan, Thomas Devin Reilly, Charles Gavan Duffy—were Catholic, while some, like William Smith O'Brien and John Mitchel, were

Protestant. What they had in common, inspired by developments in France, was a sense that their time had come. Unfortunately, they had a poor grasp of timing and seriously underestimated the willingness of a famine-stunted population to see 1848 as the year in which to take on the might of the British Empire. Their moment of defiant confrontation, such as it was, took place in midsummer in the tiny village of Ballingarry in Tipperary, where the Irish constabulary was attempting to arrest one of the group's leaders. Young Ireland men showed up ready to prevent that. The group envisioned an uprising across the island when the people heard of their eagerness to fight back. Nothing of the kind happened.

The "battleground" was the house and backyard garden of a local widow where the constables initially took cover and then emerged to subdue an outnumbered band of armed rebels without much difficulty. British troops hadn't even needed to be called in. The ignominy of the situation was impossible to deny. Parisians had brought life to a halt in their capital and sent a king packing; Irishmen had been vanquished by forty-odd paramilitary volunteers in Widow McCormack's cabbage patch. "Every Irishman from Maine to Texas who has taken the slightest interest in the cause," Hughes complained when he read of the pathetic rout at Ballingarry, "must blush and hang down his head for shame." The press on both sides of the Atlantic agreed.

Adding fuel to the anger Hughes felt was the fact that he had attended, in company with Horace Greeley, a rally that summer at the Vauxhall Gardens in Manhattan where he delivered a rousing speech on behalf of the growing opposition to the Crown, expressed the hope that Ireland would not wait much longer to enjoy its freedom as a sovereign nation, and contributed $500 of his own money to be sent abroad to the movement's organizers. On a visit to New Orleans to see his old friend Bishop Blanc the next month, he participated in a rally that raised $6,000. He knew that Bennett and other editors would never let him forget that summer of excitability and gullibility—and he was correct. Now he urged his parishioners to withhold money from Irish political groups and not to attend any more rallies until saner, more intelligent men were leading a movement with a better grasp of reality. Enough damage had been done by a wild-eyed "set of Gasconaders." He tried to get his $500 back and have the money sent to the Sisters of Mercy in Dublin.

Then the gasconaders started arriving in New York—Thomas D'Arcy McGee in the fall of 1848; Michael Doheny and Joseph Brenan in 1849;

Thomas Francis Meagher and John Mitchel later after they had been tried and exiled and escaped from their confinement on Tasmania. They arrived ready to put their extensive journalistic expertise to good use and—McGee especially—didn't give much thought to which opinions it might be wise to air and which to hold back. Within weeks of landing in the city, McGee found some backers and brought out the first number of the *Nation*, a paper modeled on a Dublin version with the same name. Then he started slashing away. One target was the clergy at home who had failed to rally round the Young Ireland banner. "The present generation of Irish Priests," he wrote in a January 1849 editorial, "have systematically squeezed the spirit of resistance out of the hearts of the people." All things considered, that was one opinion worth holding back.

In a series of letters published in the *Freeman's Journal* beginning the next week, Hughes responded to McGee's accusations. Rather than publishing under his own name, a response he felt might be lacking in dignity, he signed himself simply "An Irish Catholic," but he made sure that McGee was apprised of the identity of his formidable opponent. The Young Ireland crowd knew perfectly well, he asserted, "that the Irish clergy never gave [them] any reason to suppose they would join them." The priests of Ireland "had no more idea of committing themselves and their flocks to the issue of a bloody struggle with the overwhelming power of the British Empire than the people of England had . . . seeing, as they must have seen, the certain and inevitable consequences of a movement so nobly conceived but so miserably conducted." Weak men looked for scapegoats. Boys playing at soldier caused irreparable harm to serious causes. Any man who tried to lure good people away from their faith, as if deserting the Catholic Church could actually help pave the way for an independent Ireland, was not to be trusted. He also charged McGee and his crowd with having kept the Catholic clergy at a distance from their activities when it suited them in the hopes of gaining Protestant followers. McGee was no better than "the cutthroats who had expelled the Pope from his capital."

In February, a nervous McGee tried to make amends. He assured the bishop that he was a loyal son of the church and that his political and spiritual beliefs were entirely separate, and he promised to temper his remarks. He beseeched Hughes to stop the onslaught of bad press. Peace of a kind reigned for a few months, until McGee found it impossible to refrain from writing what he truly believed. After learning that many Irish bishops were planning to participate in the official welcome to Queen Victoria on her visit to Ireland, he described them in the *Nation* as "vermin engendered by bad blood and beggary." When he didn't back down a second time, Hughes went after the paper more directly, denouncing it from the pulpit as an infidel publication and instructing his clergymen to make sure that no one in their parish subscribed. He hit his mark. Readership dropped off by the week. Early the next year, the *Nation* folded and McGee left for Boston, where he made a second short-lived foray into American journalism with the *American Celt*.

Hughes wasn't the only man in New York glad to see McGee depart for another state. McGee's relations with other Young Ireland exiles, always a contentious bunch, had soured and even turned violent. Some found his anticlericalism unseemly and counterproductive, while others thought him too moderate in his Fenianism, too critical now of how the movement had botched its attempt at rebellion the previous summer. Michael Doheny, one of the most militant of the group, encountered him on the street one day and pushed him down a flight of stairs into a building's cellar. McGee took him to court. Joseph Brenan challenged him to a duel. McGee took to carrying a gun.

Daniel O'Connell had been a Gulliver, Hughes mourned, misguided though his abolitionist sympathies were. The Young Ireland men were Lilliputians. And, worse, Lilliputians who squabbled among themselves and did it in public, the last thing an Irish-wary city needed to see. He warned the Irish of New York to steer clear of them.

If Hughes's best efforts couldn't stop McGee from being himself, he did manage to make some of the other exiles think twice about following in McGee's footsteps. When Michael Doheny arrived in the United States, he was similarly vocal in his anger at the clergy of Ireland for not urging their parishioners to take a stand against the British until he saw the reach of Hughes's influence. "He was at first red hot about the priests," fellow nationalist Charles Hart wrote in his diary about Doheny, "and when he heard the sort of fix in which McGee then was owing to his contest with the bishop, [he] changed his tune." Yet Hughes's powers of intimidation extended only so far. Invited to a dinner party at the episcopal residence whose guests included Hart and Orestes Brownson, Doheny "arrived quite tipsy" and acted, Hart said, "in a very disgusting manner . . . treating the Bishop with a rude and vulgar familiarity." These Irishmen, Hughes realized, were not an easy bunch to tame.

John Hughes's life story is peopled with individuals who should have been his soul mates in a common struggle but, as a result of circumstances and timing, were not. Thomas D'Arcy McGee is potentially one of these. A prodigy of energy and nerve, he had come to the United States for the first time in 1844, for a year, to edit the *Boston Pilot* at the age of nineteen. Hughes read his columns and, in 1845, had favorably reviewed McGee's book *O'Connell and His Friends*. He might well have had hopes for a young Irishman of such fertile intellect, impressive literary and oratorical skills, and right-thinking opinions, which included a hatred of anything British and a skeptical view of unbridled capitalism. The two loved acidic language, hyperbole, unpopular causes. They even shared the same feelings about the new practice of celebrating Saint Patrick's Day. A day named after a saint that involved no religious observances but plenty of fighting, drinking, promenading, and "frothy orations" did nothing, McGee had argued in 1845, to help the reputation of Irish immigrants. Unlike Hughes, who was in a far less advantageous position to do so, McGee was willing to take Americans of Irish descent to task, often in blistering language, for their parochialism, ward-boss politics, anti-intellectualism, and indifference to education, hygiene, and middle-class decorum. Advancement, he insisted, meant putting aside a victim mentality and cultivating self-scrutiny and self-improvement. Here was a man after an Irish bishop's heart. By 1848, though, McGee was in a different place in his thinking on many issues. He was back in Ireland and had become more politicized and more radicalized. He didn't want to wax ecstatic about Daniel O'Connell anymore, and he was impatient with his countrymen who weren't ready to stand up to their British masters. Then came Ballingarry and his flight to the New World.

The antipathy between Hughes and the Young Ireland men had a profoundly ironic dimension to it in that both sides agreed on one important idea that Hughes felt should be reiterated as often as possible: namely, the validity of what the twentieth century would term a hyphenated identity.

Hughes wanted the Irish immigrant to see himself as an American with all the rights and the respect for his country's past and its potential that any native-born citizen experienced. But, at the same time, he saw nothing meritorious in any immigrant's desire to play down his Irish origins, his interest in the fate of Ireland, his love of Ireland. Irish Americans, he hoped, would form a new social/political entity in the West, and their vitality, their passion and energy, would benefit both the United States and Ireland. McGee, Meagher, Mitchel, O'Gorman, et al. would not have disagreed. In fact, in 1851, when McGee published his immensely popular *History of the Irish Settlers in North America*, the first book to be written about the Irish in the United States, he went beyond Hughes in his propagandizing on the point, producing what his best biographer called "a masterpiece of myth-making, which could easily have been entitled How the Irish Saved North American Civilization." Though the book covered its topic to the year 1850, McGee made sure to mention Hughes only in passing.

McGee's Boston paper, the *American Celt*, was likewise intended as an explicit attack on the alleged purity of the country's Anglo-Saxon roots. "In choosing the name this paper bears," he wrote, "we mean to adopt the opposite side of a popular theory, namely: that all modern civilization and intelligence—whatever is best and most vital in modern society, came in with the Saxons or the Anglo-Saxons. . . . When the 'Anglo-Saxons' cease to claim America as their exclusive work and inheritance, we will cease using the term 'Celt'—but not sooner." Thomas Francis Meagher echoed McGee: it was the Celts' "democratic antipathies . . . against the Gothic, brutish George III [which] produced the American Revolution." Nativism, John Mitchel likewise affirmed, wanted to deny the fact that "a variety of hardy races and diverse faiths" had built the real America. Like Hughes, Mitchel saw the charge that the Irish could not function in a democracy as ludicrous: "There is no section of the foreign population," he wrote, "who so truly appreciate Republican institutions as the Irish." Young Irelander Richard O'Gorman threw himself into New York electoral politics and Catholic charities.

Life in another hemisphere eventually led these young men down very different paths. Meagher, once he had renounced his erring ways, became quite friendly with Hughes and went on to become a brigadier general in the Civil War and the acting governor of the Montana Territory, where he hoped to found a New Ireland and died under mysterious circumstances in 1867. Mitchel, who had moved to Tennessee and then Virginia, became an outspoken defender of slavery and sided with the Confederacy. Hughes thought him a contemptible man. O'Gorman became a Tammany judge and Boss Tweed crony; Brenan, a New Orleans newspaper editor. McGee left the United States for Canada before the Civil War and became one of the founders of the Canadian Confederation. A member of the Canadian Parliament, he was assassinated in 1868 at the age of forty-three and is a prominent name in the history of Irish Canadian politics. Hughes's regard for these men and their colleagues was always conditional, dependent on whether or not they were eventually willing to stop criticizing the clergy and accept, if they were true Catholics, the embrace of the church.

Yet even after McGee experienced a change of heart and became a few years later an ultramontane Catholic and staunch spokesman for parochial-school education, he and Hughes maintained an on-and-off relationship, sometimes admiring and more often wary. The warmth Hughes came to feel for Meagher, a generous soul, he could never feel for McGee. In 1852, McGee gave up on Boston, too, and relocated to Buffalo, where he tried his luck—not much better—with a different bishop, John Timon.

———

THERE WAS ONE OTHER Irishman whom John Hughes was uneasy about welcoming to America in that same period. Theobald Mathew, who had been promising to bring his temperance crusade to the United States for several years, arrived in New York harbor on July 2, 1849, to be greeted on the dock by the Whig mayor, Caleb Woodhull, and a crowd of dignitaries and reporters. The bishop made sure he was at the head of the line, next to the mayor. Mathew had been through tough times since Hughes first met him in Ireland in 1840. Caught in two vicious crossfires, he had been the subject of attacks from the hierarchy in Ireland (though not from Rome) for his too-friendly relations with Protestants whom he sought to bring to teetotalism and from the O'Connell crowd who, before and after the Liberator's death, had found the friar annoyingly unwilling to link his cause to Irish independence or any other anti-British political action. Mired in debt, he had been arrested when he couldn't pay his creditors, and he was counting on a grand tour of the North and South to bring hundreds of thousands to take the pledge, while raising enough money to keep his movement afloat and himself out of jail. He hoped he would then be in a position to reject the modest 300 pound annual pension the British government had awarded him for his efforts, for which he was scorned in his homeland.

Hughes shared the concern that Mathew was being turned into a pawn of Protestant forces. The vindictiveness of the Irish bishops, some of whom had not allowed Mathew to speak in their dioceses and had thwarted his attempts to fund-raise, was not something he approved of, however. It was absurd to think that the man's program was anything other than desperately needed. Irish drinking—drinking, period—was out of control in the United States in the 1840s. What he was not going to put up with was watching Mayor Woodhull and Protestant temperance activists co-opt the national guest, determine his itinerary, and claim the lion's share of the press. He told Archbishop Eccleston of Baltimore in no uncertain terms that he would take charge of that situation and consequently informed Mathew that he had to move out of the suite of rooms he had been given by the city at the plush Irving House hotel and, as a Catholic clergyman, relocate to one of the city's rectories. Thereafter, he was able to make sure that Mathew's appearances about town to numerous Catholic churches, schools, and rallies outnumbered his appearances elsewhere and were on his, Hughes's, arm.

Hughes's writings about temperance are sufficiently thin and limited in number to suggest that this was not a cause about which he felt particularly hopeful at this stage in the history of Irish America. Nor does he seem to have commented on, or been comfortable with, the ambiguities of the temperance movement as it had evolved under Mathew's control. For instance, was support for total abstinence mandatory, or could one pledge to forgo hard liquor while still drinking beer and wine in moderation? That was a question hotly debated at the time.

It is hard to picture Hughes himself doing without the glass of wine he enjoyed at dinner (though his real addiction was to snuff, not alcohol), and his view of human frailty led him to think that asking men to take a vow they could not realistically hope to keep for a lifetime was dangerous when the inevitable backsliding would lead to a complete rejection of sobriety. Similarly, was it necessary to put all Irish and German Catholics who ran pubs and beer gardens out of business even if they were willing to halt the sale of whiskey but continue to sell beer? A secondary consideration was that the ranks of the Democratic Party continued to swell on that basis: it was Whigs, the Democrats charged, not unfairly, who wanted to end immigrant socializing in the public sphere.

Then there was the matter of the pledge itself, about which Mathew refused to be clear-cut. If the pledge was religiously based, a sacred promise made to God, any violation was a sin requiring absolution; if the pledge was meant to be a solemn vow of conscience, it carried a different weight. Nothing about these unresolved complications was pleasing to the New York bishop.

Hughes was also concerned that Mathew was going to be enlisted in the abolitionist cause when he left New York for Boston, and he warned his guest that he needed to be on his guard. The last thing he wanted was a repetition of the Daniel O'Connell situation. Irishmen in the United States would reject Mathew's message out of hand if he became involved in political questions that had nothing to do with alcoholism and temperance. William Lloyd Garrison and Frederick Douglass, two admirers, had both visited Mathew in Ireland and knew he supported their labors. The danger of their influence was real, and in Boston Garrison attempted to get Mathew to attend an abolitionist rally with him and announce his support for emancipation. When he refused, claiming that the slavery of liquor was battle enough for one man, Garrison viciously turned on him in public. Acknowledging in letters home that the abolitionist leader had tried to entrap him, Mathew nonetheless stayed above the fray. Yet that did him no good in the South, where he stopped in almost every state, as southerners who had heard of his earlier association with Garrison and Douglass turned on him from the opposite direction.

In the end, the result of Mathew's long sojourn in the United States, which brought him to twenty-five states, was an estimated half a million men and women inspired to take the pledge, but almost no money raised with which to extricate himself and his movement from serious debt. He visited Hughes again for several days and then left for Cork exhausted, seriously ill, and close to flat broke. The teetotal movement lapsed into a long period of dormancy. And that, John Hughes insisted, was exactly the problem with discussing slavery at all—other issues like Irish independence, temperance, poverty, or religious liberty invariably became lost in the din.

In August, once his harried guest had gone on his way to Boston, Hughes decamped for Saratoga Springs for a much-needed vacation. It was a cholera summer in New York, and the bishop took some criticism for leaving the city, but the illness was abating by the time he left, and, in truth, a man in his position would not have been expected by anyone other than his most determined critics to make the rounds of hospitals during an epidemic. By happenstance, Henry Clay was in Saratoga Springs at the same time and attended the local Catholic church to hear Hughes preach. He had to leave before the end of the sermon, as he was wracked by a "violent pain" that made those in the pews around him in that health-conscious month nervous, but he recovered and sent his apologies to the speaker. Ever grateful for Hughes's kind remarks about him in the past, ever mindful of the harm or the aid Hughes might be capable of in the future, Clay wanted everyone to know his admiration. He of all people recognized a great speaker when he heard one. Even a writer for the *Herald* who was in the audience commented that Hughes's sermon "was one of the most powerful I have ever heard." Bennett's rejoinder to his own reporter: "We fear he has not heard many sermons."

It was a month intended for rest and renewal in a bucolic setting, but it was also a month in which there were news stories to digest and decisions to be made. Gold had been discovered in California several months earlier—fantastic lodes, apparently—and that was a topic of conversation on every hotel porch and in every resort dining room. The United States was about to become a great deal richer. The pope was inching closer to accepting the offer of the French government of Louis-Napoleon, now in control of Rome, to move back to the Vatican. His Holiness's safety and the future of the papacy and the Papal States were cause for concern to every American priest, and Hughes toyed with the idea of writing further responses to Greeley's stream of sarcastic editorials attacking Pius IX. He also needed to decide if he wanted to conclude a business arrangement concerning the future of the *Freeman's Journal*. A twenty-nine-year-old freelance journalist who had been in New York City only a short time, James McMaster, had expressed an enthusiastic interest in taking the paper off his hands and had purportedly found the financial backing he needed. What Hughes heard about him was mixed, but his choices were limited. He had spent the better part of two years looking for a Catholic buyer, someone theologically and financially sound. In September, when he returned from Saratoga Springs, he signed ownership of the paper over to McMaster.

Whether Hughes knew in handing over control of the paper to his eager young buyer that he would ultimately be relinquishing any editorial influence whatsoever isn't clear, but he must have known James McMaster to be the extraordinarily independent and cocksure individual that he was. Born in Scotland, this son of a classics scholar and stern Scottish Presbyterian minister had been expected to follow in his father's footsteps. In preparation for his ministry, he had been schooled in Latin and Greek from boyhood and, after the family's immigration to the United States, enrolled at Union College in upstate New York. At twenty-five, though, he turned his back on his family's plan and converted to Catholicism. He studied for the priesthood in Belgium but soon enough recognized that his talents lay elsewhere. At twenty-eight, he was ready to launch into big-city journalism in a major way and began writing for various periodicals.

If it is sometimes true that converts can become the most devoted, even rigidly devoted, followers of their new faith, McMaster was the paradigm of that type. Three of his daughters would enter the religious life, to his great joy, and few men of letters were as ready to pledge fealty to Rome as the new owner of the *Freeman's Journal*. The pope was never to be criticized, under any circumstances, and peace was never to be made with erring Protestants. He also had strong opinions about what would ensure a successful weekly publication. Moderation wasn't for those with an eye on circulation. "Nobody who is anybody," he told Orestes Brownson, "likes to miss seeing a paper that presents among its dishes one or two roasts." He thought James Gordon Bennett a disgraceful Catholic but a smart publisher. He would not, of course, come close to equaling Bennett's success, and the subscription base for the paper never topped ten thousand before the Civil War.

McMaster also made it clear early on, though not to Hughes, that he wasn't going to give too much thought to the bishop's opinions about anything. When they were in agreement, all well and good. When not, McMaster said he would be happy to set him right. Or so he blustered at first. He told Brownson that he knew Hughes had choked at handing over the paper to him and that his success would be as galling to the bishop as his failure. "But my course is taken with him," he smugly concluded. "I shall never trust him, never directly oppose him, and suffer him to cease fearing me. . . . I look to weathering a good many storms, and still being the editor when the Bishop shall have entered into his eternal reward."

James McMaster was a man of wildly inflated ego, and, in truth, his paper for much of the time in its first years was nothing over which Hughes needed to lose any sleep. It would be a while before McMaster hit his stride and became as caustic as he thought he was. What Hughes felt in the autumn of 1849 was simple relief at the thought that it was someone else's problem now to figure out how to pay the printer, court advertisers, find capable writers, and meet deadlines.

He was eager to focus attention closer to home when he left Saratoga Springs, and he wasn't in a kindly mood. The German Catholics of the city were agitating for their own cemetery, a proposal he vehemently rejected. Ethnic separatism in life might have to be borne; it was not going to exist in death as well. Bennett was engaged in a renewed attack, defending Thomas D'Arcy McGee and announcing in September that it was time that the "aspiring and ambitious prelate was stopped in his career." Hughes wanted to take a few more whacks at the *Nation*. An officer at West Point had been dismissed from his post for refusing to attend Sunday services at the Protestant chapel, demanding the right to attend a nearby Catholic church, and he asked his bishop to help him in his appeal, even if he had to take it to the White House. The Church of the Transfiguration was again a problem, threatened with the auction block.

In October, Hughes showed up one Sunday evening after vespers at another troubled church, Saint Peter's, and before a congregation that must have been profoundly unnerved by the experience, took to the pulpit and attacked the leadership of their parish in blistering terms. Saint Peter's debts were on the rise again. He was sick to death of hearing about parishes that lived on the brink. Promises had been made to creditors that had not been kept. His patience exhausted, he was ready to lace into those he held responsible—in this case, their eminent pastor, Charles Constantine Pise, and even the recently deceased John Power, one of his own vicars-general. Such a level of mismanagement would no longer be tolerated, Hughes stormed. He told Pise to get rid of his brother-in-law (a vocal Hughes critic), who had been serving as the church's bookkeeper and whom he suspected of malfeasance, and to get the books in order immediately. Pise wrote to John Purcell that the humiliation of this public dressing-down was scarcely endurable. He wanted out of the New York archdiocese. Even when the diocesan lawyers convinced Hughes that he was wrong, that at the very least (while the books were indeed a mess) no financial improprieties had occurred at Saint Peter's, the bishop was willing to retract his insinuations but not to mend fences with Pise, in whom he had lost confidence.

As far as Hughes was concerned, the best way to ensure the success of any endeavor was to see that the person in charge was someone on whom he could rely absolutely, and he was adamant about not wasting time on the well-meaning or the barely competent. Sometimes that

FIGURE 9. *To lead Saint Stephen's Church, the architectural gem of the diocese and the most upscale parish established during Hughes's tenure, Hughes appointed his sometime nemesis, the independent-minded Father Jeremiah Cummings.* (Collection of the Archives of the Archdiocese of New York.)

meant working with people whom he knew he would have a hard time controlling but who seemed specially suited to the task. When he conse-crated Saint Stephen's Church on East Twenty-Seventh Street in Decem-ber (the eleventh parish he had established in Manhattan in a decade and the most beautiful church in the city), he appointed Jeremiah Cummings as its first pastor, a published author, linguist, and man about town who would be a good match for the affluent parishioners of that neigh-borhood. He and Cummings later butted heads over many issues. And sometimes that meant trusting to family. When Saint Vincent's Hospital opened in the fall on East Thirteenth Street, its first director was Ellen Hughes. The dark, ill-heated brick building had no running water, and room in its first few years for only thirty beds and four nuns to minister to the sick, but within twelve months it had served over three hundred largely indigent patients, with no attention paid to race or creed. It rep-resented the start of what Hughes hoped would someday be a citywide system of Catholic hospitals, and he was sure his sister, who had worked in the 1830s as a nurse at a Catholic hospital in Saint Louis, would be the right person to run it.

Saint Vincent's was only one of three hospitals in New York City in 1849, and it was the first Catholic hospital in the city. John Dubois had attempted to open one as early as 1834, but the funds could never be found. In reality, Hughes and his successors had rather little to do with the growth of the hospital system and nothing to do with the manage-ment of the hospitals for a variety of reasons, not least because there was no diocesan money to pay for them. The business of securing a mortgage, staffing, and sustaining the staff at Catholic hospitals, which grew rapidly in number after the Civil War, fell to the religious orders that founded them. Catholic medical care in nineteenth-century Amer-ica is very much a story in which activist nuns deserve the credit, not the hierarchy. It was all the bishop could do to fund-raise for schools, orphanages, and churches. But it is not a coincidence that the first Cath-olic hospital in Manhattan opened with a Hughes at its head. The Sisters of Charity of New York were anything but naïve. They knew that their bishop would not allow the hospital to fail if his own sister was its direc-tor. He knew the approachable donors.

Hughes was delighted to have Ellen assume this new role, relieved that Catholic patients might no longer be forced to go to Bellevue or New York Hospital, where priests were seldom admitted without difficulty (and the sacraments were never administered without opposition), and hopeful that a new model of faith-based care was being offered to the wary Irish or German immigrant. At least as important, Ellen had the same tenacity her brother exhibited when committed to a goal that she believed in. She was also, in a respectful way, willing to lock horns with her brother when she felt she had to, but he was comfortable directing philanthropically minded Catholic businessmen her way as he might not have been with a stranger.

Ellen Hughes was to become a force in New York City Catholicism in her own right. After working for four years under difficult conditions in Saint Louis, she had been transferred to Saint John's Asylum in Utica and in 1846 came to New York to work at the Saint Joseph's Orphan Asylum. Mild-mannered and affectionate, she was "the antithesis of her fiery brother," one historian of the Sisters of Charity noted, but she also knew how to get things done and cared deeply about improving the quality of life for the urban poor.

Sadly, though, Sister Angela and Margaret Rodrigue and her two sons and two daughters were the only members of his family with whom Hughes was still on warm terms. After their father's death more than ten years earlier, his relationship with his brother Michael had become one of a polite distance, and his feelings for Patrick had cooled decisively. To judge from their few remaining letters, John had lent Patrick money, which he couldn't repay, for a property in western New York, and on his rare visits there, John hadn't liked anything his brother had done with the farm. Not surprisingly, he let Patrick know that. "You never came here and said a kind or encouraging word but you took it back before you left," Patrick responded plaintively.

In the summer, while his brother was in Saratoga Springs with Henry Clay, Patrick wrote in the same spirit about a testy missive from New York: "If you thought it necessary to humiliate us, and make us feel how dependent we are, you have done it effectively." His famous sibling had always been "arbitrary and uncivil with [him]," Patrick complained to him in another letter two months later, and the next few years brought no renewal of their childhood bond. Patrick's letters from the 1830s addressed to "my dear brother" from "your affectionate brother" changed in the 1840s to communications of a hurt and more formal tone. In the absence of more letters or other evidence, it is impossible to know who was in the right, if there was a "right," in this painful dynamic—the two men having followed such different paths in life—but it is not surprising that Hughes's closest familial bonds would be with the sister who was devoting her life to the church and the sister who thought her brother one of the great men of the age.

The pace of life for a "great man," or a man irrevocably immersed in public life, and the number of volatile issues that required his attention, just seemed to increase. When he arrived in New York City in 1838, Hughes had imagined that ten or fifteen years hence some amelioration of the deplorable lot that the poorest members of his diocese endured would be evident. The inevitability of progress was, after all, part of the American story. He hadn't reckoned on—no one had reckoned on—the famine, the new immigration numbers, and the ways in which even periods of economic upturn would leave some members of society in ever-worsening straits. It was especially distressing to see how little progress industrious men and women, thrown out of work again and again, were making.

Concern for these problems sometimes forced Hughes to think in more political terms than he wanted to, terms that went beyond which candidate won a given election, and to devote some of his energies to areas of life most Catholic clerics rigorously avoided. In the late 1840s and early 1850s, Hughes was worried that the clergy were too often seen to be on the side of the wealthy. He had no wish to alienate those of his parishioners who wrote the big checks that the diocese desperately needed, but he wanted workingmen to know he stood with them and that the church was not indifferent to temporal pain caused by a defective economic system, even if the church's primary goal was the moral redemption of the individual and his ultimate salvation.

That statement about a Catholic pro-labor stance has to be attended by certain qualifications. Any endorsement of violence or hint of class warfare, any program that smacked of revolution rather than reform, any agitation for the right to strike or to disrupt the social order, Hughes opposed—just as Horace Greeley did. The one progressive, mainstream New York City journalist indisputably on the side of the workingman was no more a firebrand than Hughes. What Greeley was espousing at this stage of his varied career as a social theorist—what Hughes could readily assent to—was a more moderate critique of capitalism, taking aim especially at employers who refused to negotiate with their workers or even consider an eight- or a ten-hour workday and at the land

Figure 10. *Tribune
editor Horace Greeley
was friendly to John
Hughes on the rare
occasions when their
politics overlapped
and abusive in print
when they did not.*
(Courtesy of the
Library of Congress
Print and Photography
Collection.)

monopolies that abounded across the country, the speculative purchas-
ing of thousands of acres by men rich enough to hold on to these properties while they were kept out of the reach of the working-class or yeoman
farmer or rented to them at exorbitant rates. Indeed, the anti-rent / land
reform movement had finally achieved respectability by 1850, and supporters of a Homestead Act were no longer an easily dismissed minority.

A massive Tammany Hall rally in early March 1850 brought together,
in person onstage and by testimony read to the crowd, a range of public
figures who suggested just how broad-based the land-reform movement
had become: they included Whigs Greeley and Seward, Democrats Lewis
Cass, Sam Houston, and Mike Walsh (the former roughhouse Bowery
b'hoy and now a congressman), and the bishop of New York. Resolutions were passed at this rally calling for an end to private ownership of
vast tracts of unused land and the creation of a society "in which every
citizen is a free holder." Rich men should not be allowed to become
richer buying up property as an investment that might lie fallow for
years while poor people willing to work the land did without. Those
were values Hughes was comfortable in supporting, and a letter he wrote

was read aloud to the cheering crowd in which he expressed his concern about where unrestrained class hatred might lead, but he agreed with Greeley that "the public lands, as I take it, belong to all the people of the country, rich or poor." He congratulated the Land Reform Association for its hard work and noted that he saw "great propriety and great advantage in prevent[ing] anything like a monopoly . . . secured by great capitalists for the purposes of present speculation and as the foundation of future social preeminence." The great landowners of Britain and Ireland, passing their vast properties on from generation to generation while tenants eked out a meager living, had no place in the United States.

Yet, allies as they were for this cause, on this one evening, Horace Greeley and John Hughes cannot be characterized as strange bedfellows. They could barely stand each other by this time, and on almost every issue other than the rights of workingmen, their disagreements became more apparent each year. A Protestant who was happy to see the pope's power circumscribed and believed strongly in the public school system, Greeley refused to accept that every editorial in James McMaster's paper wasn't from the hand of the bishop and always suspected that Irish Catholics were at heart unreliable republicans. He began to snipe at Hughes in print, though in a less flamboyant fashion than James Gordon Bennett. In some ways, Greeley was more irksome to him than Bennett precisely because Hughes wanted to respect his idealism and sincerity and appreciated the fact that he was (at this point, anyway) a friend of Seward's, while Bennett was flagrantly an anticlerical caricaturist out to sell papers and a laissez-faire capitalist who evinced no empathy for the downtrodden.

Compensation was to be had for the pressures of office, though, and for the aggressions of men like "Kirwin" and Greeley and Bennett. It was to be found in the adulation he now enjoyed from a rising generation of the faithful who had no memory of the days, or the leadership style, of John Carroll or John Dubois, young people for whom John Hughes was the face of the Catholic Church in America. His files began to fill with letters from people who didn't even live in New York but had heard of his willingness to speak for the faithful and for the immigrant, no matter how vocal or insidious the opposition.

The daughter of the Catholic Ohio senator and current cabinet member Thomas Ewing was one. Ellen Ewing was especially eager to meet Hughes on her honeymoon trip to New York City in May 1850. Though she had married a childhood friend, a Protestant who declined to convert and was skeptical about Catholic clergymen in particular (a matter about which she never ceased to harass him), she was as devout a young woman as any in the country and thought it a great honor to meet the man who so vigorously defended and proudly represented her church. Ellen Ewing and her bridegroom came to the episcopal residence for afternoon tea. Her husband—William Tecumseh Sherman—never comfortable with his wife's paeans to the American priesthood, was probably a little less impressed. Years later, when their only surviving son became a Jesuit, Sherman was distraught. At this point in his married life, though, he knew when to play the dutiful spouse.

9

THE CHURCH MILITANT

WITH JUST CAUSE, the midpoint of the nineteenth century in the United States felt like an apocalyptic moment to many Americans. Jefferson's "fire bell in the night" was no longer a distant threat; the fire was real, and it was near. Violent disagreement in Congress about the status of slavery in the territories acquired from Mexico led to threats of disunion, and President Zachary Taylor made it clear that, at any move in that direction by the fire-eaters of South Carolina or Mississippi or Texas, he would lead an army south himself. Taylor's sudden death in July provoked a wave of more uncertainty and anxiety, eventually quelled by the famous and controversial compromise engineered by Henry Clay and Stephen Douglas. The Civil War was postponed for a decade.

Orestes Brownson spoke for many American Catholics (for once) when he acknowledged slavery to be a regrettable institution but hailed the new law as a bulwark against "destructive fanaticism" and insisted that only a check on free-soil radicalism could "save American society from utter dissolution." In November, Hughes was invited to Washington to meet Taylor's successor, who firmly supported the Compromise of 1850. Millard Fillmore impressed him favorably, and Hughes stayed to dine with the Fillmore family. Fillmore's invitation implies that the new president understood that his well-known antipathy toward Catholics and Irish immigrants, and toward Hughes in particular, might need to be modified now that he occupied the nation's highest office and hoped to obtain support for his administration wherever he could find it.

Compromise in politics was vital, Hughes agreed. He had always been, and always would be, a Clay man at heart. Except to those abolitionists concerned about the fate of America's slaves and outraged at the tightened fugitive slave laws, everything about the Compromise of 1850 encouraged the feeling of a crisis thankfully and narrowly averted. Compromise was the lifeblood of politics. In religious life, however, compromise was a different matter entirely, and with the announcement from the Vatican that fall that he was to be named an archbishop and New York elevated to the status of an archdiocese, with Boston, Burlington, Hartford, Albany, Buffalo, and Newark as suffragan sees under his authority, John Hughes felt the swelling of a great need to make clear just how he and his embattled church felt about the topic. He informed his congregation from the pulpit of Saint Patrick's Cathedral that he would go to Rome to receive his pallium (the insignia of office) personally, and it wasn't long before rumors began to circulate that the Vatican had an even greater honor in mind for the church's most pugnacious representative in the United States. Thus emboldened, Hughes made what for many people, supporters and detractors, was his most memorable sermon, "The Decline of Protestantism and Its Causes."

In some ways, it is unfortunate that this particular address, given before an overflow crowd at the cathedral on the evening of Sunday, November 10, 1850, just after his return from Washington, should be one of the speeches for which John Hughes is best known. It is neither his most carefully written nor his most erudite. It was, however, a forceful statement about spiritual confusion, about a contemporary contest between vigor and desiccation, and what he saw as historical inevitability. For his admiring listeners, he painted a portrait of a religion founded in a spirit of rebellion and negation—the egoism of Henry VIII, Luther, and Calvin—that had divided and subdivided itself past any hope of a unity and clarity such as Catholicism offered, that had rejected the idea of universal authority and so could have no means to correct the errors of its myriad wayward preachers, and whose missionary efforts were notoriously feeble compared to those of the Catholic Church. One encountered far more Protestants in our own era turning toward Rome, he noted, than Catholics turning *from* Rome. And, indeed, this was a fact. Catholic numbers were growing at a formidable rate in the United

States. It would soon be the largest Christian denomination in the country. He imagined for his audience a time—suggesting that it might be as near as the turn of the century—when all that would be left of the Anglican, Presbyterian, Lutheran, Methodist, Baptist, and other false faiths would be "the spectacle of the wreck of what had been Protestantism."

Hughes then wound to what he knew would be his most quoted lines, facing nativist paranoia head-on: "Protestantism pretends to have discovered great secrets. Protestantism startles our eastern borders occasionally on the intention of the Pope with regard to the valley of the Mississippi and dreams that it has made a wonderful discovery. Not at all. Everybody should know it. Everybody should know that we have for our mission *to convert the world*, including the inhabitants of the United States, the people of the cities and the people of the country, the officers of the navy and the marines, commanders of the army, the Legislatures, the Senate, the Cabinet, the President, and all." Conversion, not invasion or subterfuge—conversion by truth and example—was the Roman Catholic goal, and that was a goal mandated by God. He invoked the example of John Henry Newman more than once, the paradigm of possibility for the man of open mind and heart. He asked his listeners to unite in prayer for their "unhappily wandering brethren," the Protestants, and to look forward to the day when they would know "the sweet communion" of the true church, when the combined efforts of the faithful and the returned-to-the-faith could finally see to it that "every species of darkness would have vanished before the approach of the heralds of the Cross."

Unstated, but surely not lost on everyone in the bishop's audience, was the implication that the Catholic Church, like the recently tested federal government, stood for wholeness; Protestantism was a breakaway entity, founded on an act, or various acts, of theological secession, and as such it was an unstable entity, unable to offer the cohesiveness that all rational believers, like all rational citizens, must desire.

Catholics, predictably but not unanimously, applauded the speech. Protestants were dumbstruck by its hubris. Ministers around the country called it inflammatory. A group of Protestant clergymen in Philadelphia elected one of their number to deliver a counterattack in a public address and published the rebuttal, that of a David before the mitred Goliath, as Rev. Joseph Berg put it. In the *Herald*, Bennett went to town: "King Solomon has said that there is a season for everything. History bears him [out]. . . . Barnum from time to time has opened upon us with a black whale, a Fejee mermaid, a Buffalo hunt, Santa Anna's wooden leg, a sickly ourang outang, a spotted negro, a giant or a dwarf . . . a double-headed calf or a pig with five legs. . . . Bishop Hughes has opened the religious campaign of the season with a powerful argument on the 'decline of Protestantism.' . . . There is a season for everything and every season must have its opening."

Rarely had John Hughes shown less concern for the press response to his language or to any of the usual calls for a more moderate tone. He had a point to make, and he made it: let the Protestants stop harping on our "secret" plans to seize control of the nation; our mission is loftier than they imagine, and it is not secret, nor does it involve, except in the overheated imagination of a Lyman Beecher or a Samuel F. B. Morse, "seizing" anything. Let readers take the address as they would. A few days later, he was on a boat for Europe, having insisted that his good friend Terence Donaghoe come all the way from Dubuque—Hughes paid his way—to accompany him. Once again he passed through London, Paris, and Marseille, before arriving, tired but exultant, in the Holy City on Christmas Eve.

Rome was always restorative for Hughes, happily distant from the acrimony of New York. Here was a center of pleasing architecture, great paintings, and committed souls that gave him a much-needed sense of being part of a sacred community, one of "the heralds of the Cross." He joined in the celebrations for the festival of Saint Thomas à Becket held at the English College, was invited to preach at churches in Rome on at least two occasions (once on the martyrdom of the breast-severed Saint Agatha, a particularly vivid subject), and was delighted to note that "The Decline of Protestantism and Its Causes" was being translated into Italian for some of the leading journals. His rooms were constantly crowded, his secretary noted, with dignitaries and clerics who wanted to meet the remarkable man who had the nerve to suggest that America might one day be a nation with Catholic legislators and a Catholic president. With Donaghoe and John Purcell, who had come from Cincinnati to see his friend made an archbishop, he raced about the city to see his favorite sites once again. "His Grace is on the wing," one observer noted.

The ceremony of investiture was performed on April 3, not in the traditional manner, by the cardinal vicar of Rome, but by the pope himself. It was an honor that deeply affected the new archbishop and augmented his already strong attachment to this pontiff. It was a source of relief, too, to see the pope back in his rightful place, looking calm and confident after his exile, though this particular American witness to the defeat of republicanism was not apt to dwell on what other commentators in 1850–1851 regularly noted—namely, a marked sullenness among the male citizenry of Rome. As politically astute as he was, Hughes surely sensed that the pope's continued reign as a temporal ruler of any significant portion of Italy was, in fact, anything but secure.

The most satisfying ending to these four months in Italy, from at least one perspective, should have been a cardinal's hat, the appointment of America's first prince of the church. Why that did not happen may never be fully or completely known, but it would appear that the Vatican took seriously some of the concerns that had made their way to Rome from those who claimed to know Hughes and their country best. On March 15, 1851, Francis Kenrick wrote to his brother Peter, now Bishop of Saint Louis, "It seems established from sources public and private that the Archbishop of New York is to be clothed in the purple: the plan will hardly work out for the good of religion." To Father Tobias Kirby at the Irish College in Rome, he wrote more bluntly two days later and with the expectation that Kirby would see that his sentiments found their way to the right listeners: "I cannot say I am well pleased with the prospect of our having a Cardinal in the U. States, but I suppose all remonstrance is too late. Otherwise I would implore delay." Kenrick also directed Purcell to convey his view to the pope that such an appointment would be "inexpedient." Rumor had it that he wasn't the only American prelate to express reservations that had to do with the possible elevation of John Hughes.

The two ostensible reasons for an informed opposition by the American bishops were timing and nationality: first, that the tense political-religious climate in America was likely to be exacerbated by the news that the pope had named the church's first American cardinal. Nativists would take to the streets again. Second, should the Holy Father feel this move was essential, then a native-born American—Archbishop Samuel Eccleston of Baltimore was mentioned—would make more sense than a naturalized citizen. The ailing Eccleston was a poor red herring; he was dead the following month.

The real reason, of course, as everyone knew, was Hughes himself. Most of his fellow bishops respected him. A few liked him. Bishop

William Walsh of Halifax regarded him as a close friend, and Purcell thought highly of him. But no one wanted to be under his authority, and a fair number of his peers found his overbearing manner and the public persona he cultivated not at all to their taste. The pope remarked to Purcell, who was brave enough to inquire about the situation, that the American government had, in fact, expressed an interest in seeing an American made a cardinal but that the church had a sufficient number of cardinals already and that no vacancy was about to occur, and so the matter was put to rest. Ironically, Hughes was engaged in his own more successful lobbying efforts on this European trip, doing his best to be sure that John Timon of Buffalo was not named to replace Eccleston in Baltimore. Between Timon—a friend of Dubois—and Hughes, no love was lost, ever, and Timon remained in Buffalo.

John Hughes was sorely disappointed not to be returning to the United States as Cardinal Hughes. As the subject had been the talk of Rome for many days, the embarrassment was profound. As Kenrick's reluctant messenger, Purcell felt it his duty to let his friend know what had transpired from that quarter. But to have indicated anything in public other than great pleasure at receiving the pallium of an arch-bishop from the hands of the pope himself would have been a lapse inconceivable to a man of Hughes's beliefs and background. He was only fifty-three, in any case, and the future was wide open. He surely returned to his homeland with a heightened sense of how deeply he had alienated some of the fellow American bishops, for the views of Kenrick and others were an open secret by that time. When it became known that Hughes was leaving Rome without that particular honor, Francis Kenrick's letter to Father Kirby expressed a relief bordering on uncontained joy.

Nonetheless, there was sufficient cause to feel proud and refreshed, and Hughes looked it. The travelers en route home made brief stops in Austria, Germany, Ireland, and England. In London, he and Donaghoe spent a day enthralled by the exhibits in the Crystal Palace at Hyde Park and dined with Cardinal Wiseman. In Liverpool, a banquet was held in his honor by the leading Catholics of that city. They arrived back in New York City in June. The *Herald* reported that the archbishop appeared "rubicund and fresh" after his time abroad, even a little fleshier than he had the year before. He was feted by the principal Catholic gentlemen of Manhattan at a banquet at the Astor House, after which he threw himself back into work and did his best to ignore the snide innuendoes in the press about his rank in the hierarchy.

That workload was becoming a serious problem. Crushing mountains of paperwork—official correspondence, financial reports, letters seeking employment or counsel or personal help, letters from parishioners complaining about their pastors, letters from pastors complaining about their priests—awaited him when he returned from any trip. He had parish visits to make from one end of the state to the other (it was not until 1853 that his superiors finally agreed on the separation of what are today Brooklyn, Queens, and Long Island from the New York archdiocese and that northern New Jersey was also detached to become the new diocese of Newark). He had social obligations to honor and real-estate deals to watch over. He had churches to dedicate and, even though an archbishop now, an endless stream of baptisms, marriages, and funerals at which to officiate. The condition of the orphanages and schools was something about which he insisted on being kept abreast. There was always fund-raising to do, which meant more speech writing. "The Catholic Chapter in the History of the United States," delivered on the occasion of a benefit for the House of Protection of the Sisters of Mercy, was a cogent exposition of the responsibilities of citizenship and faith, which need not be mutually exclusive, and raised $1,600 for that charity.

Sometimes the fund-raising was for a foreign cause, which irked some of his priests who believed that any money raised in New York should stay in New York, but their leader made it plain that it wasn't likely he would overlook a worthy Irish enterprise. The two Irish priests who had come to the United States to raise funds for the establishment of a Catholic University in Ireland were welcomed and helped. Hughes gave a speech on their behalf at the Stuyvesant Institute, urging his clergymen to put their pulpits at the disposal of their guests and his parishioners to be liberal in their giving. During his tenure, as he made clear again and again, education was never going to be a secondary concern. Indeed, in a pastoral letter he had composed just before his trip to Rome, Hughes suggested that "the time has almost come when it will be necessary to build the school-house first, and the church afterward." Not everyone in his flock saw the sense to those emphatic, seemingly hyperbolic words. But Hughes meant them literally: education was a way out of poverty—the only certain way out. Catholic education was a way out of the spiritual malaise, the confusion of values, that was so marked a feature of their time.

And then there was the unending struggle to remind the laity that the church was an institution with a well-articulated structure and time-honored policies. When a congregation in New Jersey began to fund-raise and draw up plans for a new church without consulting him, Hughes wrote to them in a manner to leave no doubt about their misstep. Since the time of the Council of Trent, no churches had been built without a bishop's approval, he maintained (with questionable accuracy), and Saint Peter's of New Brunswick wasn't going to be the first. "Go ahead and build it with your own money," he wrote to the trustees, make it better than the old church, do whatever your heart desires, but do not expect Mass to be celebrated there. "Its walls shall remain unhallowed. It would be to us as a Protestant church or a Jewish synagogue."

The trouble from the church's point of view was that Americans were well-nigh obsessed with going their own way, with mavericks and zealots, renegades and freethinkers, and all manner of challenges to tradition and hierarchy. A prime example was the arrival in the United States in December 1851 of Lajos Kossuth, the leader of the failed Hungarian revolt three years earlier against the Austrian Empire. From the minute he stepped off the boat on Staten Island, the "noble Magyar," as the press took to calling him, was greeted with a Lafayette-like fervor. He was tall and good-looking, and crowds besieged him wherever he went. New Yorkers flocked to his rallies. Kossuth hats (a fur cap with a feather), buttons, banners, and flags were sold everywhere. Ralph Waldo Emerson dubbed him an "angel of freedom," and Walt Whitman went out of his way to meet him several times when he was in Manhattan. Like the Marquis de Lafayette, he was invited to address Congress (only the second foreigner to be so honored). William Seward organized a congressional dinner in his honor and accompanied him on a tour of Mount Vernon. An invitation to the White House was arranged for later in the year. Stephen Douglas, Abraham Lincoln, Harriet Beecher Stowe, and Frederick Douglass were among his admirers. Standing up to a reactionary monarchy, fighting the good fight for democracy in eastern Europe, the man embodied everything America stood for, Daniel Webster maintained. Horace Greeley wrote an introduction to a popular biography that was rushed into print.

To Hughes and many Catholic churchmen, the Kossuth visit simply confirmed the gullibility of Americans. On this, Hughes and the *Herald* were, for once, in full agreement. The man represented atheism and anarchy, his message was one of violence and discontent, and his attacks on the pope and Austria's Catholic emperor simply fed the nativist fires. To McMaster in the *Freeman's Journal*, he was nothing more than a "perfidious and talking Tartar." All so much "Hungarian blarney," Hughes termed the Magyar's speeches, and he wrote to the Austrian minister in Washington that he was proud of the Catholics of New York City, "whether American, Irish, German, or French" who, unlike their Protestant neighbors, had treated the Hungarian hero "with the utmost indifference; and in doing so [had] placed themselves in a most honorable position." The Austrian embassy's tactful efforts to neutralize Kossuth's popularity in America would reap the appropriate benefits, he assured Chevalier Hulsemann, and future sailing for the Austrian cause "would be on a smooth sea."

The archbishop took pains, though, to be sure that Hulsemann understood that he did not want to commit remarks of any greater specificity to paper and did not want to be quoted for public attribution, at least not while "Kossuth fever" was at such a pitch. More "meddling in politics" was the last charge he wanted to hear about that year. To Horace Greeley, who had taken him to task in print for his anti-Kossuth sentiments, he wrote a letter to the editor of the *Tribune* stating that he would leave the ultimate verdict on Kossuth "to public opinion in both hemispheres," with no doubt about what that verdict would be.

Hughes was right about the fever breaking rather quickly. Kossuth's lecture tour along the East Coast and through Pennsylvania, Ohio, and Illinois raised tens of thousand dollars in just a few months, but the bulk of it was unaccounted for by the time Kossuth departed the next summer; the steamship and munitions he had intended to buy to continue the fight in Europe remained a revolutionary's pipe dream. His public statements about slavery had been too watered-down to appeal to the abolitionist members of his audience, and he was embarrassingly ready to offer electoral advice. (He urged Americans to vote for Franklin Pierce, a Democrat, in the upcoming presidential election, an ungracious response to the hospitality of Whigs like Seward, Webster, and Greeley.) His calls for direct American involvement in a renewed attack on Europe's autocratic governments, keeping alive the spirit of 1848, struck many as nothing short of demented.

Kossuth's eventual meeting at the White House with Millard Fillmore was brief and strained. Public and congressional enthusiasm waned. The euphoric press coverage dried up. He received, at best, a mixed reception on his tour of the South. None of this surprised John Hughes. It was satisfying to be proved right when Americans turned against their new plaster saint, who had found an easy target in the Jesuits and the Austrian nobility, but it was annoying to have to have to harp repeatedly on the same themes of authority, order, and the danger of radical rhetoric and appeals for the raising of arms.

In the spring of 1852, Catholics in the United States had an occasion to read more about, and to ponder more deeply, what their church stood for and its implied vision for the future. The fathers of the Seventh Provincial Council of Baltimore had the year before petitioned the Holy See to authorize the holding of a plenary council, an occasion of greater moment than a provincial council. It was a request readily granted. Francis Kenrick, recently moved from Philadelphia to be Eccleston's successor as the new Archbishop of Baltimore, was named the apostolic delegate with the authority to convene and preside over the council. What this meant was that almost all the figures of importance in the hierarchy in North America would gather in the same place to review the challenges to their work that they considered paramount, to debate solutions, and adopt resolutions. Prelates from as far away as Toronto and Monterey arrived in Baltimore that spring. Six American archbishops and twenty-four bishops were in attendance for the conference in May, with their secretaries and theologians, along with the superiors of the Augustinians, Benedictines, Dominicans, Franciscans, Jesuits, Lazarists, Redemptorists, Sulpicians, and Vincentians. The week began with a High Mass celebrated by Kenrick at the cathedral and a grand procession through the streets of Baltimore. The honor of the opening sermon was given to Archbishop Hughes, who took as his subject an era "deceived by the cry of progress," a nation in thrall to change and diversity of opinion but never more in need of something timeless and unchanging as it was then of "the unbroken episcopacy of the Church."

The twenty-five decrees that the council formulated after eleven days of deliberation, all ultimately approved by the Vatican, covered a broad range, from a profession of allegiance to the pontiff to the mandate that European priests who wished to be received into an American diocese should have written testimonials from their bishops abroad.

It included directives about the publication of marital banns (which had long been a haphazard matter, though not in New York since Hughes's 1841 synod), the need to make the celebration of feast days more consistent, and the withholding of burial rites for Catholics who chose to be buried in public cemeteries when Catholic cemeteries were available. Greater attention was urged to the formation of seminaries and the overseeing by the bishops of church funds and accounting practices, two issues on which the New York diocese had long since taken the lead, and statements were made about the prohibition of administrative authority by laymen unless approved by a bishop—a hollow decree for some dioceses, perhaps, and more of a wish than a directive. Decree number 13—dearest to Hughes's heart—stated that "Bishops are exhorted to have a Catholic school in every parish and the teachers should be paid from the parochial funds." The one that probably meant the least to him was number 6: "Bishops are exhorted to choose consultors from among their clergy and to ask their advice in the government of the diocese."

An occasion like the First Plenary Council was a pleasing experience precisely because its concerns were so specific, so clarifying, suggestive—for once—of consensus among the American leadership. It was a source of renewal to pray with so many other dedicated priests, to see old friends and to meet the newer bishops, and to feel that no bishop need assume he stood alone in this awesome effort to carve out a place for Catholicity in a still-hostile culture.

That same spring Hughes delivered on Saint Patrick's Day in his home cathedral one of his most eloquent and heartfelt sermons, underscoring some of the same themes he touched on in Baltimore. As with many of his best addresses, he aimed for a layering effect, presenting to listeners ostensible topics gradually giving way to weightier underlying ones. Saint Patrick was lauded, naturally, and an occasion for praising the famed Roman convert led in turn to a consideration of Ireland's nearly unique place in the history of Catholicism. "Other nations shed the blood of their apostles," he reminded his parishioners, but Ireland had no history of martyring those who brought them the True Word: the Irish "harkened to [Saint Patrick's] teachings, weighed his evidence, and bowed themselves down at the foot of the cross which he presented as the symbol of his mission." Yet there was no denying that, to modern eyes, Ireland was egregiously suffering, dying. Where was God now? "Does it not seem strange," he asked, "to the dark reason and wisdom of man that God should not interpose—that even in our day, he should fatigue our patience so that when famine has multiplied sepulchres over the land, we should say, 'This is the end.' "

Patience pushed to its limit, *multiplied sepulchres*: even the Irish in his audience who had never set foot in Ireland or had no relatives left on the other side, who only read about and imagined the million skeletal souls left to rot by an indifferent colonial power, would have asked the same question. How could God allow this to happen? many might wonder. And that was not a query the bishop would answer, leaving it to his audience to question whether God or man was responsible for such a level of cruelty. (He had, in fact, answered that question in previous sermons.) But what Hughes did, most explicitly, want his parishioners to ponder was their own self-satisfaction about where they found themselves as they sat in the cathedral—not in ravaged Ireland but in a safer place where they were constantly told it was their manifest destiny to take all, to use all, to enjoy all that the continent—that American wealth, ingenuity, and ambition—had to offer. "There is reason to fear," Hughes suggested, "that when God permits men or nations to prosper *to the extent of their desires*, it is a mark of his disfavor," engendering uncontainable pride and a potential separation from the spiritual and the eternal. It was a sermon that managed to be both celebratory and cautionary, a homily about inexplicable pain and the dangers of living a life solely in flight from inexplicable pain. It was for opportunities like this that the archbishop knew he had been called to the priesthood.

Yet if John Hughes at many moments longed for a life committed solely to spiritual concerns and ecclesiastical duties, he knew there was no turning back now to that purer path. It was always politics, politics, politics in this most politically excitable of countries, and his influence was taken for granted at this point. The twin pillars of the Whig Party who had long aspired to the presidency—Clay and Webster—had died within three months of each other in 1852. The election that year pitted a little-known New Hampshire senator, Franklin Pierce, against General Winfield Scott, a compromise choice for the Whigs as much as Pierce had been for Democrats. Whigs leaned on Seward to get a letter of endorsement from Hughes for Scott, but Seward had no intention of asking for so crass a favor. At the same time, Hughes was assiduously courted by the Pierce men, who knew how necessary the New York Catholic vote was. They hoped for at least a tacit endorsement, a suggestion that the archbishop, in the apt words of historian Allan Nevins, "rejected warily"—"warily" because Pierce was overwhelmingly the favorite of his Irish and Democratic parishioners and clearly the man most likely to keep the South in the Union for another four years.

Yet Hughes had no intention of turning on Winfield Scott, a more principled man (whose two daughters had converted and one of whom had become a nun), a man whose attitudes toward Catholicism were, on occasion, almost as generous as Seward's. Hughes recognized the value of saying nothing about either candidate beyond making the observation that both men struck him as fit to serve in the highest office. (That year he was also asked by Scott's daughter to baptize her first child. Presumably he never got wind of Mrs. Scott's snide comment about the baptism. With so much oil-pouring and whatnot at the ceremony, she remarked to George Templeton Strong, she thought her grandson was being prepared for a salad.) It hardly mattered. Scott went down to a resounding defeat, taking the Whig Party with him. Ironically, some Whigs looked to throw blame back on Hughes. Many in the party, Ohio senator Thomas Corwin told a correspondent, were of the view that an about-face by the New York archbishop had led to a last-minute switch among immigrant voters to the Democratic candidate. Scott's followers had a hard time believing that a prelate as powerful as Hughes could not swing an election in New York City if he so chose.

A friend like Scott in the White House might have seemed all the more desirable given an unexpected and complex crisis in the new year. In April 1853, while Hughes was in Havana visiting the bishop there and recovering from a winter of ill health in New York, a letter arrived from Rome, sent to all the bishops in the United States, announcing that a guest—someone Hughes had met in Vienna, in 1840—would soon be departing Europe and would be relying on their help and hospitality. Gaetano Bedini, now an archbishop, would be in North America for an indefinite period before taking up his duties as papal nuncio to Brazil, during which time he would travel to as many dioceses as possible, escorted about the country by as many bishops as seemed feasible, and make any suggestions "for the better ordering of ecclesiastical affairs" as he thought necessary. In other words—call it what you will—an investigation of American Catholicity was on.

───────

AS IT TURNED OUT, Archbishop Gaetano Bedini's eight-month visit to the United States, which involved a somewhat panic-stricken diversion to Canada, had all the ingredients of a Bowery thriller: church pageantry and rioters out to do harm to a papal envoy, an ex-priest on a rampage, stiletto-armed assassins lurking in alleys (arriving in New York on a Sardinian frigate, no less), a riverboat getaway. Less luridly, it also had a great deal to say about the threat Catholicism was still felt to be among a certain class of Americans twenty years after the burning of the Charlestown convent. Indeed, one recent historian called the Bedini visit "unique among nativist episodes in that it exhibited the polarizing strength of anti-Catholicism and xenophobia in antebellum America."

Bedini wasn't the first ecclesiastical observer sent by the Holy See to take stock of the Catholic Church in America, but his was probably the most extensive and instruction-laden of the several missions that had preceded his over two other pontificates. He was to meet and offer the pope's compliments to President Pierce, evaluate the state of the American clergy, assess the extent of Catholic German-Irish enmity, see what could be done to put this lingering trustee dispute to rest (especially in Buffalo, where matters were getting out of hand again), and look into the validity of those annoying letters that kept arriving in Rome each year from parish priests complaining about their bishops. Pius IX also wanted Bedini to raise the issue, whenever possible, of missionary work among the black and Indian population of the United States, a topic of great interest to him. (The pope was a fan of *Uncle Tom's Cabin*.) It was a topic—not surprisingly—that his envoy was given almost no opportunity by his hosts to air for any length of time on either side of the Mason-Dixon Line.

Bedini had been told that the archbishops of New York and Baltimore were the men with whom he should coordinate his travels, and when he arrived in New York at the end of June, he was met at the dock by an ebullient Hughes and his entourage. Bedini spent a few days resting from his long voyage at the episcopal residence before the two men set out for Washington, where everything went smoothly and Bedini's meeting with Franklin Pierce was cordial. Pierce might have come from one of the most bigoted states in the country (New Hampshire voters were loath to repeal their anti-Catholic statutes), but he knew how to act like a chief magistrate. Hughes returned to New York, while Bedini went to Baltimore, where Francis Kenrick was his usual impressive self. (Impressive, yes, and always suspicious, not to say prescient. Kenrick told a fellow bishop that he was sure the stop-in-America-en-route-to-Brazil story was a cover, that Bedini's real mission was to see what was happening in the United States and that he would be departing for Europe, not Rio de Janeiro, when he was done.) By the time he had stopped in Philadelphia and was back in New York, ready to be accompanied by Archbishop Hughes on his journey west, Bedini was in good humor. He liked what he had seen in Washington and Baltimore in particular and was quite taken with Kenrick and Hughes. Asking a priest why Hughes in particular enjoyed such a lively reputation among American Catholic clergy, he was told, "I think that is because he is always game."

One of Bedini's many invitations was one from Bishop John Henni of Milwaukee to dedicate a new cathedral there. On July 27, Bedini and Hughes began the three-day, thousand-mile rail trip, stopping in Chicago to be joined by three other bishops (John Purcell from Cincinnati, Peter Lefevere from Detroit, and Michael O'Connor from Pittsburgh). The ceremony at the Cathedral of Saint John; the receptions with local dignitaries, both Catholic and Protestant; the press coverage in Wisconsin—everything proceeded according to plan. The *Milwaukee Daily Sentinel* called their Roman guest a "remarkable personage," befitting his great office—and this about a man who knew almost no English and spoke in either Latin, German, French, or Italian, or some combination, depending on his audience. Bedini was especially fascinated by stories of how untamed this region northwest of Illinois had been only twenty years earlier and how fast "civilization" was altering it. At every stop, the nuncio also made an effort to speak with as many priests and nuns, and tour as many schools and convents, as time permitted. From Milwaukee, he and Hughes traveled north to Mackinaw, toured the Great Lakes region aboard a U.S. Navy steamer the president had put at their disposal, stopped at an Indian mission, and then arrived in Detroit.

Detroit brought the first sign of trouble. One of the local newspapers made much of the fact that a ship paid for by U.S. taxpayers had no business ferrying a foreigner about who was neither an ambassador nor an "official" guest of the government. The tone was nasty, and Hughes heard that newspapers in other cities were starting to write critically about the nuncio's visit. Protests were being organized. He well knew where that could lead and had, in fact, done his best to keep Bedini's name out of the papers, even instructing the *Freeman's Journal* not to publicize his arrival in New York in June.

Lewis Cass Jr., the American chargé d'affaires in Rome, home on leave, was on hand in Detroit to greet the two men, but that proved to be anything but a pleasant meeting. The son of Michigan's powerful senator and the Democratic Party's candidate for president in 1848, Cass had a poor grasp of what was required for success in diplomacy. Word reached Hughes that Cass had been sharing racy gossip with an Episcopal bishop from Detroit about life at the Vatican, confirming some prurient nativist stereotypes. Many cardinals kept mistresses, he affirmed—the American obsession with priestly celibacy never abated—and the pope himself was said not to be above the practice. Hughes was furious when he heard about this rumormongering and confronted Cass directly. Cass, indignant or feigning indignation, offered to provide Hughes with a written statement from the man he had allegedly spoken to, denying any such improper comments. When that written statement never materialized, Hughes wrote to President Pierce and Postmaster General James Campbell, the latter a Catholic, and did his enraged best to see that Cass was fired. To no avail: the last thing Franklin Pierce wanted was to alienate Cass's father and have to answer to any editorializing about the Catholic Church dictating State Department appointments.

From Michigan, Hughes and Bedini went to Saratoga Springs in New York State, where the nuncio consecrated a church and Hughes preached a well-received sermon, and then they enjoyed, or hoped to enjoy, some rest at the famous local spa. Reporters had commented that summer on the poor complexion of the New York archbishop; a vicious chest cold he caught in Saratoga was to linger for six months, his exhaustion was evident to everyone, and it is possible that the first effects of what would eventually be diagnosed as Bright's disease, a serious kidney dysfunction, were manifesting themselves. Nonetheless, he was determined to do right by his guest, who so clearly relished his company and needed his support.

Their vacation was not as tranquil as Hughes had hoped—presumably more accounts of belligerent editorials made their way to Saratoga (including one by Greeley in the *Tribune*)—because Hughes decided at the end of the week that it would be unwise to return to Manhattan at the moment. Without any advance notice to the bishop in Montreal, the two men and their attendants abruptly boarded a train for Quebec. The ride, however, involved a very unpleasant surprise.

John Hughes knew perfectly well the source of some of the enmity Archbishop Bedini's presence in the United States was starting to arouse, and it was rattling to discover that source in the same car of their train. Alessandro Gavazzi, an ex-priest from Bologna who had left the church after the republican upheavals in Italy, was the celebrity of the moment on both sides of the Atlantic, and he was doing very nicely on a lecture circuit. Gavazzi was a showman extraordinaire—over six feet tall, with a black beard and a hard stare, he appeared onstage in his Barnabite monk's robe with a wooden cross hanging on his chest—and thousands had packed New York's Broadway Tabernacle, Metropolitan Hall, and the Stuyvesant Institute that spring and summer to hear his tirades against the Jesuits, papal cunning, the confused state of Italian politics, and Austrian tyranny. One of those listeners in March had been, incognito, John Hughes, whose suspicions about the man were painfully confirmed that evening. The worrisome aspect of Gavazzi's much-publicized performances during the summer was that they were targeting Gaetano Bedini specifically. According to Gavazzi, when Bedini was the pope's representative in Bologna, he not only consented to the occupying Austrians' torture and execution of the captured antipapal revolutionaries, but participated himself, helping to flay the skin off a priest allied with the subversives, one Ugo Bassi. Bedini was known in Europe, Gavazzi told his audiences, as "the Bloody Butcher of Bologna." The alliterative term, pure fantasy but a reporter's dream, stuck.

When Gavazzi and a few followers appeared in the same railroad car as the two prelates headed to Canada, only a couple of rows behind them, there must have been more than a few moments of anxiety in the air. Was Gavazzi tailing Bedini? Was he planning an assault? Was he on his way to his next lecture stop, and was this meeting merely the strangest imaginable coincidence? Newspaper accounts differ as to whether anything was even said between the two groups, but it appears that Gavazzi disembarked at Lake George and nothing untoward transpired.

Hughes felt enormous relief when they finally reached the safety of Canada, where both men were welcomed by the church hierarchy and local dignitaries throughout Quebec. Hughes stayed by Bedini's side for more than a week and then returned home to attend to diocesan business and his own increasingly fragile health. The plan was for Bedini to head south at his leisure, possibly stopping in New England first.

Back in New York City by the first of September, Hughes felt confirmed in his caution at taking Bedini to Canada when he was paid an unsettling visit one night by a man who identified himself as Joseph Sassi. An Italian immigrant who claimed to have information about a plot on the life of the papal nuncio, Sassi had a terrifying story to relate. A group of Italians, he said, had arrived in May aboard a Sardinian frigate, the *San Giovanni*, and were in the city for the purpose of assassinating Archbishop Bedini the next time he appeared in the vicinity of Saint Patrick's. This gang, armed with stilettos, was lodged near the episcopal residence. Though he knew his own life was in danger if they discovered his betrayal, Sassi told Hughes that he was willing to give the names of the would-be murderers. The whole thing sounded far-fetched, a ludicrous tale out of a penny dreadful, but Hughes passed Sassi's information on to the police. It was a shock when the police declared Sassi to be a credible witness and acknowledged that a Sardinian boat with that name had landed in May loaded with men deported from Italy for their revolutionary ties to Mazzini. Then Sassi was found brutally stabbed in the street a few nights later and died of his wounds in a city hospital.

Joseph Sassi didn't die before naming some names and being interviewed by a priest, who immediately wrote to the nuncio in Canada. Bedini wanted the matter dropped: there had been no attempt on his life, and so no one could be charged with attacking him; there was no hard evidence concerning the identity of Sassi's murderer, and the last thing he wanted was more inflammatory publicity. The police readily agreed to drop the case. Their interest in pursuing it had never seemed particularly strong in any event. Bishop Fitzpatrick in Boston, who was Bedini's next host upon his return to U.S. soil, told Hughes that their guest arrived in "a state of terrible trepidation under the fear of conspirators against his life."

Fitzpatrick hadn't been expecting Bedini. It would appear that Bedini was too nervous to return to New York until he heard from Hughes that the danger had passed and so detoured to the Massachusetts capital. An anti-Catholic riot there several months earlier might have given cause for alarm, but the visit went surprisingly well in terms of press coverage and social calm. The nuncio met with Orestes Brownson at his home and socialized with Senator Edward Everett at a grand reception. After stops in Providence and New Haven, he was back under John Hughes's wing. This took place not a minute too soon in the view of Bishop Fitzpatrick, who had been unmercifully harangued by Bedini throughout his stay on the subject of the pathetic quality of his principal church and rectory. It did Fitzpatrick no good to claim that all his meager funds went into maintaining the city's smaller churches. Poverty carried a fierce stigma in the United States, Bedini had learned, and in a city like Boston the lack of a suitable cathedral was a disgrace. To Fitzpatrick's mortification, Bedini had offered to start the fund-raising himself.

Saint Patrick's Cathedral in Manhattan elicited no such complaints from Archbishop Bedini, and on October 30 he ordained three new bishops—James Roosevelt Bayley as bishop of Newark; John Loughlin as bishop of Brooklyn; and Louis de Goesbriand as bishop of Burlington, Vermont—in a magisterial ecclesiastical ceremony. That month and the next included visits to Rochester and Buffalo, where Bedini was unable to make much headway at all with the rebellious trustees, to Albany and Troy, with more Masses and consecrations, interviews and cornerstone layings, receptions and sightseeing. The students at Fordham welcomed him with an elaborate dinner. Francis Kenrick wrote to John Purcell, "It is well that his movements should be sudden that his enemies may not execute their dire plots."

The final act of Bedini's visit blended the farcical and the pathetic. The nuncio was ready to leave, and Hughes's physical state was making his doctors nervous. He was talked into going south with Father Hecker, who was conducting a mission in New Orleans, and then to the warmth and sunshine of Cuba for a month, where it was felt he would be better off than he would be enduring a New York winter. Arrangements were made to stay with the bishop of Havana. Before leaving, though, he persuaded Bedini to extend his tour, drawing up an itinerary for him that included Cincinnati, Wheeling, Louisville, Saint Louis, Natchez, New Orleans, Mobile, Savannah, Charleston, and Richmond. What Bedini thought when he saw this list is not recorded. Hughes even took it upon himself to write to Rome on Bedini's behalf to receive permission for so much additional travel. Pope Pius IX thought this was an excellent idea,

but by the time his favorable response arrived, there was no point to continuing the trip. The Cincinnati Christmas Eve riot changed everything.

Cincinnati was a bastion of nativism, home for some years to Lyman
Beecher, along with a vituperatively anti-Catholic press. It had a significant German Protestant population. If everything was to fall apart,
that city was as likely a site as any. On December 24, at ten-thirty in the
evening, a mob of several hundred surrounded the cathedral and Bishop
Purcell's house, where Bedini was staying, and created havoc. They came
with noisemakers and nooses, clubs and torches, pitchforks and pistols.
The police were waiting for them, and the result of the melee was one
rioter killed, dozens injured, and almost sixty arrested in the bloody
fracas. In the end, though, none of the rioters was charged in the local
court, and the citizenry seemed more inclined to blame the police for
overreacting. Over the following days, raucous anti-Bedini demonstra-
tions were held in other cities, including Cleveland, Baltimore, Boston,
Philadelphia, and Covington, Kentucky, just across the Ohio River from
Cincinnati. The Bloody Butcher of Bologna was burned in effigy. Death
threats multiplied. It was past time for him to leave. Some of the American bishops—Hughes included—felt that a precipitous flight would be
a mistake and look like cowardice; others just hoped the nuncio was not
planning to visit their diocese when prudence suggested forgetting about
the western and southern states and effecting a swift return to New
York. Bishop Peter Kenrick of Saint Louis was dreading the prospect of
a Cincinnati-style welcome in his city.

The closing route of Bedini's wanderings included a brief stop in
Wheeling, then a part of Virginia, where the city had been flooded with
handbills threatening his assassination, and the nation's capital, where
he met once more with President Pierce and Secretary of State William
Marcy and was lavishly feted at Georgetown College. By now, the press
was dogging his heels, and it was impossible to keep his itinerary a
secret. He wanted to board a ship unnoticed, but that prospect seemed
increasingly unlikely. Taunting crowds gathered on docks in any city
where it was rumored he had been seen. A mass meeting was called in
New York for January 30 by Italian republicans to see what could be
done to bring the nuncio to trial for his alleged crimes. Dozens of armed
Irishmen serving as guards surrounded Hughes's residence when Bedini
finally arrived preparatory to his departure. City officials politely suggested that a surreptitious, rather than a public, exit would be wise. On

February 4, after seven tumultuous months in America, the Italian arch-bishop and his secretary boarded a small boat on Staten Island, which speedily transported him to the ship that waited for him much farther out of the harbor, all to the disappointment of the crowd that had rushed to the dock when word leaked out about his plans. For a man who had been graciously received the week before at the White House and had dined with the mayor of New York, it was as ignominious a leave-taking as any foreign dignitary had experienced in the United States. When John Hughes heard a description of this scene, he was livid. "The rene-gade Italians and infidel Germans have made all the trouble," he com-plained to Bishop Blanc of New Orleans. He also had to experience the pain later of reading an anguished letter from the nuncio, written on Staten Island the night before his departure, about the humiliations he had endured in America.

By the end of February, Gaetano Bedini was back in Rome. Francis Kenrick had been right: Brazil might never have been the intended final destination of the nuncio's transatlantic trip.

Bedini's report to Pope Pius about conditions in America was gen-erous, all things considered. Devout Catholics were holding their own in a nation preoccupied with personal freedom and antiauthoritarian to its core, but, the nuncio acknowledged with admirable understate-ment, "there is much to fear from Protestant fanaticism." The coun-try's energy and self-confidence sometimes took his breath away. ("The famous American motto, 'go ahead,' which means *avanti*, is like an elec-tric charge for all.") Those qualities were both admirable and unnerving, even dangerous in what seemed to him at times "a whirlpool of unbri-dled liberty." He took note of the American church's grave economic difficulties, admitting that he finally understood why so many American bishops came hat-in-hand to Rome and Vienna. He also took note of the very real ethnic division and agitation—too many German Catholics would not work with Irish priests—and of the anti-Irish prejudice in general. The church had to be realistic, though: "How much the Catholic Religion in the United States owes to the Irish. Everything! Everything!" The biggest problem to be confronted, accounting for the painfully high numbers of immigrants ultimately lost to the faith, was the shortage of priests and limited access to the sacraments. Priests and nuns were doing remarkable work with the resources they had, but those resources were inadequate. Above all, Bedini insisted to the pontiff that, with a growing population of more than two million Catholics in a country of twenty-four million people, it was time to establish a permanent diplomatic presence in the nation's capital. (The Pierce administration tentatively agreed, though a layman-ambassador rather than a nuncio was what the Americans had in mind.) What had happened to him in Cincinnati would have been less likely to occur had some formalized diplomatic relations between the two countries existed.

About American clergymen, Bedini had been open-eyed. He met many pious, committed, mostly European-born priests, but not all of them, he felt, had emigrated from motives of religious enthusiasm. Their various reasons for leaving (or fleeing) Europe meant that their capacities in their adopted country were similarly varied, and drinking among the clergy, he told the pope, was no small concern for the bishops. He had been quite surprised—and displeased—to see how few big-city priests wore the Roman collar outside their church or rectory for fear of attack or insult on the street. They did not convey the image he expected of the Catholic priesthood. He apparently did not know that Hughes himself had urged the first Christian Brothers who came to New York from France in 1848 to change their attire when they were in public, for their own safety.

Likewise, the bishops he met, about half the total number, struck him as a sturdy but mixed lot. John Hughes and John Purcell were clearly the "brilliant luminaries" of the church, and he found much to praise in Baltimore's Francis Kenrick, Pittsburgh's Michael O'Connor, Milwaukee's John Henni, Albany's John McCloskey, and Wheeling's Richard Whalen. He thought that Buffalo's John Timon spent too much time traveling out of his diocese, that Hartford's Bernard O'Reilly was rather stingy for a man of private wealth, and that James van de Velde of Chicago (recently transferred to Natchez) lacked prudence and fought too frequently with his clergy. Boston's John Fitzpatrick struck him as deficient in "zeal for action" (that modest cathedral, that humble rectory), and he was of the view that John Neumann might have done better in a humbler diocese than Philadelphia where his "lack of personality" and uncultivated manners obviously failed to do much for the cause in that wealthy, cosmopolitan city. (Neumann plaintively told Francis Kenrick that he turned into Sancho Panza when elaborate social occasions, of the kind Bedini expected, were called for.) Even the admired Hughes came in for added scrutiny. He was a "skillful orator" whose "resolute spirit" and "untiring energy" were bracing, but how much more effective an administrator he would be, Bedini judged, if he weren't so bossy. Despotism and nepotism were the charges the nuncio heard most frequently against Hughes. To which Hughes would probably have responded: "Just so."

―――――

BY NOW, JOHN HUGHES was not only reconciled—he was *content*, fully satisfied—to be the lightning rod for Protestant bigotry in America. His health might be impaired, but he trusted in his recuperative powers, and he knew he had at least a few good years left. His shoulders were broad, and his relish for combat undiminished. In fact, his notoriety in these post-Bedini days moved into a new and absurd direction, extending beyond the pamphleteers, Protestant clerical propagandists, and reporters for the daily press. By the mid-1850s, he was famous enough to earn a place in the gaudy pulp fiction of the day.

Stanhope Burleigh was a cloak-and-dagger novel published in New York by Charles Evans Lister, writing under a female pseudonym, Helen Dhu. Hughes appears as the magisterial Hubert in Lister's tale of thwarted lovers, conniving Jesuits, and a young woman's enforced confinement in a nunnery. (The heroine mercifully suffers a seizure and dies at the moment her hair is about to be shorn.) Hubert is described as "a lordly spirit . . . too restless by instinct to like repose," whom the Jesuits see as a fit candidate to govern their order. Rome is impressed with all he has managed to accomplish in inhospitable territory, crediting some of his achievements to his ethnicity: "Hubert had been bold: it was his nature. No Irishman calculates the odds pitted against him." Two other characters are patently based on Seward and Weed, politicians willing to do church bidding in exchange for Catholic votes. Edward Hinks's quasi-historical novel about the Borgias, *One Link in the Chain of Apostolic Succession; or, The Crimes of Alexander Borgia*, pointed to a line of tyranny that extended from the brutal Borgia pope to Archbishop John Hughes "down to the lowest and most fallen specimen of manhood that exists as a priest of Romanism." Hinks went Lister one better and even dedicated his novel to Hughes ("as a token of Eternal Enmity! with the hope that this will be instrumental in awakening Americans to do their duty").

The best, if most vulgar, of these backhanded compliments—acknowledgments of Hughes's stature and the fear he inspired—was published in Philadelphia and sold well enough to go through several printings within several months. The title character of Orvilla Belisle's potboiler, *The Arch Bishop*, is transparently Hughes, who sits in his "archbishop's palace" (the brick Mulberry Street building is always a palace in these stories), scheming not only for a cardinal's red cap, but for the papacy itself. His daughter lives with him, product of a youthful marriage kept secret from his public, the only relationship that humanizes a man otherwise obsessed with power. Belisle's story comes equipped with all the trappings of the genre: church basements loaded with arms, Inquisitorial tortures inflicted on renegade priests, secret passageways and forged wills, a young woman drugged and raped by a sexually voracious cleric, the hope that true Americans—in this case, the members of the emerging Know-Nothing Party—will rise up and save the country from papal control. Crossing any boundaries of taste or even decency, the book depicts Hughes's sister as a nun who never wanted to enter the convent and sees the moral horror of the priests around her but can do nothing to stop it.

The visit of the papal nuncio merits a passing reference in *The Arch Bishop* as well, providing the author an opportunity to take a few swipes at Bedini, "clothed in all the pomp and circumstance of the mockery which had bewildered the monarchies of the Old World" but a buffoonish figure taken by good republicans for what he was: a "mountebank clothed in tinsel trappings" lacking "manly virtues and honest principles . . . his hands still reeking with the blood of Italy's patriots." The insinuation is made that Hughes, for all his own pretense to manliness, had abandoned his beleaguered guest and retreated to Cuba when the protests became too much, only returning to New York "once the tempest should have passed away."

It also has to be said that these novels portray John Hughes as nothing if not clever. In the eyes of the nativist writers, he may be grotesque, he may be self-absorbed and dangerous and profoundly un-American, but he is smart. Echoing Shakespeare's Cardinal Wolsey in *Henry VIII*, the narrator of *The Arch Bishop* observes of the story's protagonist that "had he served his country with half the zeal he has served his foreign Master, his name would now have been enrolled beside that of a Washington, a Lafayette, a Clay and a Webster." (A formidable compliment, really.) Instead, his "devious ways led him where other men—even an Arnold and a Burr—feared to tread." In at least three other novels of the period, Hughes makes a cameo appearance as part of the great

Catholic threat to republican values, family life, and the sanctity of young womanhood.

Hughes would never have responded in public to the gutter insults of the fiction writers, but he was always eager to respond to criticism from more exalted quarters. He was especially eager if they came from the Cass family. The senator and the archbishop had articulated opposing views in print the previous year over the odd case of an Italian couple, Francesco and Rosa Madiai, who had been arrested in Tuscany for violating the law by holding a Bible meeting of their own without church sanction, making use of the Protestant Bible. Why this should have been of such inordinate interest to Americans isn't entirely clear, but it was, and rallies were held, the State Department asked for clarification, and President Fillmore reportedly urged the Duke of Tuscany to allow the couple to emigrate to the United States. Lewis Cass was now sponsoring legislation to guarantee the religious liberties of Americans abroad. Hughes had more than once referred to the Tuscan action as oppressive and unjust, but questioned why the Michigan senator wanted Congress to pass a law that would guarantee the religious liberties of Americans traveling in Europe while at home Mormons "were forced to seek retirement in the desert in order to enjoy what they call liberty of conscience" and thugs were allowed to burn Ursuline nuns out of their convent with impunity. (The fact that the Charlestown sisters had not been compensated by the state for the loss of their building and possessions was a never-ending source of indignation to Hughes.) Americans like Cass seemed interested in protecting Protestants and their King James Bible and no one else: not exactly an expansive idea of liberty.

Cass took his time, more than several months, to answer Hughes's statements, but he did so in a loquacious Senate speech a few months after the Bedini imbroglio had passed. Hughes then responded, at equivalent length. That Cass had spoken out in the Senate against the rough treatment Archbishop Bedini had received in the United States didn't seem to matter to Hughes; what probably mattered more was that the senator was the father of the gossipy and still-employed Lewis Cass Jr. Within ten days of his return to the city from his Cuba trip, Hughes had composed a thirty-four-page letter, published as a hefty pamphlet that month by a New York publisher, taking the senator to task for the narrowness of his vision of religious freedom.

Did Cass need to be answered at such length, or answered at all? Possibly not, but what was the point, Hughes felt, in responding to one's lesser adversaries if one neglected the bigger lights? Then there was the sheer joy of the debater's stance, of imagining himself on the floor of the Senate, holding his own. "I stand by my letter," he wrote toward the end of the pamphlet, "and I shrink not from the explosion of the great mortar [of General Cass's rhetoric] . . . as if he intended that it should not only kill my little sparrow of a letter, but also! that it should frighten away all the birds of the neighborhood. I find my little nycticorax in domicilio [caged night heron] not only chirping, but without a single featheret of its wing ruffled." Concern about the excessive oratorical flourish played no part in these jousts.

Yet signs were pointing to a resurgence of the worst of the anti-Catholic fervor of the 1830s and early 1840s, and they represented a greater concern than scurrilous pulp prose and senatorial humbug. Convents—in New Orleans, Galveston, and Charleston—were once again under attack. Churches were burned in New Jersey, Connecticut, Maine, and upstate New York. Nativist riots in Cincinnati lefts dozens of Irish Catholics dead ("a reign of terror surpassed only by the Philadelphia riots," Bishop Spalding wrote to Bishop Kenrick). Street violence in eastern cities was becoming almost commonplace. According to Ray Allen Billington, the historian who in the 1930s completed the most exhaustive study of the religious-based journalism of that era, "minor riots occurred in New York on almost every Sunday during 1854, caused by [anti-Catholic] street preachers and those who tried to heckle them." Hughes instructed his clergy to tell their parishioners to steer clear of such gatherings and ignore the curbside demagoguery, but New York newspapers were nonetheless filled with accounts of brawls that got out of hand.

When John Orr, better known as the Angel Gabriel, took his anti-popery performance from Boston to New York that June, lecturing in a long white gown and beginning his talks with a prolonged blast of a brass horn, he spoke to several thousand jubilant supporters on the steps of City Hall before leading a crowd to Brooklyn to spread the word there. Only a massive police presence kept the fistfights with the Irish to a minimum. Five months later a mob almost succeeded in demolishing the Church of Saint Peter and Saint Paul in Brooklyn before the police arrived to disperse them. That year also saw one of the ugliest assaults on a priest in the history of nativist aggression when a Jesuit father was attacked in Ellsworth, Maine, during an acrimonious debate about Bible reading in area schools. Father Johannes Bapst was stripped in public, tarred, feathered, and ridden through town on a rail. He recovered from that trauma sufficiently to serve later as the first president of Boston College but ultimately succumbed to a mental instability that left him incapacitated.

The rise in power of the Know-Nothing Party, as that nativist organization was colloquially known, was an even more pressing cause for concern, given its potential to effect national legislation. The huge midterm electoral gains of the American Party, to use the party's dressed-up name, were a surprise to everyone in 1854 as the Whig-Democratic two-party system collapsed and the future began to seem very confused; with their fiery anti-immigrant, pro-temperance, anti-Catholic platform, the Know-Nothings represented the most potent threat to the Irish and the church in the lifetime of John Hughes. They "swept the country with a hurricane force," Thomas D'Arcy McGee wrote in great bitterness.

In reality, the Know-Nothing influence proved to be short-lived, as differences about slavery divided the northern and southern wings of the party and Congress proved less agreeable to restrictive laws than the new congressmen imagined it would be. Few legislators were interested in prohibiting the foreign-born from holding public office, extending the naturalization period to twenty-one years, or mandating government inspection of convents. The northern branch of the American Party was absorbed within two years, in part and in an altered form, into the new Republican Party, but no one could have foreseen this development at the moment of the nativists' triumph. All these developments confirmed Hughes in his view that a pacific attitude did no good. Respect in the United States was extended only to those who exhibited strength, confidence, and a very vocal clarity.

What might have shocked the archbishop, though, was the hyperbolic opinion of some that he himself was a major factor in the growing strength of the American Party. Henry Slicer, the chaplain of the Senate, wrote to James Buchanan that summer pointing a finger at the New York prelate as the individual more responsible than any other in the country for Know-Nothing strength and Protestant enmity. The public-school fund controversy, the Bedini visit, the attack on Lewis Cass—Hughes never knew when to stop; the opposition gained adherents every time he became fired up, Slicer insisted. James Gordon Bennett, of course, fully agreed.

10

Authority Challenged

THE JOHN HUGHES–Orestes Brownson relationship should have been a fruitful and mutually useful one. Given the temperament and strength of personality of both parties, though, that was probably never a likely prospect. In 1845, Isaac Hecker had confided to his diary a truth about his friend Brownson: "No one loves to break a lance with him because he cuts such ungentlemanly gashes." The same could have been said at any time about Hughes. More important, their differences highlighted the new era the church was entering on this side of the Atlantic as it had passed through its first trials, established its power and capacity for endurance, and was now confronting an unexpected multiplicity of voices from within the faith.

The relations between the country's best-known Catholic prelate and best-known Catholic writer also highlighted John Hughes's dangerous need, fast solidifying in middle age, to assert that his was the voice of Catholic authority in the United States. Yet if the archbishop's Protestant antagonists accepted such an assertion—which also provided them a conveniently clarifying target—all Catholics did not. By the mid-1850s, Hughes came to feel increasingly embattled, questioned, tested at a time when his word, he felt, should have been taken as law.

Orestes Brownson had a hard time taking anyone's word as law, and even before he had relocated to New York from Massachusetts in 1855 (a relocation made with the New York archbishop's blessing), he had been the recipient of notes from Hughes about articles in his esteemed journal that, the archbishop was sorry to say, had "given [him] pain" or "cause to quarrel." A Vermont-born first-generation American who saw the newly arrived working-class Irish as a problematic group, Brownson nonetheless took all this in stride and had done his best to secure a place on his new bishop's good side, suggesting that he would be open to criticism and, if necessary, even censorship over the content of his magazine. Hughes demurred. One didn't set up to censor the only well-regarded publication in the nation with a Catholic bent, published by a man who had once been friends with Ralph Waldo Emerson and Henry David Thoreau, not unless one was willing to be taken for an intellectual reactionary and petty tyrant.

Yet a commencement ceremony at Fordham in July 1856 was the occasion for a particularly awkward encounter between Hughes and Brownson that gave the lie to any diplomatic niceties, at least on Hughes's part. Brownson was the commencement's principal speaker, and his speech dealt with his faith that the United States and Catholicism would, in the end, prove to be uniquely, even providentially, well suited to each other. He urged his listeners to think of themselves as part of a larger nationalist whole, no less bound to their church but less identified with their separate ethnic groups. He was endorsing what would later be spoken of as the Americanization of the Catholic Church. It was, for most listeners, unexceptional commencement fare.

Hughes was in attendance that day and spoke after Brownson took his seat. What followed, according to some listeners, was more a harangue than a speech, one that aimed to refute Brownson's ideas on the spot and, at least before this captive audience, put the man in his place. It provoked an uncomfortable moment for everyone present, and it could fairly be said that the archbishop had lost control of himself.

Part of Hughes's disagreement rested on the premise, not implausible, that it was a mistake to identify an eternal, transhistorical faith with any single nationality. Though he himself had often allowed the lines between the religious and the political to blur in own dealings with secular authorities in his adopted land, he felt that he was better able to judge when that was necessary; Brownson's rhetoric was designed to give credence to a larger idea, an identification that, as he understood it, gave a special weight to any Catholic's *American* identity. Reliving in his own mind battles from which Brownson had stood far apart, Hughes wanted

Fordham's students to know—even if it now contradicted some of his earlier stances—that there was nothing unique about the American character that should make Catholics feel they should more speedily adapt to American culture, forget or downplay their European origins, or try to accommodate themselves in any special way to a society that had been frequently hostile and even violent toward them. He argued that, for all anyone knew, more waves of violence might lie ahead. Catholics should not assume the proverbially open-armed country to which they pledged allegiance would not turn against them at some future time. Then they would have to be prepared to fight all over again. So much for an "American Catholic Church." And so much for a speaker who did not recognize and honor one particular ethnic group—that is, the Irish—for all that it had done to see that Catholicism took root on this side of the Atlantic.

It was part rational discourse, part extempore fulmination, part a reflection of a particularly cranky mood he was in that summer, ready to take issue with any remark he chose to view as a slur on the Irish; Hughes wanted to see Orestes Brownson humiliated that day, and he achieved his purpose. The same sad scenario would be repeated at Rose Hill four years later. A few weeks after his tirade, in light of some unflattering press coverage of his words instigated by Thomas D'Arcy McGee ("a man well-known for his power to do mischief"), Hughes felt compelled to write Brownson, stating that he hoped it was understood that no personal disrespect had been intended at the commencement ceremony and praising the high quality of the *Review*. Yet he ended his missive with still more thinly veiled aggression: "I am sure you will not take it offensively if I make a few suggestions [about your editorializing in the future]." One suggestion was to avoid "every censorious allusion to the nationality of any of our Catholic brethren." A second was to avoid any further speculation that Catholicism was "especially adapted to the genius of the American people." This was one convert, Hughes felt, who needed too many reminders about the pitfalls of independent thought on theological and political issues and whose usefulness to the faith Hughes was coming to doubt.

But converts, or converts of a certain class and educational background, were always a tricky proposition. For American Catholics, the mid-nineteenth century was the great age of conversions, and the publicity was splendid. The entry into the Catholic priesthood of George Hobart

FIGURE 11. *Philosopher and journalist, onetime member of the Emerson circle in Boston, Orestes Brownson was a convert to Catholicism but during the Civil War became a tart critic of the archbishop.* (Courtesy of the Library of Congress Print and Photography Collection.)

Doane, the son of the Episcopal bishop of New Jersey, had caused quite a stir, pleasing to the head of the New York archdiocese, and Thomas Preston, a respected Episcopal minister who converted in the 1850s, was steady enough for Hughes to employ him as his personal secretary for a time. The problem was that one could never be sure if they would stay the course. The devotion of an Isaac Hecker, a James Roosevelt Bayley, or a Thomas Preston was not always typical. When Levi Silliman Ives, the Episcopal bishop of North Carolina, entered the church, Hughes had worried that this "generous [but] impulsive, somewhat erratic" man would be an unstable figure in the pulpit, should he ever be allowed to preach, though Hughes was happy to see him appointed to a teaching position at Fordham. Hughes's doubts in this case were groundless. Few men were more certain for the rest of their lives that their decision had been the right one. Likewise, Peter Burnett, the first governor of California, was a convert who, in his post-gubernatorial years, wanted to proselytize. He conducted a lengthy, pedantic correspondence with Hughes and other bishops in the 1850s as he prepared his stultifying testament to the faith, the eight-hundred-page *The Path Which Led a Protestant Lawyer to the Catholic Church.*

On the other hand, the recantation of John Murray Forbes, a prominent Protestant rector turned Catholic priest in New York City, was a profound shock from which Hughes never fully recovered. Forbes's conversion ten years earlier had been a feather in the archdiocesan cap. His return to the Episcopal Church in 1859 devastated his Catholic archbishop, who had become a friend and blamed himself for a grievous failure of judgment. Having chastised others for rushing to ordain new converts who seemed suitable—and publicly useful—candidates for the priesthood, Hughes wrote that his "own turn of humiliation" for the very same mistake had rightly come upon him. Even Brownson expressed sympathy over the archbishop's grief and embarrassment. Hughes referred to "the fall of Dr. Forbes" as "the heaviest blow that was ever inflicted on my heart." He was not prepared to acknowledge, however, that his own high-handed manner with Forbes on numerous occasions might have been a contributing factor in this situation.

Even if he sometimes forgot the fact himself, Hughes would periodically remind his priests that they needed to be mindful of the high practical and emotional price some converts paid when they joined the church. Ives's decision left him for a long time unable to support his wife and children. The conversion in 1854 of politician Joseph Chandler, a good friend from Hughes's Philadelphia days, cost him his reelection to Congress that year. New York mayor Fernando Wood's wife had purportedly converted as an adolescent during her time abroad at a Paris school but had been instructed by her husband and wealthy Protestant parents never to let that disgraceful fact become public knowledge. Even when the family was more broad-minded than most, the adjustment was never easy. When Henry Clay's granddaughter converted and became a nun in 1849, Clay had been at pains to assure her that he respected the determination with which she had made her decision, had "no prejudice against the Catholic religion," and would always feel the deepest affection for her. Yet he admitted the "intense distress" the girl's decision to take the veil was causing her loving family.

The conversion of William Rosecrans, later a famed Civil War general, elicited no such tenderness and threw his family into turmoil, with his brother writing to him that "to enter the Church of Rome is to entangle one's soul." (That same brother converted some years later and became a priest and later the first bishop of Columbus, Ohio.) Many converts who openly professed their new faith became exiles from their own families. Vanbrugh Livingston, member of a distinguished New York family, had been disinherited when he became a Catholic, and was living in reduced circumstances. A Democrat, he was turned out of his consular position at the time of Zachary Taylor's election, but Hughes felt no compunctions about writing to then-Secretary of State Daniel Webster to entreat a State Department position for Livingston, who was earning a modest salary in a low-level New York Customs House position. The administration did not see its way toward giving a member of the opposition party a better job, but when the Democrats were back in office, Postmaster General Campbell, a Catholic, came to Livingston's aid at the archbishop's behest.

"The effect [of conversion] outside the Catholic circles is more than any but a convert can estimate," an acquaintance wrote plaintively to Hughes. Having lost his job at a Protestant college, J. V. Huntington had reason to know: "no matter what might be the capacity or industry or acquirements or previous social standing of a convert, unless he had an independent fortune," that man was in trouble. Huntington had hopes of a fresh start as a lecturer and writer and was enormously grateful for Hughes's sponsorship in the 1850s of his lectures in New York, for "to gain the ear of the Catholic public for a convert is equally impossible," he wrote, "without some such aid as Your Grace had now afforded me."

In contrast to the troublesome Brownson and the sadly straitened Huntington, one convert who brought Hughes deep satisfaction in the decade before the Civil War was Sophia Dana Ripley. One of the most remarkable women of her time, she had a past and a pedigree far removed from the bishop's experience. Her husband was George Ripley, a prominent Boston Unitarian and Transcendentalist who had abandoned his ministry in 1841 to found the egalitarian community Brook Farm and eventually, long after the demise of that utopian venture, became a leading literary light at Greeley's *Tribune*. Ripley remained a Protestant all his days, but when the couple left behind their old life in Boston for the West Roxbury farm, there was no turning back for his spouse. Ultimately, though, Transcendentalism and Fourierist socialism proved no more sustaining than Unitarianism had. Even while still at Brook Farm, Sophia had occasionally returned to the city to talk about religion with Orestes Brownson, a family friend, and had listened at Brook Farm to Isaac Hecker discuss his own spiritual journey. She furtively began attending her first Masses.

Questioning, self-questioning, fervent—"brainy," a recent Hawthorne biographer termed her—Sophia came from the prominent Massachusetts Dana family (one grandfather had been president of Harvard and the other a member of the Continental Congress), most of whom had always been uneasy with her independent ways. She had been friends with Margaret Fuller—an association that at first left John Hughes shaking his head in despair—and contributed feminist articles to the *Dial*. She was admired by her husband's cousin, Ralph Waldo Emerson, and faint traces of her appear in the nervous, uncertain Priscilla, the Veiled Lady of *The Blithedale Romance*, Hawthorne's fictional account of Brook Farm. (It should also be noted that she was not the only Brook Farm associate to find her way to the church. Transcendentalism provided more than a few converts in the 1840s and early 1850s. In addition to Hecker and Brownson, Sophia's niece Sophia Seares and Ripley disciples George Leach and William J. Davis followed suit. Seares became a nun.) When Sophia Ripley and her husband moved to New York City in 1847, she sought out John Hughes for guidance. He saw before him both the potential for a public-relations coup—another member of the Emerson circle come to Rome—and an articulate individual of exceptional need, earnestness, intelligence, and intensity.

But, like Isaac Hecker, Sophia Ripley—daughter of the Calvinist world—had found her transition to Catholicism anything but smooth. Her husband was a supportive if uneasy partner, even attending Catholic services with her on occasion, but self-doubt and a laceratingly judgmental nature left her no peace. She poured out her many qualms to Hughes, telling him that she feared her recent conversion had been more a matter of mind than heart, that hers was an essentially hard nature, alien to the caring spirit of Christ. "That your heart is not tender, is no concern of yours," he counseled her. "God does not ask from you what you have not." His message touched a nerve: *just as you are*—warmhearted or reserved, naturally loving or naturally cold, torn or whole, no matter—God embraces you if you so choose and accept the embrace of the church. What is beyond our power to change is not an impediment to grace. Many saints have grappled with coldness and dryness of heart, he reminded her. Think of Saint Jerome, think of Saint Ambrose. "God's command is to love, not with the heart you have *not*," he insisted, "but with the heart you have." She felt, she told her cousin Charlotte Dana, as if she had been ushered from "death unto Life" by a man who understood her qualms and had always been to her "kindness itself."

This was a side to John Hughes that not everyone saw or chose to acknowledge—the patient, calm, caring man who knew the difficulties confronted by thoughtful people trying to understand what Catholicism expected of them, especially highly intellectualized men and women, of whom Sophia Dana Ripley was certainly one. His words also spoke to an image of the church that was often lost in the politics and rhetorical combats of the day, a view he wished had wider currency, though his own flinty temperament often prevented that: that is, an understanding of Catholicism as a faith that accepted human frailty and failings, that was more about *caritas* than dark judgment and obeisance to Rome. Ripley spent the late 1850s, before the onset of the cancer that killed her in 1861, working with the Sisters of the Good Shepherd, an order that focused on rescuing prostitutes from the streets of New York.

Other converts could sometimes seem more trouble than they were worth. James McMaster was an ongoing irritant; he had become one of the banes of his archbishop's existence by the mid-1850s. The two men were painfully alike in some ways (something Hughes could grudgingly admit), but McMaster, the H. L. Mencken of his time, was the one New Yorker who could make John Hughes look mild-mannered. One of his editors later remarked that no one stood a chance at McMaster's newspaper, despite the man's absolute fidelity to the church, "if he was too fully saturated with the gifts of the Holy Ghost." The publisher of the *Freeman's Journal* made clear when hiring anyone that he wanted writers with a fluent pen, a disregard for consequences, and a large capacity for malice. He expected his underlings to share his prejudices—these included an unconditional admiration for the Redemptorists and a lifelong suspicion of Jesuits and Paulists, a belief in states' rights and a hatred of abolitionists—and said that he wrote "to edify such good people as are not overstocked with brains or at least not trained to follow theological discussions." He had no hesitation in including the church hierarchy in that number, nor any doubt that he knew better than anyone what was best for the Catholics of New York or, indeed, America.

When McMaster argued the case for public support of parochial schools or lambasted Thomas D'Arcy McGee or Samuel F. B. Morse, Hughes could look on with approval and feel that perhaps he hadn't made such a big mistake in selling the *Freeman's Journal* to this acerbic fellow who was equivocal about the cause of Irish independence. He regularly reprinted and praised the archbishop's speeches. But when McMaster criticized William Seward or, echoing Brownson, made jibes about the state of Catholic higher education, his patron cringed. Ultimately, in July of 1856, shortly after the Fordham commencement debacle, Hughes decided to break with the paper, informing McMaster that he must make clear to his readers that his columns were no longer to be taken as representing the diocesan view on anything. The heading "Official Organ of the Archdiocese" had to come off the masthead. McMaster was too much of a loose cannon, and his tone at times too inflammatory.

Exactly which article or editorial that spring or summer led to the rift is unclear. Perhaps Hughes felt that McMaster had been giving Brownson too much attention and too much respect in his pages of late. Perhaps he was made uneasy by the editor's statement that the brutal caning that year of Charles Sumner by Congressman Preston Brooks, while inappropriate, was actually something the abolitionist senator from Massachusetts had coming to him. Beyond a doubt, though, McMaster crossed a line by any standards in a May 31 editorial about Bleeding Kansas when he offered the view that if someone took a gun to Horace Greeley, Henry Ward Beecher, Theodore Parker, and William Lloyd Garrison, a "great relief" would be felt across the nation. That was emphatically not a sentiment the archbishop shared or that any bishop could afford to be associated with.

There had already been some ugly personal consequences to McMaster's invective through the years. Skewering Thomas Francis Meagher, formerly one of the Young Ireland men, in the paper two years earlier, referring to him as one of "a vain, blustering set of braggarts that did so much to spoil the work of O'Connell and to make Ireland a laughing-stock of the world," McMaster was delighted to know he had injured his target. That was the whole point of calling the Young Ireland men, past or present, "spouters without industry to work for their livings, without modesty or prudence to keep themselves out of scrapes with the police, without courage to strike a blow when caught in the very midst of their brag," without brains and without shame. The outraged Meagher was rebuffed when he tried to secure a retraction and subsequently assaulted McMaster with a riding whip outside his house one day. McMaster, who sometimes carried a revolver with him, fired at his attacker, grazing his forehead and leaving his face covered in powder burns. Both men were arrested as they scuffled in the street. They were later freed on bail and agreed not to press charges against the other, but the story made the papers. This was exactly the kind of conduct that mortified Hughes, whose pursuit of a solidly respectable, politically unthreatening image of Irish Catholic New Yorkers was constantly thwarted by Fenian radicals, Tammany thugs, and men who lived for a brawl in print like James McMaster.

For Meagher, though—handsome, eloquent, and at heart a good if sometimes erring Catholic—Hughes nurtured a soft spot. The following year, when Meagher fell in love with the beautiful daughter of a prominent New York family who had become a convert and was temporarily estranged from her irate father, the archbishop performed the wedding at his residence.

For another of the Young Ireland group, Hughes never evinced any desire for reconciliation. John Mitchel, the expatriate whom Hughes called the purest "vitriol slinger" of the Irish American press, could not bring himself to let go of a by-now tired theme: the Catholic hierarchy had betrayed the Irish people in 1798 and 1848. Priests and bishops were "treacherous enemies," he was still writing in the mid-1850s, and if Irish freedom were ever to be won, he insisted, "it must be won in spite of the priests." Hughes, in particular, he termed "an unworthy prelate." When Mitchel moved South, Hughes suggested that that was just where the ardently pro-slavery agitator belonged; as a Protestant, he would be comfortable around those who were used to oppressing others. Hughes was several years dead by the time Mitchel acknowledged that he had gone too far in his fulminations and might wish to retract his more aggressive statements. Interestingly, all three of his daughters converted in the 1860s, and one entered a convent, a decision he supported.

———

AT LEAST SINCE the time of Aquinas and Duns Scotus, the question of the relationship of Mary, the mother of Jesus, to the core Christian tenet that all human beings are born in need of redemption from original sin had been a topic of study and debate. At the beginning of his pontificate, Pius IX had established a scholarly commission to consider the matter further, and bishops around the world were solicited for prayer and counsel. In 1854, he issued his encyclical *Ineffabilis Deus*, recasting traditional belief as dogma and affirming what many Catholic theologians had long hoped for: a declaration to the faithful that Mary, though conceived by her parents, Joachim and Anne, by normal biological means, had nonetheless been conceived free of original sin—immaculate. The announcement that the Promulgation of the Doctrine of the Immaculate Conception would take place in December of that year was a source of great joy to American Catholics, especially to those of the clergy who believed that a greater emphasis on Mariology would not be amiss in an era when respect for women was increasingly threatened by the uprooting of families, rampant alcoholism, urban poverty, and sexual violence. Whatever was happening in New York could be put aside; Hughes had no intention of missing the ceremony in Rome. He set sail for Europe in late October, accompanied by the man who was now his trusted chaplain, Father Francis McNeirny (a man with "a superior manner and quasi-episcopal air" who made no secret of his aspirations, according to one fellow priest), and Bishop John Timon.

Immediately before leaving, though, the archbishop convened a provincial council, the first for the New York province, that brought together his suffragan bishops and numerous other priests from Boston, Burlington, Portland, Hartford, and Providence to Albany, Buffalo, and Newark. A week of Masses and conferences ended with six decrees, three of which were especially timely and highly practical, and a pastoral letter to be read in all churches in the Northeast. One decree forbade the further mortgaging of any church property without a bishop's consent. Hughes had long felt that the financial chaos of previous years had to come to an end, once and for all; at the very least, he wanted to be kept abreast of any intention to apply for funds from banks and to be involved in the terms. Another was a plea for greater efforts to establish Catholic schools through every diocese, and a third urged the building of rectories adjacent to each church, the title of which had to be in the bishop's name. This question of who should hold title to church property—bishop or lay trustees—was one that the New York state legislature was considering at that time, and Hughes knew what would be, once he was returned from Rome, the field of his next battle.

In Rome, Hughes and Timon met up with Francis Kenrick, John Neumann of Philadelphia, Antoine Blanc of New Orleans, and Michael O'Connor of Pittsburgh, where the six American bishops were joined by fifty-three cardinals and almost 150 bishops from around the world for the imposing ceremony on December 8, representing, Hughes wrote, "every tongue and tribe under the sky." Kenrick and O'Connor, whose credentials as scholars and theologians far exceeded those of Hughes, were the two American prelates who had been invited to participate in the deliberations in the week that preceded the declaration where the exact wording was hammered out. If Hughes felt any chagrin at his exclusion, he had the good sense never to allude to it, and his descriptions of the ceremony itself, watching a tearful pontiff proclaim the church's final verdict on Mary's stainless conception, border on the ecstatic. The unveiling of a statue of Mary and a column dedicated to her took place later in the week in the Piazza di Spagna, which Hughes attended and at which he felt an almost equivalent thrill. The rest of the month brought the expected and well-deserved pleasures he had been looking forward to: Christmas Week in the Holy City, a renewal of old acquaintanceships, hours spent among the city's masterpieces, with a special appreciation now of the Virgin from the hands of Giovanni Bellini, Andrea del Sarto, Perugino, and Raphael.

En route home, Hughes stopped for a time in England. He was invited to stay for several days at the country estate of Viscount Campden (later the Earl of Gainsborough), a young Whig politician who, with his wife, the daughter of an earl, had converted a few years earlier. This was an invitation that suggested something about Hughes's formidable status among Europeans now, and through the well-connected viscount, Hughes met a number of other aristocratic converts. The hope of a resurgence of Catholicism in Great Britain was on the minds of bishops on both sides of the Atlantic in the 1850s, and earlier that year Hughes had attempted, without success, to interest Cardinal Newman in a lecture tour of the United States. When in London, he haunted the House of Commons. Irish nationalist, poet, and MP Charles Gavan Duffy, who had heard plenty about Hughes from his friends in America, ran into him there one afternoon. He observed of the New York archbishop's visage that he had "a notable Roman head, the side face of which looks like the head on a coin in the time of Caesar." He also went on to record in his journal a less laudatory observation, that Hughes struck him "as shrewd and clear rather than great or impressive."

Shrewdness and clarity were needed back in New York, where, just as Hughes feared, legislation to restore the title of all church properties to the representatives of their lay congregations was being debated in Albany. State senator James Putnam from Buffalo had introduced his bill, the Church Property Act, with a speech on January 30, 1855, that aimed to make the legislation sound humane and innocuous. His purpose, he said, was to seek "uniformity in the tenure of church temporalities" while expressing concern for those Catholics suffering under an interdict because their church trustees would not truckle to their bishops. Yet his rhetoric was vintage Know-Nothing anti-Catholicism. James Gordon Bennett exulted that the city's "venerable and unterrified archbishop" had returned from Europe in time for a brouhaha: "like a true Celt, if there is a fight of the factions, you may count him in."

The idea that any member of the clergy should be the legal owner of church property, especially when it entailed tens of thousands of dollars, struck James Putnam and his supporters as a "violation of the whole spirit of [New York's] constitution and laws," further evidence that the Catholic clergy was "bold in its antagonism to our whole theory of government," antirepublican and indifferent to the American principle of the separation of church and state. This was a particularly heinous situation, he argued, when the congregation of a given church (like Saint Louis Church in his hometown) was composed of people who had been patriotic residents of the United States for many years, while its bishop, a minion of the pope, might have stronger allegiances elsewhere. Putnam claimed a sharp historical sense, alluding to the corruptions of Cardinal Wolsey, the Catholic opponents of William and Mary, the conniving clergy under the Bourbons, and priest-ridden Mexico, dangerous examples of that from which the United States must be protected. Archbishop Bedini came in for several swipes.

Despite Hughes's best efforts to secure allies of his own to lobby and vote against Putnam's bill, the legislation passed the state senate in April. He probably knew this was a foregone conclusion; his own efforts two years earlier to have the legislature consider a bill that would guarantee the bishops' rights to hold title to church property had gone nowhere. American Protestant churches had never adhered to such a policy, nor did Protestant legislators regard their involvement in the matter as an unreasonable encroachment on the right of any religion to organize its own financial structures, not when the properties in question were tax-exempt. One state senator, Erastus Brooks, was willing to argue that as "the political state is Protestant in character," the government was well within its rights to insist that all religions align themselves with native ideas—Protestant ideas—concerning civil liberty, the balance of secular and religious authority, and the status of tax-exempt property. Catholic ecclesiastics, he warned, were fattening themselves on the backs of their parishioners. Their bank accounts were filled with a form of plunder.

Brooks's prime example was John Hughes. He used the pages of a newspaper he co-owned with his brother, the *New York Express*, to give an accounting of the archbishop's vast wealth. He claimed that Hughes himself was worth several million dollars, making him one of the richest men in the state, if one totaled up the value of all the deeds in his name. His portrayal was of a man of the cloth as in thrall to Mammon as he was to God. Hughes was not about to let this pass. Brooks was not a penny-a-line writer for the daily press. He was a type Hughes particularly abhorred: a Whig turned Know-Nothing; an eager supporter of ex-president Fillmore, who was back in the ranks of the nativists and no longer pretending amity with Irish Catholics; a man with gubernatorial aspirations; an erudite, college-educated man who should have been above playing the demagogue and appealing to bigotry.

Using the *Courier & Enquirer*, the *New York Times*, and the *Freeman's Journal* as his vehicles, Hughes fought back in letters and guest editorials. If it could be proved that all the money Brooks claimed was really his to spend as he wished, Hughes wrote, he would donate it to the city to build a vast library named in honor of the state senator. But Brooks, of course, had it all wrong. He had been wrong in his tabulation at the city register's office of the exact number of properties the archdiocese owned, duplicating some entries and listing convents, schools, and hospitals owned by their respective orders as property he owned. More important, he had it wrong in the larger sense: the owners of these properties were the Catholics of New York, for whom Hughes was merely the symbolic head. The church had never permitted a bishop to act as if he personally could benefit from holding a title to anything.

Over the next few weeks in his various venues, Hughes reviewed in copious detail the sad history of those Catholic churches under the direction of lay trustees that had been run into bankruptcy, had denied their priests salaries or a lodging over their heads, been mismanaged by incompetent bookkeepers (Pise's brother-in-law came in for some licks), and had never repaid loans from their own desperate parishioners. Dealing with all of this had been for years now "a species of daily torture . . . a martyrdom" for him, he maintained. He reviewed his version of the

unending disputatiousness of the trustees of Saint Louis Church in Buffalo (Germans, so many of them, of course) and the greater security the
church enjoyed now that trusteeism was on its way out. Brooks had his
own retort to offer for every statement his opponent made.

The journalistic contest between Hughes and Brooks initially aroused
some public interest. The questions debated were important, and the
combatants didn't pull their punches, pretty much calling each other
liars. (Brooks termed Hughes "more ludicrous than wicked" and lacking in the qualities of a gentleman.) That interest faded pretty quickly,
though, as an examination of social principles gave way to a wallow-
ing in economic minutiae. Hughes in particular was besotted with the
idea of data, figures, and the wording of contracts. (His writings on the
church property controversy in his *Complete Works* run to eighty-five
pages of dense print.) Neither man understood the value of brevity, summary, or dignified silence.

Ironically, none of this back-and-forth really mattered, as the Putnam bill turned out to be a dead-letter piece of legislation. No church
in the state demanded its bishop return any property titles to its trustees, either because the new arrangement had already been accepted by
most Catholics as plausible or because the power of an interdict and the
example of Saint Louis Church was enough to set the matter to rest.
Never enforced, the Putnam bill was repealed during the Civil War. Yet
it had been another occasion to pit John Hughes against his usual enemies and to see him play his by now customary part in a public forum.
Brooks published some of his open letters in a small volume, carefully
edited to show him as the victor of the exchange, titled *The Controversy
between Senator Brooks and John Archbishop of New York*. Hughes
followed suit with his own skewed publication, more whimsically titled
Brooksiana.

The mid- and late 1850s did bring the archbishop some more pacific
satisfactions, evidence that he was appreciated, even liked. One was the
subscription taken up by friends to have G. P. A. Healy, far and away the
most respected and sought-after portrait painter of his day, do his portrait, a polished work that made its subject look handsomer and younger
by ten years. (The small toupee worn at the front of his head, purchased
a few years earlier as his hair—but not his vanity—diminished, is hardly
detectable as such.) Another positive development from these years was
Hughes's employment of John Hassard as his lay secretary. As he aged,

Hughes relied on his staff more and more, and a devoted, appropriately awestruck amanuensis had become essential to him. Hassard was that person. A highly literary young man who would go on to be a respected journalist and Wagnerite music critic (as well as Hughes's first biographer), Hassard was born an Episcopalian but had converted at the age of fifteen. A pleasing irony: he had been baptized by the soon-to-be apostate John Murray Forbes. After graduating from Fordham in 1855 at nineteen and receiving his MA there in 1857, he took a place at the episcopal residence and remained with the archbishop until his death seven years later. As Hughes became increasingly unfocused and disorganized in his later years, Hassard did yeoman's work to keep him on track.

One person who was very much on track in this period, and whom Hughes was glad to assist, was Sister, now Mother, Angela. When the Sisters of Charity of New York had to vacate their motherhouse, claimed by eminent domain for what was about to become the upper reaches of the new Central Park, he was relieved that his own sister took so energetically and confidently to the task of finding the order a new home. The property she eventually decided on was the estate, recently put up for sale, of Edwin Forrest in the Riverdale section of the Bronx, sixty hilly acres that would allow for a sizable convent and an enlarged academy with a spectacular view of the Hudson River and the Palisades of New Jersey. That transaction entailed using the church's lawyers to see if Forrest could be talked down from his exorbitant asking price of $100,000, some fund-raising help from Mulberry Street, and Hughes's meeting with the great Shakespearean actor himself. The archbishop's first viewing of the Font Hill estate with his sister was a good example of Ellen Hughes's ability to manage her brother by letting him think he was going to have his way. His first remark, on seeing the Gothic castle Forrest had erected overlooking the water, was "Well, that will have to go!" Mother Angela said nothing, no doubt nodded. The castle remains, to this day, on what is the campus of the College of Mount Saint Vincent in Riverdale.

It was a good moment for the family. Hughes was also happy when his niece, Margaret's daughter of the same name, married a widower that year, the banker Eugene Kelly, who was well heeled, well connected, and open to assisting the church with fund-raising. An immigrant himself with a lifelong interest in Irish independence, Kelly was the model of the crafty but civic-minded businessman whose help Hughes always needed; he was one of the founders of the Emigrant Savings Bank and a trustee of the National Academy of Design and Seton Hall College and later served on the board of the Metropolitan Museum of Art. His brother was a priest who had worked as a missionary in Africa. Kelly and Hughes understood each other well. This was the kind of family tie the archbishop craved. It was also a balm to a family that had suffered a deep loss when Margaret's other daughter, Angela, died after a short illness in 1856 at the age of sixteen.

On a larger stage, a relationship that began, so to speak, amid the dirt and rock piles of the Pennsylvania Turnpike over thirty years earlier had ripened and promised to yield the fruits that a Clay presidency—every Whig's hopeless fantasy—might have provided. James Buchanan enjoyed the company of men of strong opinions, worldly men who could be funny and deferential and sensible by turns. He also knew a man who might be of use to him when he saw one. He found both, he thought, in the New York archbishop.

When the two men met for a second time during the Polk years, they felt comfortable in each other's presence and remained in intermittent contact over the years. Hughes was also taken with Harriet Lane, Buchanan's beautiful orphaned niece who later served as official hostess at the White House during her bachelor uncle's tenure, a warm feeling that was reciprocated. Having been educated in a convent school, she was without any prejudice toward Catholicism, and her uncle had even speculated at one time, without undue anxiety, that she might consider conversion. On several occasions when Hughes had business in Pennsylvania, he was invited to stay at Wheatland, Buchanan's comfortable home in Lancaster. When Buchanan, who had long had his eye on the presidency, began positioning himself for the Democratic nomination while he was Pierce's minister to London in 1856, he had gone out of his way to let Britain's Cardinal Wiseman know that he thought well of Hughes, and any help from that direction would not go unappreciated.

There was really no need to drop hints for Hughes's support. On the subject of religion, Buchanan was known to be singularly unprejudiced himself, and his principal opponent, the first candidate for the presidency put forth by the new Republican Party, John C. Frémont, was not an appealing alternative, despite the rumors that Frémont was a secretly baptized Catholic. Still, nothing stopped the nativists, who were pushing Millard Fillmore as a third-party candidate, from playing up that contested angle and insisting that Frémont was secretly the archbishop's man. It would be hard to know if Hughes found the pamphleteering annoying or comical: FREMONT'S ROMANISM ESTABLISHED: ACKNOWL-EDGED BY ARCHBISHOP HUGHES read one brochure he kept for his files, detailing "How Fremont's Nomination Was Brought About / Hughes, Seward, Fremont, and the Foreigners / a most foul coalition." Anyone in New York who knew anything knew that the man from Lancaster, Pennsylvania, was Hughes's choice.

With James Buchanan's election, Hughes found an open door at the White House for the next four years. At times, he was astonished and dismayed at the vacillating nature of the fifteenth chief executive, but he let the president know that in any conflict that threatened the dissolution of the Union—the fight over the admission of Kansas as a free or slave state, a firm response to John Brown—he stood by him in his efforts to uphold the Constitution, give no ammunition to would-be secessionists,

FIGURE 12. *James Buchanan was the president with whom John Hughes enjoyed the most cordial relationship, visiting him frequently in the White House—until Hughes discovered the extent of Buchanan's weakness as a leader under fire.* (Courtesy the Library of Congress Print and Photography Department.)

admonish the wayward abolitionists, and forestall what was probably inevitable. This stance naturally made for some awkwardness with William Seward and Thurlow Weed as Whig Party politicians became Republicans and opposed Buchanan at every turn. A Seward-Buchanan contest in 1860 would have presented him with a real dilemma, Hughes knew, but that, of course, did not come to pass.

———

THERE WERE TIMES, indeed, when Hughes felt more appreciated by sympathetic Protestants like Buchanan, Seward, and Weed than he did by his fellow clergymen. Younger priests were starting to question the increasingly hierarchical nature of the American church, with its greater focus on pronouncements from Rome and the authority of the bishops immediately above them, and chafed at the many directives that came their way, such as wearing the Roman collar in public at all times and making appeals for charities they might not believe in. From Hughes's point of view, the upstarts had no sense of the immediate past—imprisoned popes, sacked convents, the need for a public and united front before those who would intimidate or mislead their flock. From the point of view of some men new to the priesthood, the church would benefit by the more relaxed and democratic culture they inhabited.

Dissent, or even simple disagreement, never brought out the best in John Hughes. In 1856, long-simmering relations between the archbishop and the Jesuits of Fordham were reaching a crisis point. Contractual matters, hammered out none too adroitly a decade earlier, were one root of the problem. As an astute twentieth-century commentator wrote, "It cannot be said that the history of this conflict between the Archbishop and the Jesuits is an edifying tale, or shows its chief characters in a flattering light." That view could be taken as a fairly generous understatement.

In 1855, Hughes had decided to replace the Jesuits at the seminary in stages, leaving them to manage the college that they certainly believed by this time they owned outright, bringing in secular priests to run the seminary, which was obviously in trouble. Teachers like Isidore Daubresse, a Belgian Jesuit whose English was rudimentary and whose fierce allegiance to the overthrown Bourbon dynasty scandalized democratically inclined American seminarians, was only one of the seminary's problems. The seminarians hated everything about life at Saint Joseph's, from its draconian rules to its primitive, unhealthy living conditions.

Hughes had the land surveyed—something that should have been done ten years previously—to clarify the exact boundaries of "his" seminary and "their" college. Not at all happy with the surveyor's findings (i.e., that the college property began right at the doorstep of the Rodrigues' house), Hughes wanted the surveyor's report "rectified" and ordered the college's board of trustees, still packed with some of his own men, including board president (and close friend) Peter Hargous, John McKeon, and Father Starrs, to see that this was done. The Jesuits understandably took umbrage at such a high-handed approach to a matter that could have been resolved with a gentlemen's agreement, nor did they find acceptable the ominous view held downtown that it was the archbishop's right to reclaim the school and land entirely if all its original debts were not retired or if the order ever decided to leave New York.

In a memorandum that December, the Jesuits wrote to the archbishop, reminding him that they had not received Fordham as a reclaimable "gift," as he seemed to want to believe, but had purchased the school with an understanding that they would make a good-faith effort to deal with the massive $40,000 debt he had passed on. They also reminded the archbishop of his promise of 1845, never fulfilled, that they would be given title to a church and rectory of their own in Manhattan (the still-standing Saint Francis Xavier on West Sixteenth Street). If the intent of the unsigned memorandum was to suggest to Hughes that Jesuits were not so easily intimidated, he reacted in a manner to make diplomacy or accommodation all the more unlikely. He was simply not used to having priests anywhere in his diocese who did not recognize his decisions, or wishes, as the last word on a subject. And the Jesuits had no intention of being that docile on so important a matter.

A significant part of the problem had to do with access and easements. Hughes hated the idea that he had hemmed in his sister and brother-in-law and their four children by leasing them a house that left them on college property the minute they stepped off their front steps. A nearby parcel of land abutted the expanding railroad, but who could say who owned that now, and who was to see that the railroad paid for the promised fence that needed to be raised alongside the tracks? Furthermore, Hughes had long since given permission for Our Lady of Mercy, the college's chapel, to be used as a Bronx parish church, which meant that carriages and pedestrians made their way every Sunday across school property.

At several points in their increasingly rancorous talks with the arch-bishop, the Jesuits indicated that they would be happy to make a gift of any contested property that Hughes believed was his, but that solution did not sit well on Mulberry Street. Hughes did not want to be given what he maintained was his to begin with. Nor was he willing to admit that, in effect, he owed the Jesuits a Manhattan church, though he was willing to abandon Our Lady of Mercy at Rose Hill as a parish church and see that another one was built nearby.

As is always the case in such situations, tone determined a great deal. Those Jesuits who found Hughes's manner offensive naturally talked about him behind his back from one end of the archdiocese to the other, which the subject of their vituperative remarks heard about, while Hughes sniped about aspects of the Jesuit academic program at Fordham he didn't like, expressed his disappointment at the mismanagement of the seminary, and insisted that he had never given the Jesuits permission to hear confessions downtown, which they sometimes did. To make mat-ters worse, they were said to attend the theater during Holy Week, and a few, he felt he had reason to believe, were too cozy with the Young Irelanders. The Jesuits, in turn, wanted to know what had become of a bequest of $10,000 to Saint John's College, made in Hughes's name, that had been left by a Mrs. McCarthy before her death in 1845, which seemed to be taking a suspiciously long time to be probated. They were also angered by the archbishop's refusal to let them fund-raise in Man-hattan—"his" territory—for the school they had opened there. A seesaw of communication and miscommunication led each side to add to an ever-widening list of grievances, some weighty and some petty.

What ensued, then, was three years of off-and-on quasi-legal wran-gling, inconclusive conferences, semantical debate, and ill will. At one point, Hughes told Father John Larkin that if he did not have his way, he would haul the Jesuits into court. Larkin told a colleague that they were dealing with a man for whom "neither reason nor law have any weight against his will." Jean-Baptiste Hus, the superior of the Canada–New York Mission (a match for Hughes in the exercise of maladroit diplo-macy), told his superior, Pieter Beckx, the Jesuit general in Rome, that he too had run out of patience and that they could expect nothing more from the archbishop. ("It's impossible to argue with him!" he exclaimed. "All must bend under his inflexible will.") It didn't help Hus's mood when Hughes, who was perfectly fluent in French by this time, switched to English during a conference he attended, leaving Hus in the dark. And it didn't help Hughes's mood when the man the Jesuits hired to represent their interests was Charles O'Conor, the lawyer who had served for several years as Hughes's own legal counsel.

In truth, all parties wanted to stay away from the courts and the glare of publicity, which everyone agreed would be a lacerating and humiliating experience. They also wanted to avoid having this dispute come to the personal attention of the pope. It took the intervention of the Jesuit general to get a real arbitration process going. One of the emissaries Beckx sent Hughes's way was Father John McElroy, the Georgetown priest who had been sent to Mexico during the war, and another was Father Felix Sopranis, an English-speaking Italian Jesuit, both of whom Hughes felt he could work with. McElroy, an acquaintance of long standing, was especially agreeable to him (a man of "patience and prudence," he judged), though others said their bond was built on less august ground—namely, that McElroy was in awe of Hughes and something of a sycophant from start to finish in the whole business.

What mattered was that the acrimony wound down and eventually came to an end. The seminary/college boundary dispute was settled to Hughes's satisfaction; in turn, Hughes agreed that the Jesuits did indeed own Fordham, and he also promised to settle the title of the Sixteenth Street church in Manhattan on the Jesuits—although, hemmed in for the moment by the Putnam bill, he would be in no position to do so for a few years. Hughes agreed to sell the seminary building his brother-in-law had built, the church, and the seminary land to the Jesuits for $45,000 (highway robbery, Hus screamed), while the Jesuits were given permission to hear confessions. (That sale took place in 1860.) It appears that Mrs. McCarthy's $10,000 was wisely given up for lost by the Jesuits. And Hughes, showing no largeness of spirit, got the abject apology from the Jesuits that he demanded. One real loser in the conflict, suggesting that word of the fracas had leaked out, was the college itself: enrollment dropped tremendously, from 180 to 124, between 1855 and 1860.

A part of Hughes's ungovernable anger in this whole matter stemmed from the frustration he felt over one of the diocese's most long-standing problems: the never-ending shortage of good priests. He needed more seminarians. He could become distraught at the idea that the progress being made in the diocese, at a cost of great labor and anxiety, was just not enough to keep pace with the spiritual and physical needs of the Catholics of New York. He desperately needed a well-run seminary, which the Jesuits had certainly not provided. He desperately needed Fordham to succeed in order to provide him with young men who might want to attend the seminary after graduation.

Numerous priests throughout the archdiocese heard about the archbishop's tirades on this and various other themes or, worse, experienced them firsthand. They had long since concluded that they were being ruled by a man whose authoritarian nature was spiraling out of control. Not many were willing to go public with their complaints, of course. One who did, anonymously, published under the name of "Equitas," and in January 1857 found a home for his withering attacks in the pages of the *New York Times*. Equitas charged Hughes with loving a fight for its own sake, pretending to be interested in the welfare of the church when in fact his own ego was his central concern, and exhibiting no capacity for effective administration. Vain and bullheaded, he never consulted his priests, the writer charged, and when he did, was quick to tell them how little their opinions were worth to him. That was the kind of man the clergy of New York had to work with. Equitas suggested that the archbishop spend "the few short days of his declining life" learning to curb his tongue and trying to remember that his was a spiritual, not a political, calling. His target was predictably dumbstruck by what he read.

In a rage, Hughes wrote to *Times* publisher Henry Raymond to express astonishment that a reputable paper would print such an article, something more appropriate to James Gordon Bennett's rag, and demanded an apology and the author's name or, denied that, his lawyers would file a libel charge. Again, the lawyers. Raymond did apologize and asked the priest who had supposedly submitted the article for permission to divulge his identity, only to learn to his embarrassment that the elderly Boston priest under whose name the submission had come in knew nothing at all about the matter. No one ever discovered or revealed the identity of Equitas, but everyone agreed that the list of plausible suspects wasn't likely to be short. Some people even felt they detected the hand of Thomas D'Arcy McGee at work.

When Raymond was abroad that summer, another Equitas missive arrived over the *Times* transom and, without the absent publisher's permission, also made its way into print. (Someone at the *Times* had it out for Hughes, obviously.) This one was even worse in its way, suggesting that Hughes urgently needed a coadjutor before madness overtook "the chaos without form and void" that was the New York archdiocese. To add to Hughes's humiliation, Equitas sent copies of his published letters to every bishop in the United States and to the Vatican, and at least one other paper picked up on the story of internecine warfare amid the city's Catholic ranks. Hughes then felt it necessary to pen a lengthy, self-justifying account of his administration to his superiors in Rome in which, feeling belittled and exhausted, he raised the subject of retirement himself. "I do not wish to die out," he wrote, "in the same turmoil in which God has so far appointed that I should live." The pope, dismissive of Equitas's insinuations, did not want to hear about a New York without Hughes at the helm. In Rome, Hughes was still regarded as even more useful than he sometimes realized. Several months later, Vatican officials entrusted him with an especially delicate task, requesting him to look into charges of mismanagement of the Boston diocese that had been leveled against Bishop Fitzpatrick, urging him to do so "secretly, as prudence directs." He was happy to be able to acquit his fellow bishop.

Friends tried to persuade Hughes just to pay less attention to the press. Praised or faulted, he sold papers by the thousands. It was a needless expense of energy to work himself up over every letter, editorial, or caricature. Appealing to the archbishop on those terms was all so much wasted breath: newspapers molded opinion in America, and John Hughes could not live with the idea of a critic, let alone one who wore the Roman collar, having the last bitter, sarcastic word.

Then, too, there were those irritants to deal with that could only be called minor if they were kept out of the papers. In 1857, Hughes had decided to give Ambrose Manahan a third chance and readmitted him to the diocese as a temporary administrator at Saint Stephen's Church. When questions of dubious bookkeeping practices arose after a lavish refurbishing of his rectory and Manahan was told to come to Mulberry Street to review the matter, the ex-Fordham president left town with all the parish's receipt books and financial records. Manahan was a quirky man by any standards. He told a friend a few years later that Hughes was "a tyrant, but with feeling," though many people would have said that description applied equally well to Manahan himself. Hughes was glad to see the back of him.

This was no time to have to explain unnecessary expenditures to skeptical parishioners. Throughout the 1840s, Hughes had discussed with myriad audiences his desire to build a truly monumental cathedral in Manhattan—wildly implausible as that notion was in that decade. By 1852, though, after his fourth trip to Europe, he was ready to raise the subject in earnest. The archdiocese had owned the land he had in mind since 1810, directly across the street from the recently built boys' orphanage (in the middle of nowhere, he was repeatedly told), and its acreage, what would become an entire city block, was ample enough. It had been the site of a small Jesuit school and chapel in the woods that lasted for a year or two, then a Trappist monastery that took in male orphans from 1814 to 1815, and it had been used for other diocesan purposes through the years. It was considered for the site of a future Catholic cemetery, and in the early 1840s housed a small frame church, Saint John the Evangelist, lost to foreclosure in 1844. That "middle of nowhere," as Hughes and anyone with an eye on Manhattan's upward momentum knew, was going to be the center of New York City soon enough.

Hughes had two architects in mind for his grand dream, and they had both been placed on salary in 1852 to begin work on preparatory drawings. One was his brother-in-law, William Rodrigue, and the other, eighteen years Rodrigue's junior, was the prodigy James Renwick. A Gothic Revivalist par excellence, Renwick had distinguished himself, at twenty-five, as the architect of Grace Episcopal Church on Broadway and Tenth Street, which opened in 1844 and mightily impressed Hughes, and two years later of the Smithsonian castle in sight of the Capitol in Washington, D.C. Off and on through 1852–1857, Hughes kept meeting with the two men to pore over drawings and exchange ideas. Money, not talent or ambition, was what slowed the pace of progress to a crawl. With the Panic of 1857, the entire project began to seem more far-fetched than ever.

As the economy tottered in the late 1850s, public debate centered more frequently not on cathedral-building, but on the subject of the famine immigrants who remained in the coastal cities. With so much land to the west and the example of the Scandinavian Protestants who were emigrating to Wisconsin and Minnesota before them, it was only natural that men who were interested in alleviating the squalor of overcrowded cities and pondering economic possibilities for the Irish elsewhere would want to talk about western colonization.

Earlier in the decade, Archbishop Hughes had not been flatly opposed to the idea, and when boys from the diocesan orphanages reached adolescence, many were sent out west or to farm families in upstate New York when willing Catholic foster parents could be found. He rarely discouraged individuals who consulted him from making the attempt. He had come close to supporting a Wisconsin colonization project ten years earlier. Spokesmen for the Irish American cause as different as Thomas Francis Meagher and Father Theobald Mathew had urged new immigrants to consider the possibilities of a land of open space, big skies, and arable land. They were farmers, not city dwellers, in Ireland—why not in their new homeland as well?

Hughes's view had changed by the late 1850s, but the arguments of the pro-colonization side were not easy to refute when considering the most hard-pressed residents of the city's worst neighborhoods. "It is not within the power of language to adequately describe, much less exaggerate, the evil consequences of the unhappy tendency of the Irish to congregate in the large towns of America," one visiting Irish journalist from Cork wrote in the 1860s. Bishop Mathias Loras of Dubuque was at that time doing his best to encourage resettlement in his state and received occasional support from New York's Irish Emigrant Aid Society, the *Boston Pilot*, and even the *Freeman's Journal*. Bishops O'Connor, Timon, and Whelan were on record as seeing merit in the idea. It was the one subject on which Hughes and Terence Donaghoe did not see eye to eye.

Hughes's shift in opinion came about for several reasons. Immigration from Europe was in a period of decline, at least compared to the worst years of the now-ended famine, and a leveling-off of the number of arrivals that the East Coast cities had to deal with meant—or might mean—that the worst was over. But if that perspective represented wishful thinking, it was an all-too-real fact that the number of churches, priests, and parochial schools west of Illinois was negligible, and the danger of Irish Catholics drifting from their faith wasn't a far-fetched concern. That is precisely what worried Hughes—that, and the fear that those who remained in the city would be the destitute and the disabled while the more vigorous and enterprising of America's newest citizens would heed the cry of "Go west, young man."

A convention in Buffalo devoted to this topic in 1856, sponsored in part by Thomas D'Arcy McGee and lavishly praised in his newspaper,

had stirred Hughes's ire with its proposal that Irish men of means purchase land in the West to sell as lots to Irish immigrant families willing
to leave the cities in the East. This occasioned a somewhat injudicious
statement by the archbishop in an article later that year to the effect that
he was tired of hearing the condition of the Irish in New York bemoaned
as if it were any "more squalid than the Irish hovels from which many of
them had been 'exterminated.'" Enemies took this to mean he was making light of the immigrant suffering in his midst, whereas he intended
something very different. Rather, he meant in "Reflections and Suggestions: The Catholic Press in the United States" to make three separate
observations: that the old life in Ireland should never be romanticized;
that American urban life, horrific as it could be, at least offered immigrants potential proximity to churches and schools, which might amelio-
rate their lot over time; and that it was absurd to pretend that an indigent
farmer's life in the Midwest was going to be in any way preferable for
most of those who attempted it. Life west of the Mississippi could be its
own kind of hell.

On the evening of March 26, 1857, the cause came to Manhattan
when one of its most determined advocates, Father Jeremiah Trecy,
appeared at the Broadway Tabernacle to deliver a lecture. He was there,
with the blessing of Bishop Loras and accompanied by McGee as publicist, to promote a settlement he was establishing in Nebraska. When
Hughes heard about it, he might have felt this gathering had the potential to be a replay of an episode that had occurred two years earlier
when James Shields, a Catholic Mexican War hero and former U.S.
senator from both Illinois and Minnesota, came east to sell the idea
of an Irish colony in Minnesota. Hughes had attended that lecture at
a local church and afterward spoke against the proposal. Shields tried
to engage him in a debate, but the conversation ended when he accused
the archbishop of not being able "to see beyond the length of his nose."
Hughes stalked out. This time around, he would take care to be more
in control of the situation.

Trecy orated that winter night about the idyllic future he foresaw for
the community that would be called Saint Patrick's, where the streets
would be named after the major cities of Ireland, where honest, hardworking men and women could raise their families in peace. When he
decided that he had heard enough, a man bundled in a scarf and long
coat in the front row of the balcony rose to present his objections. He

disagreed, he wanted the audience to know—all of whom quickly recognized the impassioned speaker—with every syllable they had heard. The Irish were being sold a bill of goods. Life at this alleged haven would be unspeakably harsh, radically different from but no less painful than what they confronted in the city. Growing potatoes in Ireland and managing acres of wheat in an inhospitable climate had nothing in common. The bloodshed following the passage of the Kansas-Nebraska Act suggested that peace would be the last thing any man would find there. Staring at McGee, seated on the stage behind Trecy, he complained about writers who knew rather little of what they were talking about, well-intentioned but misguided bishops, rapacious land speculators, the dangers of ethnic segregation, and gullible immigrants. Trecy attempted to get a word in, but Hughes cut him short. He buttoned his coat and departed the hall. Many audience members followed. Indeed, at least about this one proposed Irish settlement, Hughes was right: Saint Patrick's, Nebraska, proved to be a dismal failure.

The idea that the Irish would ultimately flourish in an urban setting, along the lines that Hughes envisioned that flourishing to take place, was a hard sell in the midst of what quickly became a major depression. But the depression would not last, Hughes insisted. Clear values, hard work, and an eye on the future were what was needed. And that future had to encompass a better-educated ethnic and religious minority. Throughout the 1850s, Hughes continued to be a popular lecturer, in New York and in cities as far north as Boston and as far west as Pittsburgh. Large numbers of people were willing to pay fifty cents a head to hear him and to write checks after he retired from the podium. He was often at his best, or his most energized, on the subject of the transforming power of education.

Speaking at the Saint James Church hall in Manhattan in the autumn of 1857, he held an audience of several hundred people rapt for the better part of two hours. His message—that there was a correlation between lack of education and the crime rate; that the foundation of a productive, middle-class life was to be found in literacy, learning, and the self-respect that learning engendered; that an educated class of Irish Americans would one day take their place in the halls of power—was not a new one. The archbishop had been speaking to that effect with increasing urgency for more than fifteen years now, and he believed every word of it. His passion could be contagious. More and better teachers "would make the duties of the judge and the policeman less arduous." More and better schools would make for a more stable, prosperous, and spiritually grounded society. That November night he raised $1,500. No one else in the city could boast a yield that great for so unglamorous a cause as a church-basement grammar school.

11

A New Cathedral

O F ALL YEARS in the second half of the nineteenth century in
which to begin fund-raising for the construction of a major
American cathedral, 1857 and 1858 were the worst. John Hughes
could not have known this when he decided to organize his archdiocese
for this massive, groundbreaking project. The economy in the first half of
1857 was stable. There was no hint of a looming financial crisis beyond
signs of a minor recession at the end of the previous year and a concern
about questionable loans that some overextended banks had trafficked in.
President Buchanan's new administration was much more preoccupied
with ongoing violence over slavery in Kansas and the ramifications of
the *Dred Scott* decision than by anything to do with the economy. By the
time Hughes was ready to begin active solicitations, however, the financial
health of the city and the nation was everyone's first topic of concern.

When the mismanaged Ohio Life Insurance & Trust Company, the
largest and most respected bank in Ohio, with a branch in New York
City, announced its suspension of specie payment in August, the ripple
effects "acted as a clap of thunder in a summer sky." A panic ensued
over the next two months, which led to the drying up of credit at other
banks (particularly hard on western farmers now that the Crimean War
had ended and Europe needed fewer U.S. imports), bank runs, declining
stock prices, and retrenchment in almost all industries. Only the South's
cotton market continued to do well. Building construction, shipyards,

and railroads were especially hard hit. Wage cuts of 20 to 30 percent were not uncommon. By December, a thousand merchants in New York had closed their doors. To many, it seemed like 1837 all over again. The most popular melodrama on the New York stage later that year, Dion Boucicault's *The Poor of New York*, set in 1837 and 1857, based its plot on that very analogy.

With some estimates suggesting that layoffs might reach fifty thousand in the city that autumn, Mayor Fernando Wood proposed hiring more men to labor at public works, such as the construction of Central Park, which was then well under way, paying them with potatoes and flour. Fiery rallies were held in Tompkins Square Park, and fear of labor violence gripped the city in October, especially in the aftermath of the Fourth of July altercation between the Irish Dead Rabbits and the nativist Bowery Boys, a nasty riot that had involved almost one thousand combatants, resulted in twelve deaths, and caused considerable property damage in and around the Sixth Ward.

Hughes's reaction to the situation was realistic, at first. "I had made arrangement to commence the new cathedral in New York this autumn," he wrote to a friend not long after the first banks failed. "But I shall be obliged to postpone it for the present. What is called a commercial crisis has burst upon New York as a hurricane and fortunes that were almost fabulous but a few weeks ago have been utterly prostrated. . . . The prospects are that we shall have unexampled sufferings among the poor during the coming winter."

Within a few months, though, Hughes concluded that if he didn't begin active fund-raising, at least in a tentative way, crucial momentum would be lost. He had found one hundred subscribers who were willing to pledge $1,000 each to enable work at the site to commence. The builders were stipulating that 25 percent of the projected costs had to be paid up front. By May 1858, Hughes had to report to the board of the cathedral that he had "scant hopes" that all of those one hundred donors would fulfill their pledges. Too many were pleading financial constraints. (Sixty-two came through in the end.) Just enough money was coming in to allow construction to start, but thereafter, he wrote, "We must 'pay as we go' as far as materials and workmen are concerned." This was a practice Hughes hated; he had refused to allow the orphanage across the street from the site of the new cathedral to open until it was fully paid for, and in general new churches were not consecrated until paid for.

Yet following that principle in this instance might mean no cathedral would be built before the end of the century. Payments by protracted installments and long-term debt would have to be borne. In that case, Hughes knew, "[the cathedral] shall never be consecrated in my lifetime"—he underlined the word *lifetime* in his memorandum to the board—"but if, when done and consecrated," $200,000 or $300,000 is owed, "I should not think that much." Worried about "the caprices of quarry owners & quarry men," he broached the idea of buying, for $10,000, the small quarry in Westchester from which much of the stone that would be used would be taken. He had worked at a quarry in Chambersburg in his youth. He knew something about stone, and he knew something about that business and the questionable men who profited by it.

He set the financiers he had brought together to work. Every contract would have to make provision for the possible suspension of operations, for a given time. If the committee ran out of money and needed to stop work to fund-raise, no damages were to be claimed. (Of course, it didn't turn out that way, and off-again/on-again litigation troubled the diocese right up until the time of Hughes's death.) The construction of Saint Patrick's Cathedral was going to be, then, a slow, painstaking, even potentially embarrassing fits-and-starts operation.

There were no alternatives, though, other than to abandon the project and leave it for a future generation to inaugurate—something Hughes would not consider—or to keep asking, cajoling, begging, praying. A few New Yorkers, like Lorenzo Delmonico, owner of the famed restaurant, were still flush and in a generous frame of mind. Others could not afford to be. Writing to Judge Charles P. Daly in 1858, one of the most respected Irish Catholics in a public position in the city, Hughes asked if he could meet in person so he could describe his plans for "the new St. Patrick's Cathedral, to be created . . . worthy of our increasing numbers, wealth, and intelligence in the community." The archbishop knew he wasn't approaching a regular communicant. Daly was an "Easter Sunday Catholic," but he was reputedly well-off and was on enough charitable lists around town—including some for Jewish charities—to seem a very plausible person to approach. Here, too, the tenor of the times worked against that hope. The judge put the archbishop off for a good while and ended by contributing $500, considerably less than Hughes had been after.

A show of healthy bravado was planned for the summer of 1858, when the cornerstone was to be laid. Once an elaborate ceremony had taken place marking the spot where the open ground would one day see a cathedral, more people might make the effort to dig deeper into their pockets. It was a reasonable theory. The event would play on ethnic as well as religious ties. Throughout the spring, Hughes kept meeting with James Renwick and his brother-in-law to go over the ever-changing drawings, to consider their estimates, to talk about the reliability of the companies they would work with. Everything about the planning stages, Hughes knew, had to inspire confidence. This was to be no ordinary church. It was to be a house of worship talked about for generations, visited by the faithful in centuries to come—a building "worthy of God, worthy of the Catholic religion, and an honor to this great and growing city, Babylon though it be," he wrote to Marc Frenaye in Philadelphia.

He also knew that fund-raising for a cathedral in hard times would mean less money for other religious commitments, and that dilemma gave rise to some serious awkwardness. From Italy, Father Bernard Smith, the Irish Benedictine who was to serve as acting head of the North American College scheduled to open the next year in Rome, reminded Hughes that he had promised a good-size contribution in 1858. Hughes indicated that he would need to put off sending any money for a year, given the grim situation in New York and his conflicting commitments. Smith was not so easily deterred. "A year makes little difference for the Cathedral, but it is not so with the College. I hope you find means without difficulty to fulfill your promises," he wrote back. Nor was he averse to some heavy-handed emotional blackmail: the pope had always been impressed by Hughes's "liberality and zeal," he reminded his friend, and it would be a shame to lose the goodwill of the pontiff. "I only wish to see you stand well with Rome and that you do not lose your justly merited high character. Do not consider from this that Rome does not like to see your grand cathedral completed," Smith added, but promises were promises. He also brought up a sore subject—Bedini's visit of several years ago—and commented thoughtfully on how the Italian archbishop had in a recent lecture "vindicated the Americans of the false impressions that were made against them." What a shame if those bad impressions were reawakened. Decisively checkmated, Hughes ordered collections in all diocesan churches in mid-December, which raised a total of $5,000 for the seminary in Rome that would serve North America. He was at least able to use the occasion for another sermon on the importance of schools and the church "as the fond mother of education." Irish, British, and Scottish seminarians had their own national colleges in Rome and, after their period of study there, went back to serve as priests in their native land, and it was time that the same was true for Americans.

Hughes also heard from all sides in these dark days that a cathedral was a dubious undertaking in a metropolis with so many unmet social needs. He was told repeatedly that Protestant efforts to aid the indigent were outstripping Catholic efforts—given their numbers and resources, hardly a surprise—and, equally troubling, that the Protestants were active in proselytizing for their own faith when they reached out to the needy. Protestant reformers often denied the latter charge, though they did complain that the Catholic Church of New York failed to do enough for its poor even as they acknowledged that the church's funds were spread thin in a time of school and church building.

Charles Loring Brace, founder of the Children's Aid Society, was typical. "I certainly had no prejudice against the Romanists," Brace recalled in 1872 in *The Dangerous Classes of New York*. (By "dangerous classes," he meant, in the main, the impoverished Irish immigrant class.) Yet his classic account of charity work in the city is saturated with prejudicial statements about Catholicism and the way in which the destitute Irish "seemed stamped with the spiritual listlessness of Romanism." He asserted that too many priests were indifferent to the growing poverty around them, while willing to admit on the same page that other valuable priorities—their churches, their schools—would suffer if they did channel more of their limited funds to the indigent masses.

Even before the collapse of the national economy, a bad situation had been growing worse for certain raw segments of Hughes's community. Hard times meant layoffs, and the first men laid off were the Irish; layoffs meant the breakup of families, evictions, desperation, despair, and, what was visible to everyone, more prostitutes on the streets and on the stoops of brothels, more pimps ("Broadway statues," as they were called) on the prowl. This was a problem Hughes had chosen to ignore for years. He would have preferred to ignore it indefinitely. He alternated between two extremes in his reaction. On the one hand, he insisted on occasion that the numbers, at least among Irish women, did not justify the labor and expense that seeking a solution, or remediation, would entail. And the archdiocese and its overworked priests and women religious, he argued, had enough to do with the churches, schools, orphanages, and the hospital whose establishment he had overseen. On the other hand, he was heard to complain, more honestly, that the numbers were too great to hope to effect any change at all.

The unspoken part of the problem was the unease that the topic itself evoked in a man of Hughes's background and values. The subject of sex made him profoundly uncomfortable. "To the Irish," one Catholic writer wrote in 1907, "the whole path of honor seems so natural and easy for a woman that they can find no excuse for she who leaves it. . . . This natural and supernatural horror of the desolating vice was strong in the Irish-American archbishop."

The thought that the Sisters of the Good Shepherd, the order that traditionally worked with "fallen women" in the Magdalen houses they staffed in other cities, lived in close daily contact with those who had practiced the "desolating vice" was repugnant to him. So, too, was the public admission that opening a shelter would represent: the widows and daughters of Irish immigrants by some estimates made up a third or more of the city's prostitute population, and (unlike native-born or German girls) the majority of them were streetwalkers, the most abused prostitutes, rather than occupants of a protected parlor-house brothel. Yet there were more compassionate men and women around him who wanted the archbishop to look past his own sexual anxieties and face the church's responsibility in this painful area. William Starrs, who had been working under Hughes since Hughes's arrival in New York, was one of them. He brought the subject up numerous times over a two-year period. A redemption project was not, after all, anything that would cost the archdiocese money if it were privately funded and the sisters were available to take charge. On the other hand, every dollar that was given for one cause, Hughes kept arguing, meant money lost to another, and his pleas for giving and more giving from Catholic New Yorkers were wearing even him out by this time.

Father Starrs was clever. When he had decided he had done his best in presenting his case and could do no more, he sent in a woman. Flora Foster (*Miss* in some sources, *Mrs.* in others), fiftyish and as sure of herself as was the archbishop, was the longtime matron of the Tombs municipal jail, and she firmly believed the city needed a Magdalen house. Though not a Catholic, she was Irish-born, stern but caring, and she wasn't used to being lightly dismissed. Hughes was in a despondent mode when she saw him: there were too many Magdalens in New York to deal with. "They will swamp us," he told her. Her arguments were more persuasive: What did it matter if only a few out of every thousand were saved? Those few mattered. The one lost lamb and the ninety-nine? And she had reason to know that time spent in prison did nothing to redeem any of these poor women. They came out, not repentant, she told him, but hardened, worse than when they began their sentence, and only too ready to resume their old life. How could it be otherwise if no one cared about them and they had no hope for a different future and no skills to seek employment in a different form? They were women failed by the state and the church. Sophia Ripley, the Brook Farm convert so dear to the archbishop's heart, then added her voice as well. Hughes dragged his feet a while longer and finally relented.

Starrs found a large house on Fourteenth Street that could be rented for $1,000 a year, and Ripley undertook responsibility for finding contributors to meet the bills. She knew enough well-heeled, socially conscious women in the city to keep her end of the bargain. With the barest necessities, the House of the Good Shepherd opened on Four-teenth Street in the fall of 1857, serving seventy-five girls and women in its first year, many in their early to mid-teens. Within a few years, thanks to a $16,000 donation from a Catholic businessman, it relocated to a much larger building with ample grounds a few blocks from Gracie Mansion—and far from downtown temptations—that could accommo-date several times that number. (Within fifty years, according to the order's records, the sisters served over 13,000 women, 8,581 committed to them by the courts and 4,457 who had asked admittance on their own.) Life in both facilities was spartan, to put it mildly, and Hughes insisted that he meant it when he told the sisters they were on their own in their search for funds. He did, however, in 1859 give them a onetime donation of $4,000 from his annual collection appeal.

A Fifth Avenue cathedral to rival those of Europe, with massive bronze doors and stained-glass windows from France and spires even-tually rising hundreds of feet above the street; a shelter for the most wounded young women on a judgmental social ladder: neither had existed or even been contemplated when Hughes arrived from Philadel-phia to assist John Dubois. They were the poles of the American Catholic experience in the 1850s. One would be rightly credited to him; for the other, he deserves very little credit. The twenty-first-century view of their respective importance, of the greater need to serve the poor and despairing, is clear. The same was not true in antebellum America. In any event, John Hughes accepted that his job involved making choices and ordering priorities he believed in; and once those decisions were made, he rarely looked back.

———

TO HONOR NEW YORK'S most famous prelate on his sixty-first birthday in 1858, a new publication, *Harper's Weekly: A Journal of Civilization*, put Hughes on its June 26 cover. The article, a glowing homage that had to have pleased its subject and his circle inordinately, was illustrated with an etching, taking up most of the front page, based on a photograph by Mathew Brady. The picture made the archbishop appear considerably healthier and younger than in fact he was at that time. He stands tall in episcopal robes, one hand resting on a fat book, the other in the fold of his cassock, looking—not angry or determined, but calm and steadfast. The toupee looks almost natural.

"No individual, perhaps, in this country," the writer maintained, "in office or out of it, wields a larger influence over a greater number of minds than the Most Rev. John Hughes, D.D., Archbishop of New York." The article reviewed his tenure just as he wished it to be seen—"in his diocese he has reduced discordant elements to at least a passive harmony and enjoys an undisputed supremacy, derived as much, perhaps, from his intellectual as official eminence"—and acknowledged that his "vast power" was wielded, "however imperiously, in loyal subservience to what he regards as the interest of his Church." The *Harper's Weekly* profile abounded in inaccuracies, some no doubt attributable to the interviewee: a year was shaved off his age, his youthful employment as a gardener was termed an "apocryphal story," he was referred to as a tactful administrator (what hoots that statement must have occasioned), and the business of some Welsh ancestry was raised again. Two sentences probably stung, the reference to the fact that so many Catholic families still believed the public school system was preferable for their children to the parochial schools Hughes had to offer, and the view of his writing as of a "transient or fragmentary nature."

Yet the rhetorical flourishes could have come from his own pen: "We find him ever ready for any emergency. He always has his harness on . . . he has the chivalry to be foremost in the conflict, and he scorns proxies. . . . The sum of his labors is prodigious. He seems endowed with tireless energy." No mention was made of the cathedral cornerstone laying scheduled for two months later, but one hope behind this publicity tour-de-force, from the diocesan point of view, was the suggestion that Catholics of all nationalities were lucky to be led by a man capable of bringing a project of the kind he had undertaken to fruition. The idea, the expectation, was that a Catholic family of means that had not yet contributed would read the article and think twice about their duty to their city and their faith.

Attention from *Harper's Weekly*, giving Hughes national publicity of the highest order, came at the right moment, because that same month he was engaged in another, less dignified dispute with a journalist. Hughes was suing James Swain, editor of the *Albany Statesman*, for printing an article he considered libelous. He had been sensibly advised over the years that James Gordon Bennett, Horace Greeley, David Hale, William Stone, and any number of other Manhattan newspaper men could say what they wanted in print, but that to take them to court on any provocation would only delight those men at the increase in circulation for their papers that would result and would embarrass the church. Charles O'Conor, his legal counsel, would never have let him contemplate such a thing. But the tiny *Albany Statesman*—who had heard of it outside the Albany area? He would draw the line there. Someone had to hold these vicious scribblers accountable. Yet it might also be asked, if the paper wasn't well known, why go after it? Logic in this instance was not the point.

The offending short article was printed under a pseudonym ("Mentor"), still a common practice in American papers at the time, and it claimed that John Hughes was the head of a secret society, the Circle of Jesus, that was plotting the Catholic takeover of the United States. The author was possibly Nathan Urner, a peripatetic Manhattan journalist and mischief-maker whom P. T. Barnum described as a "facetious" sort. The charge was vaguely comical, certainly threadbare. Yet Hughes had had enough of this kind of thing and wanted James Swain, editor of the paper, to prove the accusation or pay for the libel. The grand jury in Albany refused to indict, insisting that the article was so ludicrous no sensible man would take it seriously and hence no damage to the archbishop's reputation could be claimed. In the mood he was in, that wasn't good enough for John Hughes. He had Swain arrested when he was in New York City a short time later. Swain was released on $1,000 bail, a hefty amount, leading one to suspect an Irish judge at work for his archbishop. Yet it does not appear from any newspaper records that summer that the case went to trial in New York City, either. Hughes had to console himself by studying his robust, intellectual image on the cover of a periodical with a six-figure circulation.

The biggest misconception the *Harper's Weekly* article conveyed, though, did not have to do with his administrative skill or early history; it had to do with his health. For a year, Hughes had been hinting to Rome that he was not well, that he was exhausted much of the time, and that the day was approaching when he would have to ask to be relieved of his duties. Exactly when Hughes was diagnosed with the Bright's disease that would kill him five years later is unclear, but it seems as if the beginnings of that fatal kidney failure had started by the mid- or late 1850s. Cardinal Barnabo, cardinal-prefect of the Propaganda Fide, let him know that the hierarchy was unreceptive to this news. The pope would approve a coadjutor, if the work was too much—a thought not really to the archbishop's liking, though he was too diplomatic to say so—but resignation was out of the question. Baltimore had recently been given by the pope "prerogative of place" in the United States, which meant that the archbishop there had the authority to head any national councils or assembles (a development that probably did not sit well on Mulberry Street), but no one in the Vatican wanted Hughes to think that Rome did not know what he was up against in New York, how ably he had acquitted himself over the last two decades, and how irreplaceable they regarded him.

It was around this time that Hughes moved out of the rectory behind the old cathedral and relocated farther uptown, to a quieter area and to the care of the one person in the world who loved him most, his married sister. The diocesan purchase of a town house on the corner of Madison Avenue and Thirty-Sixth Street had been preceded earlier by the purchase of a country house in Manhattanville, farther north, where the archbishop could retreat for periods of rest. He never made much use of the Manhattanville property, it was duly sold, and the new house was acquired as an official residence. It was spacious enough for receptions and other fund-raising efforts, and it comfortably accommo-dated the archbishop, his now-vast library, and the Rodrigue family, who had already moved from Rose Hill back to Manhattan. Having William

Rodrigue living under the same roof with him meant that his architect need not commute from Fordham anymore; they could confer about the cathedral-in-the-making at any time. Margaret could regulate his meals and rest periods. A carriage ride to inspect the progress on "his" cathedral would take him only twelve blocks away.

Looking back on 1858, wondering at the end of that year how much longer he might be able to remain in his position of leadership, Hughes felt both somber and hopeful. The unexpected death of William Walsh, the fellow bishop with whom he felt most comfortable ("he understood me"), was a painful blow, made worse by the fact that he had wasn't well enough to make the trip to Halifax, where he had been asked to deliver the funeral oration. A heartening development was the founding of the Missionaries of Saint Paul the Apostle—the Paulists—by Isaac Hecker, and their decision to base themselves in New York, declining an offer from Bishop Bayley to locate in Newark. Hughes granted them a parish far uptown, centered at Fifty-Ninth Street and Ninth Avenue. Hecker, a convert, had been a Redemptorist but left that order in the belief that what the United States really needed at this moment was a new order less concerned with its German roots and with a greater missionary presence to secure more conversions. Approval from the Vatican was a long time in coming, and Hughes had played an equivocal part in that political drama (in part because he was uncertain of the hierarchy's attitude toward this unusual man, the very independent Hecker), but now he could look forward to a new community of dedicated men in his archdiocese.

That year had also seen marks of respect from unexpected quarters. He had been invited by Mayor Wood to be one of the speakers at the municipal banquet celebrating the laying of the transatlantic telegraph cable. Then, most movingly of all for Hughes, there was that August afternoon in an open field on Fifth Avenue when he asked a crowd of tens of thousands—some said the largest gathering the island had ever seen, certainly the largest Irish gathering ever held in Manhattan—to envision the towering cathedral that would rise on that spot. The city's transportation system had all but shut down bringing people to the site.

Held on the Feast of the Assumption, the ceremony for the laying of the cornerstone of the new Saint Patrick's Cathedral was a piece of theater of the kind Hughes reveled in, and it allowed him to do what he did best: express a deep enthusiasm that he could convince others to share. He had 3 archbishops, 7 bishops, 130 priests, musicians, and 20 altar boys in red cassocks serving as choristers on the huge, two-tiered platform around him. The Stars and Stripes waved alongside a green flag emblazoned with a golden harp of Ireland, Saint George's banner, the French tricolor, and other flags of Christian nations. "Hughes's folly," as the popular press had dubbed the idea when it was first aired, suddenly didn't look like such a folly, after all. It was clear that Fifth Avenue would in the not-too-distant future be the city's most prestigious boulevard; the first mansions had gone up two years earlier on Forty-Second Street across from the Croton Reservoir. He had picked his site well—and it was equally evident that with such fervent belief behind it, the building would rise, eventually, though its completion would require, he reminded everyone, "steadiness and indomitable resolution."

The spiritual descendants of Saint Patrick have been "outcasts from their native land and have been scattered over the earth," Hughes told the crowd, or that portion of it that could hear him, "and though there may be no mark to designate the graves in which they slumber, still the churches which they have erected . . . are most fitting headstones to commemorate . . . the honorable history of the Irish people." Now they could "laugh to scorn" at those who derided them as a people without culture, without ambition, without accomplishments and spiritual depth. His audience was ecstatic. The *New York Times* thought Hughes in bad taste to bring a political edge to his remarks (a bad taste "which has, more or less, characterized everything His Grace had said or written outside the immediate sphere of his arch-episcopal duties"). His constituency thought otherwise. The Irish press and the Catholic press thought otherwise. The afternoon closed with a Te Deum, followed by a band playing "Hail, Columbia" and "The Star-Spangled Banner."

Throughout the next year, nothing was so agreeable to the archbishop as to visit the site and note its progress. Except that that progress was more sputtering than swift, and he lived in dread of the day the coffers would run dry. Moving beyond the $75,000 that had come in thus far—approximately one-tenth of his estimate of the cathedral's total cost (a number that was ultimately far wide of the mark, of course)—proved more difficult than he had imagined, even with clergymen like Father Starrs and Father Hecker joining the list of $1,000 donors. He tried not to think about it. He appointed historian John Gilmary Shea to keep records about the construction, as he wanted an archive to document its

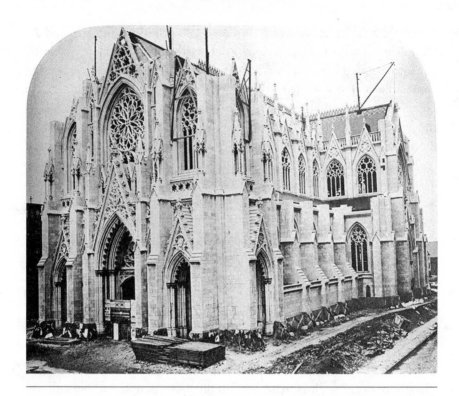

history. He dined with Seward and Weed in the spring, talking excitedly about the new Saint Patrick's and wishing Seward well on the extended European trip he was about to undertake before plunging into presidential politics the next year. He happily furnished his friend with a letter of introduction to Pius IX. At the end of the summer, he spent time on the Saint Lawrence River with the widow and sons of his brother Patrick, who had died four years earlier. Fishing and boating on the Thousand Islands with his nephews was a new experience he found rejuvenating.

An experience he found odd and uncomfortable that same summer was testifying in court on behalf of Jeremiah Cummings when a crazed parishioner at Saint Stephen's claimed she had had a child by the priest who had been abducted and was being kept hidden from her in the rectory. Cummings was an irritant a good deal of the time. He was an abolitionist, he thought the world of Orestes Brownson, he was a vocal critic of the standards of Catholic higher education and American seminaries, and he didn't believe immigrants should maintain too strong an

FIGURES 13 AND 14. *"Hughes's folly": Saint Patrick's Cathedral on Fifth Avenue under construction, c. 1860, and Saint Patrick's Cathedral completed more than two decades after John Hughes's death.* (Courtesy of the Archives of the Archdiocese of New York.)

attachment to their previous homeland—four views that put him profoundly at odds with his superior. He had also displeased Hughes when
he found the burden of maintaining a parochial school at his church to
be too much and one day marched all the pupils down Third Avenue to
enroll them in the nearest public school, a story that made the rounds of
the diocese. When he made a trip to Rome, his archbishop remarked that
he would not be heartbroken if Father Cummings decided he wanted
to stay in Italy. But there was no question that he had to be stood by
when under attack. The archbishop took the witness stand. The case
was dismissed.

In Washington to dedicate a church in the fall, Hughes visited President Buchanan, and while he was at the White House he heard the
frightening news of John Brown's raid on the U.S. arsenal at Harpers
Ferry. Buchanan looked crushed. This madman's act, Hughes wrote in
anxiety to Bernard Smith in Rome, "though insignificant, threatens to
become, if not the beginning of the end, at least the end of the beginning, of our federal system." It was clear, too, that the president was
near to overwhelmed by the burdens of his office and the direction of
national affairs.

Physical stamina was becoming a problem for Hughes as well. Yet he
simply could not bring himself to stop traveling when he felt the urge. In
the spring of 1859, he paid a second visit to his beloved Terence Donaghoe in Iowa, stopping on the way back for several days as the guest of
Bishop Henni in Milwaukee, where he said Mass in that city's cathedral.
He was in this period making an effort to cut back his speaking engage-
ments, as Margaret and his staff had been insisting he do for some time,
but the requests kept pouring in. One invitation he was especially eager
to accept arrived in the new year.

The Hibernian Society of South Carolina had beseeched him to speak
at its 1860 Saint Patrick's Day banquet, not an occasion he usually celebrated in a festive way in New York, but the invitation to the man who
was building the greatest cathedral in America was flatteringly worded,
and the city's new bishop, Patrick Lynch, assured him a warm welcome.
Lynch suggested he come early, allowing the two of them a week of
vacation at Saint Augustine in Florida. After a New York winter and a
fierce bout of rheumatism, the prospect was inviting. The realization that
he was only several weeks away from running out of money for the new
cathedral and the fact that an unresolved wage dispute with the laborers

had already called a halt to the work, a dilemma he did not want widely advertised, made a respite even more desirable. Hughes knew the South well, had visited all its major cities over the years—loved the hospitality he was always shown there, loved its climate in winter, loved the beaches and the palmettos and the pace of life. At times, it was pleasing simply because it wasn't New York.

Feted at a lavish banquet in the Hibernian Hall on Meeting Street on Saint Patrick's Day, Hughes used his time at the podium to take a shot at the stage Irishman and the stock character of popular novels then in vogue, the butt of easy jokes, the good-hearted buffoon with a brogue. He reminisced about how many Irish-born men he had met on his travels who occupied positions "just next to the throne," providing service to European monarchs, like Marshal Laval Nugent, who helped to subdue the Hungarian rebels and restore order to the Austrian Empire, or those of Irish descent like Marshal Patrice de MacMahon, the French hero of the Crimean War and bulwark for the church in anticlerical France. If Great Britain had recognized the latent talent of the most ambitious men of Ireland, he told this appreciative audience, if "like a wise government, [Britain] had encouraged the cultivation of the national talents of the Irish people, and had done them justice, she would at all times have had a nursery of statesmen, generals, and orators." Yet he was in a mood to feel sanguine—"in my advanced age." In years to come, he was certain, "the original, strong-minded, superabundant intellect of the Irish peasantry will break forth in a light brilliant enough to eclipse all that which has been taken from them. . . . Let the Irish people become educated, let them preserve the vigor of their natural character and intellect, and they may bid defiance to the slang of pretended novel-writers. Their position already entitles them to the admiration of impartial and enlightened minds throughout the world." To great applause, he proposed a concluding toast: "To the Land of the Shamrock. No one born within its borders need be ashamed of his birthplace."

Hughes thoroughly enjoyed his time with Lynch. Bishop Lynch was actually the closest thing he had to a southern counterpart, an immigrant from Northern Ireland with a strong personality and vociferous opinions, though his fame and influence were not as great. They shared some of the same problems as they coped with local nativists and parishioners who expected them to do all things and to be everywhere at once. Three thousand of the city's twenty thousand white residents were

Irish, and Lynch even had his own strong-willed journalistic version of James McMaster to deal with. They could commiserate and share notes. Hughes was to see Lynch again in three months as he had, against his doctor's wishes, accepted an invitation to deliver the commencement address at the University of North Carolina in June. Even after collapsing in exhaustion at a Mass he was celebrating in Albany in May, he refused to cancel that commitment. Boarding his train to head north now, Hughes had no suspicion that that would be the last time he would set eyes on Charleston or that, after their meeting in Chapel Hill, he would never see Lynch again, either. Momentous events would determine a different future for John Hughes and Patrick Lynch, for New York and Charleston.

A MONTH AFTER HUGHES'S departure, the Democratic national convention met a few blocks from Lynch's episcopal residence, and the first indications of an imminent national crisis were apparent. Stephen Douglas was the front-runner entering the convention, and most Americans, Hughes included, assumed he would be the Democrat to run against the Republican candidate, whoever that would be. Passions ran high in Charleston, the most determinedly pro-slavery city in the country, and enough southern delegates were opposed to Douglas's concept of "popular sovereignty," which would allow settlers in any new territory to decide the slave question, to deny him the two-thirds majority of delegates he needed. After fifty-eight ballots, everyone gave up in sweaty exhaustion and went home. At a second convention, held more sensibly in Baltimore, Douglas was finally nominated, but the party then split. In a third gathering, Democrats who would rally only behind the banner of unlimited expansion of slavery, including the acquisition of Cuba, if necessary, turned to Buchanan's vice president, John Breckenridge, as their candidate. The divisions didn't end there. Another group of mixed Democrats and former Whigs who found both Douglas and Breckenridge unacceptable turned to John Bell of Tennessee to found a third party, the Constitutional Union Party, whose premise was to support slavery but to limit it to where it currently existed. The November race would now be a four-man competition.

The Republican convention in Chicago in May yielded an even bigger surprise. Hughes assumed this was his friend's moment. Thurlow Weed and many other Republican politicians assumed the same, as did Seward himself. The whole point of Seward's trip to Europe the year before had been to keep him distant from any situations that might compromise his candidacy. But many people who should have known better had failed to reckon with several factors, including how skilled at horse-trading and backroom dealing the Lincoln men were and how long was the memory of the former Whigs and nativists who were now Republicans and made up a healthy percentage of the delegates. When the subject of Seward's attachment to Irish immigrants and Catholic education was raised among that group, his fate was sealed. (One might also ask why Weed and the Seward men agreed to hold the convention in Chicago, Lincoln territory.) The most important presidential election of the century began.

No letter indicating Hughes's preference has come to light, but it seems reasonable to conclude he placed his hopes in 1860 on Stephen Douglas—the only Democrat after Buchanan he was ever heard to say a good word about—as the man who might hold the Union together. He was seen at a Douglas rally at Cooper Union that year, though he later claimed he merely happened to be in the area and stayed only a few minutes. The other candidates were out of the question. Breckenridge refused to see that the era of slavery's expansion had passed and even that its days where it now existed were rightly numbered, Bell was an anti-Catholic Democrat-turned-Whig of no distinction, and Lincoln—Lincoln made Hughes very nervous, indeed. Republicans still had hopes of garnering his tacit support for their man, but, as always, the archbishop insisted that a clergyman must stand above partisan politics, though by this time no one believed him.

Another Catholic dismayed at Lincoln's unexpected ascendancy, but more comfortable airing his views, was Orestes Brownson. A Douglas supporter as well, he wrote that he would have respected the Republicans had they shown some minimal integrity by nominating William Seward, a man for whom he had scant regard but one who at least represented their dangerous values in a plausible way. The choice of an honest, amiable nonentity like the former one-term congressman from Illinois suggested to him that the Republican Party was scarcely taking itself seriously and would probably be a short-lived organization.

Brownson was becoming more outspoken all the time on a range of topics, and the day when he had offered the archbishop the right of censorship to his journal seemed far distant by 1860. In July, Hughes attended the Fordham commencement ceremonies, as he had every year for most of the last decade, and delivered a lengthy address to the graduates, the friends and families, and the faculty with whom he had so recently been at odds. Also present on the stage that day were Orestes Brownson, Bishop Loughlin of Brooklyn, and Bishop John Quinlan of Mobile, who was paying a visit to New York. By now the electrifying presence at the podium that had been the Hughes trademark was fading, and more often than not even sympathetic reporters commented on the speaker's querulousness and verbosity. He regarded a captive audience as truly captive, even at outdoor events in the summer sun.

Hughes found it all but impossible now to refrain in any major address from digressions and public corrections. After praising many of the student speakers, he reproved one for a joke he found inappropriate, and he took the opportunity afforded by Brownson's presence to allude to a recent article in an unnamed Catholic publication with which he disagreed. The unsigned article had offered a comparison of the standards of Protestant and Catholic university education and found the latter wanting. Acknowledging that he knew that the editor of the unnamed journal in question did not author all its articles (he hadn't in this case—it was Cummings's article), he wanted his audience to know that he wasn't insinuating Brownson had written it himself, and then he offered his target a backhanded compliment. When a man like Mr. Brownson points out our faults, the archbishop declared, it is for our own good—for "we all know he never flatters us," he added, eliciting a round of knowing laughter—and he concluded by reminding his listeners that every good Catholic should subscribe to *Brownson's Quarterly Review*.

That afternoon represented a last occasion for two occurrences. It was the last time John Hughes would ever, even half in jest, say something positive about *Brownson's Quarterly Review*. He would soon be infuriated by other articles and demand that all loyal Catholics in his diocese refrain from reading it. It was also the last time he would socialize with a bishop from the Deep South. Within several months, he and John Quinlan would be citizens of a nation and a would-be nation at war.

Brownson's lack of respect for Seward and Hughes's deep sorrow that Seward had been passed over for the presidential nomination were factors in Hughes's irascibility that summer. Yet as historians sifting through the voting patterns of 1860 have convincingly demonstrated, William Seward, if nominated, would probably not have been elected. The Republican margins of victory in Indiana, Illinois, and Michigan were slender, and those were not states in which Seward was popular. The deadlocked contest might well have ended up being decided in the House of Representatives, where Seward stood no chance at all. So the victory was Lincoln's in November because he was able to carry every state but one north of the Mason-Dixon Line, with Douglas taking New Jersey and Breckinridge and Bell dividing the southern states between them. Clarifying in his own mind what he hoped or surmised would happen, how he would respond to events as they unfolded, was as painful a process for John Hughes in the autumn of 1860, once the votes were counted, as it was to everyone who dreaded the thought of the dismantling of the Union. Few people assumed Southerners irate at the election of a "red Republican" were bluffing about the extent of their anger or their intentions.

In December, after South Carolina had announced it would hold a state convention that month to approve secession, President Buchanan delivered his final annual message as chief executive. It was a response to the crisis to make John Hughes conclude that he had never fully grasped the weakness of the man he had supported for that high office. Buchanan deplored what was happening but insisted that the federal government had no legal authority to stop this violation of law, no matter how many states chose to secede. William Seward was then led to quip that Buchanan's message "shows conclusively that it is the duty of the president to execute the laws—unless somebody opposes him—and that no state has the right to go out of the Union—unless it wants to." The "last juiceless squeeze of the orange," James Russell Lowell called the speech in the *Atlantic Monthly*. With three critical months to wait until Lincoln was sworn in, true leadership was not to be expected from the White House. The "secession winter" had begun.

More disunion within his own ranks confronted Hughes that autumn. For most of his time in office, the Irish and the Germans, and to a much lesser extent the French, had represented the ethnic range of New York Catholicism. The first Italian parish, such as it was, hadn't opened until 1857, and the Church of Saint Anthony of Padua managed to struggle on for only three short years. It occupied a rented building on Canal Street, and its congregation had trouble meeting the rent. When they lost access to that building, the almost four hundred parishioners, led by their immigrant priest, Father Antonio Sanguinetti, looked to Hughes to help them secure a new house of worship. Some awkward exchanges resulted, but Hughes let them know that while he would not stand in the way of their efforts, he could not offer any means to a solution.

Hughes and Sanguinetti never saw eye to eye about much, and the difficulties went beyond the Italian priest's very limited English. Sanguinetti's flock was small in number—there were probably no more than four thousand Italians in New York City at the time (official census figures put the number much lower), out of a population of eight hundred thousand, and the majority of those immigrants did not attend church—and Hughes thought very much in terms of numbers. He also sensed, no doubt accurately, rather little interest among the Italians in the fate of the pope back in Italy; their republican sympathies for a united Italy were fairly well known. The city's one Italian newspaper, *L'Eco d'Italia*, was vociferously pro-republican and anticlerical. Finding a building for Sanguinetti's four hundred parishioners to worship in was not in his view a primary concern, when they could just as well attend other churches, and he wasn't sure why Father Sanguinetti had to minister to an exclusively Italian parish of such limited size when other Italian or Italian American priests were doing well in less ethnically segregated places. Charles Constantine Pise had moved to Brooklyn to found Saint Charles Borromeo in Brooklyn Heights, and a Sicilian Franciscan, Francesco Caro, was happily settled in at Saint Stephen's. Before leaving for Hoboken to found a church, Antonio Cauvin had been by Hughes's lights an effective priest at Saint Vincent de Paul for four years. Sanguinetti, though, had a different perspective. He was a man on a mission.

When Hughes heard that Father Sanguinetti had taken it upon himself to solicit funds without his approval from among the city's Irish Catholics, he was not pleased. Hughes was also of the impression that the Italian priest had not been entirely honest with the people he approached about the purpose of his fund-raising. Sanguinetti "lacks judgment," Jeremiah Cummings told Cardinal Barnabo, who eventually inquired into the conflict. Even his allies admitted that Sanguinetti could be aggressive and unyielding, though Cummings was willing to be kind and call his defect one of "heroic obstinacy." In 1860, Sanguinetti went back to Italy to see if the pope might be inclined to take his side in the dispute and order Hughes to help him establish an Italian parish, and he

let everyone he spoke to at the Vatican know that he thought Hughes was
an Irish bigot and disgracefully anti-Italian. That was a fatal misstep.
Hughes was adamant now; the man could stay in Europe or go where
he wanted. He would set foot in his diocese again over his archbishop's
dead body, and if he attempted to do so, he would have him arrested
for financial malfeasance. The pope, in any event, was not interested in
Sanguinetti's cause.

There were times when an act of rebelliousness could earn Hughes's
quiet respect or at least his understanding—that is, when the subject
was political, not religious, and when it involved Ireland. The visit to the
United States of the Prince of Wales, the future King Edward VII, was
the great social and political event of the season that autumn. "Bertie"
was feted in New York, and a mammoth parade up Fifth Avenue was
staged in his honor. City officials were concerned about Irish protests,
but Hughes, while insisting he could not, of course, vouch for the behav-
ior of all Irish New Yorkers, told anyone who asked that he was sure
nothing untoward would take place. One nonviolent protester, though,
did make a newsworthy statement. Thomas Corcoran, a Fenian and
the colonel of the Sixty-Ninth Regiment, an Irish division of the state
militia, flatly refused to march his men before Victoria's son. Nothing
could induce him to change his mind, and his men followed his lead.
City and state officials were irate. Corcoran was jailed prior to being
court-martialed for his defiance.

As a public figure, Hughes had to insist that all Irishmen, especially
those occupying public positions like Corcoran, conduct themselves in a
proper civic manner. As a private citizen, Hughes had no more interest
than Corcoran did in honoring the representative of a nation he saw
as imperialistic and genocidal, but he reluctantly attended some of the
festivities. He was fine with letting John Mullaly, the editor of the *Metropolitan Record*, the newspaper that had replaced the *Freeman's Journal*
that year as the official voice of the archdiocese, speak for him. Mullaly's
editorials noted that Irish Catholics felt no particular enmity toward the
"mild, amiable, and inoffensive youth" who a guest of the nation, but at
the same time, no one should presume a gracious welcome meant that
British sins were ever to be forgotten or that any special relationship
existed between Great Britain and the United States.

Disappointments that struck close to the heart followed quickly upon
one another in 1860. The time had come to close down the failed Saint

Joseph's Seminary, sell the property to the Jesuits, as promised, and begin again. It would be two years before Hughes found an affordable location, upstate in the town of Troy, and could begin working in earnest to establish a new Saint Joseph's on the grounds of what had been a Methodist college. Hardest of all to bear was a ride up to Fifth Avenue and Fiftieth Street to see the white marble outlines of a building that was suddenly going nowhere, piles of stone lying about, excavations abandoned, remnants of scaffolding standing but the workers' sheds empty and no men at work. The walls were almost four feet thick and rose to the height of two stories, but the structure resembled nothing so much as "a large open box," one later commentator noted.

Hughes tried—poignantly or pathetically—to put the best face possible on the inevitable when it became clear that he couldn't pay the workers' higher wage demands and couldn't even pay them at their previous salary any longer. It was known to all the Catholics of the city, he had written in a letter to the *New York Times*, that "whether it should ever be completed or not . . . I will never allow the laborer to be defrauded of his wages in carrying on the work, and, consequently, whenever the funds are too low to pay the laborer the work must stop"—as if the laborers would have continued to work a single day without salary. It was the wrong moment in all ways to push for more donations, anyway, he maintained. The hot weather, his own health, the absence of so many important families from the city all urged delay. Mightily embarrassed, he insisted there was nothing to be embarrassed about. Everything would right itself in a few months, he told a reporter, and there was no cause for undue worry: "I do not think it is much to be regretted that the building should have a little repose, and time to settle on its foundations." That "little repose" would not be interrupted until seven hundred thousand Americans were dead and a national nightmare ended at Appomattox.

12

A House Divided, a Church Divided

THE CIVIL WAR divided more than families and friends, and more than the United States as a political entity—it divided institutions, the American Catholic Church among them. As late as the autumn of the election, clergy on both sides of the Mason-Dixon Line refused to contemplate the possibility of a rupture and what that might mean to their relations. Early in the new year, Patrick Lynch expressed the hope to Hughes that his friend William Seward would be the real power behind the throne and might curb what he viewed as Lincoln's warmongering instincts. A civil war would quickly assume "a frightful character," Francis Kenrick agreed, making life for everyone almost unendurable. One thing that became clear very quickly, though, was that Catholic bishops were not, in the main, pacifists; nor were they lacking in strong regional political opinions.

Southern bishops—many still slave owners, and not an abolitionist among them—saw Lincoln's post-Sumter call for volunteers as an outrageous act and disputed the legality and morality of forcing any part of the country to remain in a union it no longer supported. They were as incredulous as many antiwar factions in the North that the South might be invaded and that Americans would begin killing other Americans. John McGill, bishop of Richmond, wrote to Bishop Lynch on May 15, 1861, "Is Justice not on the side of the South? . . . I feel that the party in power has shown no disposition to respect the just claims of the South.

They seek to humiliate & subjugate her. . . . I cannot be blind as to which side seeks to domineer and oppress." McGill was agog that the North would "sustain Mr. Lincoln and fight for him without requiring him and his party to give up their unjust sectional and aggressive principles." Lynch shared that view. "Let the union be broken—we at the South will suffer to some extent," the Charleston bishop proclaimed in a letter to Hughes before the attack on Fort Sumter, "but the North will have to drain the cup, [from] which they have but taken a sip as yet."

Bishop William Henry Elder of Natchez maintained that it was the duty of Southern Catholics to support their new government under Jefferson Davis "without reference to the right or the wisdom of making the separation." (Elder was to be detained by Union forces in 1864 for a time for "encouraging . . . treasonable practices.") Jean-Pierre Augustin Verot of Savannah, arguing that slavery had always "received the sanction of God" if one's slaves were treated humanely and their right to marriage and family respected, assured his parishioners that Northerners were the true rebels—"not we of the South." John Quinlan of Mobile agreed that the South should not and "would not purchase Union at the expense of Justice," and Jean-Marie Odin of New Orleans, who owned two slaves, censured and suspended any of his priests who expressed antislavery sentiments.

Augustus Martin, bishop of Natchitoches, was willing to go further. The North was not just anti-Southern; it was anti-Catholic, he told his Louisiana parishioners, and by opposing slavery and invading the South, Northerners were setting themselves in opposition to God's plan, which had always been to raise the darker races by separating them from their pagan tribal beliefs and providing a sanctifying exposure to the Christian faith. A people cursed by nature were being saved by the American South, and their enslavement was one path to salvation. Acting as if he had never read *In supremo apostolatus*, Martin was sufficiently pleased with his pastoral letter to send a copy to Rome in 1861 in expectation of praise from his superiors, only to be told that no pontiff had ever declared that God had willed the enslavement of Africans nor did the Vatican endorse the belief that blacks represented a "cursed" people.

In New York, John Hughes made the boldest statement he could at the moment: he had the American flag raised over the cathedral. He was not the only bishop to fly the Stars and Stripes from his church as a show of support for the federal government. Philadelphia's James Wood (John

Neumann's successor in 1860), Milwaukee's John Henni, and Pittsburgh's Michael Domenec—the last somewhat more reluctantly—followed suit. John Purcell did the same in Cincinnati, in what was a far more dangerous setting than Mott Street in Manhattan. John Timon flew the flag over his Buffalo residence and delivered a strong sermon to his parishioners, calling the conflict regrettable but clearly a calamity initiated by the South, making the Northern cause "a war of duty, of lofty patriotism, of obedience to our country's call." John Fitzpatrick gave the governor of Massachusetts his support for the formation of an Irish regiment to answer Lincoln's call, a display of patriotism that led Harvard University to confer an honorary doctor of divinity degree on him.

A bishop like Peter Kenrick was forced into a position of somewhat more studied neutrality in Saint Louis, given that he owned several slaves who worked as domestics in his rectory and lived in a border state with pronounced Confederate sympathies (which he shared) but was under the constant eye of a watchful federal government. At one point late in the war, Seward raised the topic with Hughes of having Kenrick replaced for his resistance to the loyalty oath Missouri called on all its citizens to make. Bishop Martin Spalding of Louisville took the loyalty oath Kentucky demanded, but under protest, and excoriated abolitionists as "destructive fanatics" who would replace one evil—slavery—with another, equally damaging to society. One prelate, James Whalen of Nashville, found the tension between his equivocal beliefs and the strongly pro-Southern views of his congregation in Tennessee too great and felt it necessary to resign his office. Richard Whalen of Wheeling eventually risked arrest for his public support of the Confederacy, an outcome prevented only by the intervention of Francis Kenrick with the White House.

The flag flying, which was a rare occurrence in a Catholic church before this time, proved to be a more contentious issue than modern-day Catholics might imagine in an era when national flags are ubiquitous in churches. The religious press was divided about its appropriateness once the hostilities actually began, and Francis Kenrick's *Catholic Mirror* was only one of many voices raised in protest. "We disagree with those priests who have girded swords on their Catholic brethren," that paper's editor wrote, "with priests who have baptized cannon; with priests who have denounced such of their flock as did not volunteer for the war . . . with priests who have undertaken to raise Irish brigades . . . who have made [the sacred walls of their churches] conspicuous with flags outside," turning houses of God into a "barracks on a gala-day."

James Whalen was astounded when he heard that the American flag was flying above Saint Patrick's Cathedral in New York. "It could very likely involve the churches in ruin," he wrote to Hughes. This was a dangerous precedent, and he felt it was typical of the hubris of that section of the country. "Trust not to the strength of the North," he warned his onetime friend. "You may suffer no less than Virginia and the South." James McMaster, in fact, agreed with Hughes's critics.

The reference to priests blessing cannons was not, unfortunately, apocryphal or hyperbolic. One overzealous priest from Hughes's diocese, Thomas Mooney of Saint Teresa's Church, had accompanied the first Irish troops out of the city. Sprinkling holy water on a cannon before a crowd of Catholic soldiers at their encampment, he noted that babies sometimes cried at baptisms, but that the subject of his fervent blessing "has his mouth wide open, evidently indicating that he is anxious to speak, which I have no doubt he will soon do, in a thundering voice, to the joy of his friends and the terror of his enemies." Hughes ordered him back to his Manhattan parish. "Your inauguration of a ceremony unknown to the Church, viz., the blessing of a cannon was bad enough," he wrote to him, "but your remarks on that occasion were infinitely worse." When writing to Francis Kenrick, though, who had complained about Mooney, Hughes refused to be defensive or apologetic. Southern priests who sang Te Deums after the bombardment of Fort Sumter were worse.

Hughes was also worried about how the war would affect the nation's seminaries and schools. Fordham had always had a significant number of students who came from the South. Southerners studying in Northern seminaries would not be likely to remain where they were. He had already heard that a "party spirit" was dividing the American College in Rome. Peter McCloskey, the rector there, shared this concern and had been raising a good point since the time of South Carolina's secession convention: What was to be done about those seminarians who were no longer, or no longer considered themselves, citizens of the United States but natives of a separate country, the Confederate States of America? Five of the thirty-eight seminarians were from the South. Do I keep them or send them home? he wondered. Hughes had no answer just yet.

In New York, very little of a "party spirit" was evident once the bombardment of Fort Sumter commenced, though an intense ethnic spirit still prevailed. The German community established recruiting stations throughout the neighborhood known as Kleindeutschland, filling the ranks of the Steuben Guard and the German Rifles. Local Swiss and Hungarians formed the First Foreign Rifles, later joining with Italians to merge into a Garibaldi Brigade. A Polish Legion was formed. Bowery b'hoys rallied behind the banner of Elmer Ellsworth and his flamboyant Zouaves with their billowing red pants, tunics, and turbans. "Torrents of men," Walt Whitman exclaimed, were on the march. "I have witnessed my cities electric; / I have lived to behold man burst forth and warlike America rise."

Yet "no group surpassed the Irish in enthusiasm," as New York historians Edwin Burrows and Mike Wallace summarized the enlistment situation in *Gotham*. Waves of Irishmen, native and immigrants, rushed to join the ranks of the Sixty-Ninth Regiment and unanimously elected Michael Corcoran as their leader—Corcoran, who had refused to lead the regiment on parade before the Prince of Wales the year before and was still in jail awaiting his court-martial. Thurlow Weed helped to arrange his release and the dismissal of all charges. Overnight, an uncivil Irishman was a warrior and potential hero. Judge Charles Patrick Daly took an active role in fund-raising for the enlistment campaign, and Daniel Devlin, the Donegal immigrant who owned the city's largest men's clothing store after Brooks Brothers, offered to provide uniforms for free for the Irish recruits. Thomas Francis Meagher, looking to raise his own company of Irish Zouaves, which he hoped to attach to the Sixty-Ninth, reminded his compatriots that enlistment was "not only our duty to America, but also to Ireland." Ireland could be made a republic by way of the military and political skills its sons acquired in the United States.

It didn't hurt that recruiting posters plastered across Irish neighborhoods referred to the conflict as a dual cause: an attack on treasonous Southerners and a blow against Great Britain and its dependence on the "cotton lords" of that region. The *Irish-American*, which earlier in the year had been skeptical about the war, proclaimed that the American flag "shall never be trailed in the dust if Irish-American hearts and heads can keep it gloriously aloft." Nationwide, almost 150,000 Irish and Irish American men would serve in the Union ranks between 1861 and 1865.

On April 23, 1861, Hughes stood on a platform in front of Saint Patrick's Cathedral and, before an enthusiastic crowd that filled the streets, windows, and rooftops, blessed the one-thousand-man Sixty-Ninth as they marched from Great Jones Street through the Lower East Side to the downtown ferry that would begin their journey to Annapolis. It was the first time in his life he had performed such a task, and these men would be among the first in the nation to see action. He and John Timon visited them in early July at the makeshift "Fort Corcoran" they had erected on the outskirts of Washington, and the two prelates were "enthusiastically received by the regiment." It was a shock, then, to read two weeks later about the debacle of the Union army's initial encounter with the enemy, a humiliating rout for the North. The Sixty-Ninth met its share of suffering at the First Battle of Bull Run at Manassas Junction in Virginia. Corcoran was wounded and captured. Thirty-eight of his men were killed, fifty-nine were wounded, and ninety-five were missing in action. Their Jesuit chaplain, Father Bernard O'Reilly, who had been on the field aiding the wounded through the thick of the fighting, escaped capture by playing dead until Confederate patrols left the area. New Yorkers read the news accounts with dismay.

Bull Run was a shock to the entire nation. In the Mexican War, thirteen thousand men had died, the overwhelming majority from disease. Fewer than two thousand Americans had lost their lives in battle. At Manassas Junction, in a single day, almost nine hundred men from both sides were killed and twenty-seven hundred seriously wounded. The first fears were expressed that the United States had embarked on a crusade that might be more prolonged and blood-soaked than most people on either side of the Mason-Dixon Line had ever imagined. The length of the enlistment periods the government had authorized—three months—began to seem shortsighted.

There was some consolation to be had in the reports that, while they had eventually turned and run all the way back to the District of Columbia like every other U.S. regiment, the Sixty-Ninth had acquitted itself honorably. At Colonel William Tecumseh Sherman's order, they "dashed into the enemy with the utmost fury. The difficulty was to keep them quiet," wrote a reporter for *Harper's Weekly* who was with the troops. The paper's account of the fray in its August 10 issue, reprinted in other publications in the North, depicted the Irish soldiers as frighteningly enthusiastic fighters, many shirtless in the summer sun. It could be argued that this perspective played into the old ethnic stereotypes—in peacetime, that natural aggressiveness was just what concerned people about the Irish immigrant—but in the context of the defense of the nation, the Irish

troops could be more accurately viewed as exactly what Lincoln was asking for. For the moment, the customary renderings of the Irish as simian,
lazy, and oblivious of their poverty had no place in the national press.

Like many citizens, before Bull Run, Hughes had tried to keep a
hopeful spirit, writing to a correspondent in June, "I trust the war will
soon be over, and I have no doubt as to the final result, which will be to
make what they commonly called the Union more united and prosperous than it has ever been." The news from the front quickly made that
optimism sound naïve, but at least an opportunity was being presented,
Hughes believed, that had to be seized, was being seized—an opportunity for the Irish to establish themselves in the American mind, for all
time, as a loyal and brave people—fully as patriotic and dependable as
any native-born citizens. The memory of the San Patricio Brigade could
be expunged. The slurs and taunts of a generation of anti-Irish bigots
would be relegated to the past. "Let us hear no more 'nativism,' " the
editor of the *Boston Pilot* proclaimed, "for it is now dead, disgraced,
and offensive, while Irish Catholic patriotism and bravery are true to the
nation and indispensable to it in any point of consideration."

Strong as the enlistment figures were in the first year of the war, this
is not to say that all Irish Catholics were happy with Hughes's way of
thinking and its potent influence. A Massachusetts sergeant in a regiment
of Irish volunteers, thirty-two-year-old Peter Welsh, went off to war very
much over his wife's protests. She wondered why this was his fight at all.
"We have St. Paul for authority," Welsh instructed his wife, evidently
having been told by one of his priests about Hughes's lectures on Paul
and biblical injunctions against rebellion. "he says that he who unjustly
rebels rebels against the will of God and draws upon himself eternal
damnation did the rebels have a just cause, no for a decision of this question you have only to refer to the political doctrine of Arch Bishop Hughs
one whose abilitys as a statesman as well as an eclisiastic are second to
none in the land." The sergeant's spouse let him know that she didn't
give two figs about what a first-century evangelist or the famous prelate
in New York had to say on the subject. Her husband's place was at home.
"Dear wife," Welsh wrote back two weeks later, "I am sory to hear from
you that you do not care what St. Paul or Bishop Hughes says." No,
indeed, she did not care. Wounded at Spotsylvania, Welsh died in 1864.

Hughes also wanted the government to know that the church stood
ready to help, and he wrote to Winfield Scott that he could supply twelve

chaplains for the army for free, their salaries and expenses paid for by the archdiocese. He boasted that he could have them packed and on the road in twenty-four hours. Scott felt that they were not needed yet, as the Jesuits of Georgetown College were on hand and willing to serve, but he let the archbishop know that nuns to work as nurses would be needed for the army's hospitals soon enough. Francis Kenrick heard of Hughes's offer and made the veiled suggestion that it might be better if the archbishop of New York minded his own business. Unhappy with the direction of national events, he told Hughes that life in Maryland was becoming more unpleasant by the week. "We are as a conquered people under surveillance," he wrote, expecting sympathy from an unlikely quarter. From his correspondent's point of view, Maryland would be left in peace if she would simply prove her loyalty and quell the agitation of the Copperheads, as the antiwar faction was now being termed.

Scott's reference to an imminent need for nurses caused some consternation in New York, as Hughes feared the effect on his own programs—schools, hospitals, shelters—if too many nuns left for the front. When several nuns contacted the War Department indicating their willingness to do so, the archbishop let them know that he would be the judge of the right time to offer their services.

At this point in the hostilities, the antiwar faction in New York, with money first and foremost on its mind, was drowned out rather easily. When Mayor Fernando Wood invited Hughes that summer to attend a reception to meet Prince Napoleon on the first leg of his royal visit to America, the archbishop had one reason to accept—Napoleon III's cousin was an ardent supporter of the Union cause—but two reasons to decline. The prince was known in France as a leading anticlerical liberal, and Wood had attempted to convince the Common Council before Fort Sumter was attacked that, in the event of war, Manhattan should effect its own mini-secession and declare itself a "open city," keeping trade going with all sides. Businessmen who were in a panic about lost revenues and frozen assets found merit in the idea. Hughes, like most New Yorkers, deplored it. But, then, he deplored everything about the unscrupulous Fernando Wood and declined participation at most events where the mayor was present.

The ensuing months allowed Hughes to articulate to a wider public his own thoughts about what was happening, who was to blame, and the terms on which it would have to end. In September, the *Metropolitan Record* published a long letter from Patrick Lynch to Hughes, written in August, along with Hughes's lengthy reply. There is some question as to whether Lynch knew a private communication was going to be made public, but he was presented with a fait accompli and ultimately agreed that it was a clarifying statement of the opposing viewpoints. Bishop Lynch's view was that a prosperous, stable country was being torn asunder by a Yankee culture that insisted on "taking up anti-slavery, making it a religious dogma, and carrying it into politics." He saw the Confederate States of America as an established fact that would have to be accepted by the North eventually and asked why blood had to be spilled when it would change nothing in the long run.

In his response, Hughes went out of his way to express his personal regard for Lynch, whom he truly esteemed, and acknowledged that the South might have cause to feel uneasy about the future of slavery. But Lincoln's election, he insisted, did not justify secession, and talk about a Northern desire to subjugate the South was pure delusion. There was no "established fact" to be accepted; there was, however, a flagrant illegality to be fought against by all men who loved their country. He opposed any compromise that would restore the antebellum drift, the old uncertainties and threats. The South would have to concede defeat and rejoin the Union before the hostilities could end.

The exchange between the two prelates—two friends—was widely discussed that month in papers around the country. It epitomized for many what they were living through: a heartrending rupture that would not be easily mended. When the Cathedral of Saint Finbar in Charleston was destroyed by a fire unrelated to the war that December, Hughes was deeply saddened. He had celebrated Mass there and knew what that beautiful church meant to Bishop Lynch. Yet he was amazed that Southerners couldn't see what was coming if they didn't relent: a juggernaut of destruction that would leave many churches and homes in ashes and take a generation to mend.

There was an ugly side of war on the home front, too, and it made itself felt in a new way as arrests without warrants proliferated at a brisk pace throughout the North. Even if one discounts as apocryphal the oft-quoted remark by Seward to British ambassador Lyons that the U.S. secretary of state's power to imprison at will exceeded that of the Queen of England, there is no doubt that Hughes's friend in Washington exercised with relish his authority to decide in wartime what was treasonous and what was not. Newspaper editors who opposed the war were especially vulnerable.

On September 14, 1861, Seward ordered the arrest of James McMaster on charges of editing a disloyal newspaper, and, after a scuffle, McMaster was taken from his office in Manhattan and brought to Fort Lafayette, an offshore military prison in Brooklyn. His wife, facing bankruptcy and frightened that she and her two children would be put out on the street, wrote a pleading letter to the president, asking that the paper be allowed to continue under her management and promising to keep her husband in check in the future (a comic thought to anyone who knew the couple). Hughes decided to put past differences aside and visit McMaster in prison, perhaps at Gertrude McMaster's urging, but was denied entry as he arrived without the proper military pass.

McMaster spent several weeks at Fort Lafayette before finally agreeing to take an oath of allegiance to the Union and resumed work on the paper in June 1862, two months after the order banning the *Freeman's Journal* from the mail was rescinded. It wasn't likely that he would emerge from prison in a more temperate frame of mind, though, and soon the paper was filled with more lacerating attacks on Lincoln and Seward, jibes at Sumner and Greeley, inflammatory stories about Irish workingmen laid off to be replaced by African Americans, reprints of speeches (with admiring commentary) by Confederate politicians like Alexander Stephens, and advertisements for Copperhead "badges of liberty" (fifteen cents apiece, ten dollars per one hundred). Many New York papers, including Hughes's own *Metropolitan Record*, became by stages critical of the war effort, but none surpassed McMaster's publication in its ferocity. Surprisingly, the paper was allowed to continue to do business for the rest of the war, presumably on the assumption that its distribution in the South was now limited and thus its "aid and comfort to the enemy" negligible. For a time in 1863, Union general Nathaniel Banks forbade its delivery to Louisiana, thus depriving McMaster of six hundred badly needed subscribers, but Seward chose not to make a martyr of the Catholic editor. He understood that John Hughes had no control over James McMaster at this point. No one did. As far as Hughes was concerned, Seward had been right to jail McMaster.

THE COMING OF THE CIVIL WAR meant that John Hughes had had to revise his stance on violence, and that change was not something he undertook lightly. Though he had tacitly and painfully approved of the violence exercised by the United States against Mexico fifteen years earlier, he had spoken from the podium many times in the intervening years about the need to resolve grievances and achieve social change without resorting to force of arms or disruptive civil unrest. Now he had to fall back on the church's teachings about the difference between a just war and an unjust war, its assertion that both the Old Testament and the New Testament acknowledged that there were times when violence was preferable to injustice and therefore acceptable to God. In that case, the cause had to be a moral one, not for profit or revenge; the taking of life had to be authorized by a recognized civil authority; all other means of peaceful resolution had to have been tried and exhausted; a probability of success had to be evident; and an openness to renewing efforts for peace had to be present at all times in the midst of the violence. All those criteria were met by the Northern side of the present conflict, Hughes felt, and no Catholic need worry that he was fighting in a questionable cause.

This public acknowledgment that violence was sometimes the only means by which an injustice could be rectified meant that Hughes also felt the need in 1861 to reconsider his antipathy—the church's antipathy—toward Fenian radicalism. In truth, what had bothered him most about the failed Irish rebellion of 1848 was its ineptness, its ignominious failure before the eyes of the world, and had the Young Ireland men succeeded in sending the British packing—which was not even a remote possibility, given their lack of arms or any widespread support among the populace—he would have kept quiet about the methods used. Yet the church's attitudes toward Fenianism had hardened throughout the 1850s. The whole cause was judged by the anticlericalism and Protestantism of some of its leaders; no priest in Ireland, under the firm control of Cardinal Paul Cullen, was supposed to express support for political agitation against Great Britain or give aid to those who attempted it.

Yet if Hughes was urging Irish American men to enlist and fight for the Union cause, he was aware that he needed to be perceived as equally sympathetic to Irish interests overseas, and what it might take to end a long-standing injustice there, as he was now more than sympathetic to American interests being battled over that summer in Virginia, North Carolina, and Missouri. He took the occasion of a funeral to make a stand on that issue and to renew his position as an ardent ally of the cause of Irish independence.

Back in January, one of the Young Ireland rebels, Terence Bellew McManus, had died in San Francisco. He had fought at Ballingarry and was caught a short time later and tried by the British alongside Thomas Meagher. His death sentence commuted, he had been transported with Meagher to Tasmania, and upon their escape in 1852, the two men parted company once they reached the United States—Meagher settling in New York, McManus in California. Unlike Meagher, McManus never found his footing in his new homeland and died impoverished in his forties, but he was nonetheless a beloved figure in the Irish and the Irish American community. Though he had been buried in San Francisco, plans were made that summer to send the body back to Ireland for a final burial, with stops on both coasts to serve as rallying sites for the Hibernian cause. He was exhumed in August and the body placed in a new coffin, thus beginning what amounted to a six-thousand-mile, four-month wake, extravagant even by Irish standards. Cardinal Cullen let it be known that McManus, a troublemaker in his view, like all of his kind, would be buried without benefit of clergy if he had anything to say about it. One funeral and burial was all a Fenian deserved, and he had had that in California. Cullen insisted the church's stand concerning the men of 1848 was unchangeable.

Hughes thought otherwise and was willing to risk the displeasure of his ecclesiastical peers, especially Bishop Wood of Philadelphia. Meagher, who had been lecturing about the life of McManus all along the Eastern Seaboard that year, was appointed by his peers in the movement to approach the archbishop about the possibility of holding a second funeral for the deceased at Saint Patrick's Cathedral. He readily agreed, though he declined to give a eulogy, never having met the deceased, but was open to making some laudatory remarks, especially as McManus was an Ulster man. His only stipulation was that no secret societies were to enter the church in their full regalia. Cullen was no doubt incredulous when he heard the news. If Pius IX was informed, he was probably less than pleased. Even some New Yorkers were surprised that Hughes had granted permission to use his cathedral for an occasion that was more explicitly and audaciously political than it was religious. But Hughes was sure he was making the right decision.

On September 16, 1861, the cathedral was full to capacity—with faithful parishioners, with sometime Catholics, with men who had never set foot inside the church, with everyone in the city who had the faintest interest in Fenianism. Father Starrs officiated at the solemn high requiem Mass, which exhibited as much pageantry as any funeral Mott Street had ever seen. Contradicting his initial statement about not delivering a eulogy, Hughes did just that and spoke well of McManus, commending him as a man of noble intentions whose abiding passions were his love of God and his love of his country, the latter a value the church recognized as even more important than a man's love of his family and his friends. A listener could be forgiven for wondering if he had imagined the archbishop's fulminations about Young Ireland thirteen years before. Meagher wasn't surprised, but Thomas D'Arcy McGee, Michael Doheny, and John Mitchel would have been. Hughes also spoke about armed resistance, reviewing for his audience Thomas Aquinas's writings on the nature of just wars—a reference that everyone understood as offering his imprimatur for what both the Union armies and the Fenians were attempting to do. He was now willing to see them as similar causes. Fenians of all faiths or degrees of faith were effusive in their praise of John Hughes.

"The spectacle turned into an Irish city milestone," one recent historian has written, "a landmark interaction between the Church and the radicalized elements within the flock." Now no one could charge Hughes with inconsistency, supporting Americans who used force to end an injustice in their land while disparaging Irishmen who tried to do the same in theirs. (McManus was a name never forgotten by Irish nationalists: sixty years later, the Irish clergy's "dishonor[ing] of his ashes" is a hot topic at the Daedalus dinner table in James Joyce's *A Portrait of the Artist as a Young Man*. Had the New York hierarchy's respect for the martyred nationalist entered the conversation, Stephen's father and uncle might well have had a good word to say about John Hughes.)

In November, Hughes departed for Europe on his mission for Lincoln and Seward, the trip—his last abroad—that would take him away from his city and his diocese for nine months. Before leaving town, he made one very bad mistake that would follow him to Europe. It troubled him, far more than it should have at this point, that Southerners did not realize that Northern intentions had nothing to do with the forcible ending of their "peculiar institution" and everything to do with preserving the Union. It troubled him, too, that an influential Catholic like Orestes Brownson was rethinking in print his longtime opposition to the abolitionist cause. He wanted to be the spokesman for what he thought of as the sensible middle ground.

An unsigned editorial appeared in the *Metropolitan Record* on October 12. But whether it was signed or not, even when Hughes later chose to be evasive on the subject, few people had any doubts about its authorship. The style, content, and venue pointed to Hughes, and the *Boston Pilot* identified him as the author a week later. The article referred to slavery as a "calamity" that never should have come into existence and to the breaking up of black families as a monstrous wrong, but it upheld constitutional reform ratified by the states as the only proper means to deal with the matter and pointed a finger at those abolitionists who attacked the Constitution as the instigators of the current crisis. He brought up the murderous consequences of the Santo Domingo slave revolt and worried about white working-class jobs in the North once a large number of emancipated black men moved north. He compared the condition of the black man in the South and the black man in the North and claimed to see nothing inherently preferable in the poverty and degradation that characterized the life of the freedman in New York.

There was a passage that went well beyond this well-worn thread, however. Dwelling on the violence of tribal life in Africa, the supposedly anonymous editorialist went so far as to ignore Pope Gregory XVI's bull on the subject and question whether the slave trader was necessarily a morally transgressive man if he brought the unwilling captive to a new life and a Christian culture, sparing him a worse fate at the hands of "the savage king of Dahomey." "We, of course, believe that no genuine Christian—no decent man—would be engaged in that kind of business," he offered, but it was possible to imagine a view of the slave trader that called forth something other than a blanket condemnation. Then, on the other side of the Atlantic, "men of conscience" who bought these transported slaves could—or should—for reasons of financial self-interest as well as common decency "take care of these unfortunate people." If they did, Hughes claimed that there was little to fault them with, either. In part, he was speaking here to bishops Lynch, Verot, Odin, to Francisco Solaus of Havana—to the many prelates and priests he knew who owned slaves, in the American South and in Cuba, who did not mistreat or rape their chattel. He was thinking of his in-laws, the Rodrigue family. The terrible feature of the slaves' lot was that their captivity should be passed down from generation to generation, yet Hughes insisted that even such a fate was not "alien from the condition of mankind in general," subject as all human beings were to the transmission of original sin of which they had no part in causing.

The editorial was one of the most perfect pieces of idiocy ever penned by a Northern Catholic who insisted he was not a pro-slavery man. In particular the passage about the potential benefits of slavery was a sad commentary to come from the pen of a priest. It ignored completely the horrific reality of the Middle Passage. It ignored the truth that many slave owners in the United States and Cuba were not "men of conscience" but were just what Harriet Beecher Stowe had said they were. It ignored the fact that the enslaved people he was writing about were individuals who had been ruthlessly denied any say in their fate or were not even allowed to learn to read the Bible into whose light they had been brought.

Brownson responded aggressively in the January issue of his journal, suggesting that Pope Gregory XVI would have had something to say about the archbishop's retrograde views if he meant them to be taken literally. He was willing to concede that it was inaccurate to call Hughes a pro-slavery man pure and simple, but he dismissively quoted at length from the infamous "king of Dahomey" passage to embarrass his target. It was a sloppy piece of prose, he charged in a line he knew would hit home, "for a public whose taste and judgment had, to a great extent, been formed by the *New York Herald* and kindred journals." Brownson delivered a serious scolding, a lecture on church doctrine about the slave trade to a misinformed prelate, and a lament that a smart man was willing to appear heartless and was falling so far behind the times. Brownson was getting a bit of his own back: at the Fordham commencement exercises the previous summer, he and the archbishop had exchanged words on this very topic, and to his mortification in front of the Jesuits, Brownson had been told to sit down and hold his tongue.

Hughes had to answer for the article when he was in Europe as well. Augustin Cochin, a prominent French politician of liberal beliefs, questioned him pointedly about it when they met in Paris, and a Parisian newspaper, the *Journal des Débats*, accused him of a being an unqualified defender of slavery, a charge he felt he had to respond to in its pages. Slavery was "the sick man of the United States," he told the editors, and was on its way to extinction, but the abolitionist lens was flawed. Violence and ostracism awaited the liberated black man, and economic disruption awaited the United States and those who traded with her (like France), if the war led to the immediate emancipation of four million men and women unprepared for freedom and unable to support themselves. Hughes hoped that word of the *Journal des Débats* attack would not reach New York, but of course it did.

During his time abroad, while he was doing his best to influence the power brokers of the Tuileries and the Vatican, Hughes was supplied with diocesan, local, and political news from a variety of correspondents. A huge winter gale had unroofed the Orphan Asylum across from the cathedral site, which was going to require money and immediate attention. Sunday collections were down, as unemployment among the Irish was suddenly on the rise, but his sister's order was winning a name for itself among all denominations for its care of the war wounded. Some of the nuns had returned to their old property at McGowan's Pass on the eastern edge of Central Park, which had been claimed by the government as the site of a military hospital. Walt Whitman, veteran hospital visitor, paid a call on the young men there and, having seen the godawful range of government medical facilities between Washington and New York, declared the one run by the Sisters of Charity to be decidedly "well managed." Women he had once derided as "the refuse of [European] convents" were now seen by the poet as angels of mercy.

On the political front, Hughes heard about the fear that war with Great Britain was inevitable, given the acrimony of the *Trent* crisis and anger over British sympathies for the South. He learned that the inertia of George McClellan, who had taken over from Winfield Scott as commanding general of the army, was becoming a national scandal; that Thomas Meagher was energetically filling the ranks of his newly formed Irish Brigade; that criticism of Lincoln was growing; and that the abolitionists were trying to gain the upper hand now that the South was digging in its heels. John Mullaly of the *Metropolitan Record* wrote to him about John Phelps, an abolitionist from Vermont, now a Union general whose troops had taken control of an island off Mississippi. He was asking his commander, Benjamin Butler, for permission to arm the many black slaves who had swarmed to his camp while he refused to employ them as laborers, claiming he was a U.S. officer, not an overseer. A "red-hot abolition proclamation calculated to rouse the indignation of every Catholic in the country," Mullaly termed the whole business. Hughes no doubt agreed. (General Butler would later show more sympathy for the African American plight but at the time refused Phelps's request, commenting to an aide that the man was "mad as a March hare on the nigger question.")

At this point, Mullaly, Hughes, and Butler were still part of a nation-wide majority: the Civil War was not about emancipating black Americans, let alone putting rifles in their hands. Mullaly praised Lincoln for keeping the "incubus of abolition" at bay, and James Gordon Bennett was proposing in the pages of the *Herald* that any slaves who fled behind Union lines be held by the federal government and then sold back to their former masters at half price to finance the war effort.

Yet signs were pointing to a subtle shift in public opinion about slavery, and Hughes could see where that shift would take the country. Abolitionism wasn't regarded by everyone as the province of fanatics and cranks any longer, the faith of a lunatic fringe. Sumner, Chase, Greeley, and those Republicans who urged emancipation, both as a moral necessity and a useful war measure, were making inroads with Lincoln. Army officers who before the war had never dreamed of supporting emancipation spoke of the strategic damage it could inflict on the wounded enemy. Bishop Purcell had embraced the cause. Brownson, while honestly acknowledging that he would never be able to purge himself of his ingrained racism, was becoming more outspoken on the topic with each issue of his journal. The admirer of John C. Calhoun had once referred to freed blacks as "the pests of our northern cities" and argued the constitutionality of the Fugitive Slave Law and the illegality of the Missouri Compromise. Now he was emphatic that the war had changed everything. It was time to agitate the slavery question, he wrote in April 1862. Slavery had produced the national crisis, and there was no point in acting otherwise. To the consternation of his more conservative subscribers, he was willing to go further: slavery was "an outrage upon [the slave's] manhood, an outrage which disfigures and debases in him that very image of God after which he was created. . . . On this point, the abolitionists have exaggerated nothing." Abolition was the Banquo's ghost of American life, Brownson asserted in the summer of 1862, and nothing could subdue it.

The allusion to Banquo's ghost said it all. The United States, like the Scottish king, had waded too far into a pool of blood to consider returning to the shore left behind. Metaphors mixing images of blood and water, lakes and streams of it, were on everyone's mind. "Your bleeding country rejoices [at your return]," Father Terence Donaghoe, his childhood friend, wrote to Hughes a few days after his ship docked, "and your friends are consoled by your presence . . . [but] what awful days we have fallen on! Rivers of blood will continue to be shed!"

As bad as the thought of those rivers could be, the question of what that blood would be shed for suddenly become a very real concern. On September 22, 1862, five days after the momentous battle of Antietam, Lincoln fulfilled Hughes's worst fear and announced that, as of January 1, all slaves in Confederate-held territory would be declared "forever free." What the *Irish-American* called Lincoln's "Negrophilism" was out in the open, and Hughes worried that Irish Catholic support for the war would dry up in the new year. Few men in his diocese had signed on to shoot and be shot at for that end. Father O'Reilly, chaplain of the Sixty-Ninth Regiment, was of a similar frame of mind. To save the Union, the Irish were "as willing as any to make sacrifice," he wrote to Judge Daly, but surely, terrible as slavery was, "they might well pause before [the abolitionist] wheels they were exhorted and commanded to cast themselves, their families, their fortunes, and the conscience to boot." Fordham's first professor of German, Maximilian Oertel, now an anti-abolitionist editor, was likewise doing his best in a torrent of articles in *Katholische Kirchen-Zeitung* to persuade the city's German Catholics to turn on Lincoln. Even Thomas Francis Meagher, the most charismatic of speakers at recruitment rallies and an antislavery man, was troubled about how this development might affect his success.

THROUGHOUT THE FALL, once Hughes had sufficiently recovered from his voyage, the usual round of duties and projects required his attention. Michael Corcoran, released in a prison exchange and now much lionized throughout the North, had recruited more soldiers to rebuild his decimated regiment. Hughes reviewed those troops at their training ground on Staten Island and gave communion to several hundred (looking impressive "in his splendid robes, [with] his mitre on his head, his golden crozier in his hand, and his benevolent countenance," a guest who had made the journey with him commented). Maria Daly, the young wife of Judge Charles Patrick Daly, found the archbishop to be a "most gentlemanly, agreeable man. After I felt a little at home with him, I had a very pleasant time."

He also had to deal with those directly under his supervision, mercifully few in number at the moment, who now actively opposed the war. A priest had been caught urging young men in his parish to resist the call to arms and was arrested for obstruction of enlistment. Hughes wrote to John Kennedy, superintendent of the Metropolitan Police, to see what could be done. Kennedy replied reassuringly that he would hold Father Boyle for a day or two in the Tombs to teach him a lesson and then let him go. Hughes was less concerned about Boyle than he was about the arrest making the papers. A similar episode a year earlier had been publicized in the *New York Express* under the embarrassing heading "The Adventures of a Priest." Hughes's advice to Kennedy at that time was to give the erring cleric a sentence of life in prison or, to be more exact, "97 years and four months," mainly for stupidity.

Some of what occupied his attention these days was heartening and constructive—literally constructive. A fire that destroyed the Catholic Orphanage in Brooklyn and the wartime deaths of so many breadwinners had increased the number of homeless children in New York. Richard O'Gorman, former Young Irelander and now a Manhattan politician, approached the archbishop with several other prominent Catholic laymen with a plan to open a protectory for boys "in circumstances of want and suffering, of abandonment, exposure or neglect, or of beggary." The idea was not to establish a reformatory for juvenile delinquents but to open a place for those who were on their way to becoming that, to reach them before a life of crime had started and educate them for a trade. Hughes wholeheartedly endorsed the idea and claimed a central role in the planning. The Roman Catholic Orphan Asylum tended, for want of space for younger children, to ease its charges out into the world by the age of twelve or thirteen. That was problematic for obvious reasons. Hughes had even offered to take a boy into the episcopal residence himself if a home or job could not be found for him. A protectory could focus on those boys who were too old for the orphanage but by no means ready to manage on their own.

Hughes also spent a fair amount of time considering the preparations to open the new seminary upstate in Troy to replace the moribund Saint Joseph's at Rose Hill. For $60,000 he had purchased the campus of a Methodist college. It now had to be revamped as a Catholic seminary and properly staffed. But it had pleasing grounds, the requisite number of buildings, a chapel with a good organ, and a library, though he hoped the vacating Methodists would have the sense to take their books with them, or, of course, they would have to be "commit[ted] to the flames." He proposed to send John McCloskey to Europe to secure a first-rate faculty. About both developments, the seminary- and the protectory-to-be, Hughes felt good. Then came a ferocious blast of criticism out of nowhere.

In October, Orestes Brownson had decided that the time had come to unleash the dogs of war with his archbishop, to settle in a backhanded way every grievance he had been nursing for years. Turning his attention yet again to the year-old editorial Hughes had written the previous fall, the editor of *Brownson's Quarterly Review* declared that "the archbishop of New York, who we have good reason for believing, is a strong anti-slavery man," had committed a colossal error in that article, which he must not be allowed to forget, in not recognizing that the time for abolition had come and that the war effort, if nothing else, demanded it. Hughes had done precious little, Brownson charged, to educate Catholics on that point, which is precisely what his office called on him to do. Moreover, that ill-advised editorial had proved him "nearly as short-sighted and as weak a statesman as Mr. Seward himself," and, if the Union lost the war—a distinct possibility in the autumn of 1862— "few men in the country will have incurred a heavier responsibility for it than he."

The gloves were off: "No man has contributed more to keep up the old party divisions," Brownson wrote, "and to prevent the union of our people and our government on a straightforward and decided policy, such as the crisis demanded. We doubt not his loyal intentions, but had he been decidedly disloyal, he could not have done more harm." If Irish Catholics were still blind on the subject of slavery and becoming more reluctant each month to do battle with the Confederacy, the fault could be laid at the doorstep of the archbishop of New York. Rarely, even among the writers of the penny press, has one American prelate been held responsible for more evil. That a Catholic writer would discuss a leader of his church in these terms left Hughes speechless. One mutual acquaintance told Brownson that the archbishop was "wroth—in fact, savage" over the article and would gladly have consigned the writer and his journal to a "wood-pile in full blaze," if he could get away with it.

The view from the opposite end of the political spectrum was no less forgiving, though. Support for the war among Catholic New Yorkers in late 1862 and into the first months of 1863 was—just as Hughes suspected it would be—a far cry from what it had been in 1861. Antietam in September, with twenty-two thousand soldiers killed, wounded, or captured within a twelve-hour period—and with two New York Irish brigades losing 60 percent of their number in the first five minutes of the battle—helped to change that as much as the announcement of the Emancipation Proclamation. New York elected a Copperhead governor in 1862, Horatio Seymour, and Irish Catholics voted for him overwhelmingly. As the winter wore on, Hughes's position in relation to his circle of friends and parishioners—many of whom had become outright Copperheads—grew more awkward, especially after he endorsed the idea put forth by the *New York Times* of universal conscription as a more democratic way to provide the needed manpower.

Charles O'Conor, for one, was vehemently opposed to the war. (After Appomattox, he would serve as Jefferson Davis's defense attorney). Richard O'Gorman and Judge Daly had become vituperative Lincoln critics, and businessman Daniel Devlin, the enthusiastic Union supporter who had provided the Sixty-Ninth with free uniforms, was now a peace-at-any-price man. John McCaffrey, his old school friend and president of the Mount, was, like most of the students at Emmitsburg, of a similar mind. Hughes was no longer the revered alumnus.

In March 1863, John McKeon, the former congressman and devout Catholic who served on any number of boards and committees for his archbishop, including the board of trustees at Fordham, delivered as head of the local antiwar movement a lengthy address—articulate, passionate, and well-publicized—to a huge crowd at the Broadway headquarters of the Democratic Union Association. It was the kind of speech Hughes detested, even when he agreed with some aspects of it. McKeon questioned the administration's right to continue to wage a war the people no longer supported, to free slaves without popular or congressional assent, and to close down open discussion in a country that had always upheld the right of free speech. Instead, Americans who disagreed with Lincoln were faced with "the bolt and bars of the Bastille." McKeon demanded an immediate armistice. Within a few weeks, Congress approved the nationwide suspension of habeas corpus, and a new conscription law was announced. McKeon could have been arrested for that speech and, had he delivered it somewhere other than New York City, might well have landed in a military prison.

With so many Catholic New Yorkers leaning toward the view that the Union cause was, if not misbegotten, at least hopelessly mismanaged and that it was time to enter into talks with the Confederate government to end hostilities, John Hughes's insistence that Lincoln had to be supported and the country reunited assumes almost heroic proportions. The pressure on him to disavow Lincoln and Seward, or at the very least to cease making any public statements about the war, was great. He refused to do either. Like every American, he read the newspaper reports from the front with horror. The numbers were staggering, numbing. In the words of Drew Gilpin Faust, with the Civil War, the United States had become a "veritable republic of suffering," reaping a "harvest of death." But, Hughes affirmed without hesitation, *there was no turning back*. This was not like the Mexican War, when a pretense of support was politically expedient, when everyone knew U.S. motives were largely about racism, territory, money. This was a cause Hughes believed in, that he believed God approved, and that he wished all Irish Catholics would support.

Invoking the ethnic pride that the city's Irish Catholics should feel about their contributions and sacrifices often seemed like the most feasible tactic. In January, he led a memorial Mass at the cathedral for the men of the Irish Brigade killed in action, a moving ceremony attended by city officials, bereft wives, and fatherless children, and in April he spoke at a fund-raiser for Irish relief at the Academy of Music, where the other speakers included General McClellan, Daly, O'Gorman, and Meagher. When the men of the Irish Brigade on the front line heard about the fund-raiser, they passed the hat and sent $1,200 back to New York, such was their identification with that cause.

Appreciation of his efforts outside of specifically ethnic contexts, though, was getting harder to come by. The attacks in the Catholic press, grown more vehement since the diplomatic mission to Paris and Rome, continued to plague Hughes. A lifetime as an object of scorn in the nativist press was a badge of honor at this stage of his life, but he could not accept that Catholic journalists, sometimes at the behest of the priests behind them, wrote about him so critically and sarcastically. He asked Francis Kenrick if he couldn't rein in the editor of the *Catholic Mirror* in his diocese. He didn't hate the South, he didn't love war, and he did believe he was acting as a true son of the church. Kenrick pleaded that the paper was an independent organ and that he had no authority to control its content. It was a futile request, of course. The archbishop of Baltimore agreed with his editor's criticisms.

What Hughes didn't know, and never did learn, was that Kenrick had recently written to Secretary of War Edwin Stanton, urging the United States to let some of the Confederate states go in the hope that peace would be restored, an action Hughes would have found incomprehensible. But then, suddenly, Kenrick was gone, dead in his sleep on July 7, and another door to the past closed, any hope of mutual understanding or reconciliation over. In a severely weakened state that week, Hughes attended the funeral in Baltimore. Saying a Low Mass for the departed archbishop in one of the side altars of the cathedral—the first American church he had entered upon disembarking from Ireland forty-six years ago—he was unable to continue, had to be helped to a chair, and was rushed back to his hotel by his attendants.

The time of Hughes's much-anticipated public appearances was coming to an end. Two weeks earlier, he had presided at his last church dedication in New York City. It was too great an ordeal to leave his Madison Avenue home, be helped into and out of a carriage, or stand before a crowd, especially in the heat. He had to sit in the sanctuary to deliver his sermon at Saint Teresa's and was only intermittently audible. He spoke now not about Catholicism, church-building, the pope's needs, or charitable giving. Rather, he asked the congregation—entreated them, begged them—to pray most earnestly for God's intercession in the war "to bring our unhappy affairs to some conclusion, to end the effusion of human blood." It had all gone on too long, the death toll was too horrendous to contemplate, the anguish of widows past enduring, but the South would not give in. "One side can make war, but it requires two to make peace," a peace he prayed for every day, he told his listeners. The North was ready for reunion and reconciliation, but the South was not. At this point, he feared that only a miracle would end the carnage.

13

Manhattan under Siege

THE TROUBLE BEGAN on Monday, July 13, 1863—a "deadly muggy" day, one resident noted—but the passions behind it had been simmering for months. In March, the new conscription law, registering for a draft lottery all eligible unmarried men between the ages of twenty and forty-five and all married men between the ages of twenty and thirty-five, had been passed by Congress. The new law meant that the Irish of New York City could expect to see more of their able-bodied men taken by the government to be shot at, to lose limbs, or to die, not solely to end secession now, but to free the slaves. Hughes's repeated warnings to Lincoln and Seward, that this was not a cause the Irish would fight for, or should be expected to fight for, had been soundly ignored.

Throughout the spring and early summer of 1863, the vocal questioning of the cost and ramification of a conflict that now seemed unwinnable became more pronounced. In May, Clement Vallandigham, an Ohio congressman, had given a speech attacking the abolitionist goals and constitutional violations of "King Lincoln," highlighting the concerns that worried even moderates and longtime supporters of the administration and fueled the indignation of the Copperheads. He was promptly arrested and tried by a military court. When New York City's ex-mayor, now congressman, Fernando Wood, delivered a blistering speech at a pro-Vallandigham "Rally for Peace and Reunion" in Manhattan, he was loudly cheered by an overflow crowd at Cooper Union upon condemning the president's "damnable crimes against the liberty of the citizen." In the very hall where Lincoln had delivered the speech that propelled him to his party's presidential nomination three years earlier, the president was pilloried as a tyrant and a man bent on destroying the republic.

Governor Seymour offered a similar harangue at the Academy of Music on the Fourth of July, touching on the same themes he had raised in his inaugural address a few months earlier when he called the Emancipation Proclamation "clearly impolitic, unjust, and unconstitutional." (History has not been kind to New York State's eighteenth governor or to any of Lincoln's contemporary Northern critics. But, at the time, Seymour was perceived by many as a classic Jeffersonian Democrat with a healthy concern for civil liberties.) In the heat of the moment in July, though, the governor did utter one sentence he would soon regret: "Remember this, that the bloody, and treasonable, and revolutionary, doctrine of public necessity can be proclaimed by a mob as well as by a Government."

The national Catholic press was, almost as one voice, in full agreement. Newspapers like the *Cincinnati Enquirer* and the *Catholic Mirror* relentlessly assailed the administration for its advocacy of abolition and now, adding insult to injury, of conscription. The editor of the *American Catholic Quarterly Review* called the very idea of emancipation "a measure fraught with evil . . . of the most direful character" and solicited the archbishop to add his name to a protest petition. James McMaster again approached the line of what the government regarded as treasonous journalism, but that was no surprise, and of course his pained warnings proved accurate. "The storm thickens and grows nearer," he wrote mournfully in the *Freeman's Journal* on June 13. The hardest response to assimilate for Hughes was that of John Mullaly, who, by the ferocity of his attitude toward the government, permanently alienated his one-time patron. A headline in a March issue of the *Metropolitan Record* summarized Mullaly's view: "The United States Converted into a Military Despotism: The Conscription Act the Last Deadly Blow Aimed at Popular Liberty." Lincoln was compared to the czar of Russia and the conscription bill labeled "the crowning act of despotism . . . hardly less tolerable than that which drove poor Poland to rebellion." Mullaly went so far as to suggest that Irishmen should look upon the draft as a fair excuse to refuse to fight at all. Any control Hughes had exercised over the editor of his "house organ" during the last four years was long gone, and a year later, like McMaster, the editor of the *Metropolitan Record* found himself in a cell at Fort Lafayette.

In such a climate, the preparations for the institution of a draft in June were inevitably seen as a provocation. Some Northern politicians begged the administration to wait until passions had cooled and the courts had weighed in. But military needs demanded action sooner rather than later. Matters weren't helped by the fact that returning veterans told of incompetent leadership, rancid food, widespread disease, anti-Catholic chaplains and officers, and wages in arrears. Worse still, the provision that any man who could pay three hundred dollars for an exemption or hire a substitute would be freed from service was regarded by working-class men as proof positive that their lives were considered more expendable.

The archbishop shared this sense of injustice, yet any hint of sympathy for the Confederacy, talk of suing for peace, or direct attacks on the federal government continued to rile him from his sickbed to fits of pique. There was no more pretense of standing above politics; he was a Union partisan in the last year of his life. He had no use for Congressman Wood, whom he had always regarded as a shifty politician, or Governor Seymour, believing that they gave aid and comfort to the enemy. Attending the commencement exercises at Fordham in June, one of his last outings before his health finally gave way, he had listened to the young valedictorian boldly refer to the "despotism" that ruled in Washington and then rebuked the young man on the platform after his speech, angrily reminding him of the limits respect and loyalty placed on its citizens.

Did John Hughes have some sense at the start of that summer of what the immediate future would bring, of the powder keg his city represented? Past question. Six months earlier, he had written to Seward of his "serious apprehensions" concerning how much longer New York City would remain loyal to the administration. Antipathy to the government could not be reasoned away. Negrophobia now had a political focal point for the force of its hatred: the immigrant poor, badly treated by native citizens for decades, were not going to fight to end the degradation of one group while their own went unaddressed. And the working-class Irish of New York, the archbishop's supposed flock, were feeling their muscle. In 1860, they numbered two hundred thousand, over 20 percent of the city's population. Wartime inflation and labor grievances were spiraling out of control, and the lists of dead and wounded at Gettysburg were filled with the names of local boys. With most of its militia off in Pennsylvania, helping General Meade's troops rout Lee back to Virginia, the city was vulnerable.

The first drawing of names in the draft lottery took place on Saturday, July 11. It passed off peacefully enough. A large crowd gathered outside the provost marshal's Ninth District office in the city's Nineteenth Ward at Third Avenue and Forty-Seventh Street, but the mood was jocular. Not so much as a stone had been thrown. Jokes were made as friends' names were called, sarcastic goodbyes exchanged. The men, arms crossed, cocky, loud in their disdain, looked threatening enough, but the event passed off without incident. Police Superintendent Kennedy concluded that "the Rubicon was passed, and all would go well."

That night and on Sunday, however, the mood in working-class neighborhoods turned uglier, the conversations more pointed. Talk on stoops and in saloons, along the docks and in the streets, was about resistance and revenge. The city's volunteer fireman, almost all Irish, men traditionally exempt from military duty, had been particularly roused by the drawing of their names. A Brooklyn correspondent wrote to Seward that weekend that the "barbarian Irish" were "ripe for revolt." In a letter to Edwin Stanton that Sunday, Horace Greeley warned in less excitable language that most New Yorkers did not support the draft, especially the provision that protected the wealthy who could buy substitutes. Military pay needed to be increased. The grievances of the poor had to be taken into account. He took the calm of the previous day as a misleading indicator of the mood of the city.

How right Greeley was. The first hint of what was to come was evident on Monday morning when large numbers of laborers across Manhattan failed to show up for work. Machine shops, foundries, and shipyards were eerily quiet. A mob, led by firemen of the Black Joke Engine Company, gathered mid-morning outside the site of Saturday's lottery. They had made their way up Second and Third Avenues, stopping all traffic en route, calling workers out of their factories to join them. Another group had marched up Eighth and Ninth Avenues, across to Central Park, and down Third Avenue. Within minutes of the resumption of the draft call, the provost marshal's office was under attack, the sixty policemen stationed outside and within fleeing before a crowd, armed with bricks and axes, several times larger. The building was set afire, the blaze spread to adjoining residences, and a frenzy of violence, both targeted and undirected, commenced.

Telegraph poles across the east side of Manhattan had already been cut down, severing communication lines to City Hall and the police headquarters; now railroad tracks were raised with crowbars, many wielded by women. Stirred to more destructive efforts by the vast amount of liquor being consumed, most of it handed over by tavern keepers or hotel managers who were given the choice of doing as they were told or seeing their establishment set on fire, gangs fanned out across the city and began dragging riders out of passing coaches, robbing and pummeling them in the street. Superintendent Kennedy, arriving a short time later at what remained of the draft office, was immediately identified and clubbed to the ground, as were the officers who tried to help him. When he regained consciousness, he made a run for a vacant lot across the street but was surrounded and his face beaten to a bloody, unrecognizable pulp. An attempt was made to drown him in a deep puddle of muddy water. He was left for dead.

Throughout the late morning, the enormity of what was happening was slow to register farther downtown with Mayor George Opdyke and the police force, who sent deployments of men across the city that were always too small and arrived too late. Once the extent of the violence and ferocity of the rioters became clear, all draft offices were closed, and appeals for help were sent out to West Point, the Brooklyn Navy Yard, and the governors of New Jersey and Connecticut. By afternoon, police stations, policemen, and random civilians were no longer the only targets. The homes of the wealthy, including but not exclusively those known to be Republicans and abolitionists, were being looted, and the crowd's fury had been directed toward the city's black residents, beaten and stoned in the street, and in at least one case tossed into the Hudson River. By three o'clock, the Second Avenue Armory, loaded with carbines, was surrounded, and within an hour was abandoned by its defenders after they shot and killed several of the rioters. Shortly after four o'clock, the Colored Orphan Asylum on Fifth Avenue and Forty-Fourth Street was torched, the children, all under twelve years of age, barely escaping with their lives. Numerous shops had been looted and burned along Broadway in the West Twenties by five o'clock.

Some fire companies worked to put out the fires that raged in different parts of the city. Others refused. Some that tried were forced back by

FIGURE 15. *The burning of the Fifth Avenue Colored Orphan Asylum by rioters opposed to the war and emancipation: the 1863 New York draft riots represented the nadir of John Hughes's effort to see Irish Catholics accepted by their countrymen.* (Courtesy of the Library of Congress Prints and Photography Collection.)

the rioters or saw their hoses cut and hydrants smashed. At six o'clock, the building housing the *Tribune* in Park Row was under siege amid cries to lynch editor Greeley, "the nigger's friend." The offices of Henry Raymond's *Times* and William Cullen Bryant's *Evening Post* were barricaded. By nightfall, rioters controlled the city. "The Town is taken by its rats," Herman Melville wrote.

The federal government was also uncertain about how to respond to the crisis, and throughout the week the president refused to declare martial law; but the day after the rioting began, Edwin Stanton authorized the New York militia to return home with all deliberate speed. If the draft could not be enforced in New York City, Stanton observed to a colleague when informed of the riot, it could not be enforced anywhere. With manpower shortages growing, the war effort would be doomed. And that would not be allowed to happen, Stanton insisted, even if "there should be a riot and mob in every ward in every city." He urged Thurlow Weed to publicize the Union's recent gains and appeal to New Yorkers' patriotism. Yet the implications of the situation were broader and more worrisome than Stanton acknowledged. What started as a massive protest against the draft, threatening to undermine the Union cause, had quickly escalated into a class and race war that promised profound damage to the fabric of the city and the nation. Prominent Republican businessmen demanded that federal troops occupy the city.

On Tuesday, all commerce in the metropolis had shut down. A prolonged downpour during the night raised hopes that the rain would continue and the rioting would end, but the fourteenth dawned clear and humid. The governor, who had been out of the state, finally arrived, anxiously aware that his own remarks the week before could be taken as having incited New York's citizens to rebel against the new law. After conferring with Mayor Opdyke and eighty-year-old General John Wood, the senior military officer of the region, he put out a call for volunteers and recently discharged soldiers to aid the police. At noon, flanked by Boss Tweed and other Tammany leaders, he spoke to a crowd outside City Hall.

Later reports of the content of Seymour's speech varied considerably, but it would appear that he did his best to placate both sides, a thankless task. Even addressing his listeners as "my friends" had the Republican press nipping at his heels the next day. He beseeched the crowd to remember that no one benefited from a breakdown of law and order and that those who "under the influence of excitement and a feeling of suppressed wrong" were inflicting damage to property and harm to fellow citizens were only hurting themselves in the long run. Stop the violence, he cried out, "and I will see to it that your rights are protected." The governor again questioned the legality of the draft law—something his listeners very much wanted to hear—but insisted that mob rule was not the way to rectify an injustice. The courts might well overturn the law in the coming weeks, but, if not, he would see to it that there should be no inequality between rich and poor in the enforcement of the law. Funds could be raised for that purpose. "I beg you to disperse," he concluded; "leave your interests in my hands, and I will take care that justice is done to you, and that your families shall be fully protected."

Seymour left the steps of City Hall shaken, without any idea if his words would have an effect or not. No one could even say with certainty if he had been speaking to the rioters of the day before, would-be rioters, or only the curious and concerned.

At two o'clock, the governor wrote to the archbishop in a spirit of mounting desperation. "Will you exert your powerful influence to stop the disorders now reigning in this city? I do not wish to ask anything inconsistent with your moral duties, but if you can with propriety aid the civil authorities in this crisis, I hope you will do so." The message—the plea—was not unexpected. Some wondered why the governor had waited until the afternoon of the second day of the riot to contact the archbishop. Others wondered why the archbishop had needed approaching, had not taken it upon himself to do something, try anything, to end the madness and the bloodshed overtaking Manhattan. It was a fair question for anyone who didn't know just how enfeebled he had become in recent days. Bodies lay in the street not many blocks from Madison Avenue and Thirty-Sixth Street.

One of the great anxieties of John Hughes's life had always been the dread of seeming timid, of being perceived as unequal to a demand placed upon him. He knew what almost everyone said about James Buchanan now. But the world of 1859–1860 and the world of 1863 were very different places. At the time of Harpers Ferry and Lincoln's nomination, the prospect of a civil war was a real but distant threat. By the summer of 1863, the number of dead and maimed on both sides had soared into the hundreds of thousands, with no end in sight. In December, the Union army had sustained thirteen thousand casualties at Fredericksburg; in May, seventeen thousand at Chancellorsville; in July, twenty-three thousand at Gettysburg. No one had expected suffering and loss on such a scale when the Union had mobilized against Southern secession. Authority alone could not stem the tide of blood. This was a crisis of faith, and, though loath to say so in public, the archbishop's own faith had been shaken, almost devastated, by what he saw as the betrayal represented by the Emancipation Proclamation.

Even should he be able to rouse himself from his sickbed, Hughes knew he had to face an excruciating personal reality: Did any of his once-formidable influence remain among those who were, at least nominally, a part of his archdiocese or among the powers that be? How great would be the humiliation if he had no power? What if he spoke and no one listened?

A further, embarrassing complication was his support the previous autumn for the institution of a draft. He had no intention of going back on that statement. Yet he had never imagined a system that would send more Irish laborers to war while the sons of rich men—so many of whom were Protestant, so many of whom were native Americans—stayed home or went abroad. Lincoln had made a mock of his support.

One person was only too ready to remind Hughes of his advocacy for conscription in the fall of 1862 and to take him to task for the anti-draft terror engulfing the city: Horace Greeley. In fact, at the moment the governor's communiqué arrived, Hughes had been writing a stinging reply to a recent open letter from Greeley printed in the *Tribune* on the ninth. In one of his more imprudent rants, the intemperate editor had lectured Hughes in no uncertain terms, in words that were designed to enrage him: "Your people," he wrote, are citizens of questionable loyalty. The Irish bore a formidable share of guilt for this monstrous war, Greeley argued, because of their unyielding allegiance to the pro-slavery Democratic Party of Polk, Pierce, and Buchanan and the church's refusal to speak up for abolition.

Answering Greeley while an Irish-led riot was under way tied the archbishop's hand to a significant degree, but he was eager to point out—and he did—that the *Tribune* had defended the antipapal rioters in Rome who attacked the Vatican not too many years before. He let it be known that he was sick of Greeley's "assault on the Irish." Yet the last thing John Hughes wanted was for anyone to conclude that he stood for civil unrest. He called on the men roaming the streets "to retire to their homes with as little delay as possible." If the rioters were in fact Catholics, he wrote, "I ask, for God's sake—for the sake of their holy religion—for my own sake, if they have any respect for episcopal authority—to dissolve their bad association with reckless men, who have little regard for divine or human laws." Hughes's words, meant as a counter to Greeley's and as a reply-of-sorts to the governor's request, appeared in James Gordon Bennett's *New York Herald* on Wednesday morning. Not surprisingly, they had no discernible effect on the still-escalating violence, and Hughes's attempt to define two distinct groups—the "reckless men" of murderous intentions and the Catholics who were now foolishly associating with those reckless men, whoever they were—was not lost on his readers, least of all Greeley.

What Greeley had in mind, and surely what the governor had in mind, was a stand decidedly more active and public, more in the spirit of the old Hughes. Greeley went on the offensive, reminding his readers—and his nemesis—that the archbishop of Paris had taken to the streets in 1848 during the rebellion that overthrew Louis-Philippe and, while nobly pleading for peace, had paid with his life. (Exactly, Hughes must have assumed, the fate Horace Greeley would have wanted for the archbishop of New York.) "That was an act of sublime devotion," the *Tribune*'s editor intoned. "We think the great personal influence of Archbishop Hughes could be used to advantage among 'his people' by riding among them and speaking to them on their duties." Again: *your people, his people*—language calibrated to stigmatize a vast segment of the population and to unbalance the archbishop. "Mr. Greeley treats me as if I were a head constable," he fumed to an aide. Had he considered entering the fray himself, on the arm of one of his priests or bundled in a carriage making its way through cobblestone-strewn streets, he now had another, infuriating reason not to—because Horace Greeley was telling him to, because Horace Greeley was lecturing him that "his people" were threatening the foundations of the republic.

For perhaps the first time in his life, John Hughes felt soundly defeated, crushed by a circumstance he could not hope to control.

News continued to pour in that offered cause for hope and more anguish. Hughes was heartened by the reports of many priests who were doing just what Greeley wanted, in a smaller way. Isaac Hecker and his Paulist fathers had walked the streets all night, talking and pleading with men they knew. A priest from the Church of the Transfiguration on Mott Street had stopped the lynching of an entire family of African Americans, doing the late Felix Varela proud. A priest from Saint John the Evangelist parish had talked a crowd out of sacking the buildings of Columbia College in midtown. A priest from Saint Gabriel's on East Thirty-Seventh Street had insisted on giving last rites in the street to a dying militia officer, Henry O'Brien, who had been beaten, stripped, sliced, and tortured with boiling wax on the steps of his vandalized home.

At the same time, the archbishop was dismayed as other reports came in of unspeakable acts perpetrated by Irishmen against African Americans. A black man on his way to buy groceries had been hanged from a tree in Clarkson Street, a bonfire kindled beneath his body. A black seaman whose boat was docked in the Hudson had been kicked to death on LeRoy Street. A black man on Worth Street had escaped a mob, only to have the men turn on his white wife and little boy, stripping the child in the street and beating him senseless, fatally injuring his mother, with an ax and iron cart-rung. A crippled black coachman had been hanged from a lamppost on West Twenty-Eighth Street. No one could tell how many black homes had been sacked and burned. Hughes had written angrily enough about abolitionists over the years for some people to conclude he believed in slavery, that he was indifferent to the suffering of the slaves and shared the worst racist prejudices of his times. He knew some would say that he bore a measure of responsibility for these heinous acts against black Americans. There was abundant pain in that thought.

On Thursday, finally, with troops pouring into the city, the archbishop ordered handbills to be circulated and placards put up around Manhattan, announcing that he would speak the following day at two o'clock from the balcony of his residence. He addressed his message "To the Men of New-York, who are now called in many of the papers rioters." That salutation by itself was enough to elicit a tart reaction. *Called rioters?* In the view of Protestant New York, the people Hughes was summoning to Madison Avenue most assuredly were rioters, more definitively than those who had gathered with less notice to hear Governor Seymour. But that "fact" was not at all clear to the prelate who would be speaking. His audience might be composed of the men and women who had torched an orphanage, or they might be the law-abiding Irish who attended Mass every Sunday and abhorred violence as much as anyone. Or, more likely, they would be some amorphous combination of the two. By definition, though, in the opinion of the non-Irish population, they were guilty of ravaging Gotham, and Hughes could not stomach the thought that the public was at that moment defiantly indifferent to any finer distinctions.

No mention was made on the handbills or placards of the intended topic of the archbishop's remarks—perhaps none was necessary—but one line was intended to allay some plausible fears. "I take upon myself the responsibility of assuring you that in paying me this visit, or in retiring from it, you shall not be disturbed by any exhibition of municipal or military presence." That some of his listeners might be identified as looters or assailants, and that the police might seize the opportunity for a roundup or for individual arrests or to crack a few skulls in return for what their fellows had suffered, occurred to Hughes, and he didn't intend to be made use of by the authorities in that fashion. (The editorial writers of the *New York Post*, not normally among Hughes's most aggressive critics, suggested that that was exactly what the police should do, now that "their shepherd has summoned the wolves.") "You who are

Catholic," the message ended, "have a right to visit your Bishop without molestation." It was a statement directed at Mayor Opdyke and General Wood as much as to his hoped-for audience.

According to the *New York Times*, the message aroused suspicion in many quarters. The wording of the call to gather, the manner of publicizing the speech, its timing: none of it seemed quite right. A reporter from the *Times* went to see the archbishop the next day, who assured him that what had been broadcast in the morning's papers was true: "He proposed to address such of his fellow citizens as should see fit to accept his invitation." He regretted that he couldn't give the reporter a copy of his remarks, as even one hour before he was scheduled to step out onto his balcony, he had yet to commit anything to paper. What he wanted to say would remain unclear, even to himself, until he went before the hundreds or thousands who would be there.

From the point of view of the authorities, there was little or no purpose in speaking on Friday afternoon at all. Except in isolated pockets, the riot had run its course, the omnibuses were running again, and there were more men in uniform to be seen on the avenues than laborers with crowbars and hammers. The archbishop found he couldn't stand on the balcony and was helped to a chair. Yet, strangely, he was in fine voice and clearly needed to speak. To be remembered for *not* having stood before his fellow Catholics at this moment or, far worse, for having been too frightened or feeble to do so was intolerable. The applause was enthusiastic and prolonged, the heat was terrible, the experience threatened to overwhelm the archbishop, but he was there, he drank a glass of water, removed his cap, bowed to the crowd, and began.

Some of the reporters wondered whether the spiritual leader of New York's Catholics was about to utter a rebuke or a command, but that was never a realistic possibility. Conservative estimates put the crowd at three thousand. Many, probably most, possibly all, of that number had not been among the violent gangs. Rather, the archbishop wanted to make note of a bond he felt, or yearned to say aloud that he felt, before he departed this life. He wanted to feel what link still existed, if any, between him and those he believed God had entrusted to his care.

First, he assured his listeners, no one had prompted him to speak—Seymour, Greeley, the police, the military. That was important for them to know. He was not doing any other man's bidding. The Irish had done enough of other men's bidding, he implied. Men like those he looked out on were to be relied on. Gentlemen, those of the monied and the pampered classes, were not. He would stand by, advise, and if need be die with the men he saw around him now. About the causes of the riot, he said he did not wish to dwell, merely stating that "no doubt there are some real grievances, but still I think that there are many imaginary ones." He refused to pass judgment in public on the draft inequities.

Yet, Hughes said, it pained him "grievously" to read the accusations that were made in the papers. He refused to believe that *Irish* and *rioter*, or *Catholic* and *rioter*, were to be taken to mean the same thing. He told a pointless joke about a simpleminded child who ignored his mother's commands and swallowed eggs whole until he heard the screech of a chicken from his throat as he downed one egg too many. He alluded to his visits to Rome. He talked, rambled, a good while about Ireland—"mother of heroes and poets"—and despotic John Bull, noting that all Irishmen were better off in the United States than they would have been had they stayed behind, but that true Irishmen fought defensively, never aggressively. That in America the people had a right to revolution—"every four years . . . a different kind of revolution." That life had to be based on a sound foundation. (At that moment a man in the crowd cried out, "And let the niggers keep to the South," but he was quickly shouted down by the people around him.) That many noble men had been unfairly exiled from their homeland. That Irish blood had tilled the fields of the Crimea and Balaclava. "I thank you for your kindness," he ended, "and I hope nothing will occur until you return home, and if by chance you should meet a police officer, or a military man, why—just look at him."

After being helped inside, the archbishop was called back to the balcony twice to give his blessing to his audience. The crowd then left, according to one reporter, after vociferous applause, but in a state of understandable confusion as to whether they had been exonerated for any wrongdoing, gently reprimanded, reminded that as Irishmen they were better than what they had been accused of doing that week, or simply instructed to see that the city return, if possible, to normal. Orestes Brownson was scornful. The speech, he wrote, merely showed the man's "impotence." George Templeton Strong thought it would have been more merciful if the archbishop, clearly nearing his end, had died before delivering of himself in public such a piece of "imbecility."

William Seward was confident that the "abominable sentiments" of the New York mob would, in the long run, redound to the advantage of the administration and the Republican Party. His wife, back home in Auburn, was considerably less tranquil, a rock having been thrown through a parlor window amid talk of a similar reaction to the draft lottery in their upstate New York hometown. The feeling among the soldiers in Washington, D.C., Walt Whitman told his mother, was "savage and hot as fire against New York," with talk of sending gunboats north, "cannonading the city [and] shooting down the mob." Ultimately, the New York City riots proved to be the most damaging of the responses to the draft law around the country.

Hughes was also certain that New Yorkers would neither forgive nor forget what had happened in the streets that July. "His people" were all but back where they had started. They were the "Celtic scum" the nativists had always said they were. "I am sorry to say that England is right about the Irish," George Templeton Strong noted in his diary, and he spoke for many that summer. The Irish were a "brutal, base, cruel" people, not ready for civilized life in the United States. That stigma would be attached to the Irish in America, to Irish Catholics, for generations, Hughes feared. The inspiring examples of patriotism provided by Corcoran, Meagher, and General William Rosecrans ("the greatest Catholic Civil War hero of the nineteenth century," in the words of one historian), not to mention those of thousands of soldiers whose names were known only to family and friends, would be swept away in popular memory.

Even the pulp writers weren't done with him and his. The popular hack Ned Buntline (one of the instigators of the Astor Place riots) reprinted his 1853 novel *The Convict* that summer, a melodrama in which a New York archbishop declaims, "God has given us the heretics for a spoil, and their land for a heritage." The litany of evidence in Buntline's story of the secret plot to subvert American democracy involved all the usual canards: the church's attempts to undermine the public school system by prohibiting the reading of the King James Bible, the conversion of Winfield Scott's daughters to Catholicism, the mass importation of priests and nuns from Europe. All the work, purportedly, of John Hughes and his minions.

Hughes wrote to Seward not long after the riots, unwilling that the Irish should be seen as unpatriotic, but he must have realized that another casualty of the riots was his relationship with Seward. Seward had been a friend to the Irish Catholics of the city and, in hoping to win his party's presidential nomination three years earlier, had paid a price for that friendship. Republicans like Thaddeus Stevens had made it clear in 1860 they would never support for higher office an ally of public funding of parochial schools. Now many of those same people whose children he wanted to see better educated vilified him, with Lincoln, as one of their worst enemies, and Seward was in no frame of mind to think charitably about the immigrant class that had brought New York City to its knees. And how warmly could he feel about the Catholic Church and its prelates as word leaked that Pope Pius IX was ready to receive Confederate diplomats in Rome and rethink his support of the Union?

Too much of the archbishop's correspondence in the last six months of his life was filled with disheartening communication. Jean-Marie Odin, the bishop of New Orleans and one of his few Southern correspondents still willing to write to him, expressed his concern about the hardships his parishioners were suffering under Union occupation. "Many are reduced to beg," he reported in August. "A great number of our most respectable families have been sent away in a great state of destitution." Hughes also received more letters from Catholic laymen complaining of his unseemly political posture that mocked the faith of Christ he professed. He was anguished to read about the destruction of Charleston, a city he loved, and to hear of a news report (later proved false) that Thomas Francis Meagher had been captured by the Confederates. The death of Father Nicholas O'Donnell, the friend from Philadelphia with whom he had started the *Catholic Herald*, was saddening. The election to the mayoralty of an antiwar Democrat, Charles Gunther, aided in his campaign by some of the bishop's most prominent parishioners, was a source of frustration. Closer to home, Margaret's husband, in his early sixties and ill for some time, was obviously at the beginning of a long, slow decline of his own. The great cathedral would be Renwick's doing alone.

The only good news that fall was that work on the seminary in Troy was progressing, though whether the archbishop would live to see its opening in 1864 was far from certain in his or anyone's mind. Similarly, the new home for the Catholic Protectory was almost ready on Eighty-Sixth Street and Fifth Avenue, taking the boys away from the site of the summer's mayhem, but he was not sure he would ever set foot in that building, either. Pierre de Smet, the Jesuit missionary with whom he had traveled to Belgium eighteen years earlier, paid a call that raised his spirits. He also decided that it was time to make a final peace with his old antagonists at Rose Hill and indicated that he would finally sign over the title to Saint Francis Xavier to the Jesuits now that the Putnam bill of 1855 had lapsed and it was legally his to transfer. However, it would be left to his successor to fulfill that intention.

It is likely, if not almost certain, that Hughes's secretaries would have had the sense to keep the October issue of *Brownson's Quarterly Review* out their superior's hands, as the archdiocese no longer subscribed to that periodical, though Hughes sometimes still read it. If he did, however, get wind of the editor's lengthy essay "Catholics and the Anti-Draft Riots," all of his worst assumptions would have been confirmed. "That these riots were intended to cooperate with the rebel Lee in his invasion of Maryland and Pennsylvania, and to weaken and overthrow the government, by preventing it from obtaining the forces necessary to crush the rebellion, there is and can be no serious doubt," Brownson wrote. "It is certain, also, that nearly nine-tenths of the active rioters were Irishmen and Catholics." If the better class of Catholic Irishmen were not participants, he insisted, neither was it true that all those who looted and murdered were among the drunken rabble who never attended church and should not even be called Catholics. That there were practicing Catholics among the working-class mob was proved by the fact that the priests of the diocese had demonstrated some measure of influence with them in curbing more extreme acts of violence in certain neighborhoods. The problem, Brownson maintained, was that these people were of the class Hughes and his priests had too often neglected in recent years as they courted their middle-class congregations. The rioters were the sort of people who had never been properly instructed by their priests about citizenship, civility, and their religious duties. As such, he concluded, "the clergy and their most reverend chief of this city" were not wholly lacking in responsibility for what had happened and should no more be exempted from blame than the anti-Union Catholic press and the worst of the Catholic Copperhead politicians.

As he often did in his lengthy essays, Brownson would make bold statements and several paragraphs or pages later modify them. He did not think it accurate to the refer to the events of July as "a Catholic riot," he acknowledged later in the essay, but of course the damage was done—as it always was with Brownson's tart prose—in his opening paragraphs. He meant to wound. Furthermore, he was willing to link the fate of the United States to the health of the universal Catholic Church:

"The ruin of the American republic would be the most serious calamity that could befall the Catholic Church, not only here, but throughout the world." The rioters had threatened to do just that, to topple church and state. What a charge, what a burden, was thrown in the direction of the now-dying archbishop of New York. To this, Hughes would never have had the strength, the words, to answer.

———

THERE WAS ONE LAST FIGHT to be waged, though, as his kidney functions slowed and the edema worsened and the energy drained from his body. That battle was against Lincoln's newest fiscal policies, and it made for something closer to undignified farce than meaningful drama or tragedy.

The federal government's hopes in 1861 that bank loans and the sale of war bonds would finance the lion's share of the war effort proved unrealistic. The conflict was costing the government a million dollars a day by 1862. That cost was climbing, promising to double within a year or two, and the Internal Revenue Act was intended to deal with an approaching fiscal crisis. Americans were unaccustomed to the idea of a personal income tax, of course, but the terms of the 1862 bill were progressive and designed to spare the poor and the working class. Anyone with an annual income below six hundred dollars was exempt, while those who earned between six hundred and ten thousand dollars annually were to pay a 3 percent tax, and those earning above that limit would pay a 5 percent tax. Priests, ministers, rabbis—everyone—would be included in these calculations.

This was all well and good, John Hughes felt, but it had nothing to do with him. His priests might receive a fixed salary—might, in a manner of speaking, be seen as employees of an institutional structure that involved financial accountability (though hardly transparency). But a bishop, archbishop, or cardinal—no more than the pope himself—could not be seen in that light. His expenses were paid for by the diocese, but that was a matter between him and the trustees and the hierarchy. Those expenses fluctuated according to circumstances. Those expenses had to do with the exercise of his spiritual duties and were no business of the state's. That money did not constitute a "salary." The Internal Revenue Office thought otherwise.

The archbishop was as unhappy with the idea of the government looking into the church's books, blurring a line that should never even be approached, as with the idea that a man of the cloth should be considered in any way equivalent to a man of business or a clerk in an office. He also felt he had done enough for the war effort. He let the tax officials know that he had no intention of answering their queries or ever paying a personal income tax. What would follow, he wanted to know? That the monies paid to the church when a bishop officiated at a wedding or a baptism should be considered taxable income as well?

Yes—he was told—any fees paid by parishioners to his office for services rendered would, in fact, be considered taxable if the bishop's living expenses came out of those funds; but his first official correspondent, a man of goodwill, suggested that Hughes and he could simply agree on a plausible total and let it go at that. At this stage of things, New York assessor H. J. Bleeker was willing to effect any compromise to end an escalating quarrel with an old man. No, Hughes answered; he had no intention of naming sums or continuing a discussion of what he viewed as a closed matter. Churches were tax-exempt institutions in America. He *was* the church in his diocese. The harried Bleeker was forced to consult his superior in Washington.

"I regret very much that you and I differ as to what may be taxable under the income clause of the Internal Revenue laws," Bleeker wrote back to the archbishop on September 15, 1863, after receiving instructions from Washington. "If you had accepted the offer made you of a fixed salary, of course, there would have been no difficulty. . . . Unfortunately for your opinion on the subject, the Commissioner of Internal Revenue has decided that . . . marriage and baptismal fees are to be taxed." Surely, he suggested, a record of those and similarly fee-based aspects of the job had been kept, and a reasonable taxable sum figured on that basis. He wanted to make things as easy as possible, and he hastened to reassure the bishop that everything would be kept strictly confidential. His "salary" would never be made public, if that was what was bothering him, nor would anyone ever be able to question exactly where the money came from.

But that was exactly Hughes's point: he was not a salaried "employee" of anything. He wrote restating the premise from which he would not budge. It was probably also a source of mortification that he would have to admit, if pressed, that his record-keeping by this time was in scandalous shape. He had only the faintest notion of how much money came in that could be called personal to him and how much would have been fair game for the IRS. Not even his best secretaries had been able to stay on top of the paperwork. Worried as he was about his health and the state of the diocese and the nation, utterly shaken by the events of the summer, this was the last topic on his mind, and he let the assessor know that he felt he was being harassed.

To another man in the city's tax office, S. A. Duncombe, who reviewed the case, Hughes wrote a few days later in the same spirit. He would never, he declared, "submit either to state or federal government the right to investigate my income as an archbishop. . . . For myself, I have lived up till now, and ever shall live, on the voluntary contributions of my people."

His patience exhausted, H. J. Bleeker wrote once again to Hughes at considerable length, expressing frustration over his desire to "discharge the obligations resting upon me as an officer of the [Treasury Department] with all the delicacy and consideration of your exalted position." But by now, the man knew his audience. He was a Catholic himself, he finally told his archbishop, as if that were going to count for something other than a reply of "then you should know better." He begged the archbishop to remember that Mary and Joseph had traveled all the way to Bethlehem at the time Caesar Augustus had called the citizens of the empire to be taxed, and that the parents of Jesus had acquiesced, and that Jesus himself had said that rendering unto Caesar what was Caesar's was not inappropriate. He did everything but wave the flag and suggest that unpaid taxes were the greatest possible boon to Jefferson Davis.

How did the matter end? Not with John Hughes paying his taxes. Within a few weeks, he was starting to drift away from the affairs of this world, becoming more unfocused, finding it harder to read anything, needing to sleep for longer periods of time. Others took over the work of running the diocese and answering his mail. His secretaries probably wrote a check, by which time he would not even have recalled his spirited defense of his right not to be taxed.

By late November it was clear to his doctors that the archbishop would not live long, probably not even into the new year. He spent most days wrapped in blankets on a couch in his study, always cold, eating less and less, staring at his books and paintings. He did manage, apparently, to get a last note sent off to Terence Donaghoe, reflecting on all the changes they had seen in their time, but noting "yet through it all, my heart has never known a moment's change toward you, my best friend on earth."

The death of Michael Corcoran of the Irish Brigade, the cemetery dedication in Gettysburg and Lincoln's greatest speech, the president's proclamation of amnesty and reconstruction, the fierce battles in Tennessee that now opened the Deep South for a Union invasion—the national news meant nothing. Four days after Christmas, his sisters were told by his doctors that the end was fast approaching. Margaret and Mother Angela informed their brother, knowing that to be kept in the dark about his own condition would be the last thing of which he would approve. He seemed surprised. He looked intently, John Hassard commented, from one to the other and asked: "Did they say so?" Except for his final confession that day, those were his last words.

On Wednesday, December 30, Hughes received the last rites of the church from his confessor, Father William Quinn. Over the next two days, various priests came to the house to pay their final respects. By New Year's Day, he was in bed, immobile, drifting in and out of consciousness. Two days later, on Sunday morning, Father Quinn said Mass in the archbishop's bedroom. At seven o'clock that evening, as he lay surrounded by his sisters, Fathers Starrs and McNeirny, and Bishop Loughlin of Brooklyn, his chest moved spasmodically several times, and he closed his eyes. The ever-combative John Hughes had breathed his last.

EPILOGUE

LEGACY

THE WAXEN BODY of the archbishop of New York, robed and mitred, lay in state on Tuesday, January 5, 1864, in the main aisle of Saint Patrick's Cathedral, the catafalque passed during the next two days by an estimated one hundred thousand New Yorkers of all denominations. Lines formed around the block at every hour of the day until the sun set. The church where John Hughes had said Mass for twenty-five years was draped in heavy black crepe from the arched roof, twining about every arch, column, and doorway.

Eight bishops and two hundred priests from Montreal and throughout New England and New York State, from Philadelphia and Baltimore, were in attendance for the funeral on Thursday the seventh. These numbered men he had deeply respected and men he had fought bitterly with: John McCloskey and John Timon, James Roosevelt Bayley and Isaac Hecker, Jeremiah Cummings and Charles Constantine Pise, the Fordham Jesuits. The overwhelming majority of the names listed in the church accounts are Irish. Margaret Hughes Rodrigue, Mother Angela, and their older brother Michael occupied a front pew along with Eugene Kelly and Margaret Rodrigue Kelly. A significant number of Manhattan's business, judicial, and political elite were part of that capacity crowd, including Mayor Gunther, General George McClellan, John McKeon, Judge Daly, and Thurlow Weed. William Seward did not attend, nor was the federal government represented in any official way at the funeral. Seward's note to Father Starrs, expressing his regret that he would not be able to attend the service, was short and scrupulously polite. The New York legislature passed a resolution eulogizing the late Catholic leader by a vote of 76–14. No amount of arm-twisting could make it unanimous. Even in death, Hughes left some state senators grumbling about his unwelcome influence.

Mass was celebrated by Bishop Timon of Buffalo, whom Hughes had opposed for the episcopacy of Baltimore, and the principal funeral oration was delivered by John McCloskey, his favorite who would soon be named as his successor. McCloskey took as his text the seventh and eighth verses from chapter 4 of Saint Paul's second epistle to Timothy: *I have fought a good fight; I have finished my course. For the rest, there is laid up for me a crown of justice, which the Lord, the Just Judge, will render to me at that day; and not to me only, but to them also who love his coming.* He spoke of his early mentor as "the great prelate of the American Church," its most forceful representative, advocate, and defender at a time when it most needed advocacy and defense. If that day was passing, if the power of anti-Catholicism was on the wane, it was due in part, everyone should remember, to the labors of John Hughes. McCloskey aptly acknowledged, too, that there were prejudices and animosities, "differences and collisions," to "let melt and fall away . . . in the imposing and venerable presence" of death. The "softened and gentle luster of death" should allow those present now to see John Hughes's life in its truest character, a character "that appears to rise up in even colossal sublimity and grandeur." Father Thomas Preston, an Episcopal convert and priest Hughes had been particularly fond of, delivered a second, brief eulogy.

The coffin, then filled with the floral wreaths and roses that surrounded it, was closed and carried at the end of the service on the shoulders of the undertakers to a temporary resting place in a crypt beneath the church, to be removed to the new cathedral on Fifth Avenue when it should be completed. The crowds filed out to the solemn strains of a *De profundis.*

Old antagonists found it in them to be generous, to one degree or another. James Gordon Bennett acknowledged in the *Herald* that Hughes had been loved by New York's Irish Catholics "with a sentiment scarcely short of idolatry" and that the church had lost a great champion and the country a great patriot. Henry Raymond's *Times* was studiously respectful, noting that the archbishop had "endured with fortitude" his prolonged final illness and displayed throughout his life a mantle "of virtues and abilities." His death was a "severe loss" to his fellow Catholics, but the paper also commented on his longtime affection for New York City, whose well-being and prosperity had been his "constant desire." In the pages of the *Evening Post*, William Cullen Bryant praised the departed's integrity and patriotism. Horace Greeley wasn't willing to pretend a sorrow he didn't feel. He wrote, in explanation of the scant space the *Tribune* allotted to the archbishop's death, which was just a perfunctory recital of his earlier accomplishments buried at the back of the paper, "His public services during the Rebellion are too recent to require attention."

James McMaster, difficult to the last, relegated what should have been a front-page obituary to the middle of the *Freeman's Journal*, though he did find it in himself to call his bishop "a man of extraordinary talents." Their altercations were never going to be put out of mind—McMaster was even less forgiving than Hughes—but he was willing to dwell on happier days, and on the fact that Hughes had tried to visit him in prison three years earlier, when he wrote, "In unofficial intercourse, there was a winning kindliness and a playful wit about the Archbishop that made his company charming."

In the weeks immediately after the funeral, two young men who knew him well and esteemed him to the point of reverence—Lawrence Kehoe and John Hassard—set to work laying the groundwork for the historical record. Kehoe, a bookseller and publisher, an Irish immigrant and ultramontane Catholic himself, undertook to gather as many of the archbishop's speeches, sermons, public letters, and other writings as he could collect into a two-volume work that his own firm brought out that fall. Hassard, the archbishop's twenty-seven-year-old secretary who was with him to the end, devoted most of the next year and a half to writing a biography of his employer and spiritual father. Margaret entrusted him with family letters, many of which are now known only through that biography. (Seward declined to see Hassard or share any letters he had.) Hassard's book is a typical nineteenth-century biographical product—sizable, discreet, hagiographic—but without it, research into Hughes's life in future years would have been impossible.

Orestes Brownson's final words came many months later, when Lawrence Kehoe published the *Collected Works*, and they were both honest and unexpectedly gracious, given his attacks on the archbishop in the past two years: "We were no blind admirer of his during his life, and we confess that we often did him injustice in our thoughts and words too freely spoken. . . . Though we never fell under his official censure, we did fall under the lash of [his] unofficial censure, which was not at all pleasant." Yet Brownson conceded, in that self-abnegating way he employed on occasion to signal his supreme dutifulness as a Catholic convert, that "time and events have proved that he was right in many things in which we thought him wrong, or at least injudicious, at the time, and it is not for us to say that he was not always right, wise, and judicious. We are laymen, and not judges of episcopal administration."

John McCloskey might have wondered if the shoes he was being asked to fill when the Vatican announced his succession were going to be a problem, but many in the diocese and throughout Catholic America were ready for a calmer, steadier, less pugnacious style of leadership. Hughes's long, slow decline had taken its toll on more than just his body and mind; it had frayed the nerves of everyone around him. He left a fair number of people, including many Catholics who had never met him, battle weary. When the *Atlantic Monthly* referred to him a few years after his death as "a politician and one of the shrewdest and ablest of his class . . . always in the saddle," praise was not the intention.

Yet at the opening fifteen years later of the new Saint Patrick's Cathedral, steeple-less but still majestic, his name was once again invoked with something close to awe, or at least great pride. A vision mocked in the 1850s was a magnificent reality in 1879, and that was thanks to John Hughes. Time softened the memory of rough edges. A monograph by Father Henry Brann, published as a part of a *Makers of America* series in 1892, took an entirely laudatory view of the late archbishop, as did all the histories of the church that began to pour forth from the pen of John Gilmary Shea and assorted lesser lights in the late nineteenth and early twentieth century. In 1891, the noted sculptor William R. O'Donovan completed a full-length version of Hughes in bronze, which today stands on an imposing pedestal opposite the administration building on Fordham's campus, a statue that even Walt Whitman said exhibited "a recommendable faithfulness, I guess."

In sum, Hughes's respectable niche in history—Catholic history, New York City history, American and Irish American history—was secure for a good part of the next century, even if it was somewhat less imposing than some in his own day might have expected it to be. An exception to this chorus came from a secular source in 1938, Ray Billington's excellent *The Protestant Crusade: 1800–1860*, which saw Hughes as aggravating problems with the nativists that were bad enough without a counter-militancy of such force and anger.

By the late twentieth century, however, the laudatory tide had turned. There wasn't a chance of rescuing from the judgment of post–Vatican II posterity a man of outmoded racial values, attitudes toward women not even advanced enough to call sexist, and ultramontane beliefs. Every compliment came with a caveat—"a cleric of first-rate mind and third-rate temperament"—and the compliments were few and far between. (One notable exception was the positive references in Sidney Ahlstrom's 1972 classic, *A Religious History of the American People.*) Hughes's distasteful personality was a given in most accounts: not a man anyone could really like or would want to spend time with. His authoritarianism was unpardonable in a more pluralistic, ecumenical age. His intransigence was embarrassing in a more fully developed, less contentious democracy that—still—rarely acknowledges how little the brutal, untamed America of the 1840s has in common with the America of the twentieth and twenty-first centuries. His two or three most strident statements were much repeated and taken as sufficient evidence to define and condemn.

The most frequently quoted of these lines is the alleged response made to some recalcitrant priests in his diocese who questioned his reading of canon law—namely, that if they didn't know their place, he would "teach them [County] Monaghan canon law and . . . would send them back to the bogs from whence they came." Surely not an impossible sentence for John Hughes to have uttered, though it is worth noting that the sole source for this perfect gem of vitriol is Ambrose Manahan, the Fordham president fired by Hughes who later absconded with the parish receipt books from Saint Stephen's, and that this line attributed to him is found in the 1865 diary of Father Richard Burstell, himself a tart critic of the Hughes/McCloskey/Starrs leadership in New York.

Andrew Greeley, a Chicago priest and prolific writer, was probably the most lacerating of later twentieth-century critics. In a book that judiciously goes out of its way to find something positive to say about many of the nineteenth-century prelates it discusses, Hughes is described in Greeley's *The Catholic Experience* (1967) as little short of a thug and

the originator of the unfortunate role of the American bishop as pater-
nalistic protector of a flock unable to take care of itself in the midst of a
hostile culture. He was the anti-Carroll, the anti-England, the model of
the prelate fundamentally at odds with his adopted country. His influence was a "major disaster," responsible for all Catholic reactionary
opposition to progressive thought in the next century. He was a "fierce
and terrible man."

A Catholic University doctoral dissertation from 1973, alert to
the climate of the time, mined that same vein with the statement that
"Hughes did not really have a notion of a godly community of believers;
he held, rather, an idea of [a] holy organization which dispenses the law.
His life's work was to tighten the line of command and to increase the
bishop's power within that organization." Thirty-five years of labor are
reduced to self-aggrandizement and the creation of a corporate structure. A 1998 study of class and racial politics in antebellum New York
by a reputable left-wing historian termed Hughes "a staunch defender
of slavery," a statement that is flat-out incorrect. "Ambivalent," "reluctant," and "intermittent" would be more accurate. Similarly, *New York
and Slavery: Time to Teach the Truth* (2008), prepared by a Hofstra
University professor of education and intended for use as a teacher's
classroom instructional guide, paints Hughes as an unambiguously
"pro-slavery" advocate akin to John C. Calhoun and Jefferson Davis.
Hughes's approval of legislation outlawing the slave trade and his belief
that over time slavery would justly die out, views putting him more in
line with Madison and Monroe than the leaders of the Confederacy, are
nowhere a part of that story.

The criticism of recent scholarly writers has been no less severe.
Maureen Fitzgerald's *Habits of Compassion*, published in 2006, for
example, is a vitally important, incisive work that honors and examines
in detail the activist labors of nineteenth-century Irish Catholic nuns and
forthrightly confronts their erasure from history. John Hughes, though,
is the purest of villains in this story, a man whose belief that education
was a more crucial focus than charity work in his diocese before the
Civil War is dismissed as not just wrongheaded but cruelly insensitive.
His discomfort with the lot of "fallen women" does, indeed, show him as
woefully inattentive to the example of Jesus on this topic, an observation
that could be made about almost every male in a position of authority in
the nineteenth century. He is an inexcusably egocentric figure without a

redeeming quality because he was not an early-twentieth-century progressive, a sufficiently empathetic thinker by modern standards.

To swallow this more critical view of Hughes *in toto* is to overlook
quite a bit, though. First, some part of any man's personality can be
determined by his circle of friends and admiring acquaintances. William
Seward and, even more so, the gregarious Thurlow Weed found him
anything but unlikable. (It could be argued that anyone Thurlow Weed
wanted to socialize with could hardly be without personally appealing
qualities.) Bishops John Purcell, William Walsh, and Simon Bruté—good
men, strong men—enjoyed his company. The same could be said of the
saintly Felix Varela, the tireless missionary Pierre de Smet, the Paulists'
founder Isaac Hecker, and the Jesuit academic August Thebaud. Friends
made among the clergy in his Philadelphia days, like Terence Donaghoe
and Michael Hurley, as dedicated as any priests who ever lived, thought
well of him all their days. Prelates whose political beliefs were diamet-
rically opposed to his, like Patrick Lynch of Charleston, nonetheless
respected him. Priests in need of help, like Fordham's third president,
the gentle John Harley, were taken under his wing. William Corby, the
Jesuit chaplain of the Irish Brigade, termed him "the Nestor of the Catholic Church in America" (a compliment of sorts). Boston's Bishop John
Fitzpatrick wrote to John McCloskey in 1864, "I never knew how large a
place he filled in my esteem and affection . . . until the announcement of
his death." New Orleans's Bishop Jean-Marie Odin told James Roosevelt
Bayley that he had "loved and respected" Hughes, even though they were
on opposing sides in the Civil War, and that he would remember him as
a man who "always showed me a kind affection."

Numerous letters in the Hughes archive begin with statements of
gratitude for acts of generosity or expressions of concern that the archbishop had proffered his correspondent; Sophia Dana Ripley was far
from the only person who thought him "kindness itself." Not every parish priest under his authority found him an unbearable taskmaster. Not
all of the city's Catholics thought Hughes brutish. For an adversary like
James Gordon Bennett to acknowledge at the time of his death the Irish
"idolatry" of their leader is to suggest a different image. He had an acid
tongue, he never suffered fools gladly, he hated admitting when he was
wrong, and at his worst his ego was more befitting a Tammany boss
than a servant of Christ—there would be no point in denying that. John
Hughes wanted to be a cardinal, not a saint.

Father Greeley's and Dr. Fitzgerald's portrayals really speak to issues concerning Hughes that are deeper than personality or style: namely, to Hughes's view of what was needed *in his time* as he saw it, to policy decisions he made because he believed them to be right. Greeley is more or less correct in asserting that Hughes is responsible for *originating* a certain type of undemocratic, unecumenical leadership (though Francis Kenrick did his part as well), and it might have been a type of leadership not at all applicable or useful for the decades that preceded his tenure, the supposed golden age of bishops Carroll and England, or to the decades that followed his death. It can certainly be argued that it was a type of leadership needed in the thirty years before the Civil War, or at least in the 1830s and 1840s. Indeed, in 1838 Hughes's *was* a flock that could not take care of itself, and that flock existed in the midst of a culture that *was* decidedly hostile, even violent.

From the point of view of a Catholic priest or anyone who cared about the spiritual and physical well-being of others, the New York Hughes came to was a nightmare scarcely imaginable today—in religious and civic terms, in educational and hygienic terms. Nothing about a Kenrick (either brother), a Purcell, a Timon, a Neumann, a Spalding, two Bishop Fenwicks, a Fitzpatrick, an O'Connor, a Lynch, or a Henni suggests that they would have been able to manage as well as John Hughes to knit together a community of believers who would work together to combat the ills that had to be confronted. The task required more than intelligence, energy, faith, and goodwill; it required bluster and defiance, disdain for obstacles, a propagandizing instinct, even at moments a crude and frightening but crowd-pleasing ferocity. The problem with the man who exhibits those qualities is that he is often the last person to know when the time has come to temper them and adopt others, quieter and more conciliatory, and Hughes was no exception to that truism.

More important, it hardly follows that the less pleasing, antiprogressive authoritarianism of some later bishops—qualities in men who had less need to adopt those stances in the context of their much different times—should be laid at Hughes's doorstep. Michael Corrigan, John McCloskey's successor as archbishop of New York, was an enemy of the workingman. He had no sympathy for workers' rights, wanted the pope to condemn the Knights of Labor, and urged the Vatican to place Henry George's *Progress and Poverty* on the church's *Index* of forbidden books. That is not necessarily a position Hughes would have adopted at the end of the nineteenth century. It makes no more sense to trace an unassailable link between Hughes and Corrigan than it would to imagine a line from Hughes to Cardinal William O'Connell's disparagement of Father John Ryan's social-welfare proposals (presaging the New Deal by more than a decade) or to Bishop Fulton Sheen's attacks on psychiatry in the 1940s or to any of the other regrettable forms of antimodernism that the American Catholic Church adhered to in the century after him. Those were stances adopted by the men of those later times, stances that seemed appropriate to them in their day. No one can really know what Hughes would have thought about labor unions circa 1900, Ryan's brave "Program for Social Reconstruction" of 1919, or postwar psychiatry, but Hughes is often positioned as the domino that set in motion the rigid trajectory of those who came after him, all rather implausibly arranged in a tight reactionary line.

The most distinctive difference between John Hughes and the authoritarian hierarchy of a later age is probably highlighted by responses to the pedophile scandal in our own time. The idea of reassigning priests elsewhere to continue their illegal and unethical sexual practices would never have struck him as a suitable response to a moral tragedy. Whenever a priest in his diocese was guilty, or was even plausibly charged, with a sexual transgression (always in his time, as far as the evidence suggests, with an adult female parishioner, though surely more varied, undocumented cases arose), he was summarily dismissed and told to do penance. Despite the problematic shortage of clergy he had constantly to deal with, under John Hughes a man did not continue to wear the Roman collar and celebrate Mass if he had fallen that far away from his sacred role and vows. John Hughes was no Cardinal Law.

There is a kind of modernity to Hughes's story, though, in terms of three issues we still have cause to ponder in the United States: namely, the nature of community, the utility of any form of identity politics, and our national embrace of—and, in some quarters now, new skepticism about—multiple cultural identities. Hughes gave thought to the forces that were necessary to forge a tight-knit community, and his answers, if dangerous in our own day, seemed more than reasonable to him. He did not share Bishop Benedict Joseph Fenwick's gentleness when convents were sacked or Bishop Francis Kenrick's desire to turn the other cheek when churches were burned to the ground before cheering crowds. He believed in fighting back; in calling men to arms, if need be; in adopting a distinctly American, even fiercely Jacksonian role and style of rhetoric. From the earliest days of his priesthood, he was well aware that a people under siege are more likely to come together, to forge a durable common identity, than those who feel secure and respected. The fourth archbishop of New York didn't invent or exaggerate nativist anti-Catholic, anti-immigrant rage, but he turned it to useful account.

Hughes's belief that men and women needed—craved—community of some sort was central to his life's work. A country that built a national mythology on the promotion of rugged individualism, unfettered free-market competition, and the acquisition of wealth as a validation of one's worth was, in his view, in danger of creating a world governed largely by egotism and the worship of mammon. The cost of the isolation and the alienation was frightening to contemplate. For Irish Catholics, that wider sense of community could best be found, he was certain, in heartfelt ethnic and religious bonds, celebrated with greatest resonance in an urban setting. By refusing to forget or downplay their ancestry and by becoming loyal members of the Catholic Church, *they would know who they were.* It was a wonderful thing to be an American in the antebellum period, years when the country was still defining itself, but it was not enough to be, solely, an American. American values, for one, were still in too formative a stage, too jingoistic, too focused on expansion and material growth. John Hughes was a patriot, but hardly an uncritical one.

At that same time, the ideal of community Hughes hoped would evolve over time for Irish Catholics as they fought the arsonists and the belittlers did not lean toward a separatist mentality. Modern religious scholars and social commentators have made much of the "ghettoization" of American Catholics from the late nineteenth through the mid- to late twentieth centuries. It is hard to see how that would have been pleasing to John Hughes. The point of rejecting the abolitionist creed, turning a blind eye to what Manifest Destiny really meant, or fighting to save the Union in its darkest hour was precisely to ensure that Irish Catholics were not seen as un-American, as dangerous aliens, as a people who didn't understand and love the country that had taken them in. His constant theme was that it was possible to be a devout Catholic, a heritage-minded Irish American, and a proud American at the same time in equal measure. Hughes would have found himself very much at home in the post–melting pot world where multiple identities were affirmed.

The world where he would have been less at home is the one we inhabit today—an increasingly secular society uneasy with any affirmation of religion in the public realm, a homogenizing suburban culture that has seen the gradual erosion of ethnic differences and loyalties (or at least those originating in Europe), and an American Catholic population that feels a significant measure of alienation from the papacy. It was John Hughes's fate, in any case, to pass from the scene before either the fruition of his dreams or their diminishment took place. Dying while the Civil War still raged and so soon after the hideousness of the draft riots, he had no way of knowing if "his flock," as he thought of them, would become esteemed members of society on these shores, valued for their contributions and sense of self-worth, or if they would remain, except for a small elite, perpetual outsiders, doomed—as Catholics and as Irishmen—to a derided second-class status. It was his accomplishment to have helped set in motion a process that bore remarkable fruit for the better part of a century as Ireland achieved its independence with Irish American support, Irish Americans climbed their way out of poverty, Catholicism became the single largest Christian denomination in the United States, and his adopted country elected an Irish Catholic president.

What public legacy, though, is not mixed, what place in history not equivocal and subject to opposing perspectives and repeated change? What should interest and concern us is the life lived in its time, and in that sense John Hughes takes a worthy place in the age of Webster and Clay, Whitman and Lincoln, Seward and Greeley, Emerson and the Beechers. His could even be seen as a paradigmatically American story of the nineteenth century. An immigrant forced to leave his homeland sailed into Baltimore harbor with not much more than a carpetbag of clothes and enough money to last him a few days. He died having made a transforming mark on the society he entered that day in 1817, a spokesman for his faith—the most vocal and self-dramatizing of all his ecclesiastical peers—and an unrelenting opponent of religious bigotry, exploitation of the immigrant, and self-doubt.

Acknowledgments

F OUR SOURCES were essential for the writing of this biography. One was the Archbishop John Hughes Papers at the Archives of the Archdiocese of New York, housed at Saint Joseph's Seminary at Dunwoodie in Yonkers, New York. My thanks, first and foremost, then, are to the custodians of that precious archive, Father Michael Morris (now at the Regina Coeli Parish in Hyde Park, New York) and archivist Kate Feighery, whose help was vital at every stage along the way.

A second key source was the collection of manuscripts, notes, and Hughes correspondence housed in the Rare Book Collection of Low Memorial Library at Columbia University. These materials were assembled for two biographies, both never completed, written in the 1930s and the 1950s, respectively. The generosity of Father Peter Guilday and later Francis Henry Browne in leaving for future scholars the fruits of their labors gathered many decades in the past strikes me as nothing short of remarkable. (A copy of Browne's manuscript is also in the collection of the Archives of the Archdiocese of New York.)

My work was also aided by the special collections and open stacks of the Walsh Family Library at Fordham University's Rose Hill campus (a university founded by John Hughes) in the Bronx, probably the most splendid library in New York City at which to work and browse the stacks. My thanks also to Fordham's archivist, Patrice Kane, and all the Fordham librarians.

Finally, my work benefited from the labors and insights of two predecessors: John Hassard published a biography of Hughes in 1866, hagiographic in the style of Victorian life stories but nonetheless packed with valuable information and impressions, and Richard Shaw published a second biography of Hughes in 1977, equally interesting but in a more modern vein of portraiture.

In Manhattan, I also made use of the collections, for both long out-of-print books and periodicals, of the New York Public Library, the Irish Historical Society, and the New-York Historical Society. The New-York Historical Society was particularly important for its holdings of the most obscure antebellum books and its bound collection of the *Freeman's Journal*, the nineteenth-century Catholic newspaper published in New York City from the 1840s to the 1880s. Nicholson Baker was prescient in 2002 when he warned in *Double Fold: Libraries and the Assault on Paper* that irreplaceable old newspapers, so crucial to historical research, were soon to become very rare commodities. Mercifully, the New-York Historical Society did not join in the mass discarding of old newspapers that has taken place in recent decades at other institutions.

Other useful repositories of books, newspapers, periodicals, letters, and other materials were the Archives of the Archdiocese of Hartford; the Massachusetts Historical Society in Boston; the Mullen Library at the Catholic University of America in Washington, D.C.; the Philadelphia Archdiocesan Historical Research Center on the campus the Saint Charles Borromeo Seminary in Merion, Pennsylvania (run by the dedicated Shawn Weldon); the Archives of the University of Notre Dame; the Archives of the Sisters of Charity at Mount Saint Vincent College in Riverdale, New York (run by Sister Mary McCormack and Sister Maryellen Blumlein); and the Seton Hall University archives in South Orange, New Jersey (run by Alan Delozier). My special thanks to Alan for his enthusiasm and assistance in navigating the James Roosevelt Bayley Papers there.

Doctoral dissertations, published and unpublished, proved to be a more than usually rich source of information for this project, and I want to acknowledge my debt to those writers for their expert, highly focused research, the unexpected leads they provided, and some superb bibliographic references that I would have otherwise missed. Robert Francis Hueston's *The Catholic Press and Nativism, 1840–1860* (University of Notre Dame, 1972) surveyed multiple aspects of the immigrant-nativist conflict through the pages of dozens of national newspapers. Albert Henri Ledoux's *The Life and Thought of Simon Bruté, Seminary Professor and Frontier Bishop* (Catholic University of America Press, 2005) told me a great deal about an early Hughes mentor. I also benefited from reading Father Charles P. Connor's "The American Catholic Political Position at Mid-century: Archbishop John Hughes as a Test Case" (Fordham University, 1979). Rena Mazyck Andrews's hard-to-come-by dissertation, *Archbishop Hughes and the Civil War*, was printed by the University of Chicago library in 1935 but has since disappeared from the shelves of some of the libraries that list it (including the New York Public Library). It turned up in an odd corner of the Archives of the Archdiocese of New York (box E-22, not part of the Hughes collection) just as I was completing my work.

My "day job" as a teacher of English, American studies, and art history at the Nightingale-Bamford School in New York City provides me with an opportunity to extend heartfelt thanks. Diane Neary was helpful in securing interlibrary loans and obscure online articles, and many of my colleagues were a constant source of needed support, especially Laura Kirk, Catherine McMenamin, Betsey Osborne, Brad Whitehurst, and Jennifer Zaccara. I will always be grateful to Paul Burke, head of school, and the school's travelship committee for financing more than a few of my research trips.

I was fortunate to have an opportunity to talk about John Hughes and the challenges of overseeing a vast archdiocese with Cardinal Timothy Dolan and to see the traces of Hughes and the nineteenth century—a painting I had never seen before, gifts from famous contemporaries, his pectoral cross—in the episcopal residence on Madison Avenue in Manhattan. The cardinal's reputation as a welcoming, conversational, and history-minded man is not overstated.

The opportunity to talk about Hughes and the diocese with church historian Monsignor Thomas Shelley was helpful, and I thank him for reading and commenting on the book. Monsignor Michael Sakano, pastor of the old Saint Patrick's Cathedral—now basilica—was similarly cordial. Monsignor Sakano gave me a tour of the rectory where Hughes, from his study, looked out on the troubled scene below him and of the crypt beneath the basilica where he was originally buried. Dr. Catherine O'Donnell of Arizona State University (author of a forthcoming biography of Elizabeth Seton) was supportive in numerous ways and provided useful leads. I look forward to her book. Sister Maryellen Blumlein was my guide in learning more about Hughes's sister Ellen, who became Sister, later Mother, Angela of the Sisters of Charity. Dan Burns of the Archives of the Archdiocese of Dubuque deserves special thanks for some crucial material sent my way that I would never have otherwise come upon. My good friend Steven Amarnick was, as always, endlessly encouraging, while Maya Popa was both a good friend and a source of much-needed technological counsel.

Without an agent and an editor: no book at all. So "thank you" barely scratches the surface with the tireless Cathy Hemming of McCormick Literary Ltd. in New York and Michael McGandy of Cornell University Press. I also thank the staff at Cornell University Press—Meagan Dermody, Karen Hwa, Scott Levine, and Martyn Beeny.

Lastly, special thanks are due to Thomas Orefice, whom I met in our undergraduate English class at Fordham University (where we daily passed the statues of John Hughes and Orestes Brownson, the one commanding and the other fearsome). In the acknowledgments to my first book, decades ago, I referred to him as "my lover and best friend." Several years later, in another book, I wrote of him as the person who had "enriched the last nineteen years of my life." Now, as we have reached our forty-third year together, I can thank my husband and best friend.

Notes

ABBREVIATIONS

AJHC AANY   Archbishop John Hughes Collection, Archives of the Archdiocese of New York, Saint Joseph's Seminary, Dunwoodie, Yonkers, NY

HJBP CU   Henry Joseph Browne Papers, Columbia University

PROLOGUE

1 *"The prospects are gloomy enough"*: JH to Dr. Anderson, April 9, 1860, box 1, folder 1, AJHC AANY.

1 *The archbishop's hope was that William Seward*: See McCadden, "Governor Seward's Friendship."

3 *"In a few days the bloody tragedy will begin"*: Bishop Whalen to JH, May 31, 1861, box 3, folder 9, AJHC AANY.

3 *"North and South, all eyes are turned to the Secretary of State"*: JH to Seward, April 28, 1861, box 2, folder 10, AJHC AANY.

3 *"More attention should be paid"*: JH to Seward, June 18, 1861, box 2, folder 10, AJHC AANY.

3 *"Excuse me for offering these suggestions"*: Ibid. An entire file (box 1, folder 25, AJHC AANY) contains copies of Hughes's letters to Lincoln with recommendations and suggestions.

4 *"no means have been adopted"*; *"highly gifted in their social qualities"*; *"We need active useful men"*: Ferris, *Desperate Diplomacy*, 176.

5 *"No President has ever been so severely tested"*: JH to Seward, October 15, 1861, box 2, folder 10, AJHC AANY.

5 *"without seeming to do so"*: Isham, *Born Again Episcopalian*, 207.

6 *"I accompanied the Archbishop to his carriage"*: Weed, *Letters from Europe*, 1:636.

6 *Hughes had surely heard the story*: Goodwin, *Team of Rivals*, 182.

8 *"courtly"*: Elizabeth Todd Grimsley, "Six Months in the White House," *Illinois State Historical Society* 19, no. 3 (October 1926–January 1927): 60.

9 *"the reverend hypocrite's head"*: Quoted in Reynolds, *Walt Whitman's America*, 99.

9 *"I cannot imagine a descendant of the Buchanans"*: JH to James Buchanan, March 4, 1859, box 3, folder 5, AJHC AANY.

9 *Any review of the situation in France*: Franco-American relations in this tender period are analyzed in Blumenthal, *Reappraisal*, 119–165; Case and Spencer, *United States and France*, 175–249; and Daniel Carroll, *Henri Mercier and the American Civil War* (Princeton, NJ: Princeton University Press, 1971).

10 *"lie on his oars"*: Quoted in Blumenthal, *Reappraisal*, 144.

10 *"Not since the Revolutionary War"*: Ibid., 126.

10 *In his official letter of instructions*: O'Daniel, "Archbishop John Hughes," 336–339.

11 *The author of this technically accurate*: Michael Burlingame, ed., *Lincoln's Journalist: John Hay's Anonymous Writings for the Press, 1860–1864* (Carbondale: Southern Illinois University Press, 1999), 136.

11 *Worried about his health*: Note, November 2, 1861, box 1, folder 8, HJBP CU.

11 *He did decide to write to the Vatican*: Shaw, *Dagger John*, 346; JH to Cardinal Barnabo, February 13, 1862, folder 13 A-43 (misfiled originally in the Corrigan Papers), AJHC AANY.

11 *It is a shame that the three members*: Who sailed to Europe with whom on which ship presents the classic biographer's conundrum: Shaw in his 1977 biography of Hughes says definitively that Weed and Hughes sailed together and McIlvaine was not with them. And, indeed, a letter from Hughes to Weed notes that the archbishop has booked a stateroom on the *Africa* for Weed next to his own and offers to share the services of his secretary and valet. (Of course, booking a stateroom for Weed does not mean that Weed ended up using it. Pressing business might well have delayed his departure.) More importantly, Weed in his memoirs recalls sailing on a different ship, the *Arcora*, and digresses at length about socializing with Winfield Scott on the voyage. If Hughes had journeyed with someone as famous as Scott on the same trip, he would have commented on it in a letter, which he did not. Also, an American passenger on Weed's ship made sufficiently aggressive anti-Union remarks (while mysteriously making use of a French passport) for Weed to report him to the State Department [see Leo Francis Stock, *Consular Relations between the United States and the Papal States: Instructions and Dispatches*, 2:230–231], and there is no mention of such an outspoken, offensive person in Hughes's chipper letters to Seward from shipboard. I think it safe to conclude the two friends sailed on different ships. Lacking passenger lists, I think it also safe to conclude that McIlvaine did not sail with Hughes, as his presence, which would surely have been commented on, is not mentioned in any letters by Hughes that I have seen. Weed believes he did, but his memoirs contain numerous small factual errors, and he was writing in old age, twenty years after the fact. One of McIlvaine's biographers (Isham, in *Born Again Episcopalian*, 208–209) also reports him sailing with Hughes, but has the Episcopal bishop arriving on December 7, three weeks after Hughes arrived. Richard W. Smith, the most recent McIlvaine biographer, makes clear McIlvaine did not sail with Hughes. What really matters: one way or another, they were all in Europe before the *Trent* affair was resolved.

12 *"Few passengers"*: JH to Seward, November 13, 1861, box 6, ledger 1, AJHC AANY.

12 *"Mr. Weed and Bishop Hughes"*: *Times* of London, November 26, 1861, clipping in Hughes's scrapbook in box 8, HJBP CU.

12 *He caught him in the middle of a dinner party*: JH to Seward, November 28, 1861, box 6, ledger 1, AJHC AANY.

13 *"the waste was only apparent"*: Henry Adams, *The Education of Henry Adams* (Modern Library edition), 146.

13 *Something momentous had happened*: On the *Trent* affair see McPherson, *Battle Cry of Freedom*, 389–391.

13 *"the Cuban missile crisis of the nineteenth century"*: Stahr, *Seward*, 308.

13 *"The English here are very angry"*: Father Peter McCloskey to JH, December 7, 1861, box 3, folder 2, AJHC AANY.

14 *In Paris, William Dayton was more obliging*: JH to Seward, November 28, 1861, box 6, ledger 1, AJHC AANY.

15 *"a gentleman with a very superior degree of intelligence"*: The report of the Paris correspondent for the London *Star*, "The Archbishop of New York in Paris," was reprinted in the *Metropolitan Record*, January 25, 1862.

16 *"Being a bishop"*: JH to Seward, December 27, 1861, box 6, ledger 1, AJHC AANY; see also a letter to his sister, February 27, 1861, box 2, folder 7, AJHC AANY. Several letters to Margaret about the trip are a part of that file. Hughes's trip is also reviewed in Andrews, *Archbishop Hughes and the Civil War*, 116–189.

17 *He brought into the conversation, without belaboring the point, the South's long-standing designs on Cuba*: JH to Seward, January 11, 1862, box 6, ledger 2, AJHC AANY.

17 *"I think we might have fared worse"*: Quoted in Hassard, *Life*, 471.

17 *"The Public on this side"*: Margaret Hughes Rodrigue to JH, December 27, 1861, box 2, folder 18, HJBP CU.

17 *"Archbishop John Hughes is still in Paris"*: Father Matthew Hart to Bishop McFarland, January 3, 1862, University of Notre Dame (digital) Archives.

17 *More concrete, if temporary, good was accomplished in the Eternal City*: JH to Seward, February 21, 1862, box 6, ledger 2, AJHC AANY.

18 *When the Catholic clergy of the Confederacy decided two years later*: Bigelow, "Southern Confederacy and the Pope."

18 *President Lincoln decided that the submitted bills*: Seward to JH, January 9, 1862, box 3, folder 6, AJHC AANY.

19 *"Your work in Ireland can never be forgotten"*: Quoted in Hassard, *Life*, 482.

19 *A worse morass developed*: *Metropolitan Record*, August 16, 1862, and August 23, 1862; Hassard, *Life*, 482–484.

20 *"champion of desolation, blood, and fratricide"*: *Baltimore Catholic Mirror*, October 18, 1862.

20 *An elderly friend, a priest*: Hassard, *Life*, 489.

20 *The* New York Sun *ran a satirical piece*: Clipping of article by George Francis Train, November 25, 1862, box 7, AJHC AANY.

20 *Pius IX was quoted to him*: Father Bernard Smith to JH, August 1862, box 3, folder 7, AJHC AANY; also, in Stock, *United States Ministers to the Papal States* (247), the new U.S. minister, Alexander Randall, is quoted in a June 11, 1862, letter to Seward acknowledging that "an effort had been made to impress the idea, here, that [Hughes] had injured the cause of Rome by consenting to interfere, in any manner, in favor of the government."

20 *"There is no love for the United States"*: JH to Seward, November 5, 1862, box 2, folder 10, AJHC AANY. The letter was printed in full in the *Metropolitan Record*, November 15, 1862.

1. A SON OF ULSTER

22 *"I would beg leave to state"*: JH to John O'Donovan, May 20, 1860, box 2, folder 4, AJHC AANY.

23 *"I fell into a great blunder"*: JH to John O'Donovan, April 10, 1860, box 2, folder 4, AJHC AANY. Hughes's communications with O'Donovan began, apparently, in April 1860 and continued intermittently into 1861; that he was tired of the subject was clear even by the above letter of May 1860.

23 *he had floated the idea in a newspaper statement*: John Hughes, "Letters on the Moral Causes Which Produced the Evil Spirit of the Times" (an open letter to New York City mayor James Harper), Kehoe, *Complete Works*, 1:451. This letter contained more than a few "rewritings" of its author's past.

25 *"Ulster was effectively a military camp"*: Elliott, *Catholics of Ulster*, 251. Marianne Elliott in her magisterial *The Catholics of Ulster* is also one of the strongest voices among contemporary historians arguing against the overdramatization or simplification of our perception of Irish Catholic and Protestant relations in eighteenth-century Ireland, noting that the penal laws were very haphazardly applied, and a live-and-let-live stance between faiths in the north was not entirely unknown. On life in County Tyrone in Hughes's youth see also S. J. Connolly, *Priests and People in Pre-Famine Ireland, 1780–1845* (Portland, OR: Four Courts, 2001) and Oliver P. Rafferty, *Catholicism in Ulster, 1603–1983: An Interpretive History* (Columbia: University of South Carolina Press, 1994).

26 *"a chapel was a rare thing"*: O'Donoghue, *Life of William Carleton*, 36–37.

27 *"I loved John Hughes"*: Quoted in Coogan, "Study," 44.

29 *"like some disjointed and feeble spur"*: *Irish Times*, July 21, 1862, quoted in McKenna, "Visits to Ireland," 42. This speech, delivered at the laying of the cornerstone for the Catholic University of Ireland, was reprinted in its entirety in the *Metropolitan Record*, August 16, 1862.

29 *Baltimore in 1817*: Raphael Semmes, *Baltimore as Seen by Visitors, 1783–1860* (Baltimore: Maryland Historical Society, 1953).

30 *"The Catholic Church had never enjoyed a more secure and respected position"*: Spalding, *Premier See*, 77.

31 *"superintendent of a slave plantation in his youth"*: Keneally, *Great Shame*, 89. Shaw's biography of Hughes also uses the questionable word "overseer."

31 *"worked with all [his] might"*: Hassard, *Life*, 20.

31 *"Hard is the lot of him who's doomed to toil"*: Ibid., 40–45.

32 *"marvel of stone masonry"*; *"a rough and unpleasant appearance"*: *History of Franklin County, Pennsylvania* (Chicago: Warner Beers, 1887), 496, 460.

33 *That grinding manual labor led to a meeting*: Philip Shriver Klein, *President James Buchanan: A Biography* (University Park: Pennsylvania State University Press, 1962), 29. The fact that Hughes senior might have been friends back in Ulster with Buchanan's father, a Protestant, is further evidence of Elliott's thesis that relations between the two faiths in Ireland c. 1790s were never as absolutely or universally restricted or hostile as some histories have suggested.

37 *One priest Hughes had personal contact with*: Hassard, *Life*, 23. On Hughes's acquaintance with Father Cooper see Ella M. E. Flick, "The Reverend Samuel Sutherland Cooper," *Records of the American Catholic Historical Society of Philadelphia* 23 (March 1922): 301–316. The quotations in this paragraph are from Flick, 313–314. See also Martin I. J. Griffin, "The Toothless Priest: Samuel Sutherland Cooper," *American Catholic Researches*, January 1898: 17–32.

Cooper is discussed in all biographies of Mother Seton, as well as Shaw's biography of John Dubois.

38 *The other priest Hughes met at this time*: The literature on Simon Bruté is comprehensive for an obscure historical figure. See his memoirs and journal extracts, edited by James Roosevelt Bayley, *Memoirs of the Right Reverend Simon Wm. Gabriel Bruté, D.D.* (New York: Catholic Publication Society, 1876); Sister Mary Salesia Godecker, "Right Reverend Simon William Gabriel Bruté de Remur, First Bishop of Vincennes, Indiana: Priestly Career in Maryland, 1810–1834" (PhD diss., Catholic University, 1929) and her thorough but hagiographic 1931 biography of Bruté, expanded from that dissertation; and Theodore Maynard's often maligned but still readable and useful 1942 biography, *The Reed and the Rock*. Bruté is also discussed in all biographies of Dubois, Hughes, and Seton, and there are excellent pages about him in Pasquier, *Fathers on the Frontier*. Albert Henri Ledoux's 2005 published doctoral dissertation, *The Life and Thought of Simon Bruté*, is a particularly close and valuable study.

38 *"death was a daily tale"*: Bayley, *Memoirs*, 140.

40 *At the time of the appointment, John England wondered if the church was sending the right man*: Ibid., 70.

40 *"That kind of work is continually called for"*: Ibid., 81.

2. A VOCATION

41 *"terraces planted with trees"*: *The Laity's Directory: 1822* (New York: William Greagh, 1822), 89.

42 *It is significant that Seton's most recent biographer*: Joan Barthel, *American Saint: The Life of Elizabeth Seton* (New York: St. Martin's, 2014).

42 *That arrangement, which was begrudging and humiliating*: On Mount Saint Mary's employment of slaves and manumitted slaves see Maynard, *Reed and the Rock*, 135–136.

44 *Dubois was a product of Bourbon France*: Shaw, *John Dubois*, 1–16.

44 *"I found myself in that vast country"*: Ibid., 18.

45 *"a multitude of young Irishmen"*: Pasquier, *Fathers on the Frontier*, 38. Also on Maréchal's low estimate of the Mount, White, *Diocesan Seminary*, 41.

47 *Much more intimidating*: M. Eulalia Teresa Moffatt, "Charles Constantine Pise (1801–1866)," *Historical Records and Studies* (United States Catholic Historical Society) 20 (1931): 64–98.

48 *"Mr. Hughes would at least be equal to McCaffrey"*: Mary E. Meline and Francis F. X. Sweeney, "The Story of the Mountain," chapter 9, from the *Emmitsburg Chronicle* (1911), reprinted in the Emmitsburg Area Historical Society digital archive.

48 *"That's pride, sir, nothing but pride!"*: Quoted in Hassard, *Life*, 36.

48 *"Who are you, I should like to know?"*: Ibid., 24.

49 *Dubois treated him like an unwanted stepchild*: Browne's uncompleted biography of Hughes, chapter 1 ("The Immigrant"), 27 (copy in AJHC AANY).

49 *"There's a lot of John in that one"*: From *Community History: Lives of Our Departed Mothers*, published by the Sisters of Charity, the College of Mount Saint Vincent's, 1955 (in the collection of the Archives of the Sisters of Charity in Riverdale, New York), 79.

50 *"we can conclude that Bruté leaned toward ultramontanism"*: Ledoux, *Life and Thought of Simon Bruté*, 276.

51 *"the most learned man in the United States"*: Mary Ann Hughes, "Bruté Library: Cathedral in Vincennes Has Oldest Library in Indiana," *Message*, July 13, 1990, 20.

51 *Bruté was a fount of personal lore as well*: Maynard, *Reed and the Rock*, 52–56.

54 *Father Hurley was a charismatic bundle of contradictions*: Hassard, *Life*, 46–47; Light, *Rome and the New Republic*, 88–89 (Light discusses the more colorful side of this priest); Thompson Wescott, "A Memoir of the Very Reverend Michael Hurley, D.D., O.S.A., Sometime Pastor of St. Augustine's Church," *Records of the American Catholic Historical Society of Philadelphia* 1 (1884): 165–212.

54 *"Do not make your sermons long"*: Quoted in Hassard, *Life*, 47.

55 *"though much larger, it does not show itself so well"*: Frances Trollope, *Domestic Manners of Americans* (1842; New York: Penguin, 1997), 201–202.

55 *"Distractingly regular"*: Dickens, *American Notes* (1842; New York: Penguin, 2000), 10.

56 *Conwell's domain was an absurdly fractious place*: On the Philadelphia diocese in the late 1820s and early 1830s and Conwell's troubles see Arthur J. Ennis, "The New Diocese," in Connelly, *History of the Archdiocese*, 63–112; Martin I. J. Griffin, "The Life of Bishop Henry Conwell of Philadelphia," *Records of the American Catholic Historical Society of Philadelphia* 24 (1913): 16–42; Hassard, *Life*, 46–113; Kirlin, *Catholicity in Philadelphia*, 210–276; Dale Light's excellent definitive study, *Rome and the New Republic*; Warren, "Displaced 'Pan-Americans.'"

56 *"Death would not be so frightful to me"*: Quoted in Martin I. J. Griffin, "History of Rt. Rev. Michael Egan," in *American Catholic Historical Researches* 10 (1893): 179.

56 *"From my soul, I pity you"*: Michael de Burgo Egan to JH, February 5, 1827, box 3, folder 13, AJHC AANY.

56 *"The thing was almost as impossible to believe"*: Quoted in Coogan, "Study," 44.

57 *Recent historians have argued that the trustee system*: For the standard view from an earlier time (trustees, bad guys; bishops, good guys) see McNamara, "Trusteeism"; for the more nuanced, balanced, fuller account see Patrick Carey, *People, Priests, and Prelates* and Dale B. Light, *Rome and the New Republic*. See also Jennifer Schaap, "'With a Pure Intention of Pleasing and Honouring God': How the Philadelphia Laity Created American Catholicism, 1785–1850" (PhD diss., University of Pennsylvania, 2013, available online).

57 *"something new and entirely unheard of"*: Quoted in Ennis, "New Diocese," 99.

57 *It was particularly ugly in Philadelphia*: For a good analysis of the Hogan schism and sexual assault trial that suggests how out of control matters were in the diocese see Rodney Hessenger, "'A Base and Unmanly Conspiracy': Catholicism and the Hogan Schism in the Gendered Marketplace of Philadelphia," *Journal of the Early Republic* 31, no. 3: 357–396. Light, *Rome and the New Republic*, also covers the Philadelphia schisms in engrossing detail.

58 *"Jacobinical trustees"*: Quoted in Light, *Rome and the New Republic*, 119.

59 *The two men hadn't seen each other since their schoolboy days*: T.C.M., "The Very Rev. T. J. Donaghoe," *Records of the American Catholic Historical Society of Philadelphia* 23 (1912): 69–90, and Coogan's excellent summary of the Hughes-Donaghoe relationship, "Study."

60 *"the mild and forgiving character of the Redeemer"*: *Freeman's Journal*, June 4, 1842.

60 *His own estimate of regular communicants*: Hassard, *Life*, 90.

60 *Hughes was always proud to claim that he made thirteen converts*: Kirlin, *Catholicity in Philadelphia*, 261.

61 *The Conversion and Edifying Death of Andrew Dunn*: Hughes's fictional tale is a rare text, hard to locate today, but it is reprinted in some (but, interestingly, not all) editions of Kehoe, *Complete Works*, at 1:665–691.

61 *"I do not wish the thing to make any noise"*: JH to Simon Bruté, March 2, 1828, box 3, folder 7, AJHC AANY.

62 *His next published "work"*: On the *Protestant* hoax see Shaw, *Dagger John*, 65–66.

63 *The passage of the Catholic Emancipation Bill*: Hughes's sermon on the Catholic Emancipation Act is reprinted in Kehoe, *Complete Works*, 1:29–40. On the *Church Register* attack see Hassard, *Life*, 92.

66 *That long-suffering successor*: On Kenrick's first years in Philadelphia and his style of leadership see Light, *Rome and the New Republic*, 247–263, and Nolan, *Most Reverend Francis Patrick Kenrick*, 102–167; on his relationship with Hughes see ibid., 161, 219–220; O'Shea, *Two Kenricks*, 92.

68 *Rodrigue had much to recommend him*: The Rodrigue family papers are in the collection of the Philadelphia Archdiocesan Historical Research Center on the campus of Saint Charles Borromeo Seminary in Merion, Pennsylvania. On the style of the church Rodrigue and Hughes desired see Ryan K. Smith, *Gothic Arches, Latin Crosses: Anti-Catholicism and American Church Designs in the Nineteenth Century* (Chapel Hill: University of North Carolina Press, 2006), which suggests that the rise of intense anti-Catholicism and the Gothic Revival were not coincidental, that both were about perceptions of Catholicism's growing power in the United States.

68 *"It will make all the Bishops of all the churches jealous"*: Quoted in Griffin, *Anti-Catholicism*, 360–362.

68 *"The new church bids fair to be the handsomest in the United States"*: Ibid.

69 *Without Marc Frenaye*: See "Marc Antony Frenaye: A Sketch," *Records of the American Catholic Historical Society* 38 (1927): 132–143 ("bosom friend," 131). Frenaye is also discussed in all biographies of Dubois, Hughes, and Kenrick.

70 *"would have been followed by regret for the remainder of my life"*: JH to ? (dated Saturday, 1837), box 1, folder 8, HJBP CU.

3. COURTING CONTROVERSY

72 *By one estimate, more than two hundred such books*: Billington, "Tentative Bibliography."

73 *"insidious, all-pervading, persevering"*: Quoted in Reynolds, *Mightier Than the Sword*, 33.

73 *"tracts and maps are in circulation"*: Beecher, *Plea for the West*, 56–58.

74 *Even a highly ambiguous meditation on the subject*: In *Roads to Rome*, Jenny Franchot offers an extensive account of Hawthorne's fiction as part of the "antebellum Protestant response to Catholicism." The antebellum journalism of Lydia Maria Child also offers a good example of a Protestant attempt to arrive at a balance of criticism, respect, and admitted fascination.

74 *Maria Monk's* Awful Disclosures of the Hotel Dieu Nunnery: The infamous Maria Monk is discussed in various studies of the Jacksonian era (e.g., Reynolds, *Waking Giant*); see also Billington, "Maria Monk and Her Influence." In that essay, Billington calls Monk's book "by far the most influential single work of nativist propaganda in the period preceding the Civil War." On the many smutty books that appeared in the wake of Monk's best seller see Sandra Frink, "Women, the Family, and the Fate of the Nation in American Anti-Catholic Narratives, 1830–1860," *Journal of the History of Sexuality* 18, no. 2 (May 2009): 237–264.

75 *The drive to demonize convent life*: Billington, in *Protestant Crusade*, offers a brief sketch of the burning of the Ursuline convent, 68–76; Hamilton, in "The Nunnery as Menace," provides a more detailed account. Louisa Whitney's *The Burning of the Convent* (1877) is a terse, gripping, and clear-eyed memoir of the events of that night written, when she was in her fifties, by one of the school's teenage Protestant pupils. See also Daniel Cohen, "Passing the Torch, 'Tea Party' Patriots, and the Burning of the Ursuline Convent," *Journal of the Early Republic* 24, no. 4 (Winter 2004): 527–586, which suggests that the makeup of the mob might be rethought and that many firemen were actually participants in the attack. Coverage of the attack was reported with great indignation in at least three issues of Hughes's Philadelphia paper the *Catholic Herald* (September 4, 11, and 25, 1834) and was followed by coverage of the arsonists' trial. Recent historians have stressed the class basis for the attack as a factor equivalent to religious bigotry.

76 *Rather than attempting to plead with the rioters*: Whitney, in *Burning of the Convent*, writes of the mother superior's toughness that when the selectmen visited the convent to inspect the rooms in hopes of defusing the crisis, they were met with furious indignation and a "torrent of invectives" (72). Not one to be pushed around by anyone, she also refused for years to leave the Boston area after the fire, despite Bishop Fenwick's insistence that she relocate.

77 *"the tide turned"*: Cross, *Autobiography of Lyman Beecher*, 252.

77 *"had [the Charlestown men] viewed such an outrage with indifference"*: Quoted in Kenneth Silverman, *Lightning Man: The Accursed Life of Samuel F. B. Morse* (New York: Knopf, 2004), 134.

77 *Recent scholarship suggests that the literature of tourism*: See Jenny Fauchot's *Roads to Rome*, the definitive study of the subject.

78 *Bishop Fenwick's sermons in the days following the burning of the convent*: Hamilton, "Nunnery as Menace," 48.

78 *"a man much calumniated"* and on voting for Henry Clay: JH to Cassius Clay, February 6, 1858, box 1, folder 13, AJHC AANY.

79 *"The immense circulation of Miss Monk's book"*: "Maria Monk," draft of an article for the *Philadelphia Sentinel* (clipping) in box 1, folder 28, AJHC AANY.

80 *The Sisters of Charity had pressed themselves to the limit*: Hugh J. Nolan, chapter 3, 137, in Connelly, *History of the Archdiocese*, and William Watson, "The Sisters of Charity, the 1832 Cholera Epidemic in Philadelphia, and Duffy's Cut," *U.S. Catholic Historian* 27, no. 4 (Fall 2009): 1–16.

80 *"remarkable for their pastoral solicitude"*: *United States Gazette*, September 7, 1832.

81 *"diarrhoea verborum"*: Hughes, *Controversy*, 62.

81 *Despite the misgivings Kenrick expressed*: Nolan, *Most Reverend*, 161.

82 *For the propagandizing intent of the paper*: On Nicholas O'Donnell see *Historical Records and Studies* (United States Catholic Historical Society) 2, part 1 (October 1900): 237–240, and Tourscher, *Old St. Augustine's*, 62–75. On founding the *Catholic Herald* see Foik, *Faith and Action*, 130–131; Kirlin, *Catholicity in Philadelphia*, 292; "Notes on the Catholic Herald," *Records of the American Catholic Historical Society of Philadelphia* 22 (1911): 108–110; O'Shea, *Two Kenricks*, 93, 95.

83 *"occasions of sodomy"*: Hughes, *Controversy*, 195.

84 *"the worst, the half, has not been told!"*: Ibid., 241.

84 *"I condemn it as much as you"*: Ibid., 116.

84 *Hughes was more at ease, and more adept*: Hughes's writings on transubstantiation were reprinted a few times in the *Catholic Herald* (e.g., December 12, 1833).

85 *He was invited to become a member of one of the city's elite groups*: Hassard, *Life*, 161; see also Anne Wharton, "The Philadelphia Wistar Parties," *Lippincott's Magazine*, vol. 39 (June 1887), 978–988.

86 *"He pants to do good, widespread good"*: Quoted in Shaw, *Dagger John*, 92.

87 *This wasn't a surprise*: Rodrigue family papers (box 13, folders 1–9) at the Philadelphia Archdiocesan Historical Research Center.

89 *and another, even longer book publication*: The longer book on their debate was brought out by Matthew Carey's publishing house in 1836 and, throwing any interest in concision to the wind, was titled *A Discussion of the Question, Is the Roman Catholic Religion, in Any or in All Its Principles or Doctrines, Inimical to Civil or Religious Liberty? And of the Question, Is the Presbyterian Religion, in Any or in All Its Principles or Doctrines, Inimical to Civil or Religious Liberty?* It contains material (more paragraphs, citations, and lists) both men added after the debate, and it was reprinted in 1867 by a Baltimore publisher.

89 *"won unfading laurels for himself"*: Quoted in Shaw, *Dagger John*, 100.

89 *Power claimed that when Dubois spoke from the pulpit*: Quoted in Shaw, *John Dubois*, 128, and in Browne, "Public Support of Catholic Education," 7.

90 *"Our good old prelate means well"*: Shaw, *John Dubois*, 10.

90 *Bishop Dubois had let it be known that he wanted John Timon*: Riforgiato, "John Timon," 28–29.

90 *Kenrick was probably Hughes's most damaging critic*: Kenrick to JH, January 19, 1837, box 1, folder 9, HJBP CU.

91 *"Brownson may indeed have brought rudeness to Boston"*: Schlesinger, *Pilgrim's Progress*, 44.

4. CONFRONTING GOTHAM

92 *New York City was something else, though*: The best accounts of life in New York City specific to the late 1830s and early 1840s, in this writer's experience, are Edwin G. Burrows and Mike Wallace, *Gotham: A History of New York City to 1898* (New York: Oxford University Press, 1999), 587–645; Lydia Maria Child, *Letters from New-York* (New York: C. S. Francis, 1843); Patricia Cline Cohen, *The Murder of Helen Jewett: The Life and Death of a Prostitute in Nineteenth-Century New York* (New York: Random House, 1998); Timothy J. Gilfoyle, *City of Eros: New York City, Prostitution, and the Commercialization of Sex, 1790–1920* (New York: Norton, 1992); Asa Greene, *A Glance at New York* (New York: A. Greene, 1837); and—those historian's mainstays—the diaries of Philip Hone and George Templeton Strong. See also James C. Brandow's editing of Nathaniel T. W. Carrington's journal, "A Visit to New York and Long Island in 1837," *New York History* 67, no. 1 (January 1986): 23–38, and Ernst, *Immigrant Life*. The prostitution figures from the Magdalen Society are from Cohen, *Murder of Helen Jewett*, 71.

93 *"one of the most crime-haunted and dangerous cities"*: Quoted in Reynolds, *Walt Whitman's America*, 109. Whitman's journalism is from the 1840s, but his observations apply equally well to the late 1830s.

93 *"The oyster shops swarm with them"*: Max Berger, "British Impressions of New York a Century Ago," *New York History* 27, no. 2 (April 1946): 144.

93 *One particularly disgruntled British traveler*: Richard Toby Widdicombe, ed., *America and the Americans—in 1837–1838, by an Emigrant, Richard Gooch*

(New York: Fordham University Press, 1994), 140. It should be noted that not all historians view Richard Gooch's vivid anti-American travel book as authentic (a long story, there), but this reference corresponds to similar impressions by other British visitors.

94 *"Ugly brutes"*: Charles Dickens, *American Notes* (1842; New York: Penguin, 2000), 97.

94 *"The city is virtually without any municipal government"*: Quoted in Adams, *Bowery Boys*, xiii.

94 *"pig sty"*: Brandow, "Visit to New York," 30.

94 *"but in consequence of the extreme filth"*: Ibid.

95 *several of the city's priests boycotted Hughes's consecration*: Thebaud, *Forty Years*, 284–287.

96 *"grand and imposing scene"*: Quoted in Hassard, *Life*, 185.

96 *"His manner is very good"*: Nevins and Thomas, *Diary of George Templeton Strong*, 1:102–103.

97 *The churches of the diocese labored under a collective debt*: The financial statements pertaining to Saint Peter's Church in New York City and the churches in Utica, Erie, Schenectady, and Albany are from box 2, folder 24, AJHC AANY, a random assortment of records. They are documents Hughes saved from c. 1839 to 1845, but it can be assumed that the situation was no better, if not worse, in 1838, immediately after the Panic of 1837 and before the worst period of the Panic of 1839. The reference to the financial straits of the Church of the Transfiguration is from McCadden and McCadden, *Father Varela*, 116–117. The reference to the loan that could not be paid off at Saint Joseph's Church is from Shelley, *Greenwich Village Catholics*, 38. Other records that suggest the dire financial situation of the diocese then are to be found in the Debt Association ledger, box 8, HJBP CU; the ledger titled "Collections for St. Peter's and St. Patrick's Churches in New York," box 15, folder 6, HJBP CU; and Hughes's 1840 report to the Leopoldine Society, box 1, folder 8, HJBP CU. See also Dolan, *Immigrant Church*, 47–48.

99 *"the bowels of the city"*: William Bobo, *Glimpses of New York City by a South Carolinian* (Charleston: J. J. McCarter, 1852), 12.

99 *When the first bishop of New York, John Connolly, arrived in 1815*: On the New York diocese in its early days, pre-Hughes, see McCadden and McCadden, *Father Varela*, xii–xiii (the McCaddens' biography of Father Varela is an invaluable source on the diocese in the early to mid-1800s); Shelley's *Archdiocese of New York*, 80–105; and the several volumes of *The Metropolitan Catholic Almanac and Laity's Directory* for the 1820s and 1830s. For Bishop Dubois's view of his diocese early in his tenure see "The Diocese of New York in 1830," *Historical Records and Studies* (United States Catholic Historical Society) 5 (April 1909): 216–230.

99 *"Conditions in New York might be worse"*: JH to Bishop John Purcell, February 24, 1838, Archdiocese of Cincinnati Collection II-4-g, University of Notre Dame Archives.

100 *A thin, shaggy-haired, bespectacled Cuban*: Hughes's 1855 obituary notice for him is as laudatory as anything he ever wrote about another person: box 8, folder 9, HJBP CU.

100 *"one of the best educated and most exemplary priests"*: JH to Bishop Antoine Blanc, January 3, 1839, Archdiocese of New Orleans Collection V-4-h, University of Notre Dame Archives.

100 *"fine, commanding figure"*: *Historical Records and Studies* (United States Catholic Historical Society) 2, part 2 (October 1900): 78.

101 *"I am sorry to say you know not your man"*: John Urquhart to JH, December 25, 1840, box 3, folder 19, AJHC AANY; Urquhart's letters in this folder are among the most vivid and absorbing in the collection. After a fine start with Hughes, he left the diocese to work in western New York State and left the country a few years later under a cloud of scandal when rumors, possibly unfounded, of an illegitimate child circulated.

101 *Pastors treated imperiously by their trustees were equally voluble*: Complaints from priests about trustees and vice versa are scattered throughout Hughes's archive, but one file devoted to that topic is in box 3, folder 1, HJBP CU.

102 *"taken to city life with a passion"*: Shaw, *John Dubois*, 119–120.

103 *"If you ever possessed the true spirit of a priest"*: JH to Father Philip Gillick, n.d., box 1, folder 20, AJHC AANY.

103 *"Retire and do penance"*: JH to Father Farnan (?), December 29, 1846, box 5, ledger, HJBP CU.

103 *"I hardly spoke"*: Quoted in Hassard, *Life*, 201–202.

103 *Unfortunately, truculence was more the order of the day*: On the trustee battle see Hassard, *Life*, 192–196; Shaw, *Dagger John*, 129–131. See also "Minutes of Meetings of Pewholders of St. Patrick's Cathedral by trustee Hugh Sweeny, 1839," box 8, folder 7, HJBP CU.

105 *"If so, then it is almost time"*: Quoted in Hassard, *Life*, 192.

105 *"We have brought them so low"*: Ibid., 196–197.

105 *Saint Nicholas's Church on the Lower East Side*: Dolan, *Immigrant Church*, 90–92.

107 *In 1833, he had purchased 160 acres*: *Catholic Herald*, December 12, 1833; on the Nyack, Lafargeville, and Brooklyn schools see Hassard, *Life*, 189–192; Shaw, *Dagger John*, 128–129 ("splendid folly" quoted 128).

108 *Looking to Europe in 1839*: On the Leopoldine Society and other European sources of funding see Blied, *Austrian Aid*, and Theodore Roemer, *Ten Decades of Alms* (New York: B. Herder, 1942). On the money to Edward Fenwick: Fortin, *Faith and Action*, 19–20. On the money to Kenrick for his seminary: Nolan, *Most Reverend*, 153, and Blied, *Austrian Aid*, 96–97, give two different amounts. See also the *Catholic Herald*, December 19, 1833.

109 *John Purcell had recently made one of these begging trips*: On Purcell's "begging trips" to Europe see Hussey, *Archbishop John Purcell*, n.p., loc. 1132, 1136.

5. WHO SHALL TEACH OUR CHILDREN?

111 *On October 16, 1839, John Hughes boarded a packet ship*: The best accounts of Hughes's trip are in Browne's unpublished manuscript: chapter 9 ("Mendicant and Educator"), box 15, folder 6, HJBP CU (copy also in the collection of the Archives of the Archdiocese of New York) and Hughes's letters to his sister, box 2, folder 18, HJBP CU. See also Hassard, *Life*, 206–222, and Shaw, *Dagger John*, 134–137.

111 *"The winds were howling through the cordage"*: The letters from JH to his sister describing the voyage (no longer extant, apparently) are quoted in Hassard, *Life*, 207–209 and were reprinted in part by Thurlow Weed in the *Albany Evening Journal* (see Kehoe, *Complete Works*, 1:443–449).

112 *"Great luxury and great misery"*: JH to Margaret Hughes Rodrigue, December 7, 1839, box 2, folder 18, HJBP CU.

112 *"full episcopal costume à la française"*: Ibid.

112 *Attending Mass one Sunday a few pews away from the duc d'Orléans*: See Kenrick-Frenaye Correspondence, 43–44. On the memorial service for the dauphin in New York: *Freeman's Journal*, August 6, 1842.

113 *"the sky too is all that the poets have said of it"*: JH to Margaret Hughes Rodrigue, January 30, 1840, box 2, folder 18, HJBP CU.

113 *"The Romans seem to care very little"*: Ibid.

114 *"received him with great goodness"*: Cardinal John Candolni to John Purcell, February 12, 1840, University of Notre Dame (digital) Archives.

114 *Unlike his successor, though, Gregory was not a progressive leader*: See John F. Quinn, " 'Three Cheers for the Abolitionist Pope!' " See also Joseph E. Capizzi, "For What Shall We Repent? Reflections on the American Bishops, Their Teaching, and Slavery in the United States, 1839–1861," *Theological Studies* 65 (2004): 767–791.

115 *"Other cities are beautiful, if you please"*: JH to Varela, n.d., quoted in Hassard, *Life*, 211.

116 *"that he is not in the land of his fathers"*: From Hughes's "Report to the Leopoldine Society," headed "Vienna, April 16, 1840," box 1, folder 8, HJBP CU; reprinted in Kehoe, *Complete Works*, 2:459–464.

117 *Kunz's experience with the trustees*: See *Historical Records and Studies* (United States Catholic Historical Society) 6, part 1 (February 1911): 54–55; see also Jonathan Schwarz to JH, June 16, 1840, box 3, folder 1, AJHC AANY.

117 *"city of gloom and gorgeousness"*: JH to Frenaye, June 1, 1840, quoted in Hassard, *Life*, 219.

117 *Simon Bruté had probably spoken for many*: Simon Bruté to JH, February 10, 1838?, box 2, folder 16, HJBP CU. On Bruté's personal disapproval of slavery: Ledoux, *Life and Thought*, 216.

118 *"crushed by an apostate nation"*: JH to Varela, n.d., quoted in Hassard, *Life*, 220.

118 *He wanted to go back to County Tyrone to meet with the cousins*: Patrick Hughes to JH, August 12, 1840, box 2, folder 10, HJBP CU.

119 *"wonderful things of the moral revolution"*: JH to Felix Varela, June 1, 1840, quoted in Hassard, *Life*, 221.

119 *$12,000 in all, he told Margaret*: JH to Margaret Hughes Rodrigue, May 30, 1840, box 2, folder 18, HJBP CU.

119 *"I have had every success"*: JH to Frenaye, June 1, 1840, quoted in Hassard, *Life*, 219.

120 *Not all of them worked out as planned*: On the reprobate Daniel McManus see JH to William Higgins, July 28, 1842, and William Higgins to JH, December 13, 1842, box 3, folder 4, AJHC AANY.

121 *John Power and Felix Varela had been especially busy*: On the New York City school debate of the 1840s, the definitive source is still Vincent P. Lannie's 1968 article "Public Money and Parochial Education: Bishop Hughes, Governor Seward, and the New York School Controversy." Diane Ravitch devotes many excellent pages to it in *The Great School Wars: A History of the New York City Public Schools*. See also Mushkat, *Tammany*, 198–207, and the articles by Browne, McCadden, and van Deusen listed in the bibliography. Almost every issue of the *Freeman's Journal* c. 1840–1842 contains an article on the controversy, including transcripts of the Common Council sessions, June 26 and August 7, 1841. Dozens of recent books that deal with the history of church-state relations in the United States discuss Hughes's role in the debate, including Steven Green's *The Bible, the School, and the Constitution: The Clash That Shaped*

Modern Church-State Doctrine (New York: Oxford University Press, 2012), 46–68. Hughes's speeches and correspondence devoted to this topic during a two-year period take up over 250 pages in his *Complete Works* (ed. Kehoe, 2:41–296).

122 *Parental and clerical anger went beyond the use of the King James Bible*: For a comprehensive review of the bigotry of the textbooks of the era see Fell, "Foundations of Nativism," 112–138.

123 *"A bad foundation for liberty, civil or religious"*: Child, *Letters from New-York*, 149.

124 *"Knowledge taught by a sect is better than ignorance"*: Quoted in Lannie, *Public Money and Parochial Education*, 26 (letter to William Palmer, December 17, 1840, Seward Papers, University of Rochester).

124 *"Why should an American hate foreigners?"*: Quoted ibid., 17 (letter to Harman Westervelt, May 5, 1842, Seward Papers, University of Rochester).

124 *"high, liberal, and true American views"*: Quoted in Stahr, *Seward*, 70.

125 *"a masterstroke of Whig opportunism"*: Sean Wilentz, *Chants Democratic: New York City and the Rise of the American Working Class, 1877–1850* (New York: Oxford University Press, 2004), 315.

125 *But there is no reason those motives couldn't have been both altruistic and self-interested*: See Vincent Peter Lannie, "William Seward and the New York School Controversy, 1840–1842: A Problem in Historical Motivation," *History of Education Quarterly* 6, no. 1 (Spring 1966): 52–71, and, for an opposing view, John W. Pratt, "Governor Seward and the New York City School Controversy, 1940–1842," *New York History* 42, no. 4 (October 1961): 351–364.

125 *Yet Father Power and several Whig ward politicians*: Van Deusen, "Seward and the School Question," 317 (letter of Richard Blatchford to William Seward, April 11, 1840, Seward Papers, University of Rochester).

127 *He was particularly incensed by An Irish Heart*: Kehoe, *Complete Works*, 1:52–53, 114.

127 *His performance was mixed*: Transcripts were published in the *Freeman's Journal*, June 26 and August 7, 1841.

128 *"no one could hear him without painful regret"*: *New York Observer*, November 7, 1840.

128 *"We come here denied of our rights"*: Kehoe, *Complete Works*, 1:242–246.

129 *"a landmark challenge to the Anglo-Protestant cultural power"*: Golway, *Machine Made*, 29.

130 *"That a great majority of the inhabitants"*: *Freeman's Journal*, August 7, 1841.

130 *"to see that all are protected alike"*: Kehoe, *Complete Works*, 1:269.

130 *"even the appearance of politics"*: Quoted in Browne, "Public Support of Catholic Education," 18 (JH to Felix Varela, June 1, 1840, quoted in the *Catholic Register*, June 25, 1840).

130 *"We exclude politics from our deliberations"*: Kehoe, *Complete Works*, 1:79.

131 *What Weed witnessed was a tour-de-force*: For Hughes's speech at Carroll Hall, ibid., 1:275–284.

132 *Most incredibly, the list also included the notorious Mike Walsh*: On Walsh, a remarkable New York story of its own, see Adams, *Bowery Boys*, where he figures as a prominent character.

132 *"filled the city with utter astonishment"*: *New York Sun*, November 1, 1841.

132 *The* New York Sunday Times *saw no reason*: The editorial views of the *New York Sunday Times* (not the *Times* we know today), the *New York Sun*, the *Journal*

of Commerce, and the *New York Herald* quoted in Lannie, *Public Money and Parochial Education*, 180–183, 199. William Cullen Bryant's remarks are quoted in Mushkat, *Tammany*, 203.

133 *"the Catholic Bishop and clergy of New York to come forth"*: Quoted in James L. Crouthamel, "The Newspaper Revolution in New York, 1830-1850," *New York History* 45, no. 2 (April 1964), 91.

133 *"the impudent priest . . . the abbot of unreason"*: This and following Bennett quotes from the *New York Herald*, October 31, 1841.

133 *"this cunning, flexible, serpent-tongued priest"*: Quoted in Krieg, *Whitman and the Irish*, 40.

134 *"with a deficient education and an intellect half made up of shreds and patches"*: Quoted in Lannie, *Public Money and Parochial Education*, 198.

134 *The solution of Hughes's allies upstate was to have William Maclay*: Ibid., 216.

135 *For this, Maclay, more wily Jesuit than honest Baptist*: Ibid.

135 *"into the faithless arms that have embraced and wheedled them so long"*: Quoted in Ravitch, *Great School Wars*, 79.

136 *"Had it been the reverend hypocrite's head"*: Quoted in Reynolds, *Walt Whitman's America*, 99.

136 *"the first fruits of that abominable tree"*: Nevins and Thomas, *Diary of George Templeton Strong*, 1:178.

137 *"rich and instructive"*; *"What ardent hopes, what trembling fears"*: Kehoe, *Complete Works*, 1:299–312.

138 *The chief justice of the U.S. Supreme Court, Roger Taney*: Spalding, *Premier See*, 131.

138 *"The contest in New Orleans should be a bold one"*: JH to Bishop Antoine Blanc, January 3, 1852, Archdiocese of New Orleans VI-1-7, University of Notre Dame Archives.

138 *"they are exceedingly stupid on these matters"*: Quoted in Browne, "Public Support of Catholic Education," 23 (JH to Seward, May 11, 1841, University of Rochester).

138 *When the New York senator delivered his famous "higher law" speech*: JH to Cardinal Fransoni, September 1850, box 1, folder 19, AJHC AANY.

6. "THE BAAL OF BIGOTRY"

139 *The Church Debt Association*: *Freeman's Journal*, May 15, 1841, October 9, 1841.

140 *The result did not amount to much*: Box 16, folder 6, HJBP CU.

141 *"an unfinished house in a field"*: Quoted in Scanlan, *St. Joseph's Seminary*, 19.

141 *A German immigrant and Lutheran minister*: Charles G. Herbermann, "John James Maximilian Oertel," *Historical Records and Studies* (United States Catholic Historical Society) 4, parts 1 and 2 (1906): 139–144.

141 *Ambrose Manahan was an American priest*: Schroth, *Fordham: A History and Memoir*, 9–10; Shelley, *Greenwich Village Catholics*, 52–55.

142 *"in one of the most picturesque and healthy parts of Westchester County"*: Advertisement in the *Freeman's Journal*, June 19, 1841, and subsequent issues of the paper that year.

142 *"its system of government will be mild and paternal"*: Ibid.

143 *The Irish Emigrant Aid Society was born*: See the *Handbook of the Benevolent Institutions and Charities of New York* (New York: Thomas Whittaker, 1877), 60; *Freeman's Journal*, March 27, 1841, April 10, 1841, October 16, 1841, August 27, 1842. Hughes is sometimes discussed as the "founder" of this society.

I find no evidence to consider him as such. Rather, he seems to be an early and important supporter, with the wealthy laymen (many who were members of the Friendly Sons of Saint Patrick's Society) taking the lead.

144 *Even Walt Whitman wrote plaintively*: Krieg, *Whitman and the Irish*, 53.

144 *"The previously leaky vessel of the Church in New York"*: Shaw, *Dagger John*, 180.

146 *"an eccelesiastical law which is to be general throughout this diocese"*: Deuther, *Life and Times*, 104, 108. Deuther in his biography of John Timon chronicles the Saint Louis parish interdict, from the church perspective, at length; see also Shaw, *Dagger John*, 180–181. The pastoral letter that was the end result of the synod was reprinted in the *Freeman's Journal*, October 8, 1842.

147 *The secular press in New York*: See "Bishop Hughes's Apology for His Pastoral Letter in Reply to the Strictures of Four Editors of Political Newspapers," Kehoe, *Complete Works*, 1:327–350. For the references to the dagger, ibid., 338, 343. See also the *Freeman's Journal*, November 5, 1842.

148 *"crowded to overflowing"*: *Freeman's Journal*, July 2, 1842.

148 *A report from a church near Buffalo in 1850*: *Freeman's Journal*, April 27, 1850.

149 *"The rest of the children"*: *Freeman's Journal*, March 16, 1850.

149 *A Protestant observer at Dubois's funeral*: Child, *Letters from New-York*, 246–247.

150 *At the Fifth Provincial Council in Baltimore in May 1843*: Guilday, *History of the Councils*, 120–142.

150 *John Purcell wanted to raise the matter of how to extend religious instruction*: Hussey, *Archbishop John Purcell*, n.p. (ebook).

151 *"lawyer and merchant, a contractor, a money-payer, and a borrower"*: Quoted in Dolan, *Immigrant Church*, 65.

151 *Most of those gentlemen were Catholic*: On prominent Catholic laymen in New York at this time see Thomas Meehan, "Some Pioneer Catholic Laymen," in *Historical Records and Studies* (United States Catholic Historical Society) 4 (October 1906): 292–301.

152 *A friend of the Winfield Scott family*: Gouverneur, *As I Remember*, 59.

152 *"joy in living, his love of power, and his zest for action"*: Van Deusen, *Thurlow Weed*, 31.

153 *"I do not believe Mr. Weed is an adjunct of the right reverend apostles of the papacy"*: Nevins, *Diary of Philip Hone*, 659.

153 *A cardinal's hat had, in fact, been on Hughes's mind*: On his first trip to Europe, JH wrote to his sister Margaret to tell their sister Angela that "there is not the least danger of her brother being made Cardinal": May 30, 1840, box 2, folder 18, HJBP CU.

153 *Of the six Atlantic crossings*: On Hughes's 1843 trip to Europe see Hassard, *Life*, 267–271; Shaw, *Dagger John*, 190–191; the first half of Weed's book *Letters from Europe and the West Indies, 1843–1862*, 1–307. Hughes outlined his intentions for this trip to Father Pierre de Smet in a letter of July 22, 1843; see box 1, folder 16, AJHC AANY.

154 *"For the first ten days our ship bounded gaily"*: Weed, *Letters from Europe*, 1:4.

154 *"truly impressive" sermon*: Weed, *Letters from Europe*, 1:13.

155 *"After being buried five years"*: Quoted in Joseph A. Griffin, "The Contribution of Belgium to the Catholic Church in America, 1523–1857" (PhD diss., Catholic University, 1932), 200.

156 *When Weed, his travel bag loaded with letters of introduction*: Weed, *Letters from Europe*, 1:79.

156 *"in the prime of life, with tastes and habits and aspirations which will not rest"*: Ibid., 251.

156 *All he had to show for his time in Belgium*: Griffin, "Contribution of Belgium" (cited above), 200.

157 *On the afternoon of May 6, 1844*: Billington, *Protestant Crusade*, 220–237; Feldberg, *Philadelphia Riots*, 99–119, 143–161; Kyle Edward Haden, "The City of Brotherly Love and the Most Violent Religious Riots in America" (PhD diss., Fordham University, 2012), 218–260; Vincent P. Lannie and Bernard C. Deithorn, "For the Glory and Honor of God: The Philadelphia Bible Riots of 1844," *History of Education Quarterly* 8, no. 1 (Spring 1968): 44–106; Milano, *Philadelphia Nativist Riots*.

158 *"The decisive blow has been struck"*: Billington, *Protestant Crusade*, 235.

159 *"Blame attaches to both parties"*: Harrison, *Philadelphia Merchant*, 440.

159 *A death threat came in the mail*: Feldberg, *Philadelphia Riots*, 129.

159 *"men, women, and children were compelled by American citizens to flee"*: Quoted in Stahr, *Seward*, 98.

159 *Former Philadelphia mayor and U.S. senator George M. Dallas*: Milano, *Philadelphia Nativist Riots*, 134. Dallas, an Episcopalian, was probably one of the most pro–Irish Catholic politicians of his time, a fact that helped Polk in the 1844 presidential election.

160 *With cause, Whig politicians worried*: Melba Porer Hays, ed., *The Papers of Henry Clay*, vol. 10 (Lexington: University of Kentucky Press, 1991), 414.

160 *"I look upon him as a sincere, honest . . . honorable bigot"*: JH to Henry Puttle (?) and George Prentice, July 22, 1844, box 2, folder 5 AJHC AANY.

161 *Henry Clay's surprise defeat*: Albert Kirwan, *John J. Crittenden: The Struggle for the Union* (Lexington: University of Kentucky Press, 1962), 295.

161 *"at the wave of his crozier"*: *New York Herald*, October 29, 1844.

162 *Hence, the anxiety caused him by Daniel O'Connell or the rare abolitionist priest like Father Thomas Farrell*: Shelley, *Greenwich Village Catholics*, 73–78.

162 *And what of Hughes himself and slavery*: Walter G. Sharrow's account in "John Hughes and a Catholic Response to Slavery in Antebellum America" is a fair summary; see also Rena Mazyck Andrews, "Slavery Views of a Northern Prelate," *Church History* 3, no. 1 (March 1934): 60–78. See also Diane Batts Morrow, "Righteous Discontent: Black Catholic Protest in the United States of America, 1817–1941," a paper delivered at the 2009 Annual Meeting of the Atlanta University Center; and "The Influence of Christianity on Social Servitude" in Kehoe, *Complete Works*, 1:371–385, reprinted in the *Freeman's Journal*, April 1, 1843. For a summary of the tortured and tortuous Catholic response to slavery see Joseph D. Brokhage, "Francis Patrick Kenrick's Opinion on Slavery" (theology diss., Catholic University, 1955).

162 *An Irish-Catholic abolitionist like Henry Kemp*: See *Proceedings of the Massachusetts Anti-Slavery Society, 1855* (Boston: no publisher listed, 1865), 41.

164 *"There perhaps never was a period"*: "A Lecture on the Importance of a Christian Basis for Science of Political Economy," in Kehoe, *Complete Works*, 1:513–534.

164 *"The spectacle of the starving laborer"*: See *Proceedings of the Massachusetts Anti-Slavery Society, 1855* (Boston: no publisher listed, 1865), 41.

165 *"The hero wields a sturdy pen"*: Maynard, *Orestes Brownson*, 95.

166 *Bishop Fenwick of Boston*: ?F to JH, April 1, 1843, box 1, folder 6, AJHC AANY.

166 *Hughes takes "a great interest in you"*: Gower and Leliaert, *Brownson-Hecker Correspondence*, 113.

7. WAR AND FAMINE

167 *"His modesty was of a kind"*: Farley, *Life of John Cardinal McCloskey*, 149.

167 *Cardinal James Gibbons made a biblical comparison*: Ibid., 150.

167 *That is just how the Joshua of New York wanted it*: On the Hughes-McCloskey relationship, it should be noted that McCloskey was anything but a yes-man to his demanding boss. When Hughes acknowledged that he needed a coadjutor a few years later, he made it clear that he wanted John Loughlin, the soon-to-be bishop of Brooklyn and a man with whom he worked well. McCloskey, then bishop of Albany, let him and their superiors in Rome know that he thought Loughlin was not the right man for the post. Hughes did not get his way and so ended any talk of another coadjutor in the New York archdiocese. See Francis B. Donnelly, "Erection of the Diocese of Brooklyn: A Providential Afterthought," *U.S. Catholic Historian* 1, no. 4 (Fall 1982): 106–132.

168 *"living in the wilderness and having nothing to do"*: Quoted in Coogan, "Study," 58.

168 *"Mr. Manahan has come among us full to overflowing"*: Schroth, in his history of Fordham (9), dates this letter as February 23, 1843, but it is dated February 23, 1842, in box 3, folder 26, AJHC AANY.

168 *By 1845, Charles Constantine Pise*: Pise to John McCloskey, November 14, 1845, box 2, folder 17, HJBP CU.

169 *Harley's illness was never specified*: The diary of James Roosevelt Bayley, April 6, 1845, box 1, folder 19, in the collection of the Seton Hall University Archives.

169 *"his last hope for that dear and valuable young ecclesiastic"*: JH to Bishop Antoine Blanc, November 24, 1845, Archdiocese of New Orleans Collection V-5-d, University of Notre Dame Archives.

169 *"Here in Germany"*: Quoted in Blied, *Austrian Aid*, 69.

170 *There were, he calculated now, approximately two hundred thousand Catholics*: "Report to the Propagation of the Faith," January 23, 1845, copy in box 5, HJBP CU.

170 *Harley was ill on the voyage over*: On the trip to Europe see Hassard, *Life*, 281–285, and Shaw, *Dagger John*, 206–208.

170 *"Riches and poverty are to be met side by side"*: John Harley to ?, January 18, 1846, Archives of the Archdiocese of Hartford, series 1866, box 8.

170 *"there was a cry around that some blight had struck the potato stalks"*: Quoted in Kerby Miller, *Emigrants and Exiles*, 281.

171 *"the distress likely to accrue from the potato rot"*: John Harley to ?, January 18, 1846, Archives of the Archdiocese of Hartford, series 1866, box 8.

171 *"On the whole, though we expect some serious degree of scarcity"*: Quoted in Wilson, *Thomas D'Arcy McGee*, 1:118.

172 *"The Diocese of New York is like a racer"*: John Purcell to John McCloskey, December 6, 1845, box 1, folder 13, HJBP CU.

173 *Five trustees of a church in Troy*: JH to Philip Riley (?), October 11, 1845, box 2, folder 24, AJHC AANY.

173 *"You can no longer be pastor at St. Joseph's"*: JH to Ambrose Manahan, September 4, 1845, box 1, folder 28, AJHC AANY.

174 *The relationship between Hughes and the Jesuits was not destined to be smooth*: On the Jesuits coming to Fordham see Curran, "Archbishop Hughes," Schroth, *Fordham: A History and Memoir*, and Shelley, *Fordham: A History*.

174 *"an affectionate and pleasant companion"*: Thebaud, *Forty Years*, 291.

174 *That same year, Hughes had appealed to the Common Council*: Jacoby, *Catholic Child Care*, 97–98.

175 *Smack in the midst of these successes*: On the Sisters of Charity controversy see the Hughes–Mother Etienne–Louis Deluol letters quoted in Hassard, *Life*, 289–302; the Deluol letters are in box 3, folder 12, AJHC AANY. See also Joseph B. Code's account of the problem, *Bishop John Hughes and the Sisters of Charity*; Maureen Fitzgerald, *Habits of Compassion*, 42–52; and Shaw, *Dagger John*, 209–212.

178 *"the center of power and authority"*: Quoted in Fitzgerald, *Habits of Compassion*, 47.

179 *"uncalled for, impolitic, and unjust"*: H. Brownson, *Works of Orestes A. Brownson*, 16:51.

179 *"grand and imposing, beyond anything ever before witnessed in the United States"*: United States Catholic Magazine and Monthly Review 5, no. 6: 341–343.

180 *"I desire to confer with you"*: James Buchanan to JH, May 13, 1846, quoted in O'Connor, *Fitzpatrick's Boston*, 230.

181 *"If the Catholic priests in Mexico"*: Quoted in Eugene Irving McCormac, *James K. Polk: A Political Biography to the End of a Career, 1845–1849* (University of California Press, 1922), 420–421.

181 *He may have met with Polk separately*: Ibid., 411.

181 *"a highly intelligent and agreeable man"*: Quaife, *Diary of James K. Polk*, 1:408–410.

182 *Eighteen years later, ex-president Buchanan*: Meehan, "Archbishop Hughes and Mexico," 33–35.

182 *A large recruitment rally in New York City*: Pinheiro, *Missionaries of Republicanism*, 76.

182 *"One nation is full of Christians, the other is full of Catholics"*: Ibid., 86.

183 *"If all Catholic priests were like him"*: Quoted in Kurtz, *Excommunicated from the Union*, 14. On McElroy and Rey see also Tyler V. Johnson, "Punishing the Lies on the Rio Grande: Catholic and Immigrant Volunteers in Zachary Taylor's Army and the Fight against Nativism," *Journal of the Early Republic* 30, no. 1 (Spring 2010): 63–84, and Johnson's 2012 book, *Devotion to the Adopted Country*.

183 *"because a certain Bishop of that Church"*: Pinheiro, *Missionaries of Republicanism*, 75. Pinheiro offers the best and most complete account of the Polk-Hughes meeting and its aftermath, as well as the most detailed, persuasive analysis of the anti-Catholic basis of the Mexican-American War.

183 *In reality, Hughes hadn't thought much of Polk*: McCadden, "Governor Seward's Friendship," 174 (letter from JH to Weed, August 29, 1846).

184 *"famished and ghastly skeletons"*: Quoted in Miller, *Emigrants and Exiles*, 284.

184 *The "Irish hemorrhage" started in earnest*: E. Margaret Crawford, ed., *The Hungry Stream: Essays on Immigration and Famine* (Belfast: Institute for Irish Studies, 1997), introduction, 1. The immigration and census figures are from Edwin O'Donnell, " 'The Scattered Debris of the Irish Nation': The Famine Irish and New York City, 1845–1855," ibid., 49–60. See also Hasia R. Diner, " 'The Most Irish City in the Union': The Era of the Great Migration, 1844–1877," in *The New York Irish*, ed. Ronald H. Bayor and Timothy J. Meagher, 87–106 (Baltimore: Johns Hopkins University Press, 1996).

185 *"My feelings, my habits, my thoughts"*; *"as a great personal grief"*; *"It is better that the seminaries should be suspended"*: All quoted in Hassard, *Life*, 303.

186 *"We never had, not even in the days of persecution, anything to equal the distress"*: Edward McGinn to JH, n.d., 1847, box 3, folder 3, AJHC AANY.

186 *The month after sending his seminary collection abroad, Hughes gave an angry lecture:* "A Lecture on the Antecedent Causes of the Irish Famine in 1847," Kehoe, *Complete Works,* 1:544–558.

187 *When a bill was debated in Congress:* Timothy J. Scarborough, "The Spirit of Manifest Destiny: The American Government and Famine Ireland, 1845–1849," in *Fleeing the Famine: North American and Irish Refugees, 1845–1851,* ed. Margaret M. Mulrooney (Westport, CT: Praeger, 2003), 51.

188 *"made two questionable appearances and vamoosed":* Quoted in Ernst, *Immigrant Life,* 151. Circulation figures for the *Irish-American* ibid., 279. On Patrick Lynch (and numerous other New York Irish or Catholic editors of the day) see William Leonard Joyce, *Editors and Ethnicity: A History of the Irish-American Press, 1848–1883* (PhD diss., University of Michigan, 1974; New York: Arno Press reprint, 1976), 74–143.

188 *"the interests of the Irish American":* Quoted in Hueston, *Catholic Press and Nativism,* 140.

189 *"Young countrymen from Ireland!":* *Irish-American,* May 26, 1850.

8. A WIDENING STAGE

190 *"the historical man of the day":* Maury, *Statesmen of America,* 228.

191 *The invitation—like the jubilation that greeted Pius IX's ascension:* On a John Quincy Adams speech critical of Catholicism see the *Freeman's Journal,* December 2, 1843.

191 *"menagerie of politicians and roguery":* *New York Herald,* December 13, 1847.

191 *Others suspected an ulterior motive:* On the rumormongering about Hughes's appearance in the capital and on Hughes's anger with Polk about the *Washington Daily Union* editorial see Pinheiro, *Missionaries of Republicanism,* 75, 98.

192 *"Christianity: The Only Source of Moral, Social and Political Regeneration":* The speech to Congress is reprinted in Kehoe, *Complete Works,* 1:558–573. A handwritten copy is in box 11, folder 16, HJBP CU.

192 *"a very high admiration for the character of the bishop":* Robert W. Johannsen, ed., *The Letters of Stephen A. Douglas* (Urbana: University of Illinois Press, 1961), 228–229.

192 *One member of the society who had opposed the invitation:* Connor, "American Catholic Political Position," 122.

193 *"Were I to give way to my feelings":* *New York Evening Post,* December 27, 1847.

193 *"intellectual pugilist":* Samuel Irenaeu Prime, *Memoirs of Rev. Nicholas Murray* (New York: Harper & Bros., 1862), 274.

193 *"Kirwin Unmasked":* Kehoe, *Complete Works,* 1:636–664.

194 *Whig senator John Bell of Tennessee:* Pinheiro, *Missionaries of Republicanism,* 153. Some historians have argued that anti-Catholicism was not a significant factor in the war with Mexico and that Catholic patriotism at the time helped to quell nativist bigotry and, to some degree, create a more tolerant climate after the war: see Ted C. Hinckley, "American Anti-Catholicism during the Mexican War," *Pacific Historical Review* 31, no. 2 (May 1962): 121–137. Pinheiro quite effectively refutes that view. On this topic see also Tyler V. Johnson, "Punishing the Lies on the Rio Grande: Catholic and Immigrant Volunteers in Zachary Taylor's Army and the Fight against Nativism," *Journal of the Early Republic* 30, no. 1 (Spring 2010): 63–84.

194 *An Ohio major, Luther Giddings:* See *Sketches of the Campaign in Northern Mexico by an Officer of the First Regiment of Ohio Volunteers* (New York:

George P. Putnam, 1853), 276–277. Giddings, on the other hand, perpetuated plenty of stereotypes about Mexican Catholic priests, those "pampered and frantic friars" he encountered and felt he had no reason to trust.

194 *The tragedy of the Saint Patrick, or San Patricio, battalion*: A good account is Robert Ryan Miller, *Shamrock and Sword: The Saint Patrick's Battalion in the U.S.-Mexican War* (Norman: University of Oklahoma Press, 1989). Miller points out that neither the Mexican nor the American view of these men (the one seeing them as political idealists turning their backs on an aggressor nation, the other seeing them as calculating political turncoats) quite captures the reality of their motives, which were murky, varied, and never entirely political. He also notes that the Irishmen in the battalion might have constituted as little as 40 percent of the total who went over to the Mexican side—yet, interestingly, even today the San Patricios' desertion is viewed as an exclusively Irish American action. The name, of course, furthers that impression.

194 *"madness of [Polk's] plans"*: Quoted in Amy S. Greenberg, *A Wicked War: Polk, Clay, Lincoln, and the 1846 U.S. Invasion of Mexico* (New York: Random House, 2012), 203.

196 *In Italy, this issue was especially evident*: On Pope Pius's dilemma, which was truly more of a dilemma than it is made to seem in some accounts that portray the pope as more antirepublican and pro-Austrian than he was prior to 1848, see Mike Rapport, *1848: Year of Revolution* (New York: Basic Books, 2009), 151–151, 162–163, 323–324.

197 *The Young Ireland leadership was a disparate, fractious group*: Wilson, *Thomas D'Arcy McGee*, 203–223. Wilson's biography of McGee is excellent on the nature and various stages of the Hughes-McGee relationship. On Hughes's trip to New Orleans and fund-raising for the movement: Christine Kinealy, *Repeal and Revolution: 1848 in Ireland* (Manchester: Manchester University Press, 2009), 218. On the Young Ireland men coming to the United States and interacting with Hughes see also David Brundage, *Irish Nationalists in America: The Politics of Exile, 1798–1998* (Oxford University Press, 2016).

199 *"The present generation of Irish Priests"*: *Nation*, January 6, 1849.

199 *In a series of letters published in the* Freeman's Journal: "An Irish Catholic," *Freeman's Journal*, January 13, 1849.

200 *"vermin engendered by bad blood and beggary"*: *Nation*, June 9, 1849.

200 *Daniel O'Connell had been a Gulliver*: Quoted in Hassard, *Life*, 304.

200 *"He was at first red hot about the priests"*: Brendan Ó Cathaoir, ed., *A Young Irelander Abroad: The Diary of Charles Hart* (Cork: Cork University Press, 2003), 43.

201 *Hughes read his columns and, in 1845, had favorably reviewed McGee's book*: *Boston Pilot*, March 1, 1845.

201 *"frothy orations"*: Quoted in Wilson, *Thomas D'Arcy McGee*, 92.

202 *"a masterpiece of myth-making"*: Ibid., 275.

202 *McGee's Boston paper*: The McGee, Meagher, and Mitchel quotations on Anglo-Saxon versus Celtic identity are quoted in Cian T. McMahon, *The Global Dimensions of Irish Identity: Race, Nation, and the Popular Press, 1840–1880* (Chapel Hill: University of North Carolina Press, 2015), 94–95. On Meagher's post–Civil War life see Timothy Egan, *The Immortal Irishman*, the best and most recent biography of Meagher. For an example of a Hughes missive to Meagher that is both scolding and affectionate: JH to Meagher, February 15, 1853, box 1, folder 28, AJHC AANY.

203 *There was one other Irishman whom Hughes was uneasy about welcoming*: John
F. Quinn, " 'The Nation's Guest?,' " 154–169, and chapter 7 (154–171) in his
biography of Mathew; see also JH to Eccleston, April 16, 1849, AJHC AANY.
"By 1860, much of what Father Mathew had managed to achieve during his
American tour was already undone": Quinn, " 'Nation's Guest?,' " 180.

204 *Hughes's writings about temperance are sufficiently thin*: Hughes delivered a
speech on the subject in Philadelphia in 1840 after his return from Europe and
his first experience of Mathew's influence in Ireland (*Kenrick-Frenaye Correspondence*, 30), but the record of further speeches or references to temperance
in his correspondence is thin.

205 *By happenstance, Henry Clay was in Saratoga Springs*: Hassard, *Life*, 252.

207 *"Nobody who is anybody"*: On James McMaster, his views, and editorship of the
paper see Egan, "Slight Appreciation," 19–34, for the most honest accounts, and
Mary Augustine Kwitchen's published doctoral dissertation, *James Alphonsus
McMaster*, for a more academic account.

208 *The German Catholics of the city were agitating*: JH to the trustees of the Most
Holy Redeemer Church, August 5, 1849, box 2, folder 1, AJHC AANY.

208 *"aspiring and ambitious prelate was stopped in his career"*: *New York Herald*,
September 9, 1849.

208 *An officer at West Point had been dismissed*: Box 3, folder 23 (the letters extend
from 1847 to 1850), AJHC AANY.

210 *When Saint Vincent's Hospital opened in the fall*: McCauley, *Who Shall Take
Care*, 1–15; Walsh, *Sisters of Charity*, 133–144.

211 *Ellen Hughes was to become a force in New York City Catholicism*: Walsh, *Sisters of Charity*, 182–183.

211 *"You never came here and said a kind or encouraging word"*: Patrick Hughes's
letters to his brother, box 2, folder 10, HJBP CU.

213 *A massive Tammany Hall rally*: See Helene Sara Zahler, *Eastern Workingmen
and National Land Policy, 1829–1862* (New York: Columbia University Press,
1941) for the antebellum politics of land reform. Terry Golway in *Machine Made*
(51) has Hughes attending the rally at Tammany Hall (which would indeed have
been a radical gesture), while Zahler has him sending a letter of support to
be read instead (141). Newspaper accounts (e.g., *New York Tribune*, March 2,
1850) support Zahler. Golway is correct, though, in suggesting that Hughes's
willingness to address the issue, at the risk of offending his wealthy allies in
the business world, "spoke to the growth of Irish political consciousness in
New York" (51). On Greeley's moderate brand of radicalism c. 1850: Williams,
Horace Greeley, 133.

214 *The daughter of the Catholic Ohio senator*: Anna McAllister, *Ellen Ewing:
Wife of General Sherman* (New York: Benziger Books, 1936), 66. McAllister
describes Sherman as being fully as impressed as his wife with the bishop; given
Sherman's lifelong skepticism about priests and Ellen's zealotry, that observation
should be taken with several grains of salt.

9. THE CHURCH MILITANT

216 *"destructive fanaticism"; "save American society"*: H. Brownson, *Works of
Orestes A. Brownson*, 17:38–39.

216 *Fillmore's invitation implies*: Fillmore was showing an expedient hospitality
to Hughes; another example of the new president's need to downplay, for the

moment, his anti-Catholic ardor was the fact that he joined the procession in 1851 that accompanied Archbishop Eccleston's body from Georgetown College, where he died, to the capital's train station (see Spalding, *Premier See*, 152)—not the kind of thing he would have done when he was a politician in nativist Buffalo!

217 *"The Decline of Protestantism and Its Causes"*: The sermon is reprinted in Kehoe, *Complete Works*, 2:87–102. Hughes's claims that the United States would eventually become a Catholic country were at the time less far-fetched than they would appear to be to later generations. One foreign visitor and travel writer, Frederick Marryat, had voiced the same opinion thirteen years earlier, noting that, even aside from the immigration figures so favorable to Catholics, Protestant fervor seemed on the wane in a country that most Europeans had previously assumed to be a deeply religious, devoutly Protestant nation. Many of the people he encountered west of the Alleghenies, Marryat wrote, were either Catholic or simply indifferent to religion: see Sydney Jackman, ed., *A Diary in America: With Remarks on the Institutions by Frederick Marryat* (New York: Knopf, 1962), 304–305.

218 *a David before the mitred Goliath*: Joseph F. Berg, *Lecture Delivered in the Musical Fund Hall in Answer to Archbishop Hughes on the Decline of Protestantism* (Philadelphia: C. Collins Jr., S. Sherrerd, and A. Dumont, 1850).

218 *"King Solomon has said that there is a season for everything"*: *New York Herald*, November 14, 1850.

219 *Rome was always a restorative for Hughes*: Hassard, *Life*, 339.

219 *His rooms were constantly crowded*: Ibid. Also on the 1850–1851 trip to Rome: Coogan, "Study," 59–60.

220 *"It seems established from sources public and private"*: Kenrick-Frenaye Correspondence, 315.

220 *"I cannot say I am well pleased with the prospect of our having a Cardinal"*: Francis Kenrick to Tobias Kirby, March 17, 1851, quoted on page 59 of chapter 9 (Browne's MSS of his unpublished Hughes biography), box 15, folder 5, HJBP CU.

221 *The pope remarked to Purcell*: Hassard, *Life*, 340.

221 *Between Timon—a friend of Dubois—and Hughes, no love was lost*: A good account of this energetic politicking is in Riforgiato, "John Timon," 27–42.

221 *As Kenrick's reluctant messenger*: John Purcell to John Hassard, September 17, 1865, box 1, folder 13 (a), HJBP CU.

221 *"rubicund and fresh"*: Clipping from the *New York Herald*, box 3, folder 11, AJHC AANY.

222 *"the time has almost come"*: Quoted in Hassard, *Life*, 338.

223 *"Go ahead and build it with your own money"*: JH to the congregation of Saint Peter's, March 13, 1852, box 2, folder 8, AJHC AANY.

223 *A prime example was the arrival in the United States*: Komlos, *Louis Kossuth in America*; also, Holt, *Rise and Fall*, 692–697; Wilentz, *Rise of American Democracy*, 661–662; Williams, *Horace Greeley*, 142–147. One historian has written that Fillmore rescinded his invitation to the White House, but for Fillmore's awkward reception of Kossuth see Komlos, *Louis Kossuth in America*, 103. See also Gouverneur, *As I Remember*, 156–157; Arthur J. May, "Seward and Kossuth," *New York History* 34, no. 3 (July 1953): 267–283; and William Warren Rogers, "The 'Nation's Guest' in Louisiana: Kossuth Visits New Orleans," *Louisiana History* 9, no. 4 (Autumn 1968): 355–364.

224 *"perfidious and talking Tartar"*: *Freeman's Journal*, July 7, 1855, 4.

224 *"whether American, Irish, German, or French"*: JH to Chevalier Hulsemann, December 11, 1851, box 1, folder 22, AJHC AANY.

224 *"to public opinion in both hemispheres"*: Kehoe, *Complete Works*, 2:467.

225 *In the spring of 1852*: On the plenary council see Guilday, *History of the Councils*, 167–186; Kari, *Public Witness*, 22–24; O'Shea, *Two Kenricks*, 173–174.

226 *That same spring Hughes delivered on Saint Patrick's Day*: "Sermon on St. Patrick's Day, 1852" is reprinted in Kehoe, *Complete Works*, 2:174–179.

228 *"rejected warily"*: Nevins, *Ordeal of the Union*, 2:33.

228 *Hughes recognized the value of saying nothing about either candidate*: On Hughes not wanting to endorse either Pierce or Scott see *New York Evening Post*, September 27, 1852, and JH to D(?)H Chadwick, September 6, 1854, box 1, folder 13, AJHC AANY.

228 *That year he was also asked by Scott's daughter to baptize her first child*: Nevins and Thomas, *Diary of George Templeton Strong*, 2:104.

228 *Many in the party*: Albert Kirwin, *John J. Crittenden: The Struggle for the Union* (Lexington: University of Kentucky Press, 1962), 296.

229 *"for the better ordering of ecclesiastical affairs"*: Connelly, *Visit of Archbishop*, 10. The best sources for the Bedini visit to the United States are Connelly's exemplary account and Guilday's essay "Gaetano Bedini," though Guilday's summary of Bedini's report to Pope Pius IX omits many of Bedini's interesting negative comments; see also Condon, "Constitutional Freedom," Endres, "Know-Nothings," and Shaw, *Dagger John*, 278–287.

229 *"unique among nativist episodes"*: Endres, "Know-Nothings," 1.

229 *He was to meet and offer the pope's compliments to President Pierce*: Connelly, *Visit of Archbishop*, 12–14.

229 *The pope was a fan of* Uncle Tom's Cabin: Reynolds, *Mightier Than the Sword*, 32. The Italian translation of the novel turns Tom into a devout Catholic!

230 *Kenrick told a fellow bishop*: Ibid., 21.

230 *"I think that is because he is always game"*: Quoted in Lannie, "Profile of an Immigrant Bishop," 366.

230 *"remarkable personage"*: Connelly, *Visit of Archbishop*, 29.

231 *Lewis Cass Jr., the American chargé d'affaires in Rome*: On Hughes's wish to see Cass fired see JH to Joseph Campbell, November 25, 1853, box 1, folder 12, AJHC AANY. Campbell's response, claiming that Pierce cannot fire Cass's son: Joseph Campbell to JH, December 23, 1853, box 3, folder 22, AJHC AANY.

231 *To no avail*: Guilday, "Gaetano Bedini," 123–124.

232 *Alessandro Gavazzi, an ex-priest from Bologna*: Billington, *Protestant Crusade*, 301–305; Gavazzi, *Father Gavazzi's Lectures*; Marraro, "Italians in New York."

232 *When Gavazzi and a few followers appeared in the same railroad car*: Connelly, *Visit of Archbishop*, 33–34.

233 *An Italian immigrant who claimed to have information*: Connelly, *Visit of Archbishop*, 38–39, and Condon, "Constitutional Freedom," 455.

233 *"a state of terrible trepidation"*: John Fitzpatrick to JH, September 29, 1853, box 2, folder 21, AJHC AANY.

233 *It would appear that Bedini was too nervous to return to New York*: JH to Father Bernard Smith, November 25, 1853, box 2, folder 11, AJHC AANY.

234 *"It is well that his movements should be sudden"*: Connelly, *Visit of Archbishop*, 84–85.

236 *"The renegade Italians and infidel Germans made all the trouble"*: JH to Bishop Antoine Blanc, November 24, 1845, Archdiocese of New Orleans Collection V-5-d, University of Notre Dame Archives.

236 *"there is much to fear from Protestant fanaticism"*: Connelly, *Visit of Archbishop*, 200.

236 *"The famous American motto"*: Quoted ibid., 270.

236 *"a whirlpool of unbridled liberty"*: Ibid., 219.

236 *"How much the Catholic religion in the United States owes to the Irish"*: Ibid., 250.

237 *Above all, Bedini insisted to the pontiff* : For Bedini's report to Pope Pius, ibid., 210–240.

237 *Hughes himself had urged the first Christian Brothers who came to New York from France in 1848 to change their attire*: Gabriel, *Christian Brothers*, 106.

237 *Neumann plaintively told Francis Kenrick*: Connelly, *Visit of Archbishop*, 23. What a splendid irony that the person Bedini was least impressed with on this trip was the one American bishop of his era later declared a saint.

238 *Despotism and nepotism*: Connelly, *Visit of Archbishop*, 235.

238 *"a lordly spirit . . . too restless"*: Dhu, *Stanhope Burleigh*, 131, 175.

238 *"Hubert had been bold"*: Ibid., 130.

238 *"down to the lowest and most fallen specimen of manhood"*: Susan Griffin, *Anti-Catholicism*, 111.

239 *"clothed in all the pomp and circumstance"*: Belisle, *Arch Bishop*, 348.

239 *"mountebank clothed in tinseled trappings"*: Ibid.

241 *"I stand by my letter"*: Hughes, *Archbishop Hughes to General Cass, in Self-Vindication* (copy in the Special Collections at the Walsh Family Library at Fordham University).

241 *"a reign of terror surpassed only by the Philadelphia riots"*: Condon, "Constitutional Freedom," 448.

241 *"minor riots occurred in New York"*: Billington, *Protestant Crusade*, 319.

241 *When John Orr, better known as the Angel Gabriel*: Ibid., 306.

241 *Five months later a mob almost succeeded*: Ibid., 309.

242 *Father Johannes Bapst was stripped in public*: Condon, "Constitutional Freedom," 445–446; O'Shea, *Two Kenricks*, 181–182; Gerard C. Treacy, "Father John Bapst, S.J., and the 'Ellsworth Outrage,'" *Historical Records and Studies* (United States Catholic Historical Society) 14 (May 1920): 7–19.

242 *The rise in power of the Know-Nothing Party*: Billington, *Protestant Crusade*, 380–436; McPherson, *Battle Cry of Freedom*, 135–143; Nevins, *Ordeal of the Union*, 2:323–346; Potter, *To the Golden Door*, 248–261.

242 *"swept the country with a hurricane force"*: Quoted in Wilson, *Thomas D'Arcy McGee*, 327.

242 *What might have shocked the archbishop*: Nevins, *Ordeal of the Union*, 2:324.

242 *James Gordon Bennett, of course, fully agreed*: *New York Herald*, November 17, 1854.

10. AUTHORITY CHALLENGED

243 *"No one loves to break a lance with him"*: Quoted in Maynard, *Orestes Brownson: Yankee, Radical, Catholic*, 143.

244 *"given [him] pain" or "cause to quarrel"*: John Hughes to Orestes Brownson, July 1, 1854, box 2, folder 10, HJBP CU

244 *a commencement ceremony at Fordham in July 1856*: Henry Brownson discusses the Fordham commencement episode and quotes from Hughes's letter to his father in the third volume of his biography of his father, *Orestes A. Brownson's Latter Life: 1856 to 1876* (67–74); see also the various biographies of Brownson

(e.g., Peter Carey, *Orestes A. Brownson: American Religious Weathervane*, 242–243; Maynard, *Orestes Brownson: Yankee, Radical, Catholic*, 248–250; Ryan, *Orestes A. Brownson: A Definitive Biography*, 532–534). Hassard (*Life*, 383), at his most hagiographic, if not dishonest, refers to Hughes that day as "kindly but decidedly" refuting Brownson's views. For the best study of Brownson, the reader should go to Carey.

245 *"a man well-known for his power to do mischief"* and *"I am sure you will not take it offensively"*: JH to Brownson, August 29, 1856, box 1, folder 6, AJHC AANY.

246 *"generous [but] impulsive, somewhat erratic"*: Quoted in Shaw, *Dagger John*, 262.

246 *Likewise, Peter Burnett, the first governor of California*: Burnett's letters to JH, box 3, folder 21, AJHC AANY.

247 *"own turn of humiliation"*: Quoted in Shaw, *Dagger John*, 328.

247 *Even Brownson expressed sympathy*: On Brownson's letter to Hughes about Forbes, Hughes's reply, and the tensions in the Hughes-Forbes relation that Hughes papered over see Henry Brownson's biography of his father, *Orestes A. Brownson's Latter Life*, 190–193. See also JH to Orestes Brownson, November 29, 1859, box 1, folder 6, AJHC AANY.

247 *The conversion in 1854 of politician Joseph Chandler*: Frank Gerrity, "The Disruption of the Philadelphia Whigocracy: Joseph R. Chandler, Anti-Catholicism, and the Congressional Election of 1854," *Pennsylvania Magazine of History and Biography* 111, no. 1 (April 1987): 161–194.

247 *New York mayor Fernando Wood's wife had purportedly converted*: Father Bernard Smith to JH, January 20, 1861, box 3, folder 7, AJHC AANY.

247 *When Henry Clay's granddaughter converted*: "Henry Clay's Letter to His Granddaughter," *American Catholic Historical Researches* 14 (1897): 39.

247 *The conversion of William Rosecrans*: Anne C. Rose, "Some Private Roads to Rome: The Role of Families in American Victorian Conversions to Catholicism," *Catholic Historical Review* 85, no. 1 (January 1999): 41–43, 54.

248 *Vanbrugh Livingston, member of a distinguished New York family, had been disinherited*: "Letter of Archbishop Hughes to Daniel Webster," *American Catholic Historical Researches* 13 (April 1896): 94–95. Also: JH to Postmaster General Campbell, November 25, 1853, box 5, ledger, HJBP CU, thanking him for finding Livingston a job.

248 *The effect [of conversion] outside the Catholic circles*: J. V. Huntington to JH, November 29, 1859, box 3, folder 26, AJHC AANY.

249 *"brainy"*: Brenda Wineapple, *Hawthorne: A Life* (New York: Knopf, 2003), 144.

249 *she was not the only Brook Farm associate to find her way to the church*: Gower and Leliaert, *Brownson–Hecker Correspondence*, 117.

249 *But, like Isaac Hecker, Sophia Ripley*: The Sophia Ripley–Charlotte Dana letters (some dated, some not, some partially dated) are in the Dana Collection of the Massachusetts Historical Society. See Franchot, *Roads to Rome*, 302–320 and Crowe, *George Ripley*, 215–225.

250 *"if he was too fully saturated with the gifts of the Holy Ghost"*: Maurice Egan, "Slight Appreciation," 8.

250 *"to edify such good people"*: Ibid., 12.

251 *"great relief"*: *Freeman's Journal*, May 31, 1856, 4.

251 *There had already been some ugly personal consequences*: Timothy Egan, *Immortal Irishman*, 151–152; Wylie, *Irish General*, 95–96.

252 *For another of the Young Ireland group*: See James Quinn, *John Mitchel* (Dublin: University College Dublin Press, 2008), and Bryan P. McGovern, *John Mitchel:*

Irish Nationalist, Southern Secessionist (Knoxville: University of Tennessee Press, 2009); Hassard, *Life*, 365; Shaw, *Dagger John*, 302–303.

252 *"vitriol slinger"*; *"treacherous enemies"*; *"it must be won"*; *"an unworthy prelate"*: All quoted in Quinn, *John Mitchel*, 59–60.

253 *"a superior manner and quasi-episcopal air"*: Seton, *Memories*, 163.

254 *"every tongue and tribe under the sky"*: Quoted in Hassard, *Life*, 371. Also on the ceremonies in Rome see *Kenrick-Frenaye Correspondence*, 377–385.

254 *Kenrick and O'Connor, whose credentials as scholars and theologians far exceeded those of Hughes*: Szarnicki, *Michael O'Connor*, 144.

254 *"a notable Roman head"*: For Duffy's impressions of Hughes see Charles Gavan Duffy, *My Life in Two Hemispheres* (New York: Macmillan, 1898), 2:126.

254 *State senator James Putnam from Buffalo*: On the Putnam bill and the church property controversy see Kehoe, *Complete Works*, 2:549–632; Shaw, *Dagger John*, 292–297.

255 *"venerable and unterrified archbishop"*: *New York Herald*, April 23, 1855.

255 *"violation of the whole spirit"*: Speech of James O. Putnam of Buffalo, on the Bill Providing for the Vesting of the Title of Church Property in Lay Trustees, January 30, 1855 (Albany: Van Benthuysen Printer, 1855), 3, 6–7.

255 *"the political state is Protestant in character"*: Quoted in Shaw, *Dagger John*, 292.

256 *"a species of daily torture"*: Kehoe, *Complete Works*, 2:561.

257 *"more ludicrous than wicked"*: Hughes, *Brooksiana*, 167.

257 *One was the subscription taken up by friends to have G. P. A. Healy*: The G. P. A. Healy portrait of Hughes is now in the collection of the Arizona State University Art Gallery in Tempe.

257 *Another positive development from these years*: Kelly, "John Rose Greene Hassard," 19–37.

258 *When the Sisters of Charity of New York had to vacate their motherhouse*: On the purchase of Font Hill by the Sisters of Charity see Walsh's *Sisters of Charity of New York*, and the Mother Angela files in the Archives of the Sisters of Charity, the College of Mount Saint Vincent, Riverdale, New York.

259 *When Buchanan, who had long had his eye on the presidency*: Jean Baker, *James Buchanan* (New York: Times Books, 2004), 68.

261 *In 1856, long-simmering relations between the archbishop and the Jesuits*: The most detailed account of this labyrinthine mess is in Curran, "Archbishop Hughes and the Jesuits," 174–221; see also Schroth, *Fordham: A History and Memoir*, 51–54; Shaw, *Dagger John*, 321–324; Shelley, *Fordham: A History*, 84–90, 97–102. See also Hughes's November 9, 1857, letter to Peter Hargous with notes summarizing the situation, which he wanted Hargous to read to the college's board of trustees (box 1, folder 22, AJHC AANY).

261 *"It cannot be said that the history of this conflict"*: Curran, "Archbishop Hughes," 214.

263 *"neither reason nor law have any weight against his will"*: Quoted in Shelley, *Fordham: A History*, 99.

263 *"It's impossible to argue with him!"*: Quoted in Thomas J. Shelley, "Anniversary," *Catholic New York*, July 6, 2000.

265 *One who did, anonymously, published under the name of "Equitas"*: *New York Times*, January 9, 1857 (clipping, box 3, folder 24, AJHC AANY) and July 15, 1857; Shaw, *Dagger John*, 306–315.

266 *"I do not wish to die out"*: Quoted in Hassard, *Life*, 411.

266 *"secretly, as prudence directs"*: O'Connor, *Fitzpatrick's Boston*, 183.

266 *In 1857, Hughes had decided to give Ambrose Manahan a third chance*: JH to Manahan, December 9, 1857, box 1, folder 28, AJHC AANY.

266 *"a tyrant, but with feeling"*: Burstel diary, vol. 1, July 24, 1865, AJHC AANY. Thomas Shelley recounts Manahan's checkered career in his histories of Fordham and of the New York archdiocese.

267 *Hughes had two architects in mind for his grand dream*: Walter Knight Sturges, "Renwick, Rodrigue and the Architecture of St. Patrick's Cathedral, N.Y.C.," *U.S. Catholic Historian* 1, no. 2 (Winter/Spring 1981); Shaw, *Dagger John*, 306–315.

267 *As the economy tottered in the late 1850s*: On the colonization dispute see Browne, "Archbishop Hughes and Western Colonization"; Kehoe, *Complete Works*, 2:751–755; Kelly, *Catholic Immigrant Colonization Projects*, 210–270; Shaw, *Dagger John*, 310–314; Wilson, *Thomas D'Arcy McGee*, 348–353. See also Henry W. Caspar, *History of the Catholic Church in Nebraska* (Milwaukee: Catholic Life Publications, 1960), 67–70.

268 *"It is not within the power of language"*: John Francis Maguire, *The Irish in America* (New York: D. & J. Sadlier, 1867), 214.

269 *"more squalid than the Irish hovels"*: Kehoe, *Complete Works*, 2:692.

270 *Speaking at the Saint James Church hall*: Hughes's speech on Catholic education was reprinted in the *Freeman's Journal*, November 28, 1857.

11. A NEW CATHEDRAL

272 *1857 and 1858 were the worst*: On the Panic of 1857 see Burrows and Wallace, *Gotham*, 842–851; James L. Huston, *The Panic of 1857 and the Coming of the Civil War* (Baton Rouge: Louisiana State University Press, 1987); and Kenneth Stampp, *America in 1857* (New York: Oxford University Press, 1990), 213–238.

272 *"acted as a clap of thunder in a summer sky"*: Huston, *Panic of 1857*, 14.

273 *With some estimates suggesting that layoffs might reach fifty thousand*: On Mayor Wood's proposal see Huston, *Panic of 1857*, 25, and Mushkat, *Fernando Wood*, 77–78.

273 *"I had made arrangement to commence the new cathedral"*: JH to Bernard Talbot, n.d., 1857, box 2, folder 10, AJHC AANY.

273 *Within a few months, though, Hughes concluded*: Notes to the board of Saint Patrick's Cathedral detailing the finances of the construction are located in box 1, folder 5, AJHC AANY.

274 *"[the cathedral] shall never be consecrated in my lifetime"*: Ibid.

274 *"the new St. Patrick's Cathedral, to be created"*: Quoted in Harold Earl Hammond, *A Commoner's Judge: The Life and Times of Charles Patrick Daly* (Boston: Christopher Publishing House, 1954), 127–128.

275 *"worthy of God, worthy of the Catholic religion"*: Quoted in Hassard, *Life*, 405.

275 *"A year makes little difference for the Cathedral"*: Bernard Smith to JH, September 11, 1858, box 3, folder 1, HJBP CU, and copy in box 2, folder 12, AJHC AANY.

276 *He was at least able to use the occasion for another sermon*: Hughes's sermon for the collection for the American College in Rome is reprinted in Kehoe, *Complete Works*, 2:271–274.

276 *"I certainly had no prejudice against the Romanists"*: Charles Loring Brace, *The Dangerous Classes of New York* (New York: Wynkoop & Hallenbeck, 1872), 155.

276 *Even before the collapse of the national economy*: On the founding and development of the House of the Good Shepherd see Katherine Conway, *In the Footprints of the Good Shepherd* (New York: Convent of the Good Shepherd, 1907),
and Jacoby, *Catholic Child Care*, 198–202.

277 *"the whole path of honor seems so natural and easy for a woman"*: Conway, *In
the Footprints*, vi. (Despite pretending otherwise, Hughes was well aware of the
number of prostitutes in the city. In his debate with John Breckinridge in 1833,
he had made reference to the New York Magdalen Society's disturbing statistics.) Along with Sophia Ripley, Father William Starrs is an unsung hero of this
endeavor amid a generally indifferent hierarchy; when he died in 1873, he also
left the Magdalen House $5,000 in his will.

278 *"They will swamp us"*: Conway, *In the Footprints*, 37.

279 *To honor New York's most famous prelate*: *Harper's Weekly*, June 26, 1858.

280 *Hughes was suing James Swain*: Box 9, folder 4, subseries 1, HJBP CU, and the
Albany Atlas and Argus, June 19, 1858, *New York Evening Express*, June 24,
1858, and *Albany Morning Express*, June 28, 1858. P. T. Barnum on Nathan
Urner: P. T. Barnum, *The Life of P. T. Barnum: Written by Himself* (Buffalo:
Courier Co., 1888), 42.

282 *"he understood me"*: JH to Rev. Hannan (1859), box 1, folder 22, AJHC AANY.

282 *A heartening development was the founding of the Missionaries*: JH to Father
Smith, December 29, 1857, box 2, folder 11, AJHC AANY. On his initial uneas-
iness about backing Hecker's break with the Redemptorists, wanting first to see
what the Vatican thought about it: JH to Cardinal Barnabo, October 30, 1857,
box 1, folder 8, and JH to Hecker, July 7, 1859, box 1, folder 22, AJHC AANY.

283 *The spiritual descendants of Saint Patrick*: The speech at the cornerstone laying
is reprinted in Kehoe, *Complete Works*, 2:263–270. On the ceremony: Burton,
Dream Lives Forever, 32–37; *New York Times*, August 16, 1858; Young, *New
World Rising*, 21–23.

283 *He appointed historian John Gilmary Shea to keep records*: Peter Guilday, *John
Gilmary Shea: Father of American Catholic History, 1824–1892* (United States
Catholic Historical Society, 1926), 66–67.

284 *An experience he found odd and uncomfortable*: On the Jeremiah Cummings
scandal see the *New York Herald*, August 23, 1859. On Hughes's statement that
if Cummings stayed in Rome he would not be heartbroken see H. Brownson,
Orestes A. Brownson's Latter Life, 191.

286 *"though insignificant, threatens to become"*: JH to Bernard Smith (n.d., 1859),
box 3, folder 7, AJHC AANY.

286 *Physical stamina was becoming a problem*: On Hughes's trip to Iowa and Milwaukee: Coogan, "Study," 65–66.

286 *The Hibernian Society of South Carolina*: Hughes's speech is reprinted in Kehoe,
Complete Works, 2:756–759.

288 *Even after collapsing in exhaustion at a Mass he was celebrating in Albany in
May*: Hassard, *Life*, 382.

289 *He was seen at a Douglas rally at Cooper Union*: Connor, "American Catholic
Political Position," 246.

289 *Another Catholic dismayed at Lincoln's unexpected ascendancy*: Orestes Brownson, "Politics at Home," in H. Brownson, *Works of Orestes A. Brownson*,
17:104.

290 *Hughes found it all but impossible now*: On his speech at the 1860 Fordham
commencement see the *New York Times*, July 12, 1860.

291 *Yet as historians sifting through the voter patterns of 1860*: Stahr, *Seward*, 209.

291 *William Seward was then led to quip*: Quoted ibid., 211.

291 *"last juiceless squeeze of the orange"*: Quoted in Kenneth M. Stampp, *And the War Came: The North and the Secession Crisis, 1860–1861* (Baton Rouge: Louisiana State University Press, 1950), 56.

292 *Hughes and Sanguinetti never saw eye to eye*: Tomasi, *Piety and Power*, 66–71; Dolan, *Immigrant Church*, 23.

293 *The visit to the United States of the Prince of Wales*: *Metropolitan Record*, October 20, 1860, and November 17, 1860.

294 *"whether it should ever be completed or not"*: *New York Times*, August 9, 1860.

294 *"I do not think it is much to be regretted that the building should have a little repose"*: Ibid.

12. A HOUSE DIVIDED, A CHURCH DIVIDED

295 *Early in the new year, Patrick Lynch expressed the hope*: Patrick Lynch to JH, February 26, 1861, box 1, folder 10, HJBP CU.

295 *"a frightful character"*: Francis Kenrick to JH, April 26, 1861, box 12, folder 9, HJBP CU.

295 *"Is Justice not on the side of the South?"*: Wight, "War Letters of the Bishop of Richmond," 262.

296 *"Let the union be broken"*: Wight, "Some Wartime Letters of Bishop Lynch," 24 (letter dated January 6, 1861). Wight mistakenly cites this as a letter from Lynch to John Mullaly of the *Metropolitan Record*, but it was addressed to Hughes; see Heisser and White, *Patrick N. Lynch*, 80–82.

296 *"without reference to the right or the wisdom of making the separation"*: Wight, "Bishop Elder and the Civil War," 290.

296 *"encouraging . . . treasonable practices"*: McGreevy, *Catholicism and American Freedom*, 74.

296 *"received the sanction of God"*: Wight, "Bishop Verot and the Civil War," 154, 156.

296 *"would not purchase Union at the expense of Justice"*: Quoted in Hennessey, *American Catholics*, 151.

296 *Augustus Martin, bishop of Natchitoches, was willing to go further*: Woods, *History*, 290, and McGreevy, *Catholicism and American Freedom*, 55. Bishop Martin also overlooked the fact that the church had never opposed interracial marriage and, indeed, insisted on its validity (McGreevy, *Catholicism and American Freedom*, 55). For the broadest view of Southern Catholics and the Civil War, chapter 8, "From Aliens to Confederates: Catholics in the South, 1845–1865," in James M. Woods's fascinating study *A History of the Catholic Church in the American South*, is excellent.

297 *John Timon flew the flag over his Buffalo residence*: Deuther, *Life and Times*, 283, 285. See also Leonard R. Riforgiato, "Bishop Timon, Buffalo, and the Civil War," *Catholic Historical Record* 73, no. 1 (January 1987): 62–80.

297 *A bishop like Peter Kenrick; Bishop Martin Spalding; James Whalen of Nashville*: Hennessey, *American Catholics*, 152–154. On Richard Whalen: Kurtz, *Excommunicated from the Union*, 34.

297 *"We disagree with those priests who have girded swords"*: Quoted in Frese, "Catholic Press and Secession," 81.

298 *James Whalen was astounded*: Blied, *Catholics and the Civil War*, 40.

298 *"It could very likely involve the churches in ruins"*: Whalen to JH, May 3, 1861, box 3, folder 9, AJHC AANY.

298 *The reference to priests blessing cannons*: Kurtz, *Excommunicated from the Union*, 73; Shelley, *Archdiocese of New York*, 206.

298 *"party spirit"*: JH to Peter McCloskey, April 9, 1861, box 1, folder 17, AJHC AANY.

299 *"Torrents of men"*: Walt Whitman, *Leaves of Grass* (New York: Modern Library), book 21, 235–236.

299 *"no group surpassed the Irish in enthusiasm"*: Burrows and Wallace, *Gotham*, 870.

299 *"not only our duty to America, but also to Ireland"*: Quoted in Bruce, *Harp and the Eagle*, 52. Susannah Ural Bruce's superb 2006 book is the definitive study of the Irish American volunteers in the Civil War.

299 *"shall never be trailed in the dust"*: *Irish-American*, June 15, 1861.

300 *"enthusiastically received by the regiment"*: Cavanagh, *Memoirs of Thomas Francis Meagher*, 388.

300 *"dashed into the enemy with the utmost fury"*: On the *Harper's Weekly* reportage of Bull Run see Bruce, *Harp and the Eagle*, 76.

301 *"I trust the war will soon be over"*: JH to Dr. McNally, June 15, 1861, box 1, folder 26, AJHC AANY.

301 *"Let us hear no more 'nativism'"*: *Boston Pilot*, October 19, 1861.

301 *"we have St. Paul for authority"* and *"Dear wife . . . I am sory to hear"*: Kohl and Richard, *Irish Green and Union Blue*, 65, 73.

301 *Hughes also wanted the government to know*: JH to Scott, May 13, 1861, box 3, folder 3, AJHC AANY.

302 *"We are as a conquered people under surveillance"*: Francis Kenrick to JH, box 1, folder 9, HJBP CU.

302 *When Mayor Fernando Wood invited Hughes that summer*: Box 3, folder 5, AJHC AANY.

302 *In September, the* Metropolitan Record *published a long letter*: The letter in the *Metropolitan Record* was originally written as a personal letter to Hughes, who passed it on to the newspaper's editor, purportedly without Lynch's permission, with his own rebuttal attached. Unless he was being sarcastic, Lynch took no umbrage at Hughes's use of his epistle: See Patrick Lynch to JH, September 25, 1861, box 1, folder 10, HJBP CU. Interestingly, Francis Kenrick claimed that when he met with Lynch earlier in the year, immediately before secession, Lynch indicated that he had no confidence in the idea of a Southern secessionist confederation (*Kenrick-Frenaye Correspondence*, 458).

304 *On September 14, 1861, Seward ordered the arrest of James McMaster*: *New York Times*, September 24, 1861; on Gertrude McMaster's letter to Lincoln see *The Papers of Abraham Lincoln* (digital archive), box 7, RG 59, entry 93. See also JH to John McCloskey, October 8, 1861, ledger in box 3, HJBP CU.

304 *Many New York papers*: On the drift of the *Metropolitan Record* toward its anti-Lincoln, anti-Union stance see George, "'Catholic Family Newspaper.'"

306 *Back in January, one of the Young Ireland rebels*: Louis R. Bisceglia, "The Fenian Funeral of Terence Bellew McManus," *Eire-Ireland* 14, no. 3 (Autumn 1979): 46–64; Cavanagh, *Memoirs of Gen. Thomas Francis Meagher*, 417–421; Dolan, *Irish-Americans*, 185–186. See also Oliver P. Rafferty, *The Church, the State, and the Fenian Threat, 1861–1875* (London: Macmillan, 1999), which discusses efforts in the early 1860s by the American hierarchy, especially Bishop Wood of Philadelphia, to follow Cullen's lead and categorically condemn any involvement with Fenianism. Hughes and the hierarchy were parting company on this issue.

307 *Contradicting his initial statement about not delivering a eulogy, Hughes did just that*: The text of Hughes's funeral sermon was reprinted in Cavanagh, *Memoirs of Gen. Thomas Francis Meagher*, 419–421.

307 *"The spectacle turned into an Irish city milestone"*: Mary G. Kelly, *Catholic Immigrant Colonization Projects*, 135.

308 *An unsigned editorial appeared in the* Metropolitan Record *on October 12*: It was reprinted in the *Boston Pilot* of October 19, 1861.

309 *Brownson responded aggressively*: *Brownson's Quarterly Review*, January 1862, reprinted in H. Brownson, *Works of Orestes A. Brownson*, 17:179–210 ("for a public whose taste and judgment," 180).

309 *"the sick man of the United States"*: Quoted in Hassard, *Life*, 350.

310 *"well managed"*: Walt Whitman (digital) Archive, from Whitman, "Hospital Visits," *New York Times*, December 11, 1864.

310 *John Mullaly of the* Metropolitan Record *wrote to him about John Phelps*: John Mullaly to JH, December 17, 1861, box 3, folder 28, AJHC AANY.

311 *"incubus of abolition"*: *Metropolitan Record*, January 25, 1862.

311 *James Gordon Bennett was proposing*: On Bennett's suggestion about reselling the slaves to their masters see the *New York Herald*, May 30, 1861.

311 *It was time to agitate the slavery question*: H. Brownson, *Works of Orestes A. Brownson*, 17:253 – 272.

311 *"Your bleeding country rejoices"*: Terrence Donaghoe to JH, September 3, 1862, box 3, folder 12, AJHC AANY.

312 *"as willing as any to make sacrifice"*: Quoted in Samito, *Becoming American*, 128.

312 *"in his splendid robes"*: Hammond, *Diary of a Union Lady*, 187.

312 *He also had to deal with those directly under his supervision*: On the priests accused of anti-enlistment efforts: JH to John Kennedy, n.d., box 3, folder 27, AJHC AANY, and box 2, folder 12 (clipping of "The Adventures of a Priest"), HJBP CU. In the latter case, the priest does not seem to have been from the New York diocese, and his actions, as reported in the press, sound somewhat unstable.

313 *Some of what occupied his attention*: On the protectory, the orphanage, and the Catholic orphan situation in New York during the Civil War see Jacoby, *Catholic Child Care*, 115, 118, 123–157.

313 *Hughes also spent a fair amount of time*: On the seminary in Troy see Scanlan, *St. Joseph's Seminary*, 25–27 ("commit[ted] to the flames," 25).

314 *In October, Orestes Brownson had decided that the time had come to unleash the dogs of war*: *Brownson's Quarterly Review*, October 1862, reprinted in H. Brownson, *Works of Orestes A. Brownson*, 17:317–352 (quotations on 323).

314 *"wroth—in fact, savage"*: Quoted ibid., 360.

314 *Antietam in September, with twenty-two thousand soldiers killed, wounded, or captured*: For the Irish death toll at Antietam see Bruce, *Harp and the Eagle*, 119.

315 *John McCaffrey, his old school friend*: Kurtz, *Excommunicated from the Union*, 44.

315 *In March 1863, John McKeon*: McKeon's speech, "Peace and Union, War and Disunion," New York Democratic Anti-Abolition States' Rights Association (March 3, 1863), printed by the Democratic Union Association, New York, reprinted in the Samuel J. May Anti-Slavery Collection, Cornell University, digital archives.

316 *"veritable republic of suffering"*: Drew Gilpin Faust, *This Republic of Suffering: Death and the Civil War* (New York: Vintage, 2009), xiii.

316 *When the men of the Irish Brigade*: Kohl and Richard, *Irish Green and Union Blue*, Father Corby's memoirs, 147–148.

316 *What Hughes didn't know, and never did learn*: On Kenrick's letter to Edwin Stanton see Heisser and White, *Patrick N. Lynch*, 90.

317 *Hughes attended the funeral in Baltimore*: On Kenrick's funeral see Hassard, *Life*, 499.

317 *"One side can make war, but it requires two to make peace"*: Quoted ibid., 498.

13. MANHATTAN UNDER SIEGE

318 *"deadly muggy"*: George Templeton Strong, quoted in Schecter, *Devil's Own Work*, 128.

318 *When New York City's ex-mayor, now congressman, Fernando Wood*: Mushkat, *Fernando Wood*, 137.

319 *Governor Seymour offered a similar harangue*: Schecter, *Devil's Own Work*, 26–27, and Stewart Mitchell, *Horatio Seymour of New York* (Cambridge, MA: Harvard University Press, 1938), 304–306.

319 *"a measure fraught with evil"*: N. J. Richardson to JH (December 1862), box 3, folder 17, AJHC AANY.

319 *"The storm thickens and grows nearer"*: *Freeman's Journal*, May 13, 1863.

319 *"The United States Converted into a Military Despotism"*: *Metropolitan Record*, March 4, 1863; Mullaly is discussed in Klement, "Catholics as Copperheads," 48, and George, "'Catholic Family Newspaper,'" 112–132. Given Mullaly's virulent racism, it is interesting to note that contemporary bloggers have urged the renaming of New York City's Mullaly Park in the Bronx.

320 *Attending the commencement exercises at Fordham in June*: H. Brownson, *Orestes A. Brownson's Latter Life*, 413–414.

321 *A Brooklyn correspondent wrote to Seward*: Ibid., 104.

321 *In a letter to Edwin Stanton*: Williams, *Horace Greeley*, 240.

321 *A mob, led by firemen of the Black Joke Engine Company, gathered mid-morning*: The literature on the New York draft riots is extensive, but certain sources are now standard: e.g., Adrian Cook's *The Armies of the Streets: The New York City Draft Riots of 1863* (1974) remains a good, highly detailed narrative history of the events; Iver Bernstein's *The New York Draft Riots: Their Significance for American Society and Politics in the Age of the Civil War* (1999) considers the riots in their broadest historical and sociological context; and Barnet Schecter's *The Devil's Own Work: The Civil War Draft Riots and the Fight to Reconstruct America* (2005) is a work of original research and expert synthesis. Of earlier publications, David M. Barnes's *The Metropolitan Police: Their Services during Riot Week; Their Honorable Record* (1863), J. T. Headley's *The Great Riots of New York, 1712 to 1873* (1873), and Dupree and Fishel's 1960 editing of an eyewitness account have the advantage of greater proximity to the event itself. Several pages of George Templeton Strong's diary (Nevins and Thomas, eds., 3:334–343) capture the immediacy of the tension. One problem, though, is that very few sources, including newspaper accounts of the time, provide exactly the same daily and hourly chronology of events.

323 *"The Town is taken by its rats"*: See Andrew Delbanco, *Melville: His World and Work* (New York: Knopf, 2005), 272; Melville was actually out of town, in Pittsfield, Massachusetts, at the time of the riots but later wrote a poem based on newspaper accounts, "The House-Top," in which he imagined witnessing the violence from his rooftop.

323 *even if "there should be a riot and mob in every ward in every city"*: Quoted in Benjamin P. Thomas and Harold Hyman, *Stanton: The Life and Times of Lincoln's Secretary of War* (New York: Knopf, 1962), 282.

324 *Later reports of the content of Seymour's speech*: Cook, *Armies of the Streets*, 104–106.

325 *At two o'clock, the governor wrote to the archbishop*: Ibid., 106.

329 *he drank a glass of water, removed his cap, bowed to the crowd, and began*: Hughes's speech on July 17 was reported in the *New York Times*, July 18, 1863; see also Hassard, *Life*, 499–501; Headley, *Great Riots of New York*, 262; Shaw, *Dagger John*, 367–369.

330 *"impotence"*: Quoted in Kurtz, *Excommunicated from the Union*, 113.

330 *"imbecility"*: Nevins and Thomas; *Diary of George Templeton Strong*, 2:390.

330 *"abominable sentiments"*: Quoted in Stahr, *Seward*, 378.

331 *"savage and hot as fire against New York"*: Quoted in Krieg, *Whitman and the Irish*, 121.

331 *"I am sorry to say that England is right about the Irish"*: Nevins and Thomas, *Diary of George Templeton Strong*, 2:342.

331 *Hughes wrote to Seward not long after the riots*: Lee, *Discontent in New York*, 142; JH to Seward, July 19, 1863, box 2, folder 10, AJHC AANY.

332 *"Many are reduced to beg"*: Odin to JH, August 10, 1863, box 1, folder 12, HJBP CU.

333 *Hughes's secretaries would have had the sense to keep the October issue of* Brownson's Quarterly Review: On Orestes Brownson's observations on the draft riots see "Catholics and the Anti-Draft Riots" in *Brownson's Quarterly Review*, October 1863, reprinted in H. Brownson, *Works of Orestes A. Brownson*, 17:412–447.

334 *There was one last fight to be waged, though*: H. J. Bleeker's letters about his tax bills to Hughes: Box 3, folder 21, AJHC AANY.

336 *"submit either to state or federal government the right to investigate my income"*: JH to S. A. Duncombe, September 18, 1863, box 1, folder 17, AJHC AANY.

336 *"through it all, my heart has never known a moment's change toward you"*: Quoted in Coogan, "Study," 71; 178.

337 *"Did they say so?"*: Quoted in Hassard, *Life*, 501–502.

EPILOGUE

338 *Eight bishops and two hundred priests*: On the funeral and John McCloskey's eulogy see Kehoe, *Complete Works*, 1:17–22.

339 *"with a sentiment scarcely short of idolatry"*: *New York Herald*, January 4, 1864.

340 *"endured with fortitude"*: *New York Times*, January 4, 1864.

340 *"His public services during the Rebellion"*: *New York Tribune*, January 4, 1864.

340 *"a man of extraordinary talents"*: *Freeman's Journal*, January 9, 1864.

341 *"We were no blind admirer of his during his life"*: Quoted in Maynard, *Orestes Brownson*, 255.

341 *"a recommendable faithfulness, I guess"*: Quoted in Krieg, *Whitman and the Irish*, 188.

342 *"a cleric of first-rate mind and third-rate temperament"*: John Kelly, *The Graves Are Walking: The Great Famine and the Saga of the Irish People* (New York: Henry Holt, 2008), 288.

342 *"teach them [County] Monaghan canon law"*: Quoted in Jay Dolan, *The Immigrant Church*, 165.

343 *"major disaster"* and *"fierce and terrible man"*: Greeley, *Catholic Experience*, 102, 109.

343 *A Catholic University doctoral dissertation*: Leon Adolphe LeBuffe, "Tensions in American Catholicism, 1820–1870: An Intellectual History" (PhD diss., Catholic University, 1973), 152.

343 *"a staunch defender of slavery"*: Anthony Gronowicz, *Race and Class Politics in New York City before the Civil War* (Boston: Northeastern University Press, 1998), 165.

344 *"the Nestor of the Catholic Church in America"*: Corby, *Memoirs*, 299.

344 *"I never knew how large a place he filled"*: John Fitzpatrick to John McCloskey, January 5, 1864, box 1, folder 6, HJBP CU.

344 *"loved and respected"*: Jean-Marie Odin to James Roosevelt Bayley, January 30, 1864, box 10, folder 19, James Roosevelt Bayley Papers, Seton Hall University Archives.

BIBLIOGRAPHY

Adams, Peter. *The Bowery Boys: Street Corner Radicals and the Politics of Rebellion.* Westport, CT: Praeger, 2005.

Ahlstrom, Sydney. *A Religious History of the American People.* New Haven, CT: Yale University Press, 1972.

Alvarez, David J. "The Papacy in the Diplomacy of the Civil War." *Catholic Historical Review* 69, no. 2 (April 1983): 227–248.

Anbinder, Tyler. *Nativism and Slavery: The Northern Know Nothings and the Politics of the 1850s.* New York: Oxford University Press, 1992.

Andrews, Rena Mazyck. *Archbishop Hughes and the Civil War.* PhD diss. University of Chicago Libraries, 1935.

——. "Slavery Views of a Northern Prelate." *Catholic History* 3, no. 1 (March 1934): 60–78.

Baker, Jean. *James Buchanan.* American Presidents Series. New York: Times Books, 2004.

Bancroft, Frederic. *The Life of William H. Seward.* Vol. 2. New York: Harper Bros., 1899.

Bayor, Ronald H., and Timothy J. Meagher, eds. *The New York Irish.* Baltimore: Johns Hopkins University Press, 1997.

Beecher, Lyman. *A Plea for the West.* Cincinnati: Truman & Smith, 1835.

Belisle, Orvilla. *The Arch Bishop: Or, Romanism in the United States.* Philadelphia: William White Smith, 1855.

Berger, Max. "The Irish Immigrant and American Nativism as Seen by British Visitors, 1836–1860." *Pennsylvania Magazine of History and Biography* 70, no. 2 (April 1946): 146–160.

Bernstein, Iver. *The New York Draft Riots: Their Significance for American Society and Politics in the Age of the Civil War.* New York: Oxford University Press, 1999.

Bigelow, John. *Retrospections of an Active Life.* Vol. 1, *1817–1863.* New York: Baker & Taylor, 1909.

——. "The Southern Confederacy and the Pope." *North American Review* 157, no. 443 (October 1893): 462–475.

Billington, Ray Allen. "Maria Monk and Her Influence." *Catholic Historical Review* 22, no. 3 (October 1936): 283–296.

———. *The Protestant Crusade: 1800–1860.* New York: Macmillan, 1938.

———. "Tentative Bibliography of Anti-Catholic Propaganda in the United States (1800–1860)." *Catholic Historical Review* 18 (1932–1933).

Biographical Sketch of the Most Rev. John Hughes, D.D., Archbishop of New York. New York: Metropolitan Record, 1864.

Blied, Benjamin J. *Austrian Aid to American Catholics, 1840–1860.* Milwaukee: Saint Francis Seminary, 1944.

———. *Catholics and the Civil War.* Milwaukee: Saint Francis Seminary, 1945.

Blumenthal, Henry. *A Reappraisal of Franco-American Relations, 1830–1871.* Chapel Hill: University of North Carolina Press, 1959.

Brann, Henry. *Most Reverend, John Hughes.* New York: Dodd, Mead, 1892.

Brown, Mary Elizabeth. "John Joseph Hughes (1797–1864): Definitions of 'Assimilation.'" In *The Making of Modern Immigration: An Encyclopedia of People and Ideas,* edited by Patrick J. Hayes, 1:273–286. Santa Barbara, CA: ABC-CLIO, 2012.

Browne, Henry J. "Archbishop Hughes and Western Colonization." *Catholic Historical Review* 36, no. 3 (October 1950): 257–283.

———, ed. "The Archdiocese of New York a Century Ago: A Memoir of Archbishop John Hughes, 1838–1858." *Historical Records and Studies* (United States Catholic Historical Society) 39–40 (1952): 129–190.

———. "Public Support of Catholic Education in New York, 1825–1842: Some New Aspects." *Catholic Historical Review* 39, no. 1 (April 1953): 1–27.

Brownson, Henry. *Orestes A. Brownson's Latter Life: 1856 to 1876.* Detroit: H. Brownson, 1906.

———, ed. *The Works of Orestes A. Brownson.* Vols. 16 and 17. Detroit: H. Brownson, 1906.

Bruce, Susannah Ural. *The Harp and the Eagle: Irish-American Volunteers and the Union Army, 1861–1865.* New York: NYU Press, 2006.

———. "'Remember Your Country and Keep Up Its Credit': Irish Volunteers and the Union Army." *Journal of Military History* 69, no. 2 (April 2005): 331–359.

Bryant, William Cullen II. "No Irish Need Apply: William Cullen Bryant Fights Nativism, 1836–1845." *New York History* 74, no. 1 (January 1993): 29–46.

Burrows, Edwin G., and Mike Wallace. *Gotham: A History of New York City to 1898.* New York: Oxford University Press, 1999.

Burton, Katherine. *The Dream Lives Forever: The Story of St. Patrick's Cathedral.* New York: Longmans, Green, 1960.

Carey, Patrick W. *People, Priests, and Prelates: Ecclesiastical Democracy and the Tensions of Trusteeism.* Notre Dame, IN: University of Notre Dame Press, 1987.

Carey, Peter. "The Laity's Understanding of the Trustee System, 1785–1855." *Catholic Historical Review* 64, no. 3 (July 1978): 357–376.

———. *Orestes A. Brownson: American Religious Weathervane.* Library of Religious Biography series. Grand Rapids, MI: Eerdmans, 2004.

Case, Lynn M., and Warren F. Spencer. *The United States and France: Civil War Diplomacy.* Philadelphia: University of Pennsylvania Press, 1970.

Cavanagh, Michael. *The Memoirs of Gen. Thomas Francis Meagher, Comprising the Leading Events of His Career. . . .* Worcester, MA: Messenger, 1892.

Child, Lydia Maria. *Letters from New-York.* Edited by Bruce Mills. Athens: University of Georgia Press, 1998. First published by C. S. Francis, 1843.

Code, Joseph B. *Bishop John Hughes and the Sisters of Charity.* Miscellenea Historica, 1935.

Cohalan, Florence D. *A Popular History of the Archdiocese of New York.* Yonkers, NY: United States Catholic Historical Society, 1983.

Condon, Peter. "Constitutional Freedom of Religion and the Revivals of Religious Intolerance." *Historical Records and Studies* (United States Catholic Historical Society) 5 (April 1902): 426–462.

Connelly, James F., ed. *The History of the Archdiocese of Philadelphia.* Wynnewood, PA: printed by the archdiocese, 1976.

———. *The Visit of Archbishop Gaetano Bedini to the United States of America (June, 1853–February, 1854).* Rome: Libreria Editrice dell'Università Gregoriana, 1960.

Connor, Charles P. "The American Catholic Political Position at Mid-century: Archbishop Hughes as a Test Case." PhD diss., Fordham University, 1979.

Coogan, M. Jane. "A Study of the John Hughes–Terence Donaghoe Friendship." *Records of the American Catholic Historical Society of Philadelphia* 93, nos. 1–4 (March–December 1983): 41–75.

Cook, Adrian. *The Armies of the Streets: The New York City Draft Riots of 1863.* Lexington: University of Kentucky Press, 1974.

Corby, William. *Memoirs of Chaplain Life: Three Years with the Irish Brigade in the Army of the Potomac.* Edited by Lawrence Frederick Kohl. New York: Fordham University Press, 1992.

Cross, Barbara, ed. *The Autobiography of Lyman Beecher.* Vol. 2. Cambridge, MA: Belknap Press of Harvard University Press, 1961.

Crowe, Charles. *George Ripley: Transcendentalist and Utopian Socialist.* Athens: University of Georgia Press, 1967.

Curran, Francis X., "Archbishop Hughes and the Jesuits: An Anatomy of Their Quarrels." In *Fordham: The Early Years,* edited by Thomas C. Hennessey, 177–221. New York: Something More, 1998.

Cutler, Wayne, ed. *Correspondence of James K. Polk.* Vol. 11 (1846). Knoxville: University of Tennessee Press, 2005.

D'Agostino, Peter R. *Rome in America: Transnational Catholic Ideology from the Risorgimento to Fascism.* Chapel Hill: University of North Carolina Press, 2004.

Deuther, Charles George. *The Life and Times of the Rt. Rev. John Timon, D.D.: First Roman Catholic Bishop of the Diocese of Buffalo.* Buffalo, NY: published by the author, 1870.

Dhu, Helen [Charles Evans Lister]. *Stanhope Burleigh; or, The Jesuits in Our Homes.* New York: Stringer & Townsend, 1855.

Dolan, Jay P. *The Immigrant Church: New York's Irish and German Catholics, 1815–1865.* Notre Dame, IN: University of Notre Dame Press, 1992.

———. *In Search of an American Catholicism: A History of Religion and Culture in Tension.* Oxford: Oxford University Press, 2002.

———. *The Irish-Americans.* New York: Bloomsbury, 2008.

Dupree, Hunter, and Leslie H. Fishel Jr., eds. "An Eyewitness Account of the New York Draft Riots, July 1863." *Mississippi Valley Historical Record* 47, no. 3 (December 1960): 472–479.

Egan, Maurice Francis. "A Slight Appreciation of James Adolphus McMaster." *Historical Records and Studies* (United States Catholic Historical Society) 15 (March 1921): 19–34.

Egan, Timothy. *The Immortal Irishman: The Irish Revolutionary Who Became an American Hero.* New York: Houghton Mifflin Harcourt, 2016.

Eisenhower, John S. D. *Agent of Destiny: The Life and Times of General Winfield Scott.* New York: Free Press, 1977.

Elliott, Marianne. *The Catholics of Ulster: A History.* New York: Perseus, 2001.

Ellis, John Tracy. *A Select Bibliography of the History of the Catholic Church in the United States*. New York: Declan V. McMullen, 1947.

Ellsworth, Clayton Sumner. "The American Churches and the Mexican War." *American Historical Review* 45, no. 2 (January 1940): 301–326.

Endres, David J. "Know-Nothings, Nationhood, and the Nuncio: Reassessing the Visit of Archbishop Bedini." *U.S. Catholic Historian* 21, no. 4 (Fall 2003): 1–16.

——. "Rectifying the Fatal Contrast: Archbishop John Purcell and the Slavery Controversy among Catholics in Civil War Cincinnati." *Ohio Valley History* 2, no. 2 (Fall 2002): 23–33.

Ennis, Arthur J. "The New Diocese of Philadelphia." In *History of the Archdiocese of Philadelphia*, edited by James F. Connelly, 63–112. Wynnewood, PA: printed by the archdiocese, 1976.

Ernst, Robert. *Immigrant Life in New York City: 1825–1863*. New York: Octagon Books, 1979. First published in 1949.

Farley, John. *The Life of John Cardinal McCloskey*. New York: Longmans, Green, 1918.

Feldberg, Michael. *The Philadelphia Riots of 1844: A Study of Ethnic Conflict*. Westport, CT: Greenwood, 1975.

Fell, Marie Leonore. "The Foundations of Nativism in American Textbooks, 1783–1860." PhD diss., Catholic University, 1941.

Ferris, Norman. *Desperate Diplomacy: William Seward's Foreign Policy in 1861*. Nashville: University of Tennessee Press, 1976.

Fitzgerald, Maureen. *Habits of Compassion: Irish Catholic Nuns and the Origins of New York's Welfare System, 1830–1920*. Urbana: University of Illinois Press, 2006.

——. "The Perils of 'Passion and Poverty': Women Religious and the Care of Single Women in New York City, 1845–1890." *U.S. Catholic Historian* 10, nos. 1/2 (1991/1992): 45–58.

Foik, Paul J. *Pioneer Catholic Journalism*. New York: United States Catholic Historical Society, 1930.

Fortin, Roger. *Faith and Action: A History of the Archdiocese of Cincinnati, 1821–1996*. Columbus: Ohio State University Press, 2002.

Franchot, Jenny. *Roads to Rome: The Antebellum Protestant Encounter with Catholicism*. Berkeley: University of California Press, 1994.

Frese, Joseph, "The Catholic Press and Secession, 1860–1861." *Historical Records and Studies* (United States Catholic Historical Society) 45 (1957): 79–106.

Gabriel, Angelo. *The Christian Brothers in the United States, 1848–1948*. New York: Declan X. McMullen, 1948.

Gannon, Michael V. *Rebel Bishop: The Life and Era of Augustin Verot*. Milwaukee: Bruce Publishing, 1964.

Gannon, Robert J. *Up to the Present: The Story of Fordham*. New York: Doubleday, 1967.

Gavazzi, Alessandro. *Father Gavazzi's Lectures in New York*. New York: Dewett & Davenport, 1853.

George, Joseph, Jr. " 'A Catholic Family Newspaper' Views the Lincoln Administration: John Mullaly's Copperhead Weekly." *Civil War History* 24, no. 2 (June 1978): 112–132.

Gjerde, John. *Catholicism and the Shaping of Nineteenth-Century America*. Cambridge: Cambridge University Press, 2012.

Golway, Terry. *Machine Made: Tammany Hall and the Creation of Modern Politics*. New York: Liveright, 2014.

Goodwin, Doris Kearns. *Team of Rivals: The Political Genius of Abraham Lincoln.* New York: Simon & Schuster, 2005.

Gouverneur, Marian. *As I Remember: Recollections of American Society in the Nineteenth Century.* New York: Appleton, 1911.

Gower, Joseph F., and Richard M. Leliaert, eds. *The Brownson–Hecker Correspondence.* Notre Dame, IN: University of Notre Dame Press, 1979.

Greeley, Andrew M. *The Catholic Experience: An Interpretation of the History of American Catholicism.* New York: Doubleday, 1967.

Griffin, Martin I. J. "History of the Church of St. John the Evangelist, Philadelphia." *Records of the American Catholic Historical Society of Philadelphia* 20 (1909): 350–404.

Griffin, Susan M. *Anti-Catholicism and Nineteenth-Century Fiction.* Cambridge: Cambridge University Press, 2004.

Guilday, Peter. "Gaetano Bedini." *Historical Records and Studies* (United States Catholic Historical Society) 23 (1933): 87–170.

——. *A History of the Councils of Baltimore.* New York: Macmillan, 1932.

——. *John Gilmary Shea: Father of American Catholic History.* New York: United States Catholic Historical Society, 1926.

Hamilton, Jeanne. "The Nunnery as Menace: The Burning of the Charlestown Convent, 1834." *U.S. Catholic Historian* 14, no. 1 (Winter 1996): 35–65.

Hammond, Harold Earl, ed. *Diary of a Union Lady: 1861–1865.* Lincoln: University of Nebraska Press / Bison Books, 2000.

Harrison, Eliza Cope, ed. *Philadelphia Merchant: The Diary of Thomas P. Cope, 1800–1851.* South Bend, IN: Gateway, 1978.

Hassard, John R. G. *Life of the Most Reverend John Hughes, D.D., First Archbishop of New York, with Extracts from His Private Correspondence.* New York: D. Appleton & Co., 1866.

Headley, J. T. *The Great Riots of New York, 1712 to 1873.* New York: E. B. Treat, 1873.

Heisser, David C. R., and Stephen J. White. *Patrick N. Lynch, 1817–1882: Third Catholic Bishop of Charleston.* Charleston: University of South Carolina Press, 2015.

Hennessey, James. *American Catholics: A History of the Roman Catholic Community in the United States.* New York: Oxford University Press, 1983.

Holt, Michael F. *The Rise and Fall of the American Whig Party.* New York: Oxford University Press, 1999.

Howe, Daniel Walker. *What Hath God Wrought: The Transformation of America, 1815–1848.* New York: Oxford University Press, 2007.

Hueston, Robert Francis. *The Catholic Press and Nativism, 1840–1860.* PhD diss., University of Notre Dame, 1972. New York: Arno Press, 1976.

Hughes, John. *Archbishop John Hughes to General Cass, in Self-Vindication.* New York: Edward Dunnigan & Brother, June 1854.

——. *Brooksiana; or, The Controversy between Senator Brooks and Archbishop Hughes: Growing Out of the Recently Enacted Church Property Bill.* New York: Edward Dunigan & Brother, 1855.

——. *Controversy between the Rev. John Hughes of the Roman Catholic Church and the Rev. John Breckinridge of the Presbyterian Church.* Philadelphia: Joseph Whetham, 1833.

——. *Discussion of the Question: Is the Roman Catholic Religion Inimical to Civil or Religious Liberty?* Philadelphia: Carey, Lea, and Blanchard, 1836.

Hussey, Edmund. *Archbishop John Purcell of Cincinnati.* ebook, 2012.

Ignatiev, Noel. *How the Irish Became White.* New York: Routledge, 2008. First published in 1995.

Isham, Thomas Garrett. *A Born Again Episcopalian: The Evangelical Witness of Charles Pettit McIlvaine.* Vestavia Hills, AL: Solid Ground Christian Books, 2011.

Jacoby, George Paul. *Catholic Child Care in Nineteenth-Century New York.* PhD diss. Washington, DC: Catholic University of America Press, 1941.

Johnson, Tyler V. *Devotion to the Adopted Country: U.S. Immigrant Volunteers in the Mexican War.* Columbia: University of Missouri Press, 2012.

Kari, Camilla J. *Public Witness: The Pastoral Letters of the American Catholic Bishops.* Collegeville, MN; Liturgical Press, 2004.

Kehoe, Lawrence, ed. *Complete Works of the Most Reverend John Hughes, Archbishop of New York.* Vols. 1 and 2. New York: Lawrence Kehoe, 1865.

Kelly, Blanche Mary. "John Rose Greene Hassard." *Historical Records and Studies* (United States Catholic Historical Society) 15 (March 1921): 19–34.

Kelly, Mary C. "'A Sentinel of Our Liberties': Archbishop John Hughes and the Irish-American Intellectual Negotiations in the Civil War Era." *Irish Studies Review* 18, no. 2 (Summer 2010).

——. *The Shamrock and the Lily: The New York Irish and the Creation of a Transatlantic Identity, 1845–1921.* New York: Peter Lang, 2005.

Kelly, Mary Gilbert. *Catholic Immigrant Colonization Projects in the United States, 1815–1860.* Washington, DC: United States Catholic Historical Society, 1939.

Keneally, Thomas. *The Great Shame and the Triumph of the Irish in the English-Speaking World.* New York: Anchor, 2000.

Kenny, Levin. "Religion and Immigration: The Irish Community in New York City, 1815 to 1840." *Recorder* 4, no. 1 (Winter 1989): 4–49.

The Kenrick-Frenaye Correspondence: Selected Letters from the Cathedral Archives. Philadelphia: Archdiocese Archives, 1920.

Kirlin, Joseph. *Catholicity in Philadelphia.* Philadelphia: John Jos. McVey, 1909.

Klement, Frank. "Catholics as Copperheads during the Civil War." *Catholic Historical Record* 80, no. 1 (January 1994): 36–57.

Kohl, Lawrence Frederick, and Margaret Cosse Richard, eds. *Irish Green and Union Blue: The Civil War Letters of Peter Welsh.* New York: Fordham University Press, 1986.

Komlos, John. *Louis Kossuth in America, 1851–1852.* Buffalo, NY: East European Institute, 1973.

Krieg, Joann P. *Whitman and the Irish.* Iowa City: University of Iowa Press, 2000.

Kurtz, William B. *Excommunicated from the Union: How the Civil War Created a Separate Catholic America.* New York: Fordham University Press, 2016.

Kwitchen, Mary Augustine. *James Alphonsus McMaster: A Study in American Thought.* PhD diss. Washington, DC: Catholic University of America Press, 1949.

Lannie, Vincent Peter. "Profile of an Immigrant Bishop: The Early Career of John Hughes." *Pennsylvania History* 32, no. 4 (October 1965): 366–379.

——. *Public Money and Parochial Schools.* Notre Dame, IN: University of Notre Dame Press, 1968.

Ledoux, Albert Henri. *The Life and Thought of Simon Bruté: Seminary Professor and Frontier Bishop.* PhD diss. Washington, DC: Catholic University of America Press, 2005.

Lee, Basil Leo. *Discontent in New York City: 1861–1865.* PhD diss. Washington, DC: Catholic University of America Press, 1943.

Light, Dale B. "The Reformation of Philadelphia Catholicism, 1830–1860." *Pennsylvania Magazine of History and Biography* 112, no. 3 (July 1988): 375–405.

——. *Rome and the New Republic: Conflict and Community in Philadelphia Catholicism between the Revolution and the Civil War.* Notre Dame, IN: University of Notre Dame Press, 1996.

Lojek, Helen. "Thoreau's Bog People." *New England Quarterly* 67, no. 2 (June 1994): 279–297.

Marraro, Howard R. "Italians in New York in the Eighteen-Fifties, Part II." *New York History* 30, no. 3 (July 1949): 276–303.

Marshall, Megan. *Margaret Fuller: A New American Life.* New York: Houghton Mifflin Harcourt, 2013.

Maury, Sarah Mytton. *The Statesmen of America in 1846.* Philadelphia: Carey and Hart, 1847.

Maynard, Theodore. *Orestes Brownson: Yankee, Radical, Catholic.* New York: Macmillan, 1943.

——. *The Reed and the Rock: A Portrait of Simon Bruté.* New York: Longmans, Green, 1942.

McAllister, Anna. *Ellen Ewing, Wife of General Sherman.* New York: Benziger Bros., 1936.

McAvoy, Thomas T. "The Formation of the Catholic Minority in the United States." *Review of Politics* 10, no. 1 (January 1948): 13–34.

——. "Orestes Brownson and Archbishop John Hughes in 1860." *Review of Politics* 24, no. 1 (January 1962): 19–47.

McCadden, Joseph J. "Bishop Hughes versus the Public School Society of New York." *Catholic Historical Review* 50, no. 2 (July 1964): 188–207.

——. "Governor Seward's Friendship with Bishop Hughes." *New York History* 47, no. 2 (April 1966): 160–184.

McCadden, Joseph J., and Helen McCadden. *Father Varela, Torch Bearer from Cuba.* New York: United States Catholic Historical Society, 1969.

McCauley, Bernadette. *Who Shall Take Care of Our Sick? Roman Catholic Sisters and the Development of Catholic Hospitals in New York City.* Baltimore: Johns Hopkins University Press, 2005.

McEniry, Blanche Marie. "American Catholics in the War with Mexico." PhD diss., Catholic University, 1937.

McGreevy, John T. *Catholicism and American Freedom: A History.* New York: Norton, 2003.

McKee, Joseph. *Popery Unmasked: Showing the Depravity of the Priesthood and Immorality of the Confessional, Being the Questions Put to Females.* Lowell, MA: H. M. Hatch, 1835.

McKenna, Ellen. "The Visits to Ireland of John Hughes, Archbishop of New York, from 1840 to 1862." *Clogher Record* 20, no. 1 (2009): 19–38.

McNamara, Robert F. "Trusteeism in the Atlantic States, 1785–1863." *Catholic Historical Review* 30, no. 2 (July 1944): 135–154.

McPherson, James. *Battle Cry of Freedom: The Civil War Era.* New York: Oxford University Press, 1988.

Meehan, Thomas. "Archbishop Hughes and the Draft Riots." *Historical Records and Studies* (United States Catholic Historical Society) 1 (1900): 170–190.

Meehan, Thomas F. "Archbishop Hughes and Mexico." *Historical Records and Studies* (United States Catholic Historical Society) 19 (September 1929): 32–37.

Meenagh, Martin. "Archbishop John Hughes and the New York School Controversy, 1840–1842." *Nineteenth-Century American History* 5, no. 1 (Spring 2004): 34–65.

Miegs, Earl, ed. *Lincoln Day by Day.* Vol. 3. Washington, DC: Lincoln Sesquicentennial, 1960.

Milano, Kenneth W. *The Philadelphia Nativist Riots: Irish Kensington Erupts.* Charleston, SC: History Press, 2003.

Miller, Kerby A. *Emigrants and Exiles: Ireland and the Irish Exodus to North America.* New York: Oxford University Press, 1988.

Mitchell, D. W. *Ten Years in the United States.* London: Smith, Elder, 1863.

Mize, Sandra Yocum. "Defending Roman Loyalties and Republican Values: The 1848 Italian Revolution in American Catholic Apologetics." *Church History* 60, no. 4 (December 1991): 480–492.

Morris, Charles. *American Catholic: The Saints and Sinners Who Built America's Most Powerful Church.* New York: Random House, 1997.

Moss, Kenneth. "St. Patrick's Day Celebrations and the Formation of Irish-American Identity, 1845–1875." *Journal of Social History* 29, no. 1 (Autumn 1995): 125–148.

Mueller, Gilbert H. *William Cullen Bryant: Author of America.* Albany: SUNY Press, 2008.

Mushkat, Jerome. *Fernando Wood: A Political Biography.* Kent, OH: Kent State University Press, 1990.

———. *Tammany: The Evolution of a Political Machine, 1789–1865.* Syracuse, NY: Syracuse University Press, 1971.

Nevins, Allan, ed. *The Diary of Philip Hone, 1828–1851.* Vol. 1. New York: Dodd, Mead, 1927.

———. *Ordeal of the Union.* Vol. 2, *A House Dividing, 1852–1857.* New York: Scribners, 1947.

Nevins, Allan, and Milton Halsey Thomas, eds. *The Diary of George Templeton Strong.* Vols. 1–4. New York: Macmillan, 1952.

Nolan, Hugh J. *The Most Reverend Francis Patrick Kenrick.* Philadelphia: American Catholic Historical Society of Philadelphia, 1948.

Noll, Mark A. *The Civil War as a Theological Crisis.* Chapel Hill: University of North Carolina Press, 2006.

O'Connor, Thomas F. "Joseph Rosati, C.M., Apostolic Delegate to Haiti, 1842: Two Letters to Bishop John Hughes." *Academy of American Franciscan History* 1, no. 4 (April 1945): 190–194.

O'Connor, Thomas H. *Fitzpatrick's Boston, 1846–1866: John Bernard Fitzpatrick, Third Bishop of Boston.* Boston: Northeastern University Press, 1984.

O'Daniel, Victor Francis. "Archbishop John Hughes: American Envoy to France (1861)." *Catholic Historical Review* 3 (1917): 336–339.

O'Donoghue, D. J., ed. *The Life of William Carleton: Being His Autobiography and Letters.* London: Downey & Co., 1896.

O'Shea, John J. *The Two Kenricks: Most Rev. Francis Patrick, Archbishop of Baltimore and Most Rev. Peter Richard, Archbishop of St. Louis.* Philadelphia: John J. McVey, 1904.

Osofsky, Gilbert. "Abolitionists, Irish Immigrants, and Romantic Nationalism." *American Historical Review* 80, no. 4 (October 1975): 889–912.

Oxx, Katie. *The Nativist Movement in America.* New York: Routledge, 2008.

Pasquier, Michael. *Fathers on the Frontier: French Missionaries and the Roman Catholic Priesthood in the United States, 1789–1870.* New York: Oxford University Press, 2010.

Pinheiro, John C. *Missionaries of Republicanism: A Religious History of the Mexican-American War.* New York: Oxford University Press, 2014.

Potter, George W. *To the Golden Door: The Story of the Irish in Ireland and America.* Boston: Little, Brown, 1960.

Pray, Isaac, ed. *The Memoirs of James Gordon Bennett and His Times.* New York: Stringer & Townsend, 1855.

Prendergast, William B. *The Catholic Voter in American Politics: The Passing of the Democratic Monolith.* Washington, DC: Georgetown University Press, 1999.

Quaife, Milo Milton, ed. *The Diary of James K. Polk.* Vol. 1. Chicago: A. A. Mc-Clurg, 1910.

Quinn, John F. "Expecting the Impossible? Abolitionist Appeals to the Irish in Antebellum America." *New England Quarterly* 82, no. 4 (June 2009): 667–710.

——. " 'The Nation's Guest?': The Battle between Catholics and Abolitionists to Manage Father Theobald Mathew's American Tour, 1849–1851." *United States Catholic Historian* 22, no. 3 (Summer 2004): 19–40.

——. " 'Three Cheers for the Abolitionist Pope!' American Reactions to Gregory XVI's Condemnation of the Slave Trade." *Catholic Historical Review* 90, no. 1 (January 2004): 67–93.

Quinn, Peter A. "A Tale of New York, 1863." *Recorder* 5, no. 1 (Winter 1991): 48–64.

Ravitch, Diane. *The Great School Wars: A History of New York City Public Schools.* Baltimore: Johns Hopkins University Press, 2000.

Remini, Richard. *Henry Clay: Statesman of the Union.* New York: Norton, 1991.

Reynolds, David S. *Mightier Than the Sword: "Uncle Tom's Cabin" and the Battle for America.* New York: Norton, 2011.

——. *Waking Giant: America in the Age of Jackson.* New York: HarperCollins, 2008.

——. *Walt Whitman's America: A Cultural Biography.* New York: Knopf, 1995.

Riforgiato, Leonard R. "John Timon and the Succession to the See of Baltimore in 1851." *Vincentian Heritage Journal* 8, no. 1: 27–42.

Roemer, Theodore. "The Ludwig Missions-Verein and the Catholic Church in the United States, 1839–1918." *Franciscan Studies*, no. 12 (August 1933): 1–161.

Ryan, Leo Raymond. *Old St. Peter's: The Mother Church of Catholic New York (1785–1935).* New York: United States Catholic Historical Society, 1935.

Ryan, Thomas R. *Orestes A. Brownson: A Definitive Biography.* Herrington, IN: Our Sunday Visitor, 1976.

Samito, Christian G. *Becoming American under Fire: Irish Americans, African Americans, and the Politics of Citizenship during the Civil War.* Ithaca, NY: Cornell University Press, 2009.

Scanlan, Arthur J. *St. Joseph's Seminary, Dunwoodie, New York, 1896–1921: With an Account of Other Seminaries of New York.* Washington, DC: United States Catholic Historical Society, 1922.

Schecter, Barnet. *The Devil's Own Work: The Civil War Draft Riots and the Fight to Reconstruct America.* New York: Walker, 2005.

Schlesinger, Arthur M., Jr. *A Pilgrim's Progress: Orestes A. Brownson.* Boston: Little, Brown, 1939.

Schrag, Peter. *Not Fit for Our Society: Immigration and Nativism in America.* Berkeley: University of California Press, 2011.

Schroth, Raymond A. *Fordham: A History and Memoir.* New York: Fordham University Press, 2008.

Scisco, Louis Dow. "Political Nativism in New York State." PhD diss., Columbia University, 1902.

Semmes, Raphael. *Baltimore as Seen by Its Visitors, 1783–1860.* Baltimore: Maryland Historical Society, 1953.

Seton, Archbishop. *Memories of Many Years (1839–1922).* New York: P. J. Kennedy & Sons, 1923.

Sharrow, Walter G. "John Hughes and a Catholic Response to Slavery in Antebellum America." *Journal of Negro History* 57, no. 3 (July 1972): 254–269.

Shaw, Richard. *Dagger John: The Unquiet Life and Times of Archbishop John Hughes.* New York: Paulist Press, 1977.

——. *John Dubois: Founding Father.* Yonkers, NY: United States Catholic Historical Society, 1983.

Shea, John Gilmary. *History of the Catholic Church in the United States: 1843–1866.* Vol. 4. New York: John G. Shea, 1892.

Shelley, Thomas J. *The Archdiocese of New York: The Bicentennial History, 1808–2008.* Strasbourg, France: Éditions du Signe, 2008.

——. *Fordham: A History of the Jesuit University of New York.* New York: Fordham University Press, 2016.

——. *Greenwich Village Catholics: St. Joseph's Church and the Evolution of an Urban Faith Community.* Washington, DC: Catholic University of America Press, 2003.

——. "Orestes Brownson and Archbishop Hughes." *Essays on United States Church History: St. Meinrad Essays* 12, no. 1 (May 1959): 25–39.

Smith, Richard W. *Bishop McIlvaine, Slavery, Britain and the Civil War.* Xlibris, 2014.

Spalding, Thomas W. *The Premier See: A History of the Baltimore Archdiocese.* Baltimore: Johns Hopkins University Press, 1995.

Stahr, Walter. *Seward: Lincoln's Indispensable Man.* New York: Simon & Schuster, 2012.

Stock, Leo Francis. *Consular Relations between the United States and the Papal States: Instructions and Dispatches.* Vol. 2. New York: American Catholic Historical Association, 1945.

——. *United States Ministers to the Papal States: Instructions and Dispatches, 1848–1868.* Washington, DC: Catholic University Press, 1933.

Sturges, Walter Knight. "Renwick, Rodrigue, and the Architecture of St. Patrick's Cathedral, N.Y.C." *U.S. Catholic Historian* 1, no. 2 (Winter–Spring 1981): 68–72.

Szarnicki, Henry A. *Michael O'Connor: First Catholic Bishop of Pittsburgh.* Pittsburgh: Wolfson, 1975.

Thebaud, Augustus. *Forty Years in the United States of America (1839–1885).* New York: United States Catholic Historical Society, 1904.

Tomasi, Silvano M. *Piety and Power: The Role of the Italian Parishes in the New York Metropolitan Area, 1880–1930.* New York: Center for Immigration Studies, 1975.

Tourscher, Francis Edward. *Old St. Augustine's in Philadelphia.* Philadelphia: Peter Reilly, 1937.

Van Deusen, Glyndon G. "Seward and the School Question Reconsidered." *Journal of American History* 52, no. 2 (September 1965): 313–319.

——. *Thurlow Weed: Wizard of the Lobby.* New York: DaCapo, 1969.

——. *William Henry Seward.* New York: Oxford University Press, 1967.

Walsh, Maria de Lourdes. *The Sisters of Charity of New York, 1809–1959.* Vol. 1. New York: Fordham University Press, 1960.

Warren, Richard A. "Displaced 'Pan-Americans' and the Transformation of the Catholic Church in Philadelphia, 1789–1850." *Pennsylvania Magazine of History and Biography* 128, no. 4 (October 2004): 343–366.

Weed, Thurlow. *Letters from Europe and the West Indies, 1843–1862.* Vol. 1. Albany: Weed, Parsons, 1866.

Weigley, Russell F., ed. *Philadelphia: A 300-Year History.* New York: Norton, 1982.

White, Joseph M. *The Diocesan Seminary in the United States.* Notre Dame, IN: University of Notre Dame Press, 1989.

Whitney, Louisa. *The Burning of the Convent: A Narrative of the Destruction, by a Mob, of the Ursuline School on Mount Benedict, Charlestown, as Remembered by One of the Pupils.* Boston: J. R. Osgood & Co., 1877.

Wight, Willard, ed. "Bishop Elder and the Civil War." *Catholic Historical Review* 44, no. 3 (October 1958): 290–306.

——. "Bishop Verot and the Civil War." *Catholic Historical Review* 47, no. 2 (July 1961): 153–163.

——. "Letters of the Bishop of Savannah, 1861–1865." *Georgia Historical Quarterly* 42, no. 1 (1958): 93–106.

——. "Some Wartime Letters of Bishop Lynch." *Catholic Historical Review* 43, no. 1 (April 1957): 20–37.

——. "War Letters of the Bishop of Richmond." *Virginia Magazine of History and Biography* 67, no. 3 (July 1959): 259–270.

Wilentz, Sean. *The Rise of American Democracy: Jefferson to Lincoln.* New York: Norton, 2005.

Williams, Robert C. *Horace Greeley: Champion of American Freedom.* New York: NYU Press, 2006.

Wilson, David A. *Thomas D'Arcy McGee.* Vol. 1, *Passion, Reason, and Politics, 1825–1857.* Montreal: McGill–Queen's University Press, 2008.

Woods, James M. *A History of the Catholic Church in the American South, 1513–1900.* Gainesville: University Press of Florida, 2011.

Wylie, Paul R. *The Irish General: Thomas Francis Meagher.* Norman: University of Oklahoma Press, 2007.

Yeager, M. Hildegarde. *The Life of James Roosevelt Bayley, First Bishop of Newark and Eighth Bishop of Baltimore, 1814–1877.* Washington, DC: Catholic University Press, 1947.

Young, Thomas G. *A New World Rising: The Story of St. Patrick's Cathedral.* New York: Something More, 2006.

Zanca, Kenneth J. *American Catholics and Slavery, 1789–1866: An Anthology of Primary Documents.* Lanham, MD: University Press of America, 1994.

Index